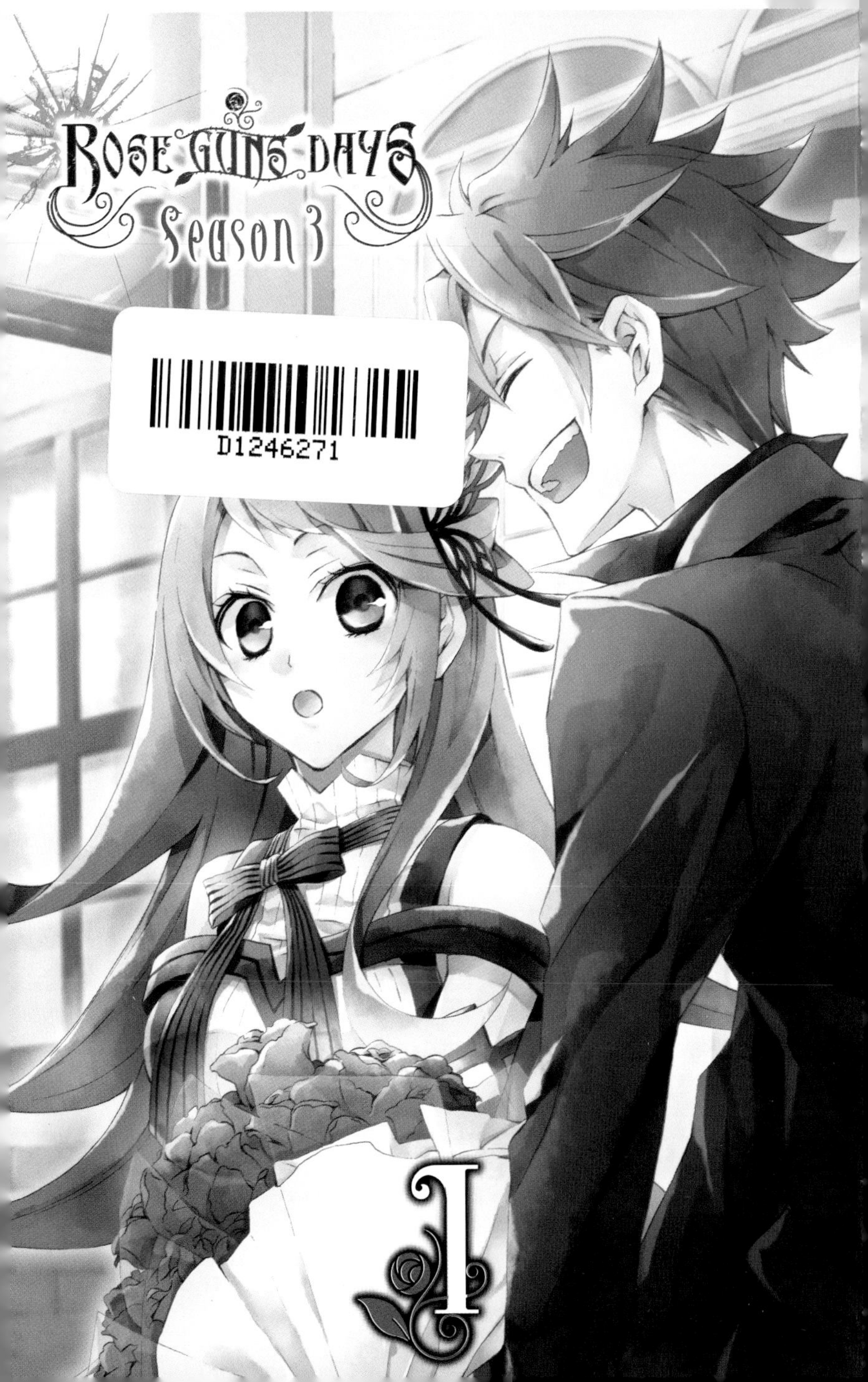
ROSE GUNS DAYS
Season 3
1

ROSE GUNS DAYS Season 3

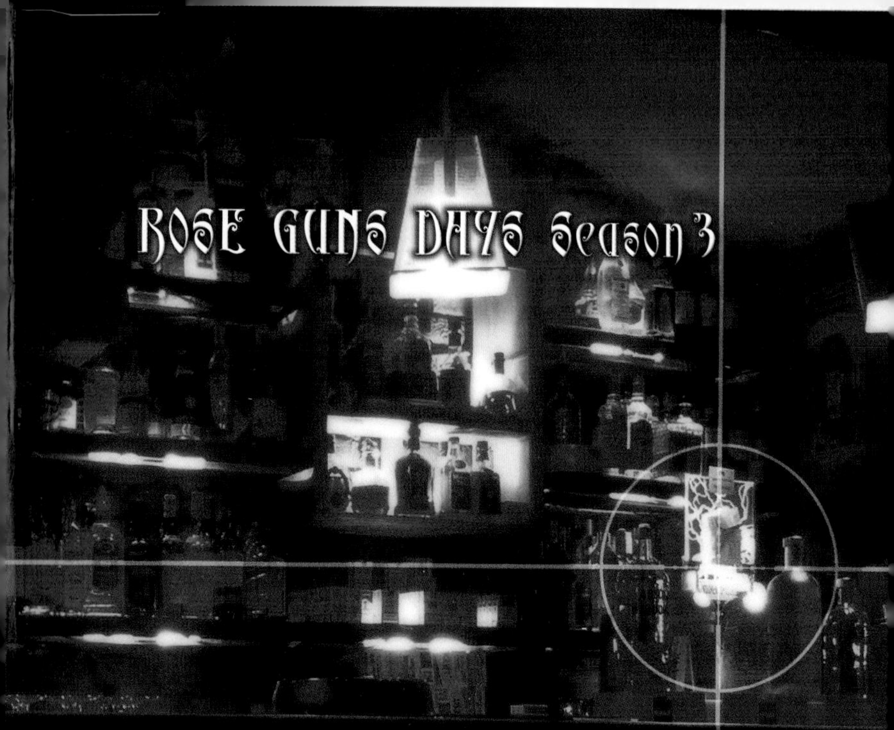

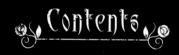

Contents

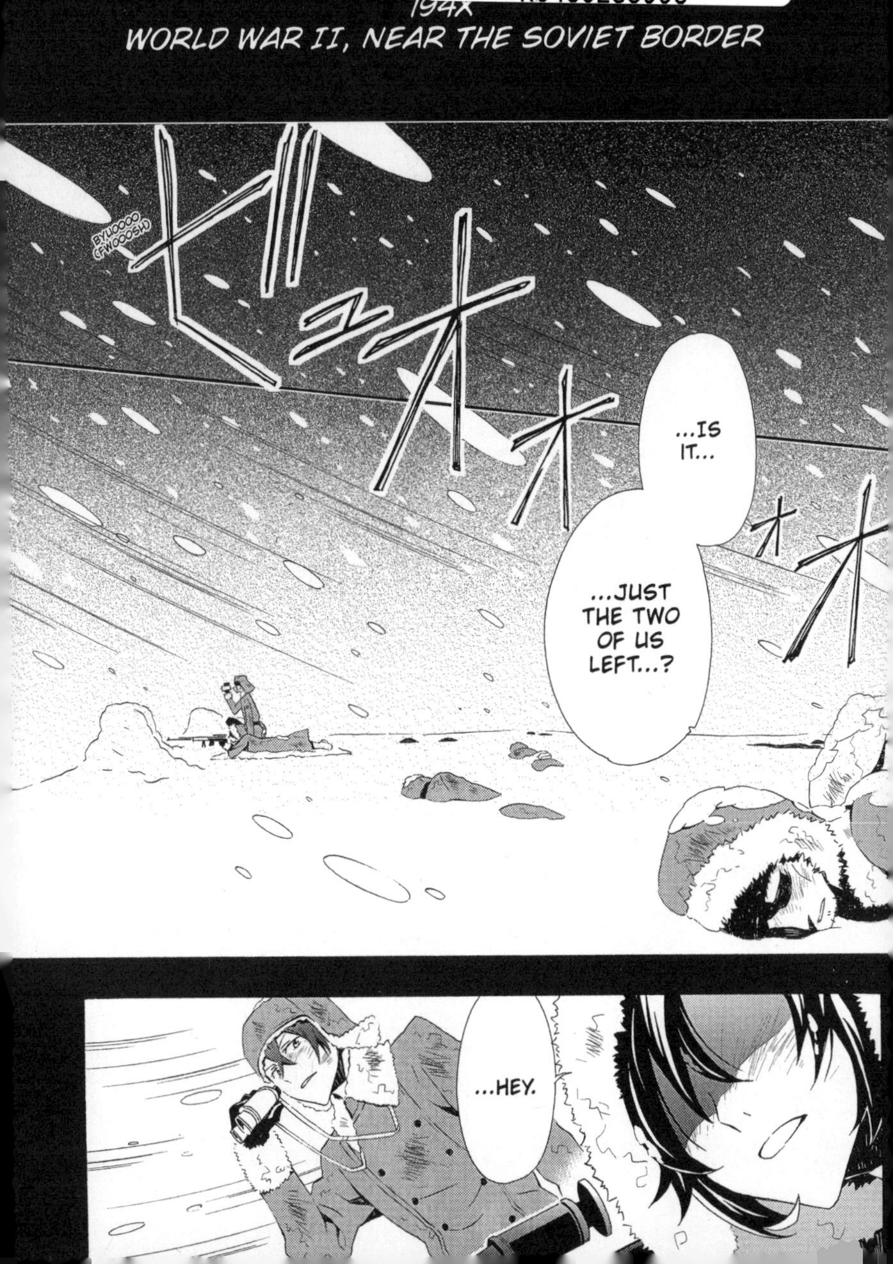
194X
WORLD WAR II, NEAR THE SOVIET BORDER
BYUOOOO (FWOOOOSH)
...IS IT...
...JUST THE TWO OF US LEFT...?
...HEY.

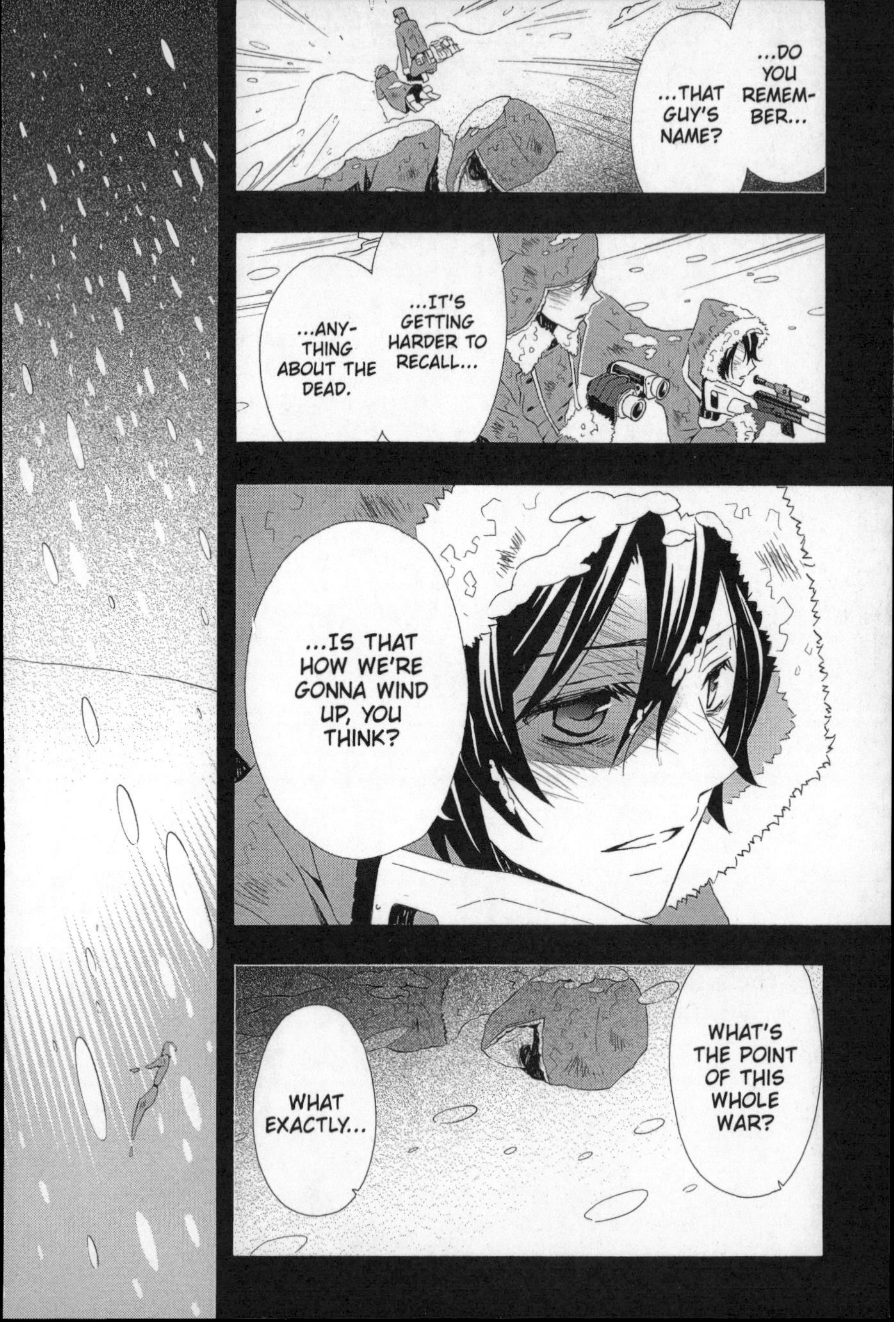
...DO YOU REMEM-BER...
...THAT GUY'S NAME?
...IT'S GETTING HARDER TO RECALL...
...ANY-THING ABOUT THE DEAD.
...IS THAT HOW WE'RE GONNA WIND UP, YOU THINK?
WHAT'S THE POINT OF THIS WHOLE WAR?
WHAT EXACTLY...

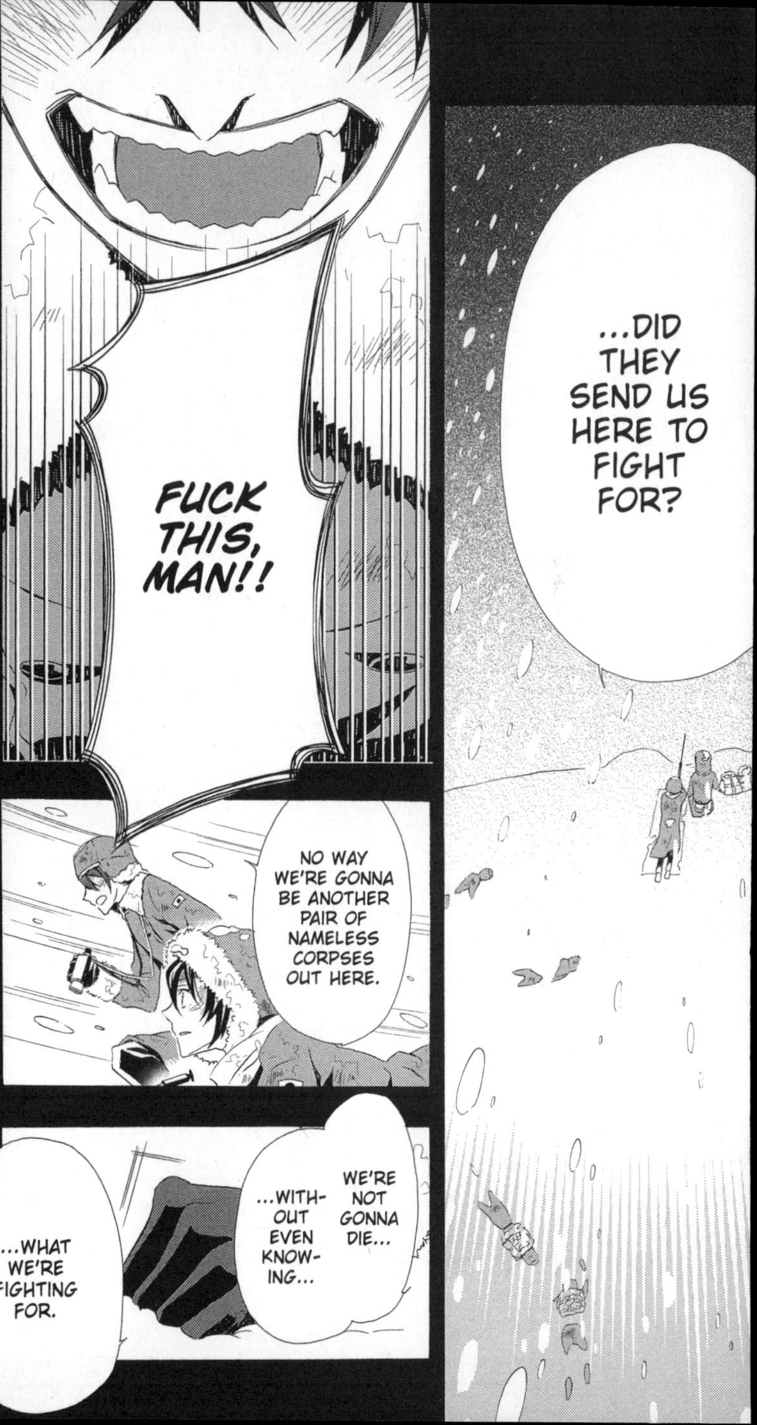
...DID THEY SEND US HERE TO FIGHT FOR?
FUCK THIS, MAN!!
NO WAY WE'RE GONNA BE ANOTHER PAIR OF NAMELESS CORPSES OUT HERE.
WE'RE NOT GONNA DIE...
...WITH-OUT EVEN KNOW-ING...
...WHAT WE'RE FIGHTING FOR.

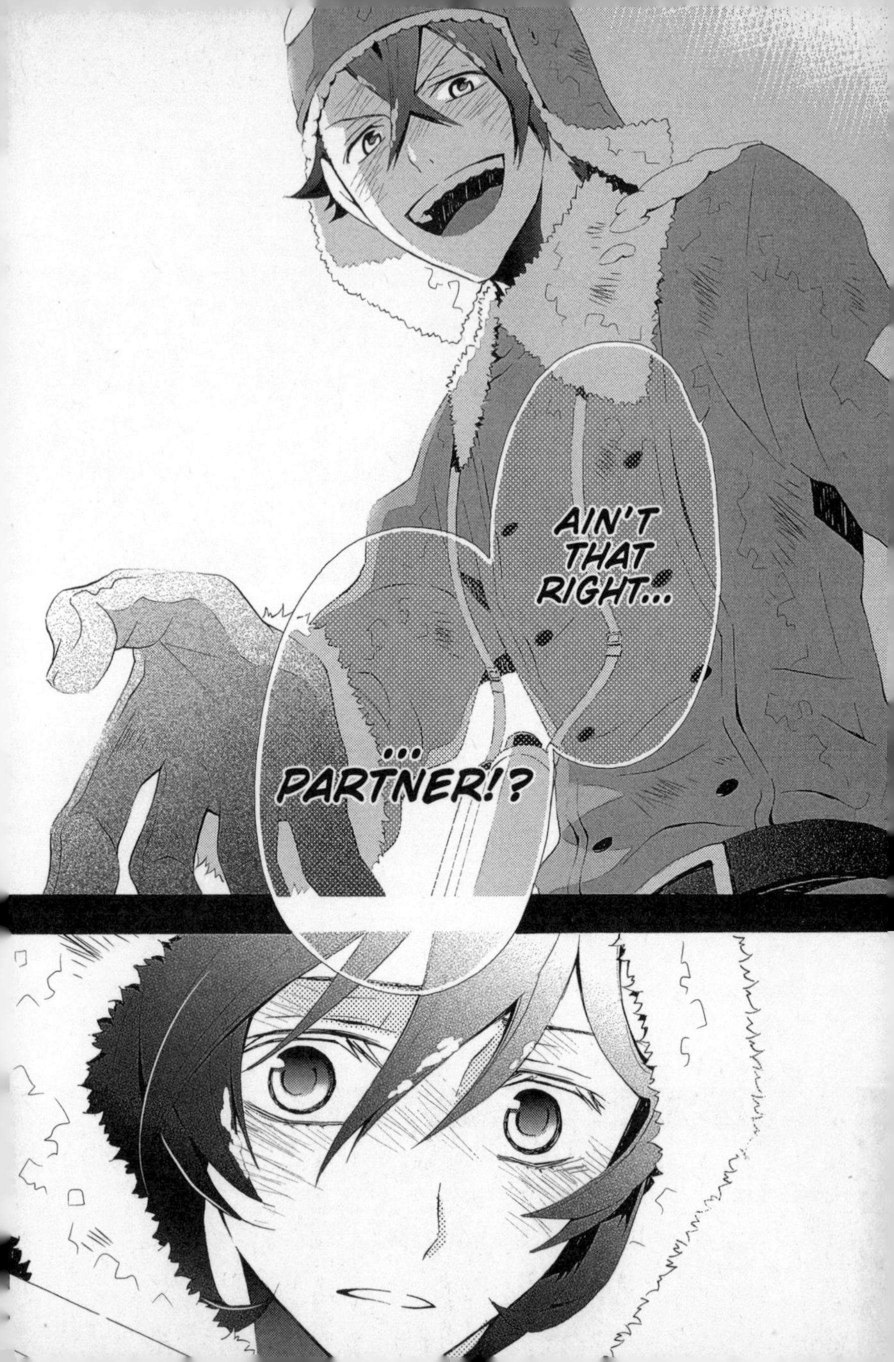
AIN'T THAT RIGHT...
...PARTNER!?

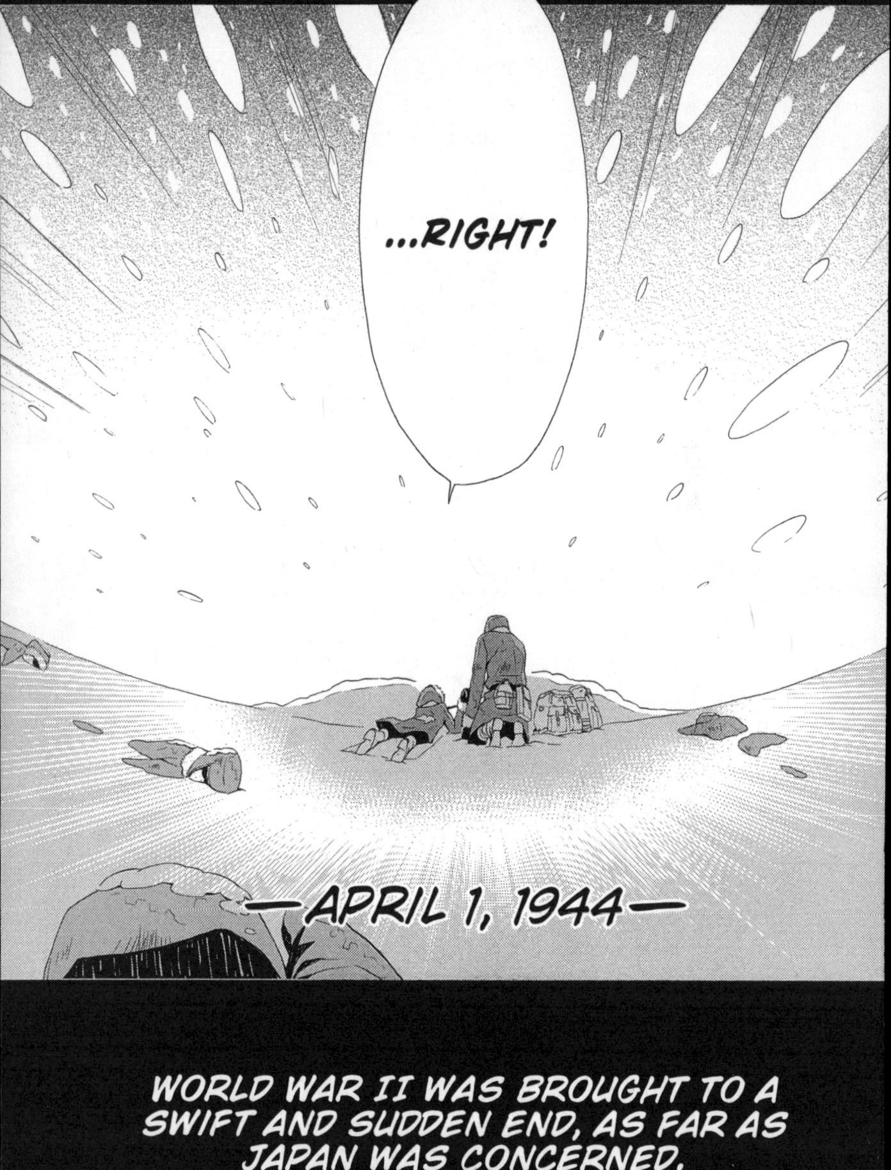
...RIGHT!
—APRIL 1, 1944—

WORLD WAR II WAS BROUGHT TO A SWIFT AND SUDDEN END, AS FAR AS JAPAN WAS CONCERNED.

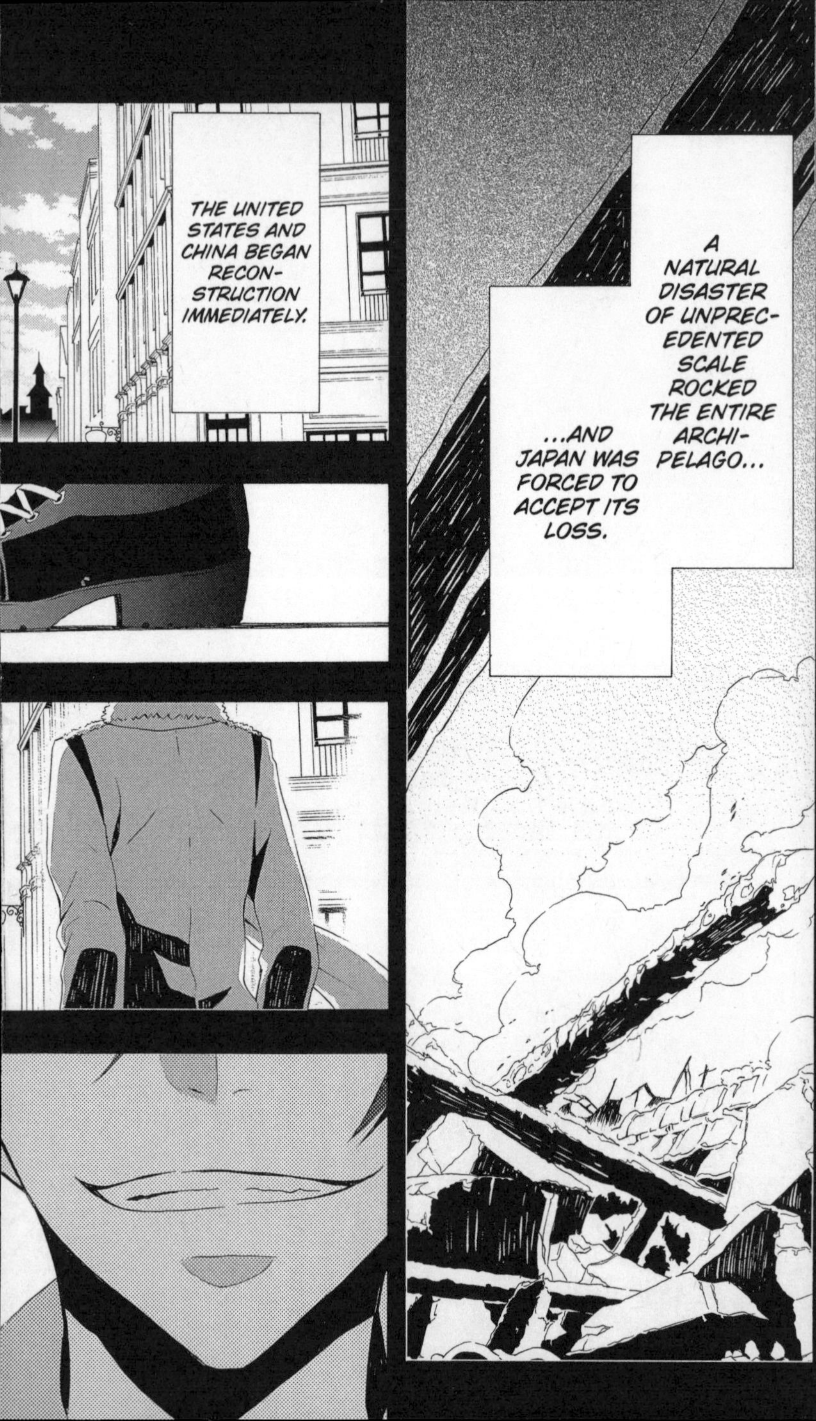
A NATURAL DISASTER OF UNPREC-EDENTED SCALE ROCKED THE ENTIRE ARCHI-PELAGO...
...AND JAPAN WAS FORCED TO ACCEPT ITS LOSS.
THE UNITED STATES AND CHINA BEGAN RECON-STRUCTION IMMEDIATELY.

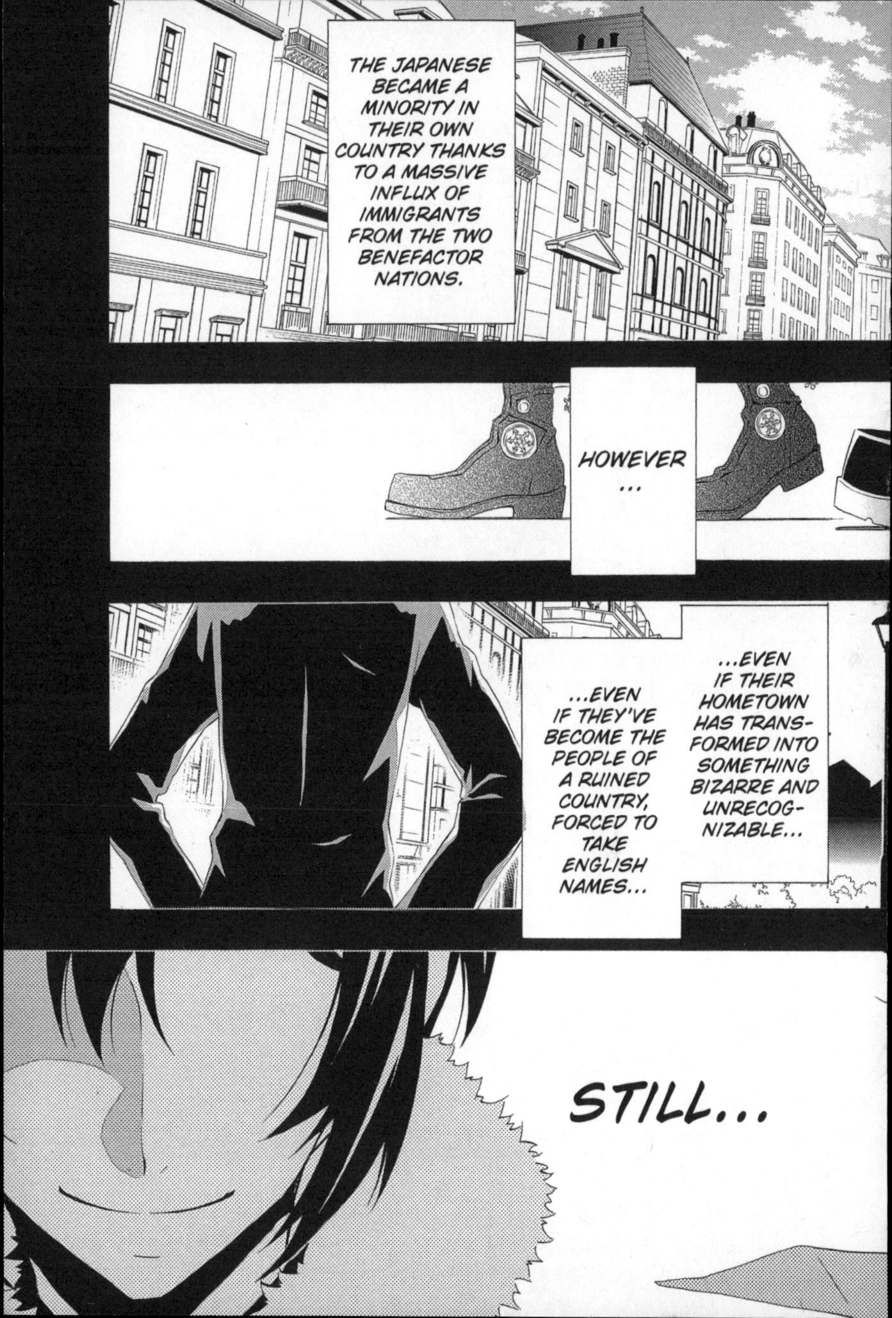
THE JAPANESE BECAME A MINORITY IN THEIR OWN COUNTRY THANKS TO A MASSIVE INFLUX OF IMMIGRANTS FROM THE TWO BENEFACTOR NATIONS.
HOWEVER ...
...EVEN IF THEIR HOMETOWN HAS TRANS-FORMED INTO SOMETHING BIZARRE AND UNRECOG-NIZABLE...
...EVEN IF THEY'VE BECOME THE PEOPLE OF A RUINED COUNTRY, FORCED TO TAKE ENGLISH NAMES...
STILL...

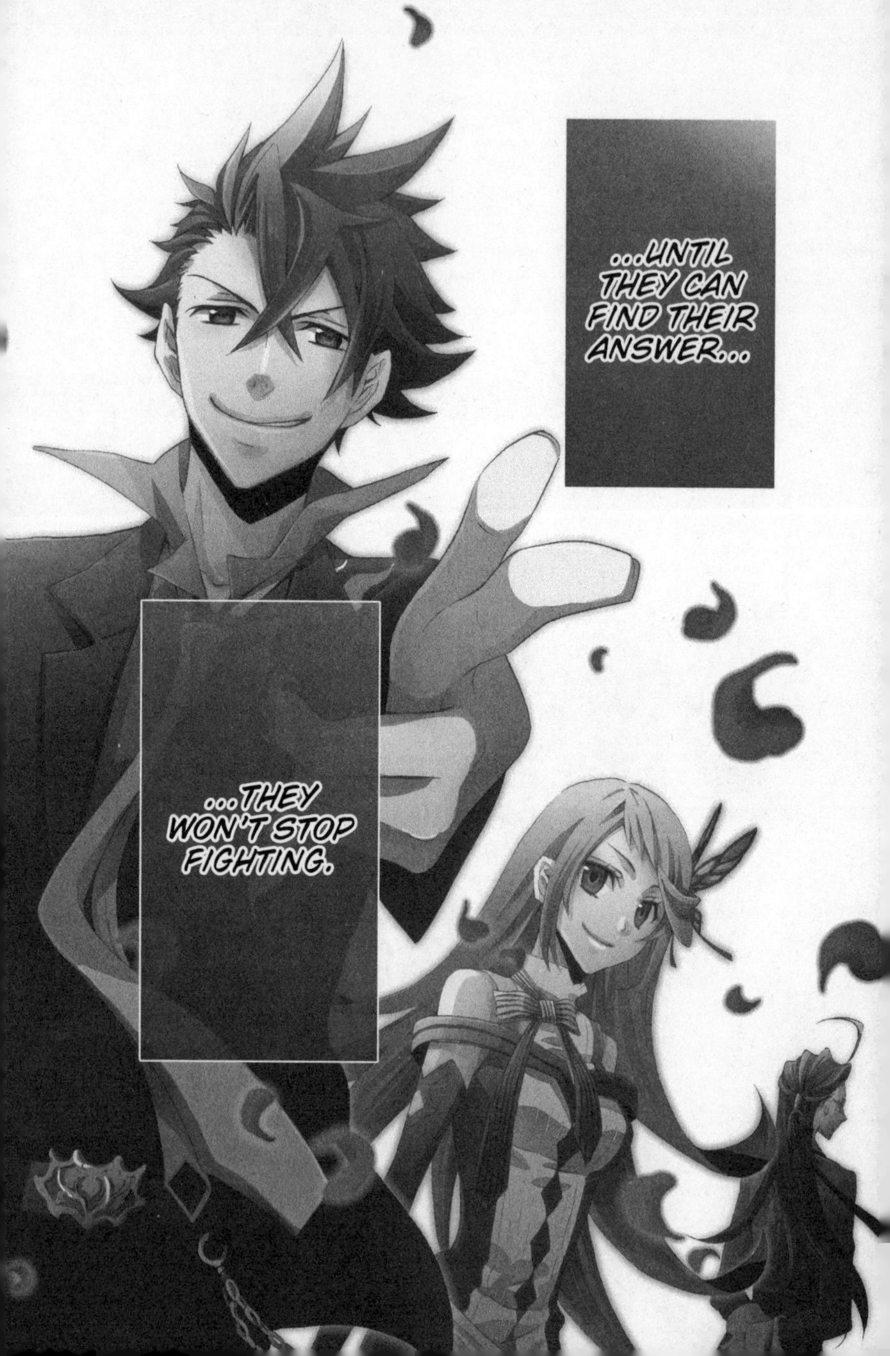
...UNTIL THEY CAN FIND THEIR ANSWER...
...THEY WON'T STOP FIGHTING.

REASON 1: On a Nameless Epitaph

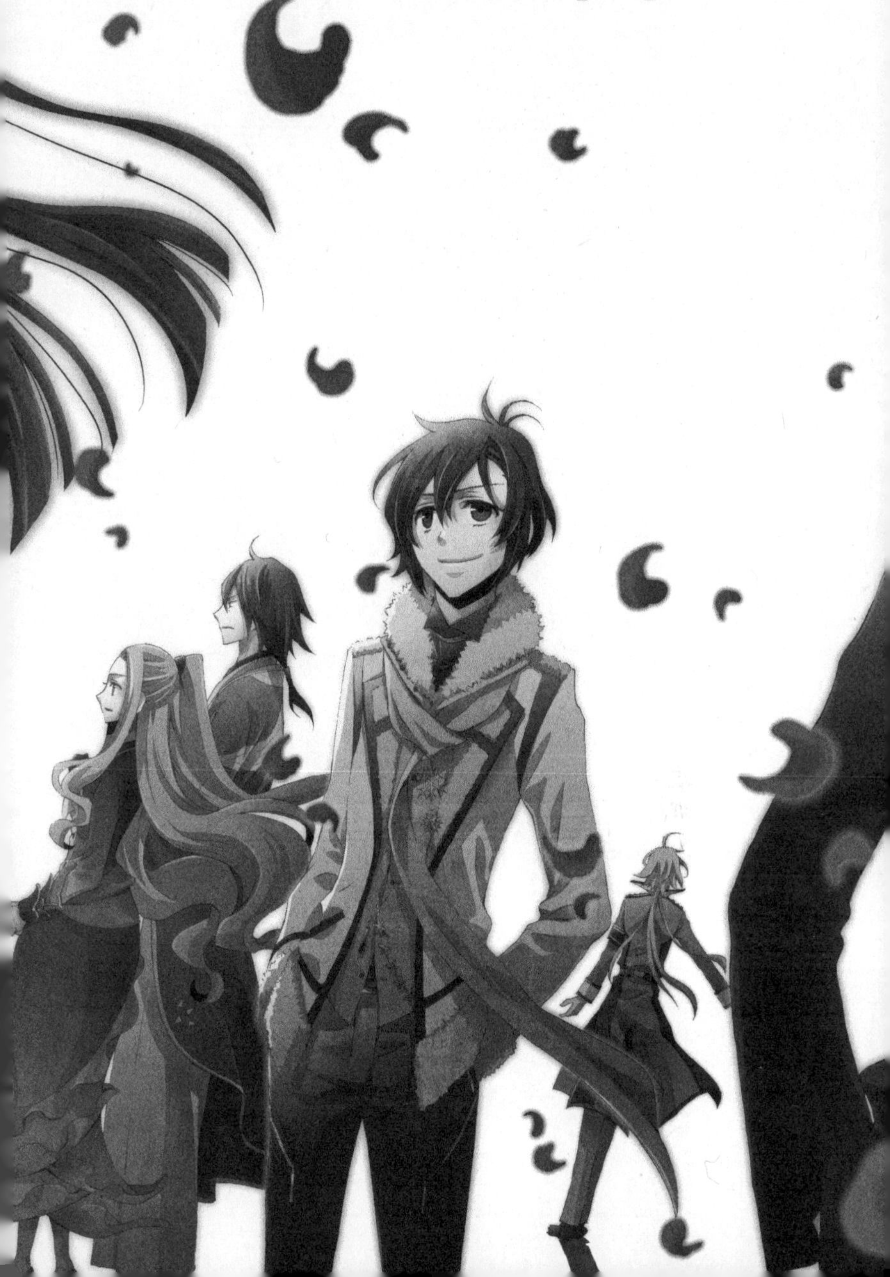

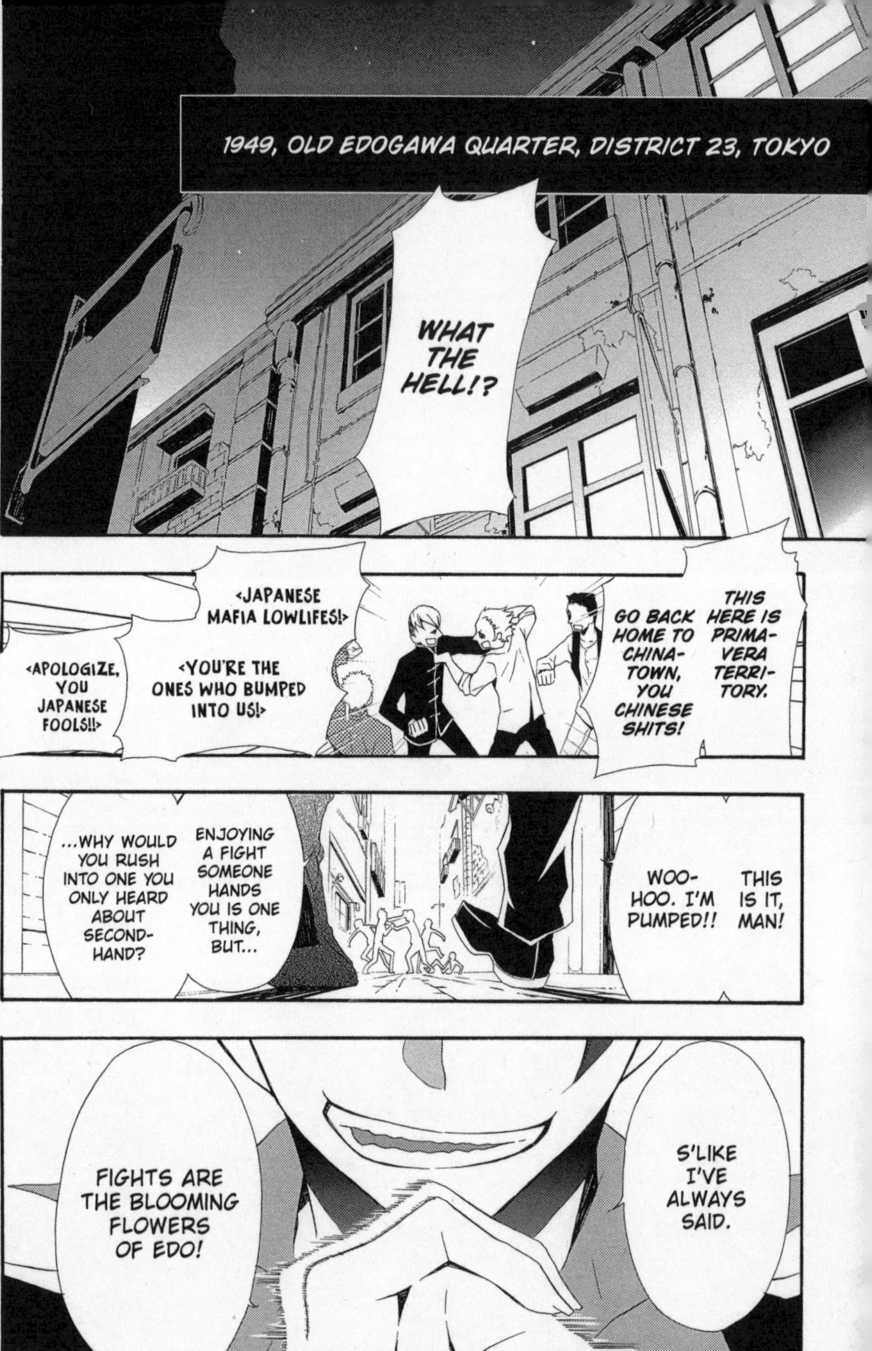
1949, OLD EDOGAWA QUARTER, DISTRICT 23, TOKYO
WHAT THE HELL!?
THIS HERE IS PRIMAVERA TERRITORY.
GO BACK HOME TO CHINATOWN, YOU CHINESE SHITS!
<JAPANESE MAFIA LOWLIFES!>
<YOU'RE THE ONES WHO BUMPED INTO US!>
<APOLOGIZE, YOU JAPANESE FOOLS!!>
THIS IS IT, MAN!
WOO-HOO. I'M PUMPED!!
ENJOYING A FIGHT SOMEONE HANDS YOU IS ONE THING, BUT...
...WHY WOULD YOU RUSH INTO ONE YOU ONLY HEARD ABOUT SECONDHAND?
S'LIKE I'VE ALWAYS SAID.
FIGHTS ARE THE BLOOMING FLOWERS OF EDO!

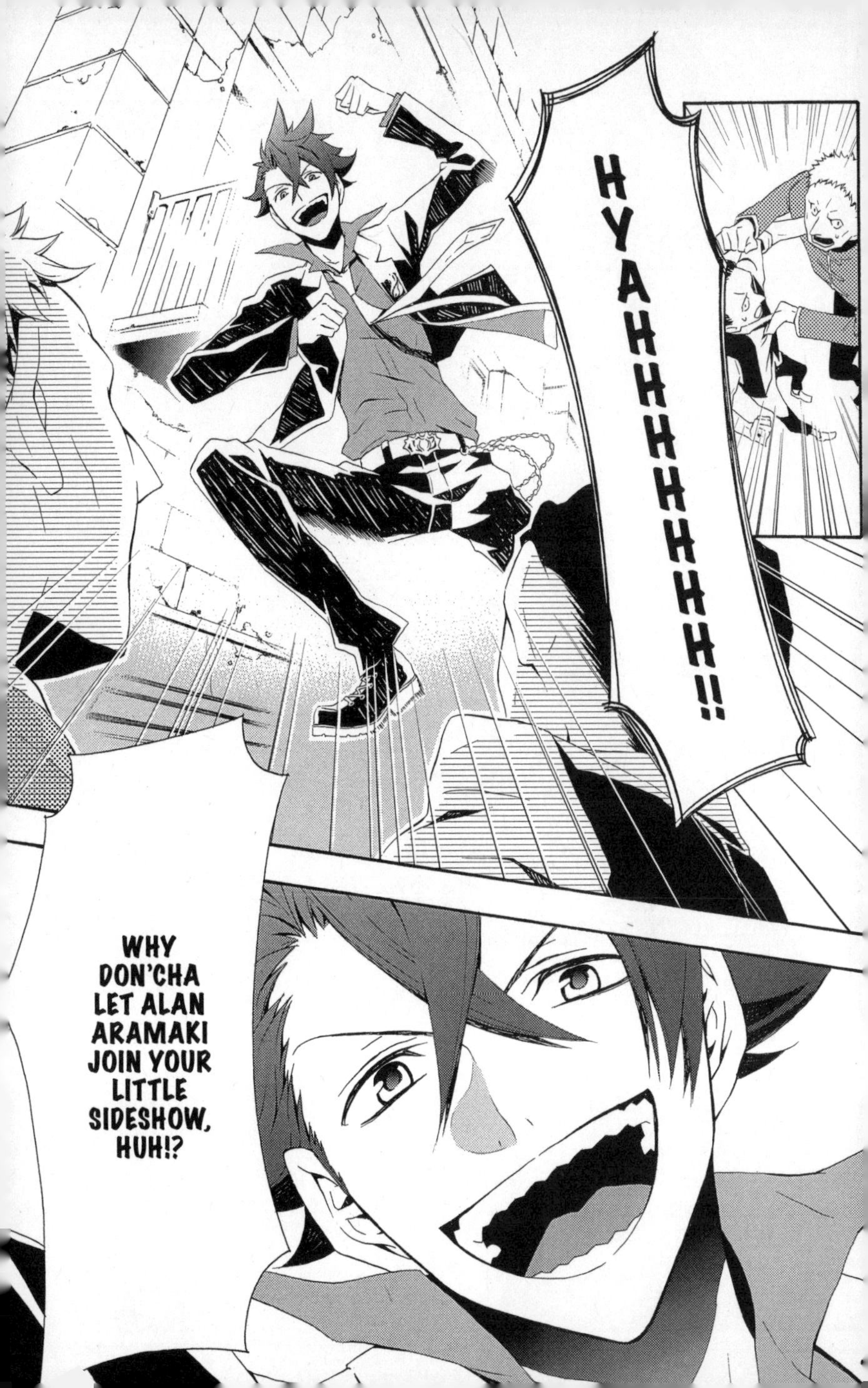
HYAHHHHHHHH!!
WHY DON'CHA LET ALAN ARAMAKI JOIN YOUR LITTLE SIDESHOW, HUH!?

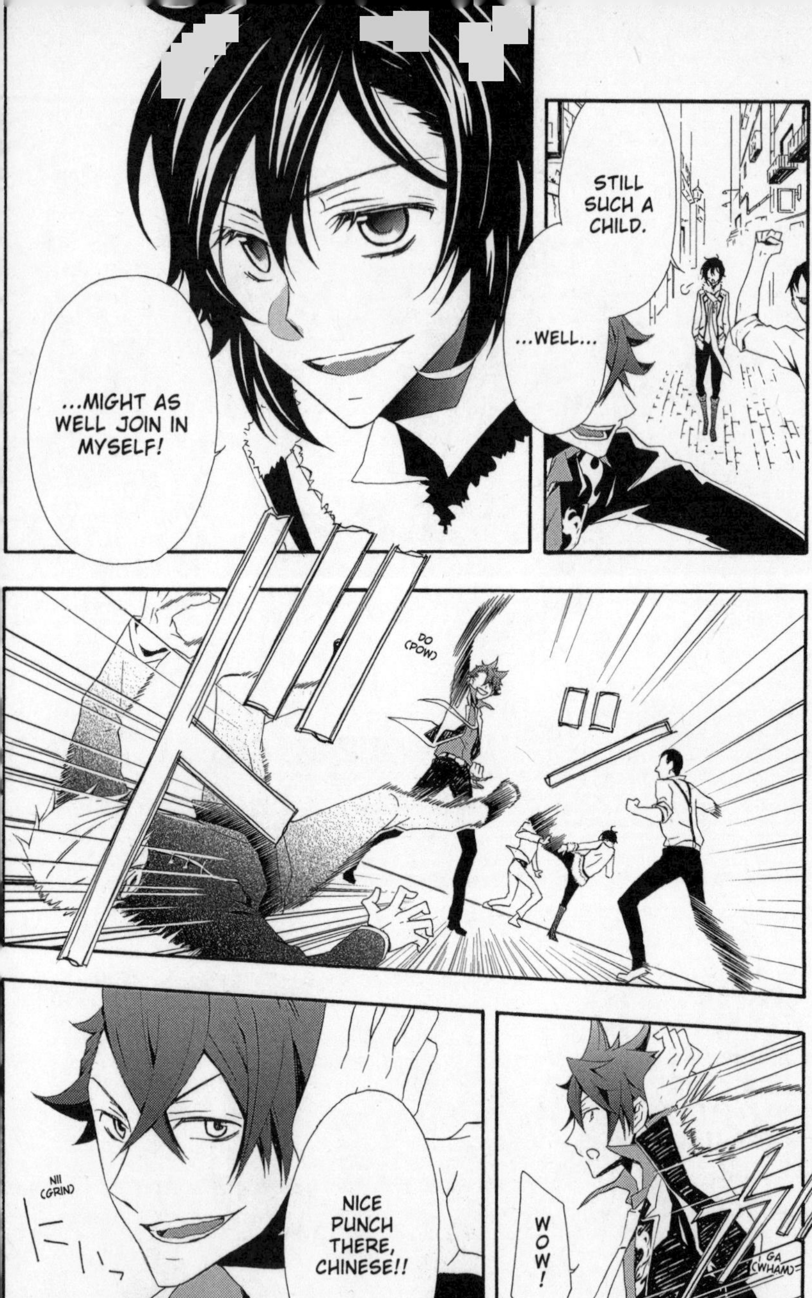
STILL SUCH A CHILD.
...WELL...
...MIGHT AS WELL JOIN IN MYSELF!
DO (POW)
WOW!
GA (WHAM)
NICE PUNCH THERE, CHINESE!!
NII (GRIN)

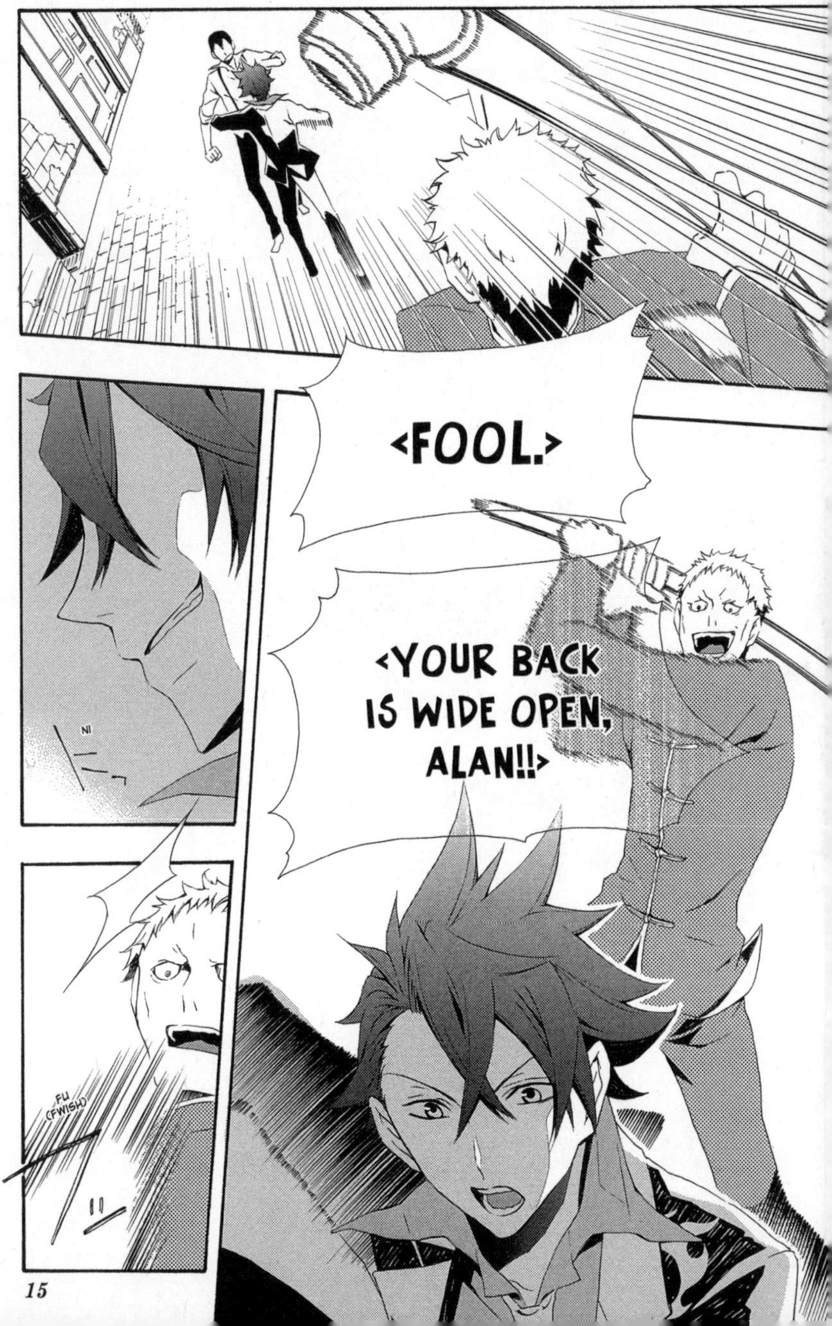

<FOOL.>
<YOUR BACK IS WIDE OPEN, ALAN!!>
NI
FU (FWISH)

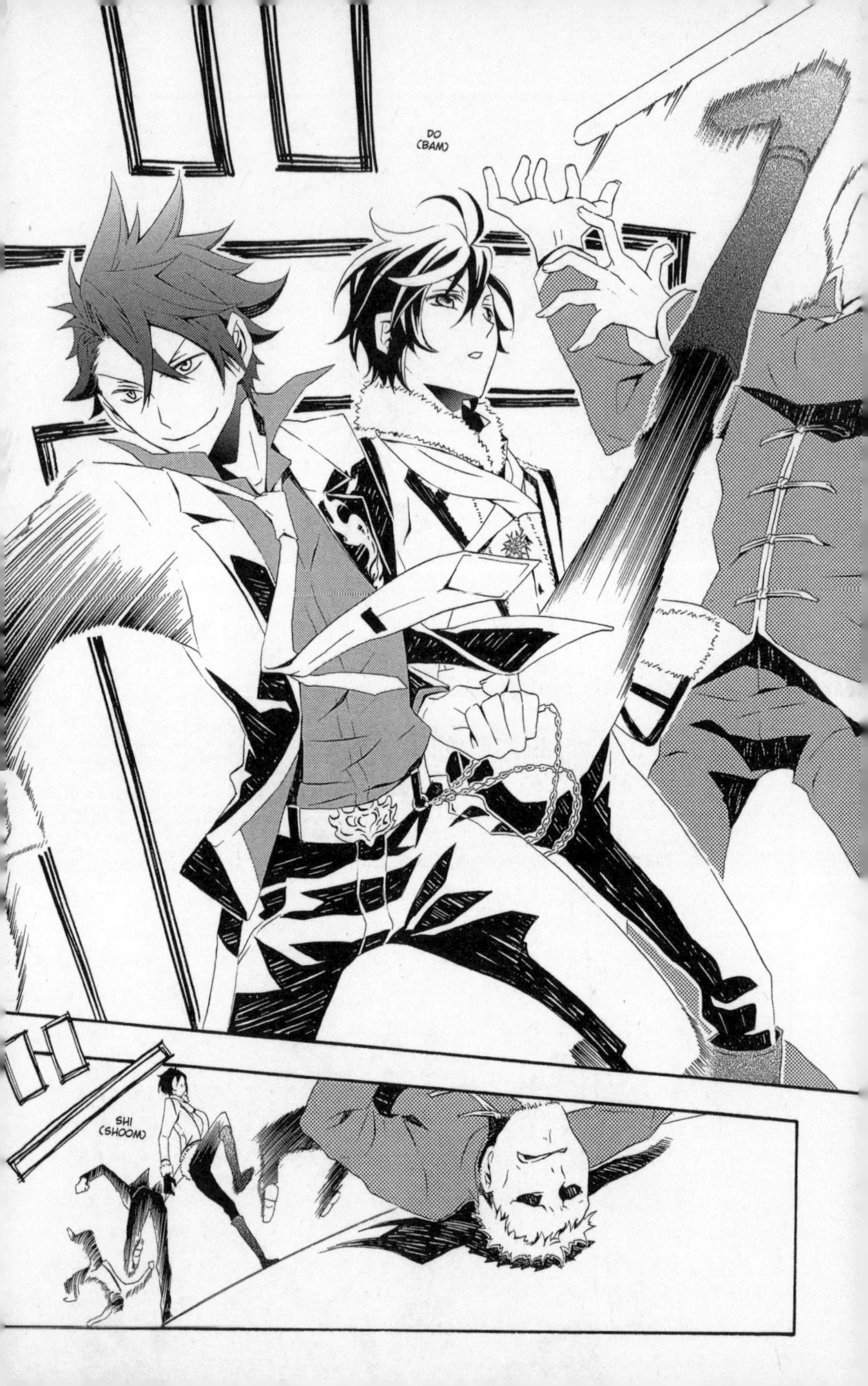
DO
(BAM)
SHI
(SHOOM)

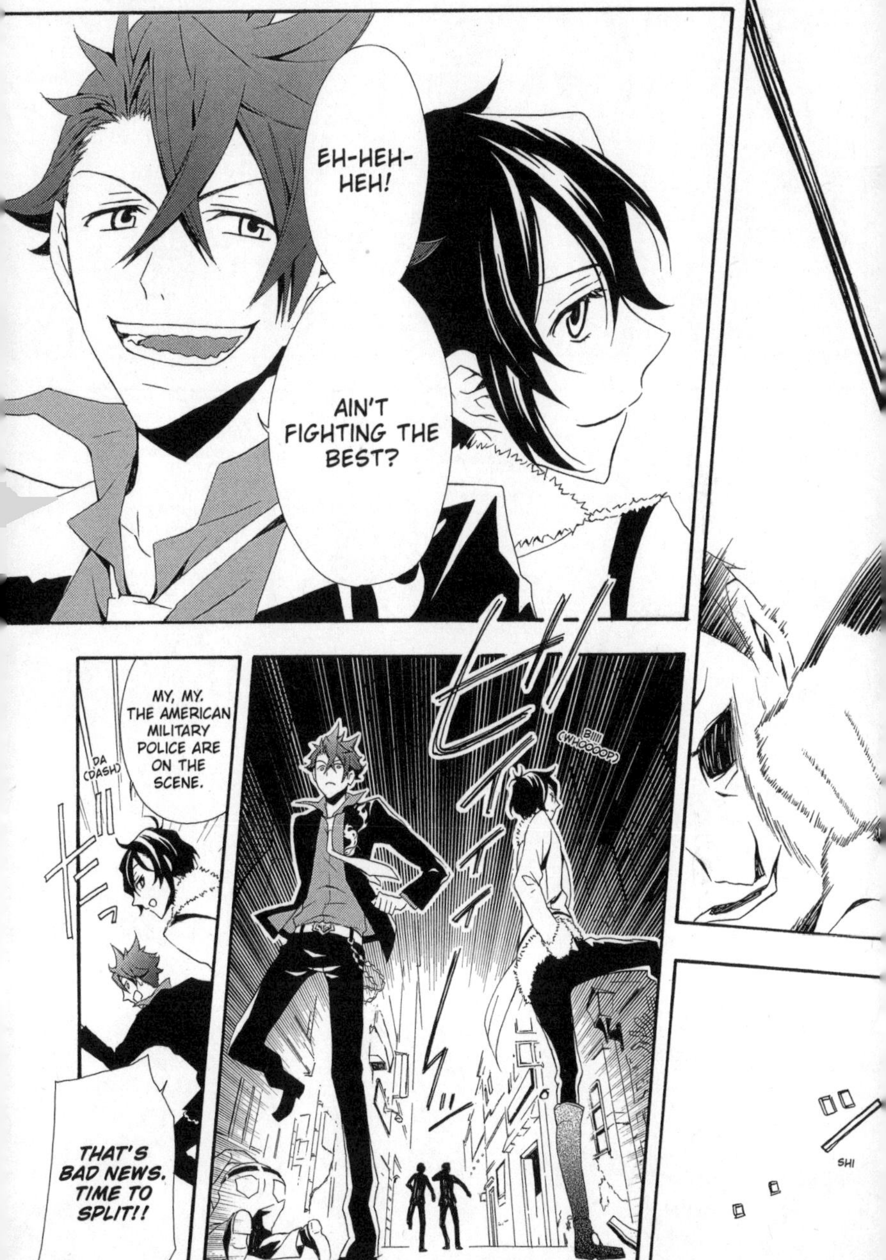
EH-HEH-HEH!
AIN'T FIGHTING THE BEST?
SHI
BI!!! (WHOOOOP)
MY, MY. THE AMERICAN MILITARY POLICE ARE ON THE SCENE.
DA (DASH)
THAT'S BAD NEWS. TIME TO SPLIT!!

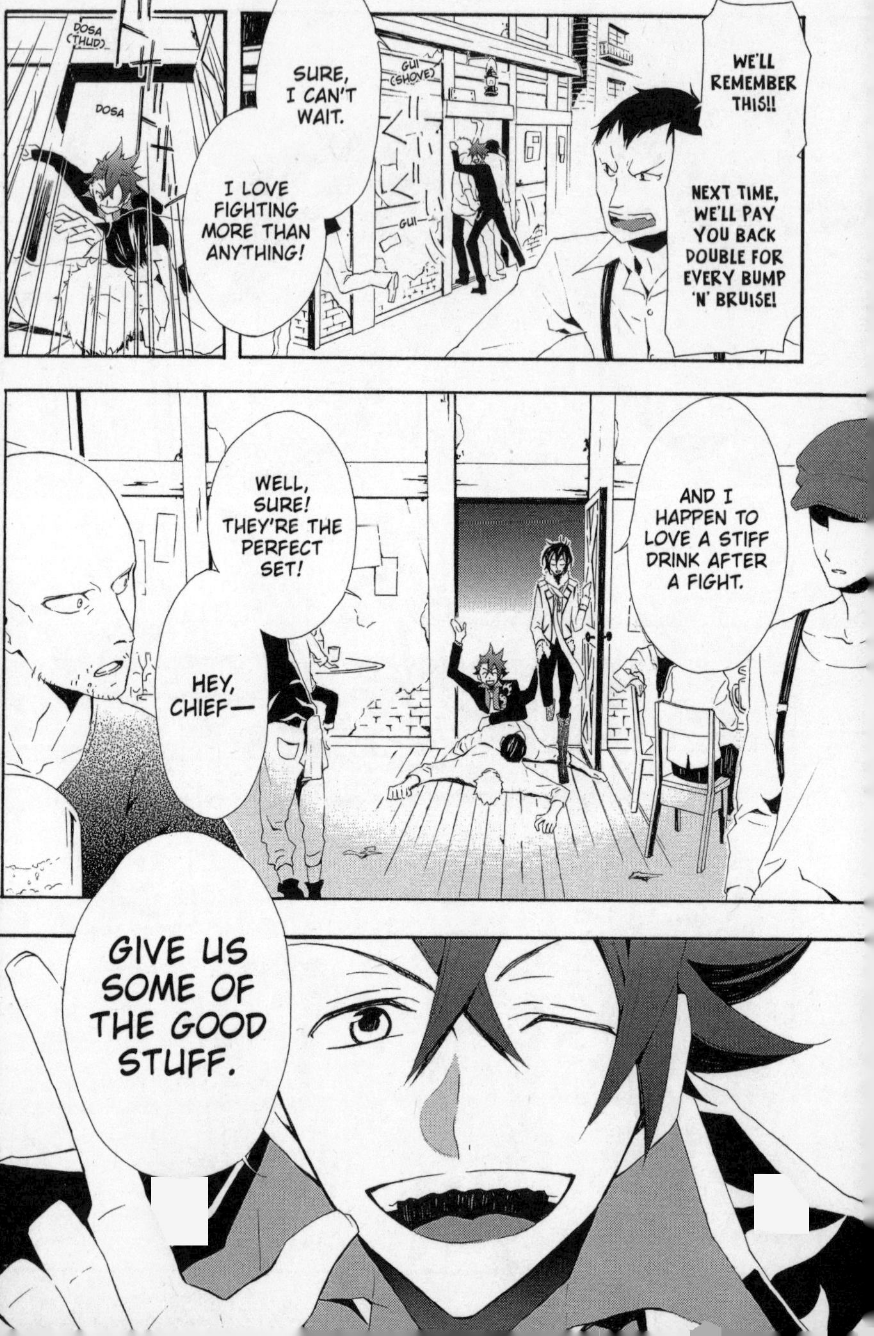
WE'LL REMEMBER THIS!!
NEXT TIME, WE'LL PAY YOU BACK DOUBLE FOR EVERY BUMP 'N' BRUISE!
SURE, I CAN'T WAIT.
GUI (SHOVE)
GUI
I LOVE FIGHTING MORE THAN ANYTHING!
DOSA (THUD)
DOSA
AND I HAPPEN TO LOVE A STIFF DRINK AFTER A FIGHT.
WELL, SURE! THEY'RE THE PERFECT SET!
HEY, CHIEF—
GIVE US SOME OF THE GOOD STUFF.

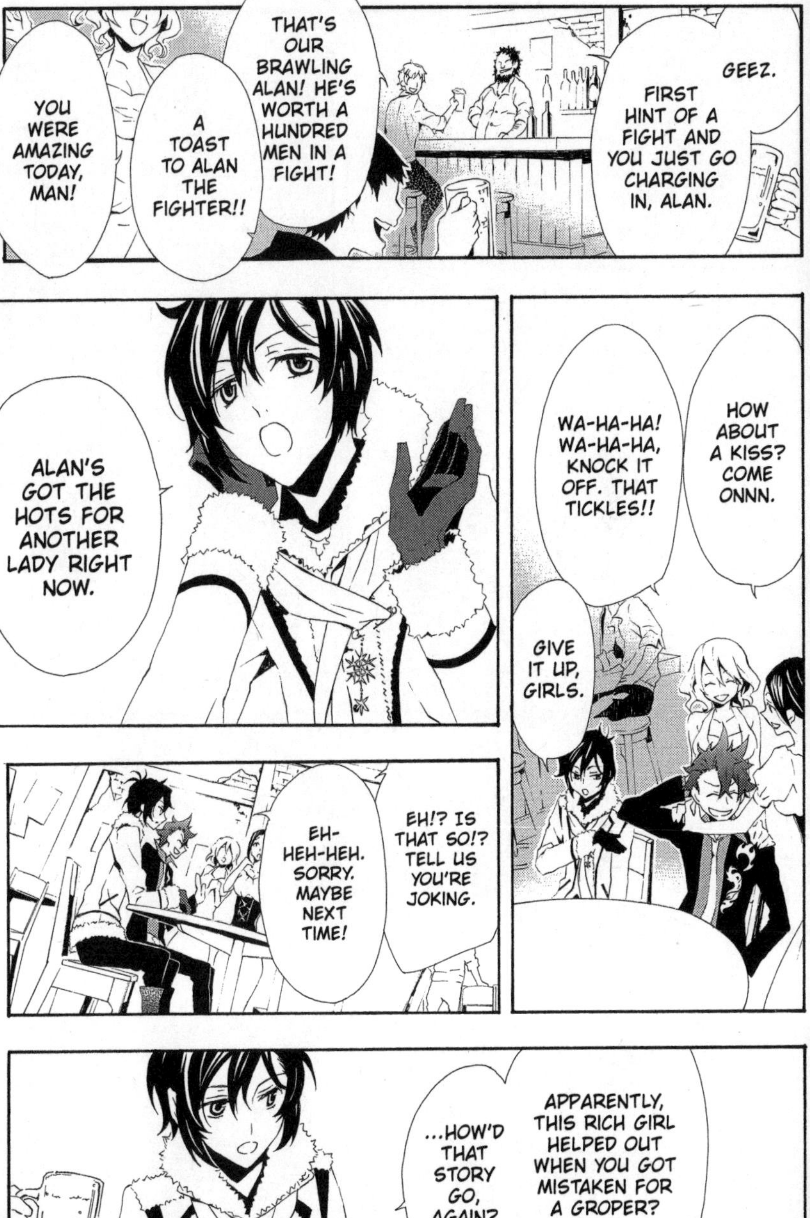
GEEZ. FIRST HINT OF A FIGHT AND YOU JUST GO CHARGING IN, ALAN.
THAT'S OUR BRAWLING ALAN! HE'S WORTH A HUNDRED MEN IN A FIGHT!
A TOAST TO ALAN THE FIGHTER!!
YOU WERE AMAZING TODAY, MAN!
HOW ABOUT A KISS? COME ONNN.
WA-HA-HA! WA-HA-HA, KNOCK IT OFF. THAT TICKLES!!
GIVE IT UP, GIRLS.
ALAN'S GOT THE HOTS FOR ANOTHER LADY RIGHT NOW.
EH!? IS THAT SO!? TELL US YOU'RE JOKING.
EH-HEH-HEH. SORRY. MAYBE NEXT TIME!
APPARENTLY, THIS RICH GIRL HELPED OUT WHEN YOU GOT MISTAKEN FOR A GROPER?
...HOW'D THAT STORY GO, AGAIN?

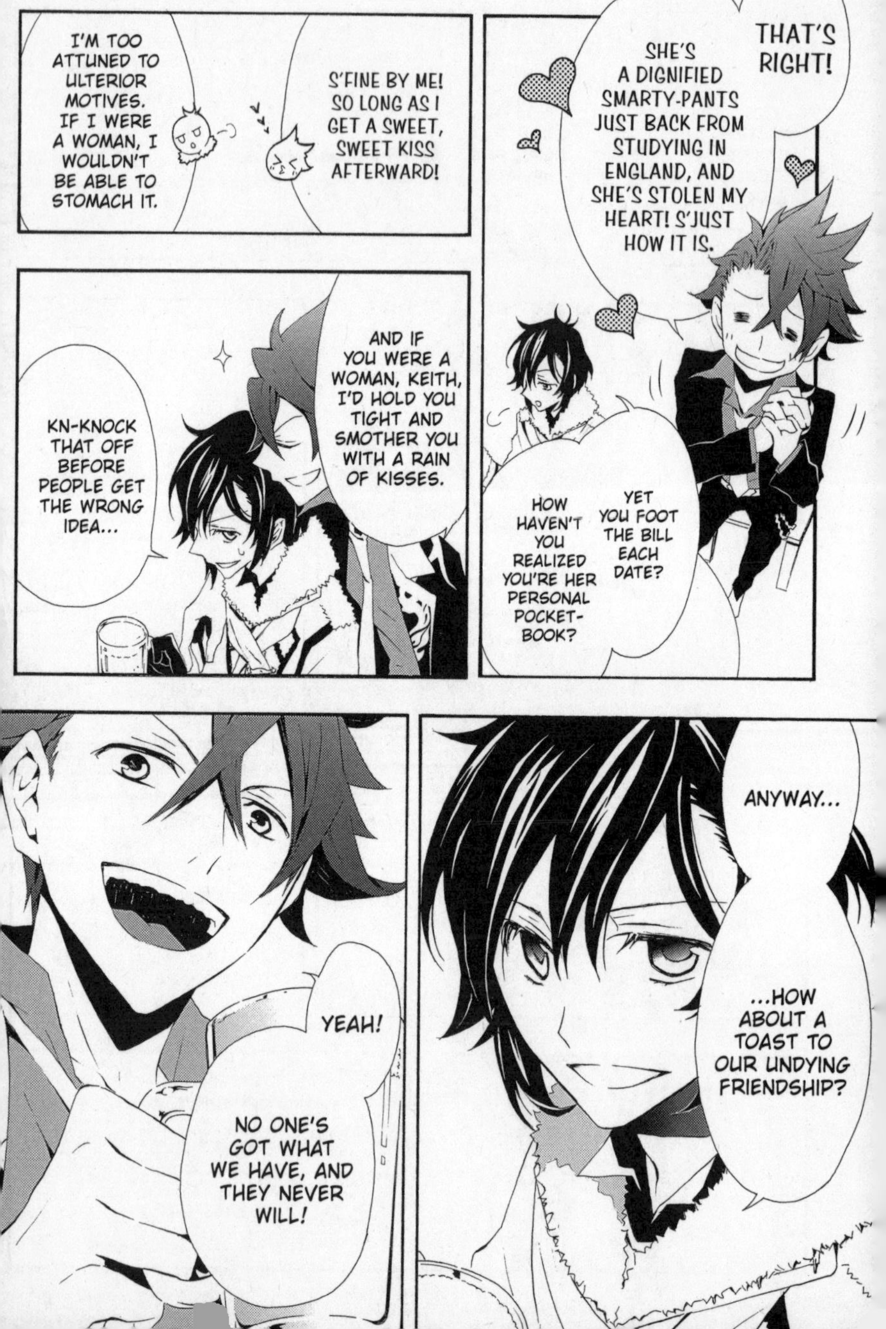
THAT'S RIGHT!
SHE'S A DIGNIFIED SMARTY-PANTS JUST BACK FROM STUDYING IN ENGLAND, AND SHE'S STOLEN MY HEART! S'JUST HOW IT IS.
YET YOU FOOT THE BILL EACH DATE?
HOW HAVEN'T YOU REALIZED YOU'RE HER PERSONAL POCKET-BOOK?
S'FINE BY ME! SO LONG AS I GET A SWEET, SWEET KISS AFTERWARD!
I'M TOO ATTUNED TO ULTERIOR MOTIVES. IF I WERE A WOMAN, I WOULDN'T BE ABLE TO STOMACH IT.
AND IF YOU WERE A WOMAN, KEITH, I'D HOLD YOU TIGHT AND SMOTHER YOU WITH A RAIN OF KISSES.
KN-KNOCK THAT OFF BEFORE PEOPLE GET THE WRONG IDEA...
ANYWAY...
...HOW ABOUT A TOAST TO OUR UNDYING FRIENDSHIP?
YEAH!
NO ONE'S GOT WHAT WE HAVE, AND THEY NEVER WILL!

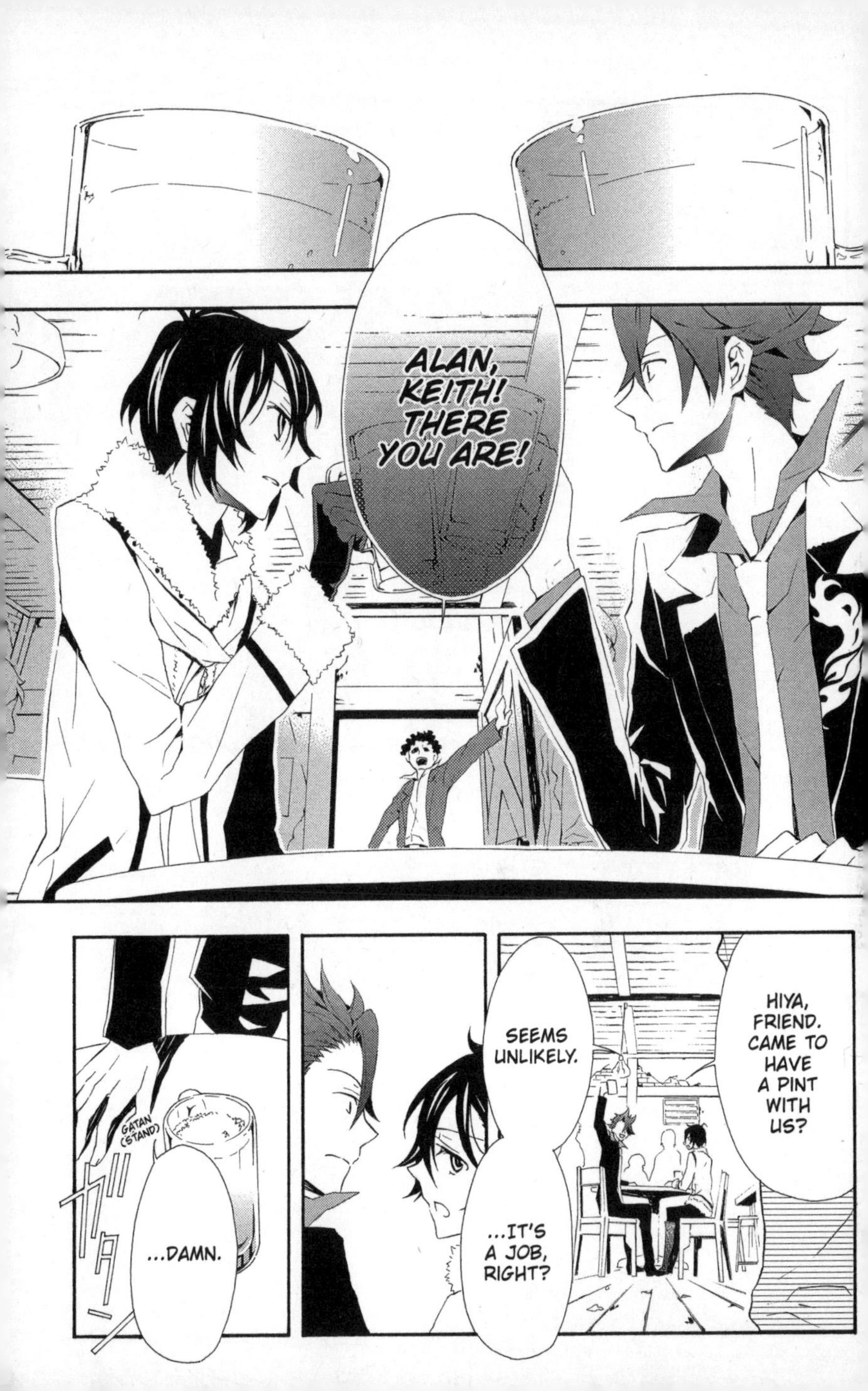
ALAN, KEITH! THERE YOU ARE!
HIYA, FRIEND. CAME TO HAVE A PINT WITH US?
SEEMS UNLIKELY.
...IT'S A JOB, RIGHT?
GATAN (STAND)
...DAMN.

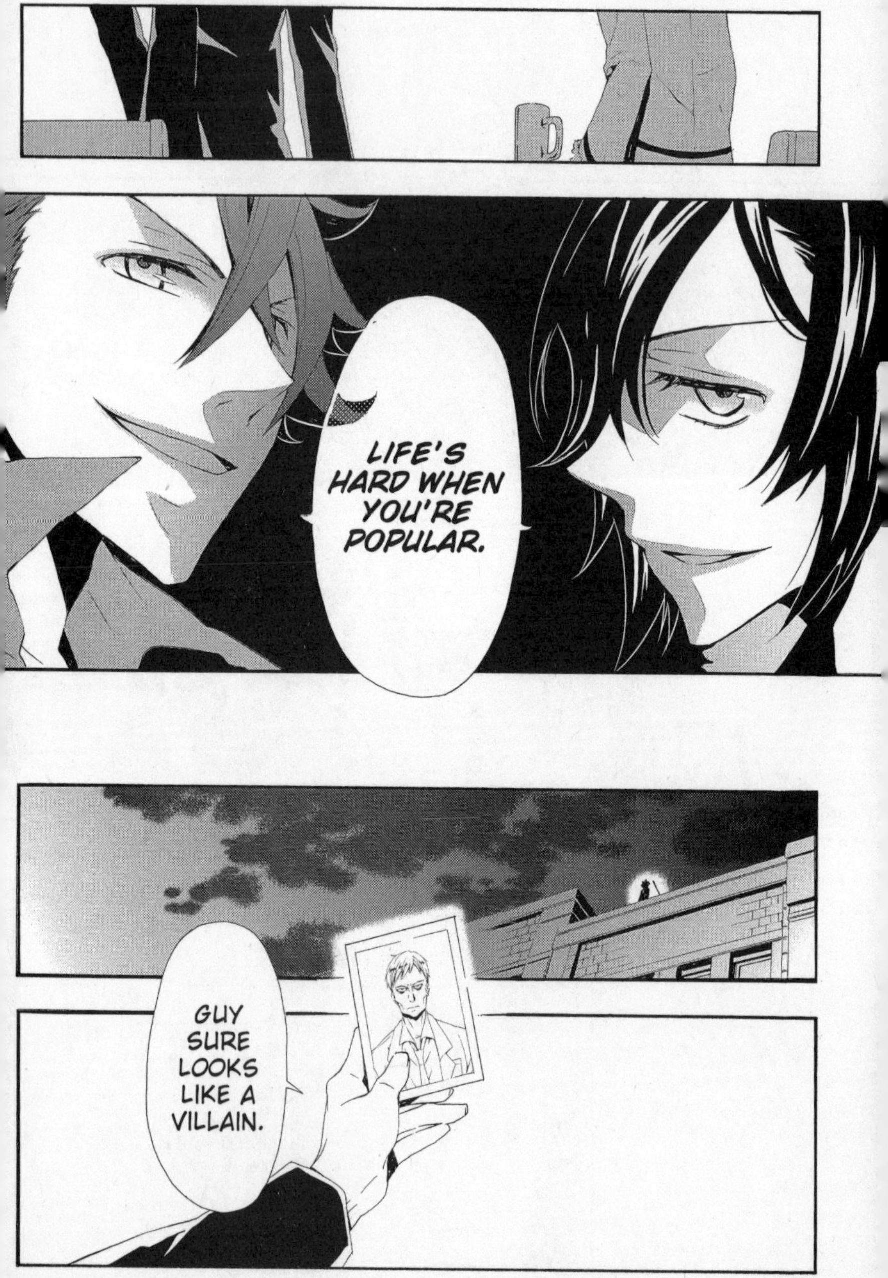
LIFE'S HARD WHEN YOU'RE POPULAR.
GUY SURE LOOKS LIKE A VILLAIN.

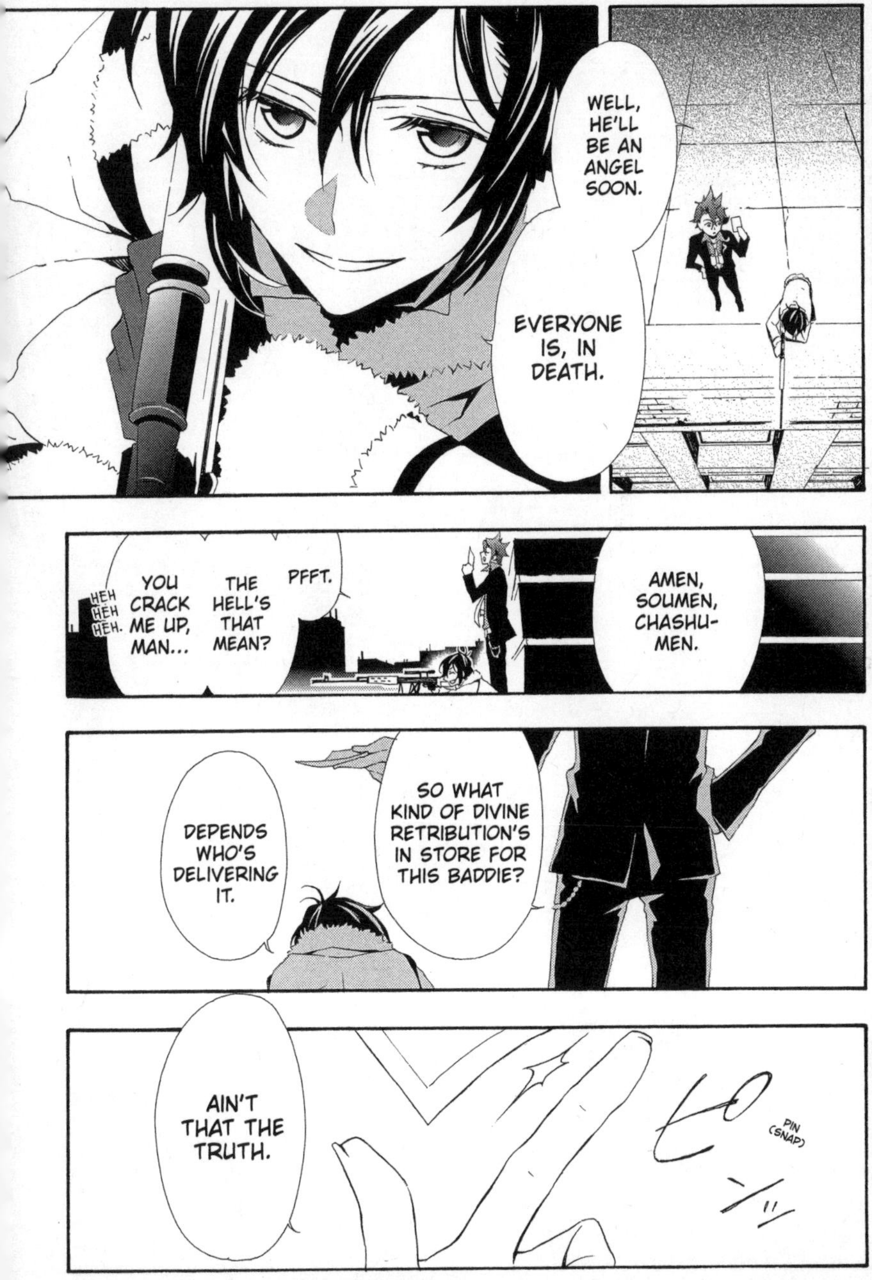
WELL, HE'LL BE AN ANGEL SOON.
EVERYONE IS, IN DEATH.
AMEN, SOUMEN, CHASHU-MEN.
PFFT.
THE HELL'S THAT MEAN?
YOU CRACK ME UP, MAN...
HEH HEH HEH.
SO WHAT KIND OF DIVINE RETRIBUTION'S IN STORE FOR THIS BADDIE?
DEPENDS WHO'S DELIVERING IT.
PIN (SNAP)
AIN'T THAT THE TRUTH.

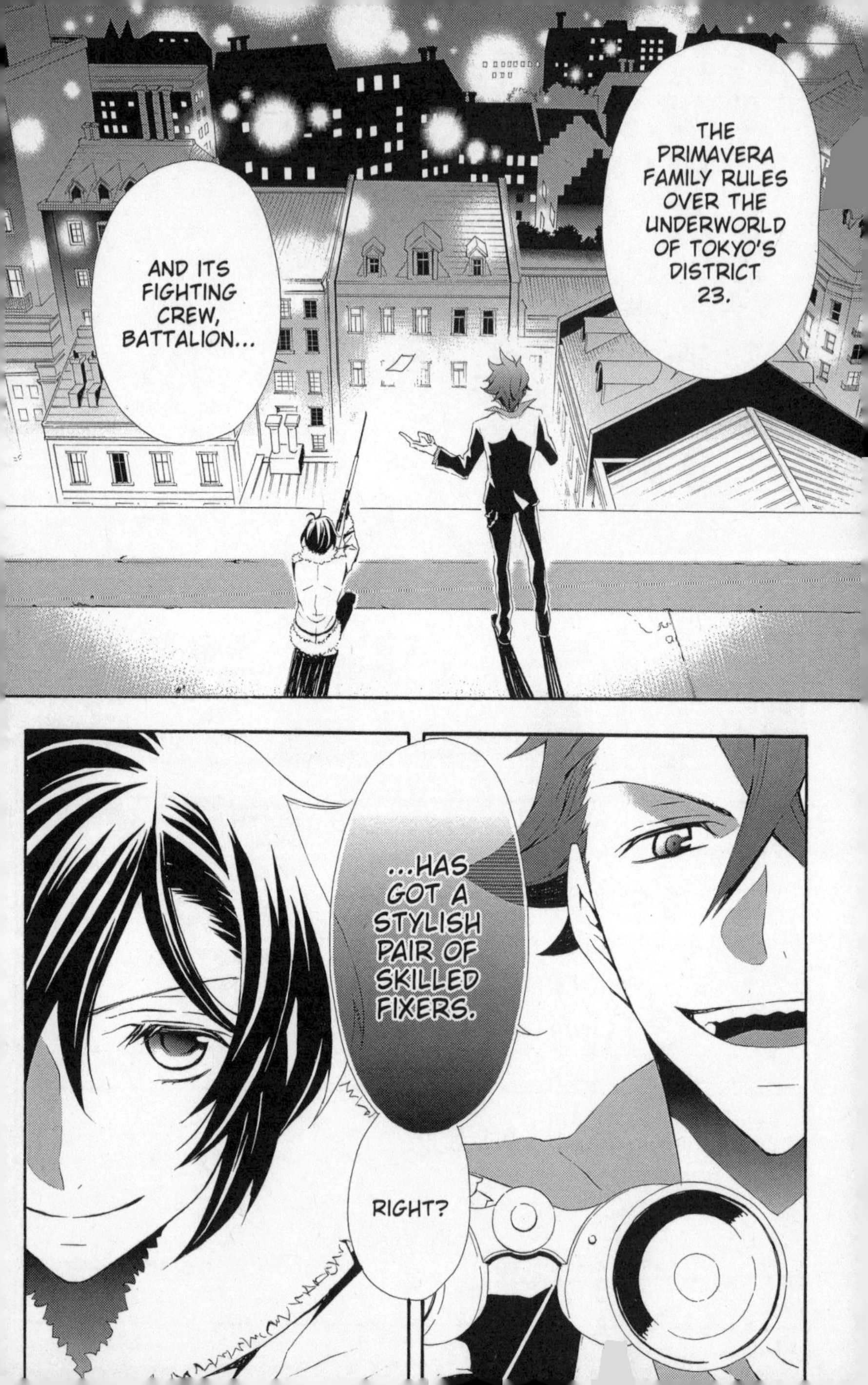
THE PRIMAVERA FAMILY RULES OVER THE UNDERWORLD OF TOKYO'S DISTRICT 23.
AND ITS FIGHTING CREW, BATTALION...
...HAS GOT A STYLISH PAIR OF SKILLED FIXERS.
RIGHT?

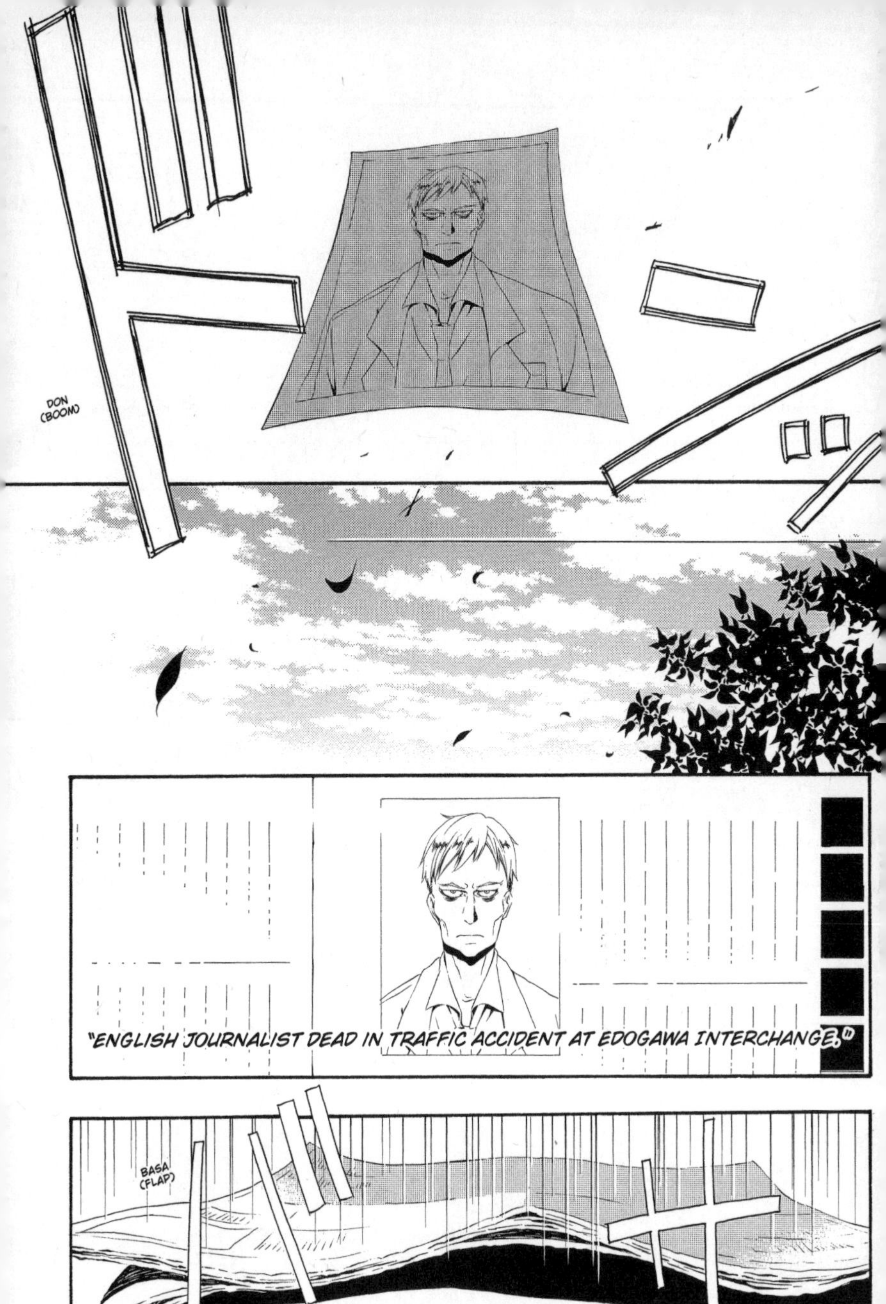
DON (BOOM)
"ENGLISH JOURNALIST DEAD IN TRAFFIC ACCIDENT AT EDOGAWA INTERCHANGE."
BASA (FLAP)

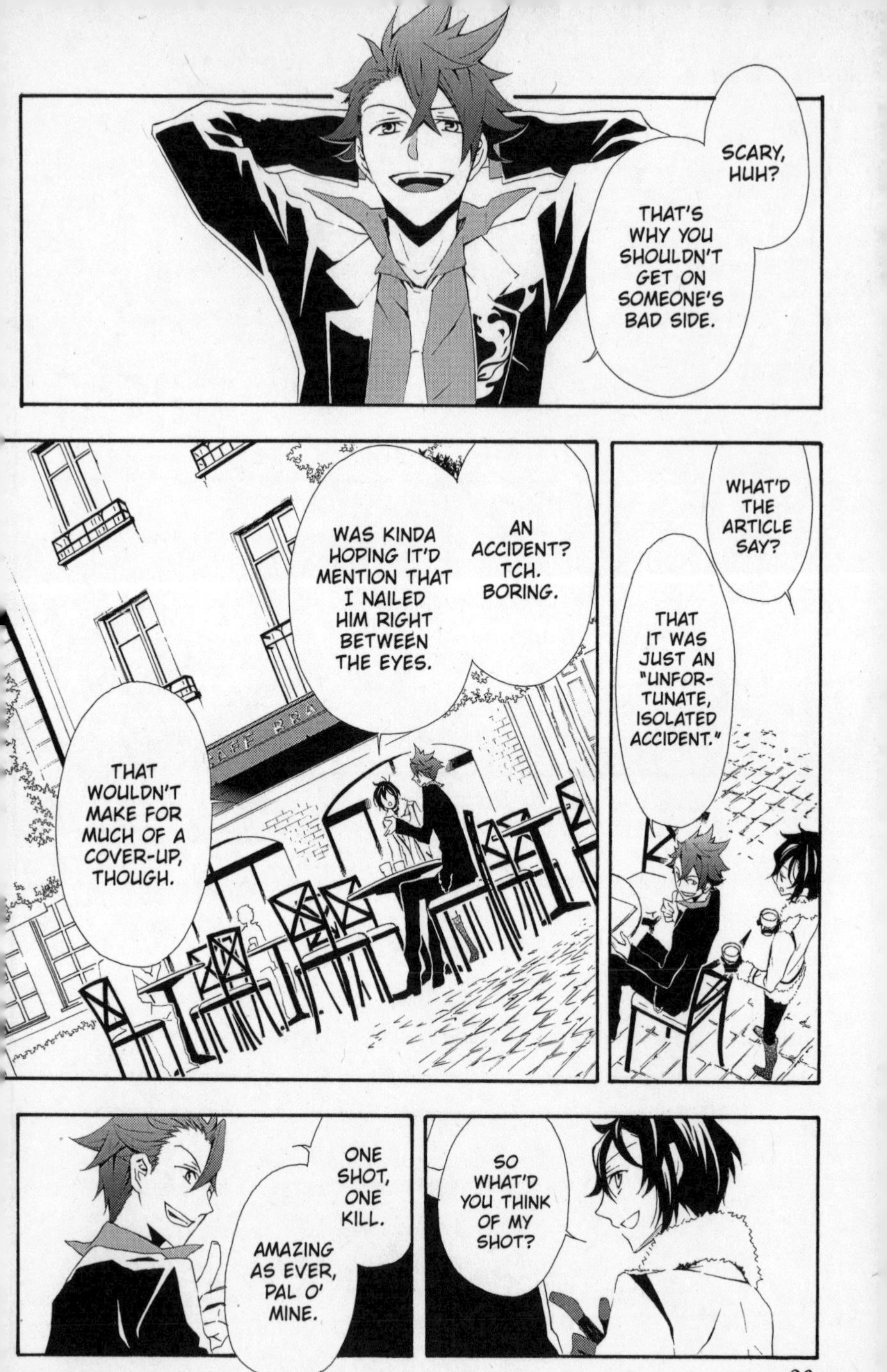
SCARY, HUH?
THAT'S WHY YOU SHOULDN'T GET ON SOMEONE'S BAD SIDE.
WHAT'D THE ARTICLE SAY?
THAT IT WAS JUST AN "UNFORTUNATE, ISOLATED ACCIDENT."
AN ACCIDENT? TCH. BORING.
WAS KINDA HOPING IT'D MENTION THAT I NAILED HIM RIGHT BETWEEN THE EYES.
THAT WOULDN'T MAKE FOR MUCH OF A COVER-UP, THOUGH.
SO WHAT'D YOU THINK OF MY SHOT?
ONE SHOT, ONE KILL.
AMAZING AS EVER, PAL O' MINE.

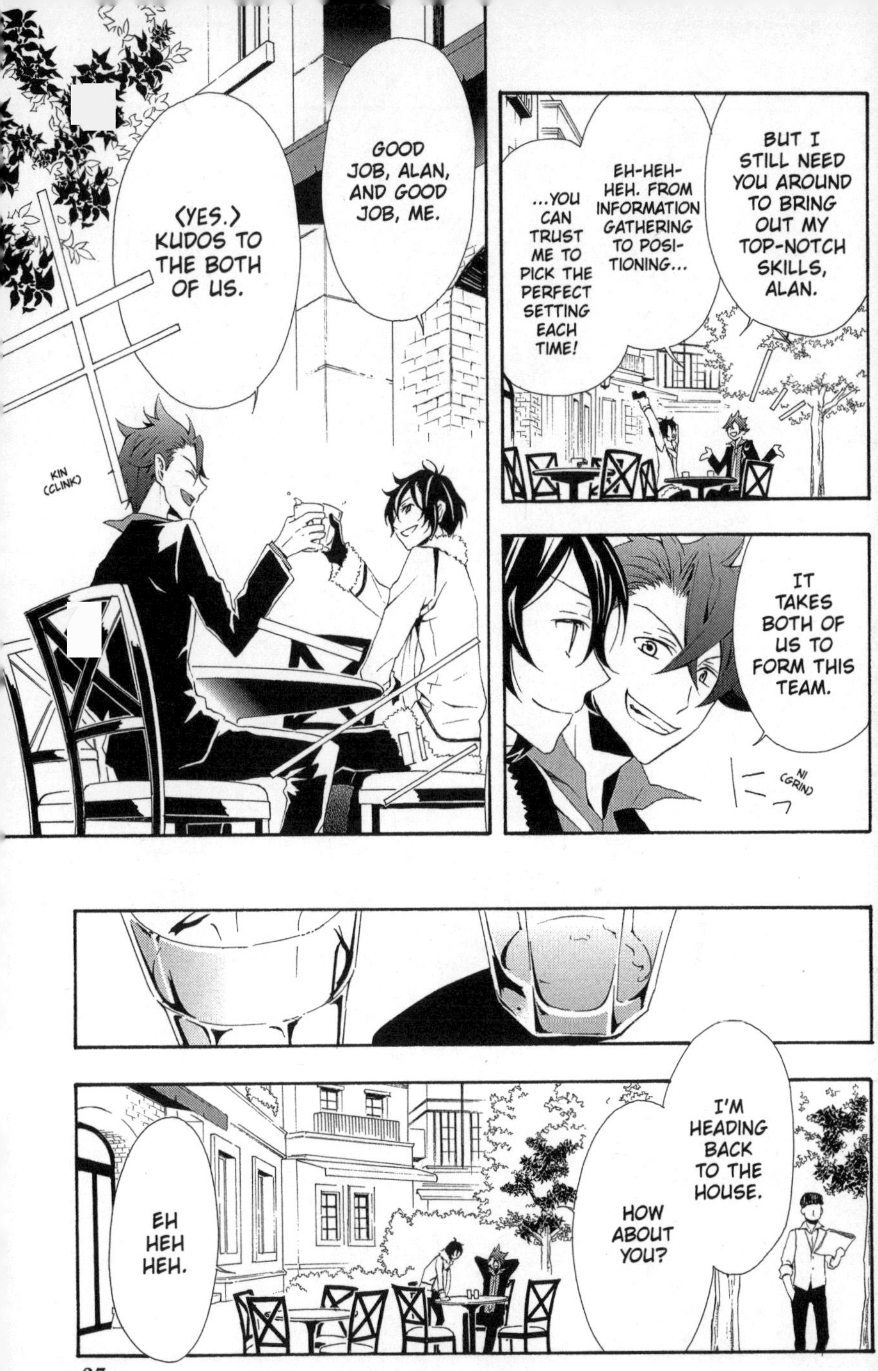
BUT I STILL NEED YOU AROUND TO BRING OUT MY TOP-NOTCH SKILLS, ALAN.
EH-HEH-HEH. FROM INFORMATION GATHERING TO POSITIONING...
...YOU CAN TRUST ME TO PICK THE PERFECT SETTING EACH TIME!
IT TAKES BOTH OF US TO FORM THIS TEAM.
NI (GRIN)
GOOD JOB, ALAN, AND GOOD JOB, ME.
〈YES.〉 KUDOS TO THE BOTH OF US.
KIN (CLINK)
I'M HEADING BACK TO THE HOUSE.
HOW ABOUT YOU?
EH HEH HEH.

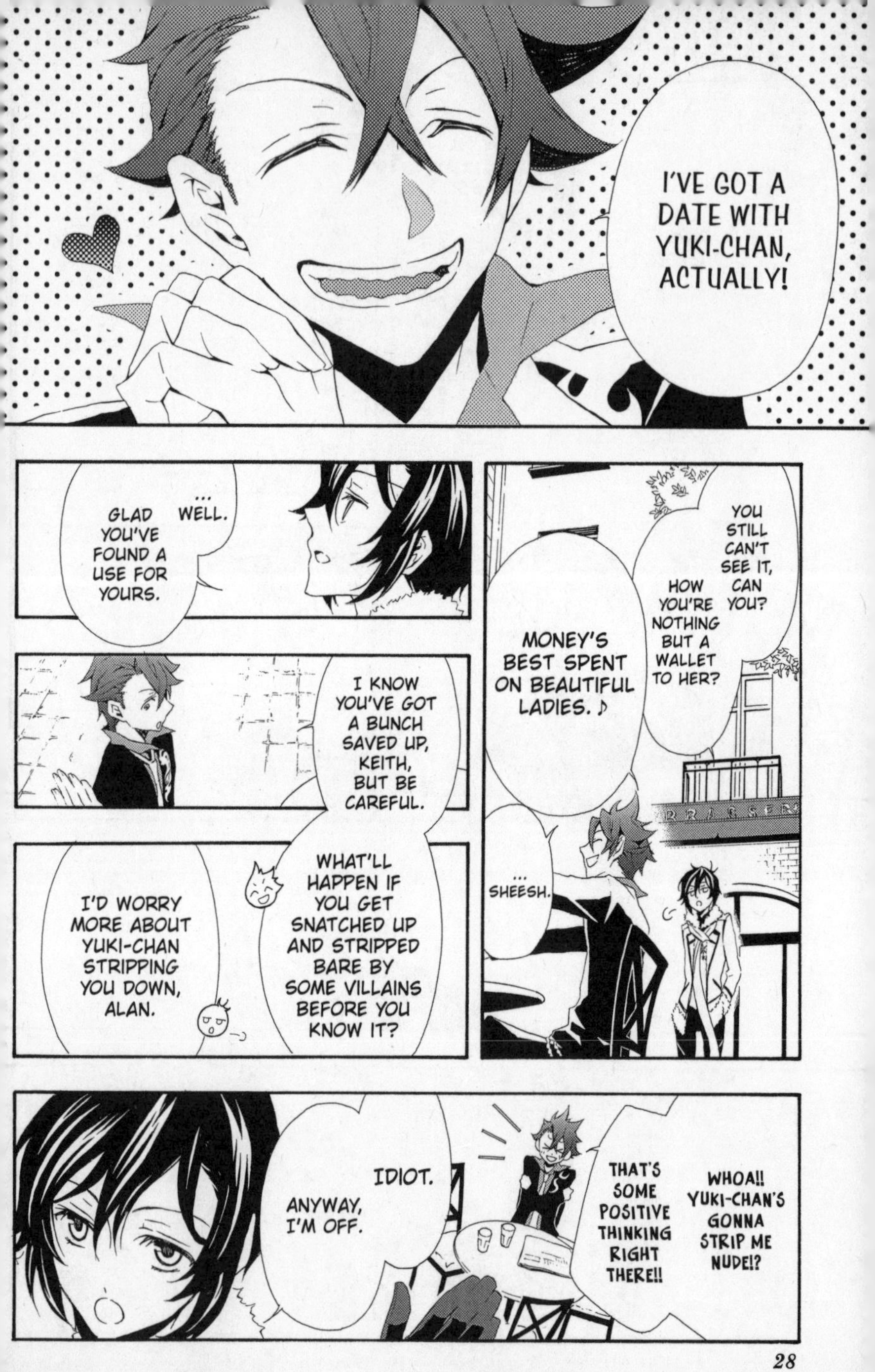

I'VE GOT A DATE WITH YUKI-CHAN, ACTUALLY!
YOU STILL CAN'T SEE IT, CAN YOU?
HOW YOU'RE NOTHING BUT A WALLET TO HER?
MONEY'S BEST SPENT ON BEAUTIFUL LADIES. ♪
... SHEESH.
... WELL.
GLAD YOU'VE FOUND A USE FOR YOURS.
I KNOW YOU'VE GOT A BUNCH SAVED UP, KEITH, BUT BE CAREFUL.
WHAT'LL HAPPEN IF YOU GET SNATCHED UP AND STRIPPED BARE BY SOME VILLAINS BEFORE YOU KNOW IT?
I'D WORRY MORE ABOUT YUKI-CHAN STRIPPING YOU DOWN, ALAN.
WHOA!! YUKI-CHAN'S GONNA STRIP ME NUDE!?
THAT'S SOME POSITIVE THINKING RIGHT THERE!!
IDIOT.
ANYWAY, I'M OFF.

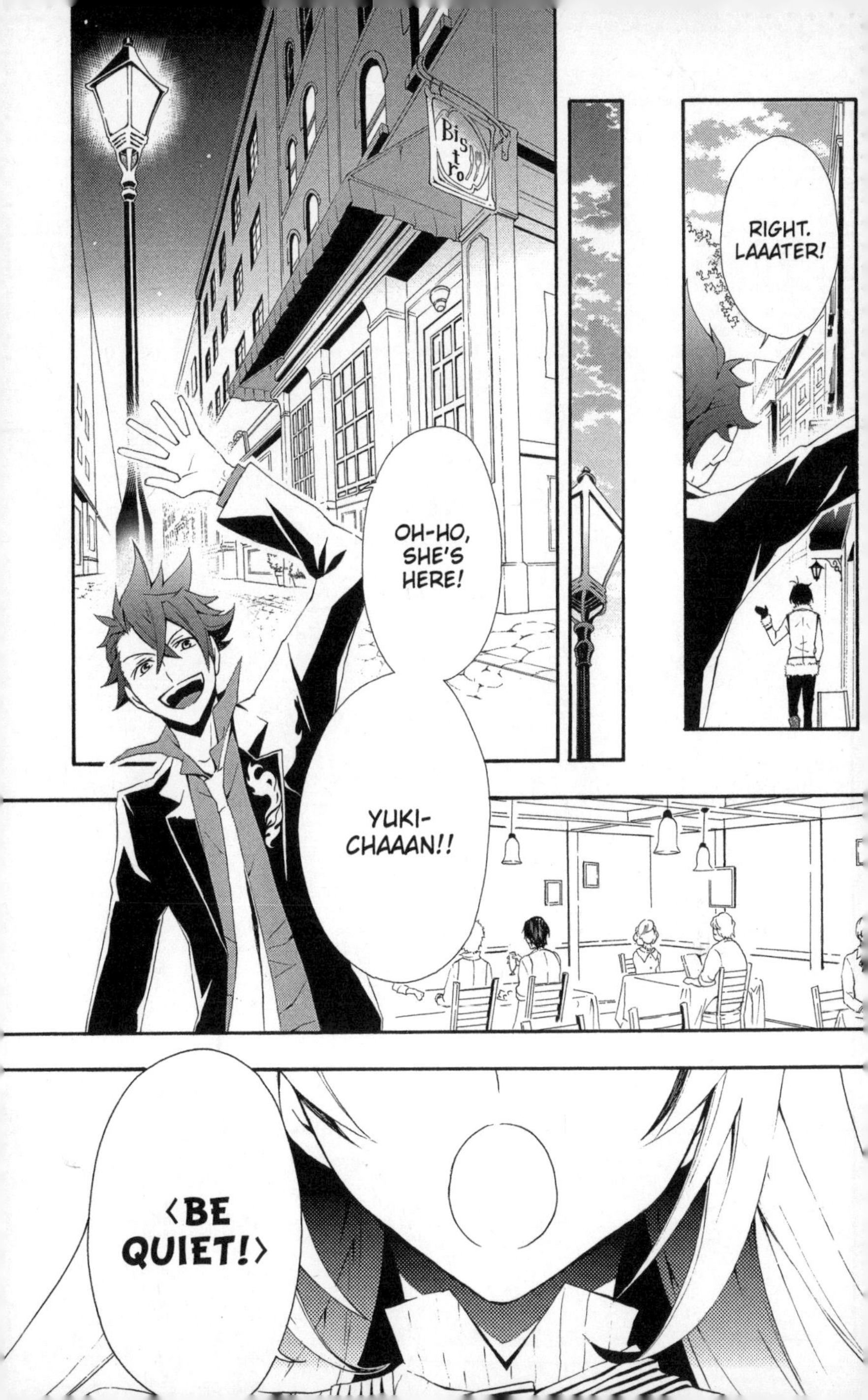
RIGHT. LAAATER!
OH-HO, SHE'S HERE!
YUKI-CHAAAN!!
〈BE QUIET!〉

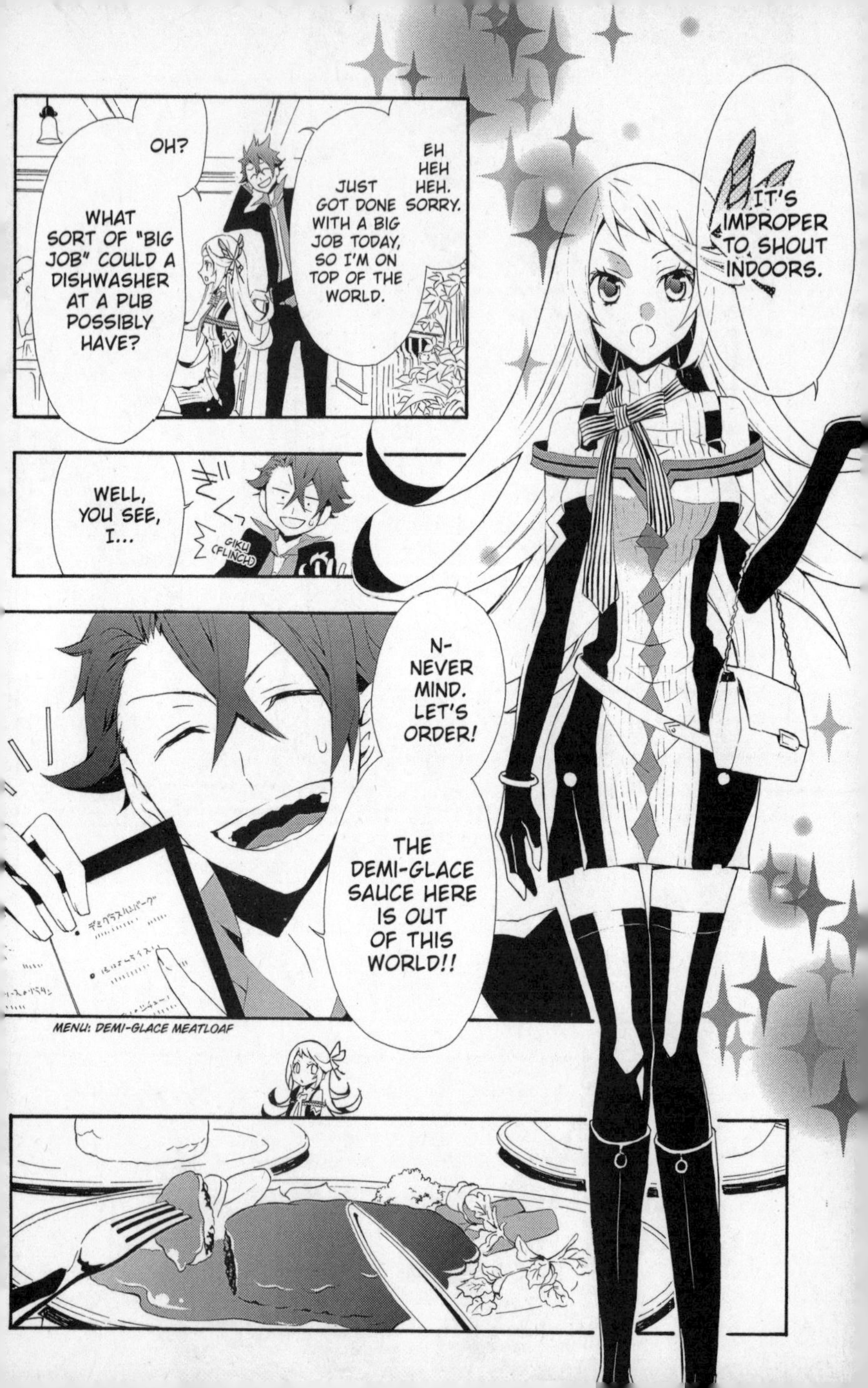
IT'S IMPROPER TO SHOUT INDOORS.
EH HEH HEH. SORRY.
JUST GOT DONE WITH A BIG JOB TODAY, SO I'M ON TOP OF THE WORLD.
OH?
WHAT SORT OF "BIG JOB" COULD A DISHWASHER AT A PUB POSSIBLY HAVE?
GIKU (FLINCH)
WELL, YOU SEE, I...
N-NEVER MIND. LET'S ORDER!
THE DEMI-GLACE SAUCE HERE IS OUT OF THIS WORLD!!
MENU: DEMI-GLACE MEATLOAF

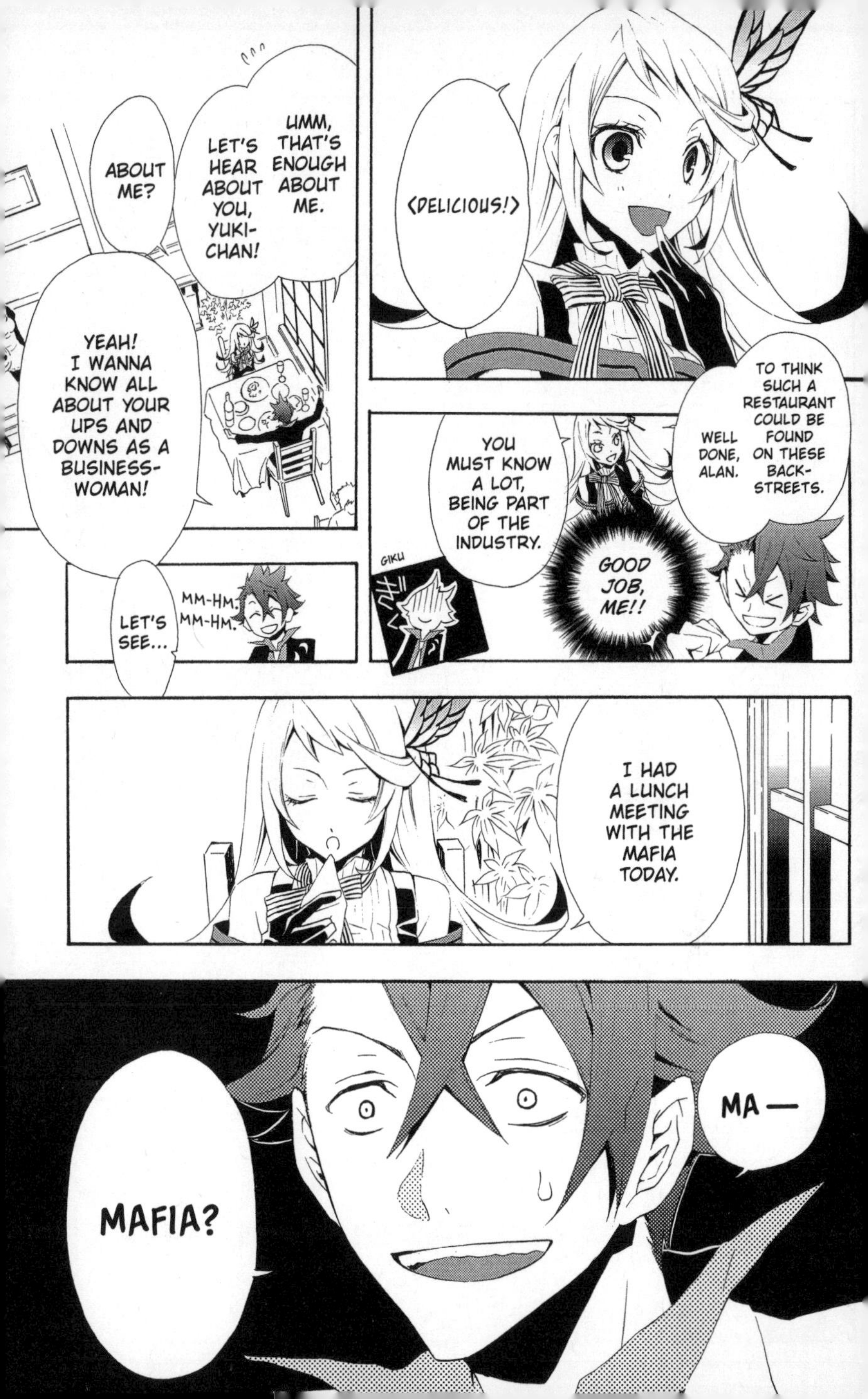
⟨DELICIOUS!⟩
UMM, THAT'S ENOUGH ABOUT ME.
LET'S HEAR ABOUT YOU, YUKI-CHAN!
ABOUT ME?
YEAH! I WANNA KNOW ALL ABOUT YOUR UPS AND DOWNS AS A BUSINESS-WOMAN!
TO THINK SUCH A RESTAURANT COULD BE FOUND ON THESE BACK-STREETS.
WELL DONE, ALAN.
GOOD JOB, ME!!
YOU MUST KNOW A LOT, BEING PART OF THE INDUSTRY.
GIKU
MM-HM. MM-HM.
LET'S SEE...
I HAD A LUNCH MEETING WITH THE MAFIA TODAY.
MA—
MAFIA?

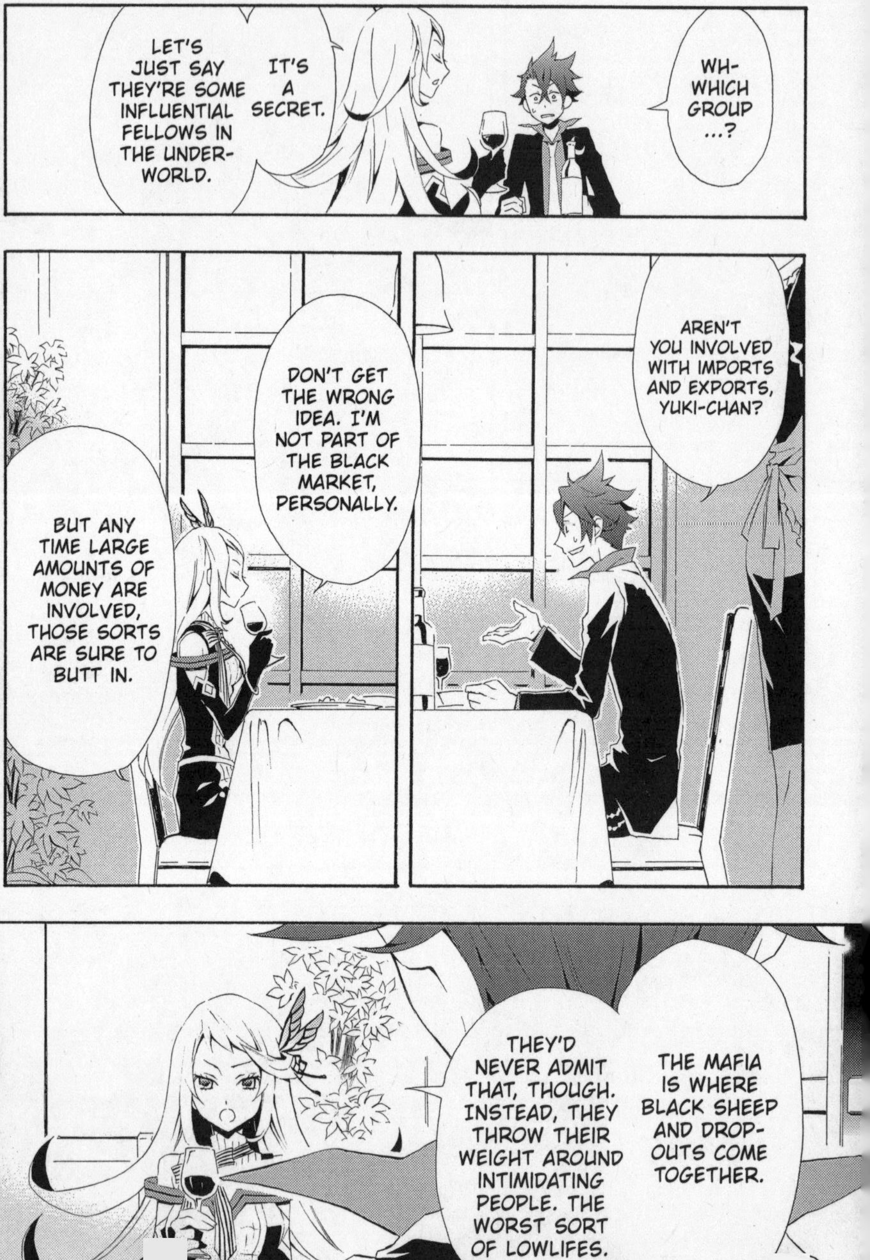
WH-WHICH GROUP...?
IT'S A SECRET.
LET'S JUST SAY THEY'RE SOME INFLUENTIAL FELLOWS IN THE UNDER-WORLD.
AREN'T YOU INVOLVED WITH IMPORTS AND EXPORTS, YUKI-CHAN?
DON'T GET THE WRONG IDEA. I'M NOT PART OF THE BLACK MARKET, PERSONALLY.
BUT ANY TIME LARGE AMOUNTS OF MONEY ARE INVOLVED, THOSE SORTS ARE SURE TO BUTT IN.
THE MAFIA IS WHERE BLACK SHEEP AND DROP-OUTS COME TOGETHER.
THEY'D NEVER ADMIT THAT, THOUGH. INSTEAD, THEY THROW THEIR WEIGHT AROUND INTIMIDATING PEOPLE. THE WORST SORT OF LOWLIFES.

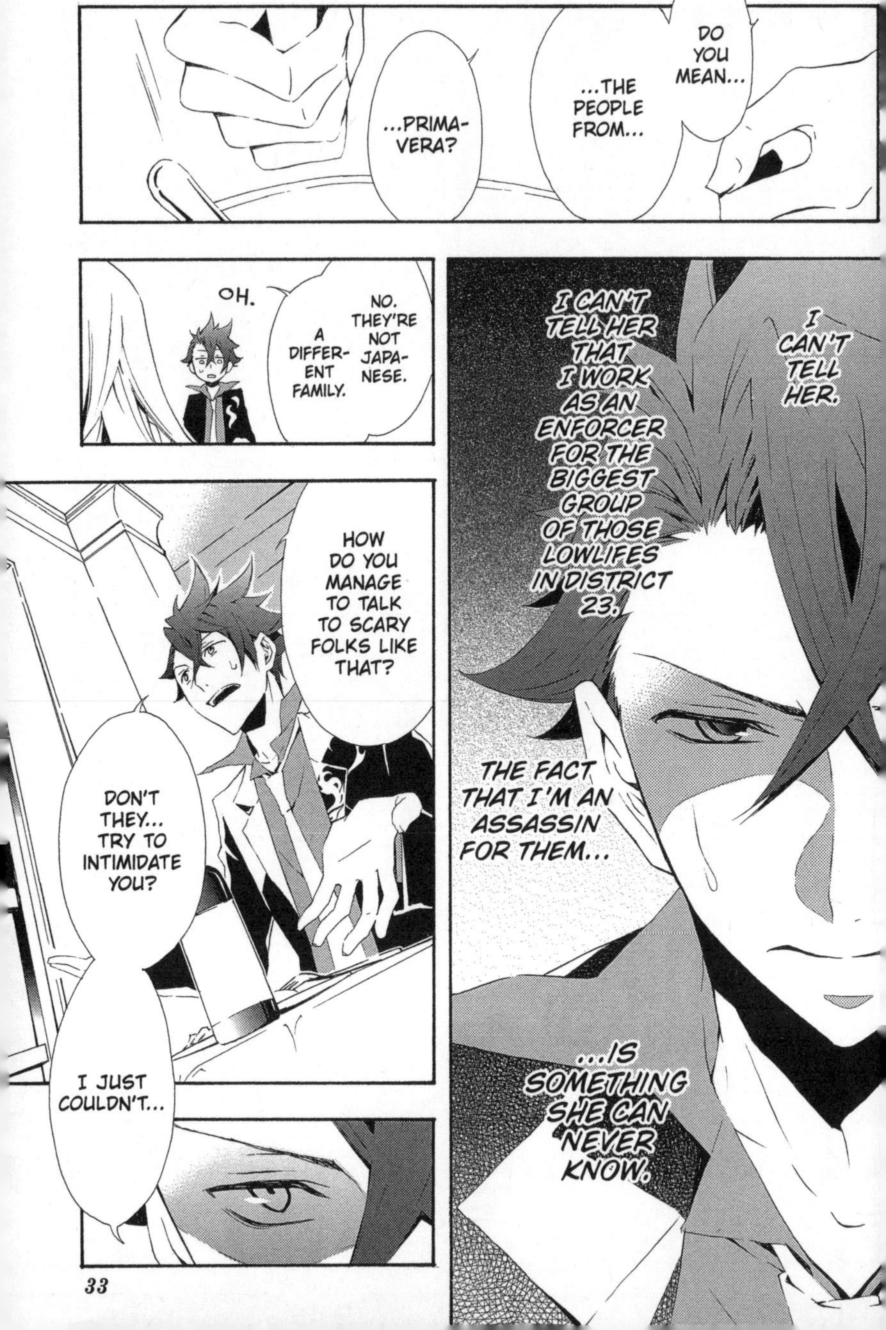
DO YOU MEAN...
...THE PEOPLE FROM...
...PRIMAVERA?
I CAN'T TELL HER.
I CAN'T TELL HER THAT I WORK AS AN ENFORCER FOR THE BIGGEST GROUP OF THOSE LOWLIFES IN DISTRICT 23.
THE FACT THAT I'M AN ASSASSIN FOR THEM...
...IS SOMETHING SHE CAN NEVER KNOW.
NO. THEY'RE NOT JAPANESE.
A DIFFERENT FAMILY.
OH.
HOW DO YOU MANAGE TO TALK TO SCARY FOLKS LIKE THAT?
DON'T THEY... TRY TO INTIMIDATE YOU?
I JUST COULDN'T...

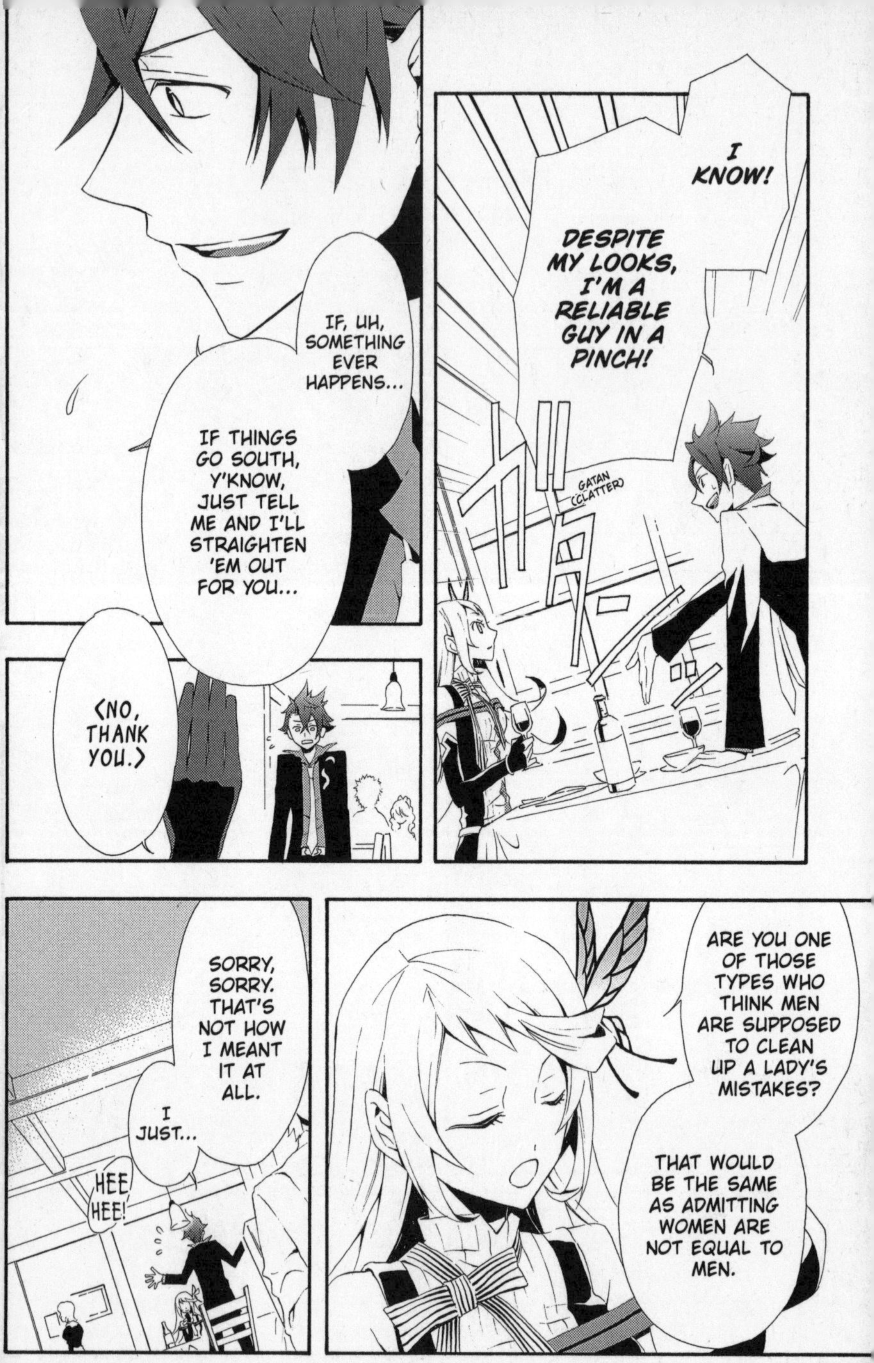
I KNOW!
DESPITE MY LOOKS, I'M A RELIABLE GUY IN A PINCH!
GATAN (CLATTER)
IF, UH, SOMETHING EVER HAPPENS...
IF THINGS GO SOUTH, Y'KNOW, JUST TELL ME AND I'LL STRAIGHTEN 'EM OUT FOR YOU...
<NO, THANK YOU.>
ARE YOU ONE OF THOSE TYPES WHO THINK MEN ARE SUPPOSED TO CLEAN UP A LADY'S MISTAKES?
THAT WOULD BE THE SAME AS ADMITTING WOMEN ARE NOT EQUAL TO MEN.
SORRY, SORRY. THAT'S NOT HOW I MEANT IT AT ALL.
I JUST...
HEE HEE!

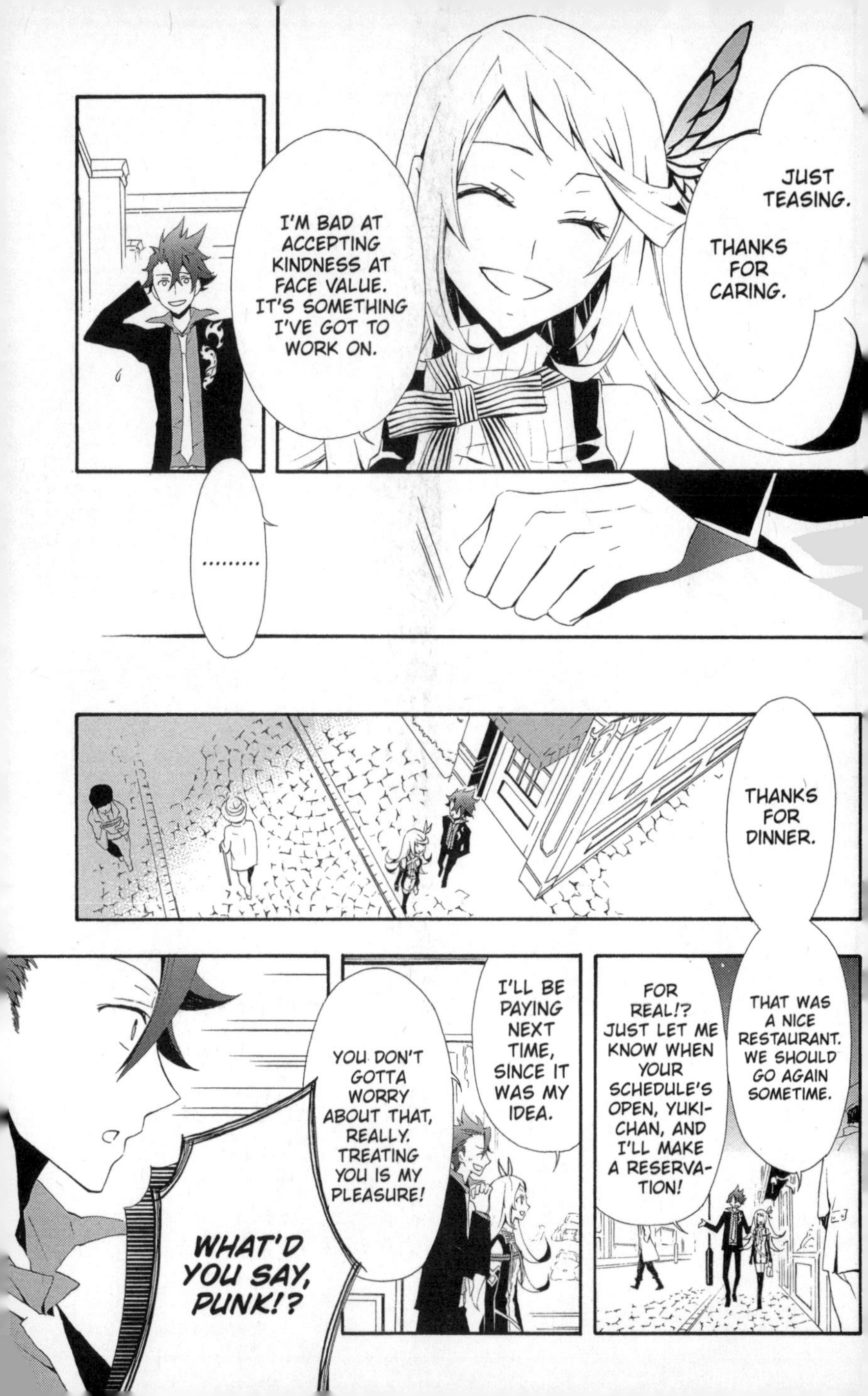
JUST TEASING.
THANKS FOR CARING.
I'M BAD AT ACCEPTING KINDNESS AT FACE VALUE. IT'S SOMETHING I'VE GOT TO WORK ON.
....
THANKS FOR DINNER.
THAT WAS A NICE RESTAURANT. WE SHOULD GO AGAIN SOMETIME.
FOR REAL!? JUST LET ME KNOW WHEN YOUR SCHEDULE'S OPEN, YUKI-CHAN, AND I'LL MAKE A RESERVA-TION!
I'LL BE PAYING NEXT TIME, SINCE IT WAS MY IDEA.
YOU DON'T GOTTA WORRY ABOUT THAT, REALLY. TREATING YOU IS MY PLEASURE!
WHAT'D YOU SAY, PUNK!?

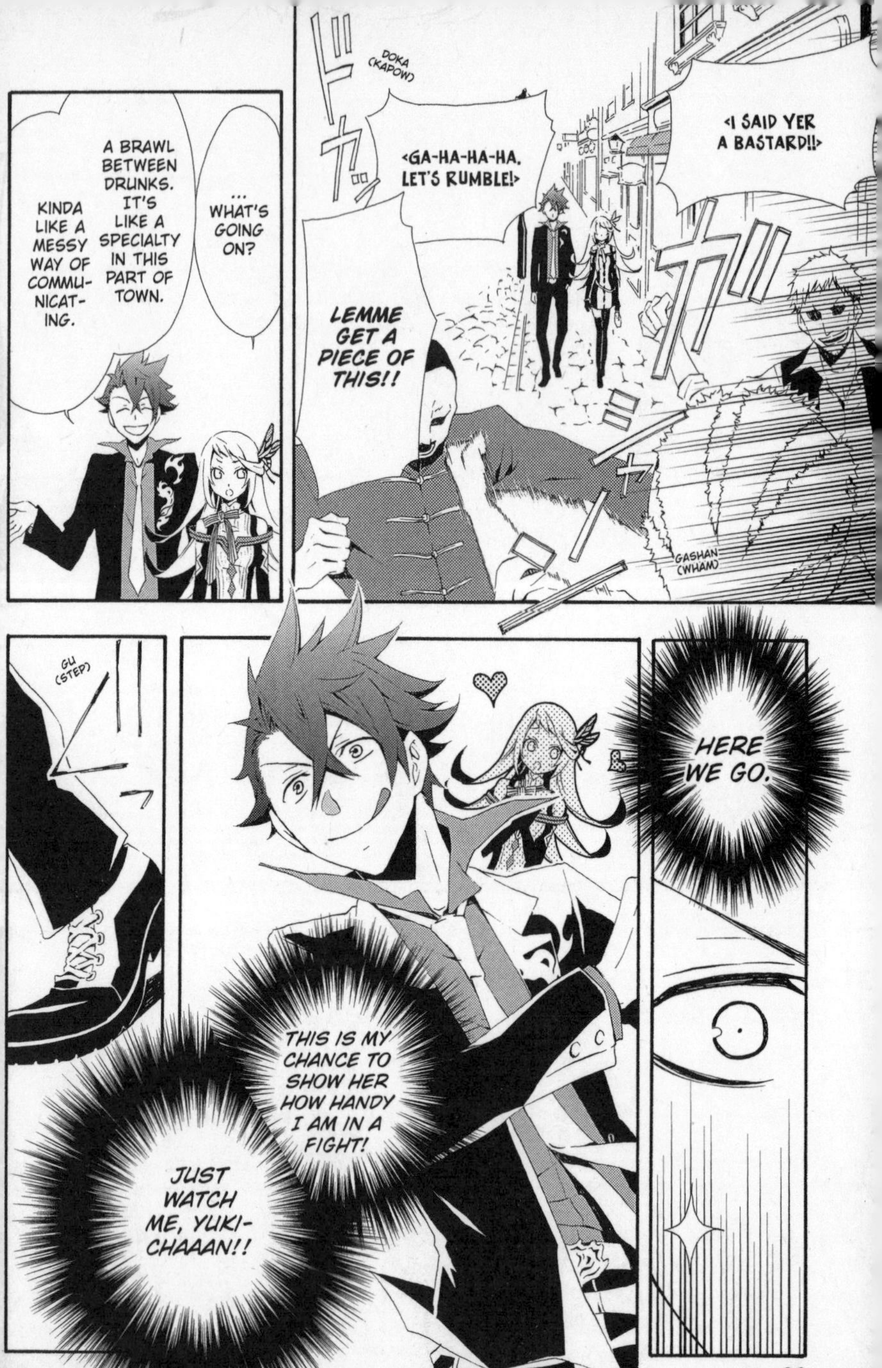
<I SAID YER A BASTARD!!>
DOKA (KAPOW)
<GA-HA-HA-HA. LET'S RUMBLE!>
LEMME GET A PIECE OF THIS!!
GASHAN (WHAM)
... WHAT'S GOING ON?
A BRAWL BETWEEN DRUNKS. IT'S LIKE A SPECIALTY IN THIS PART OF TOWN.
KINDA LIKE A MESSY WAY OF COMMUNICATING.
HERE WE GO.
THIS IS MY CHANCE TO SHOW HER HOW HANDY I AM IN A FIGHT!
JUST WATCH ME, YUKI-CHAAAN!!
GU (STEP)

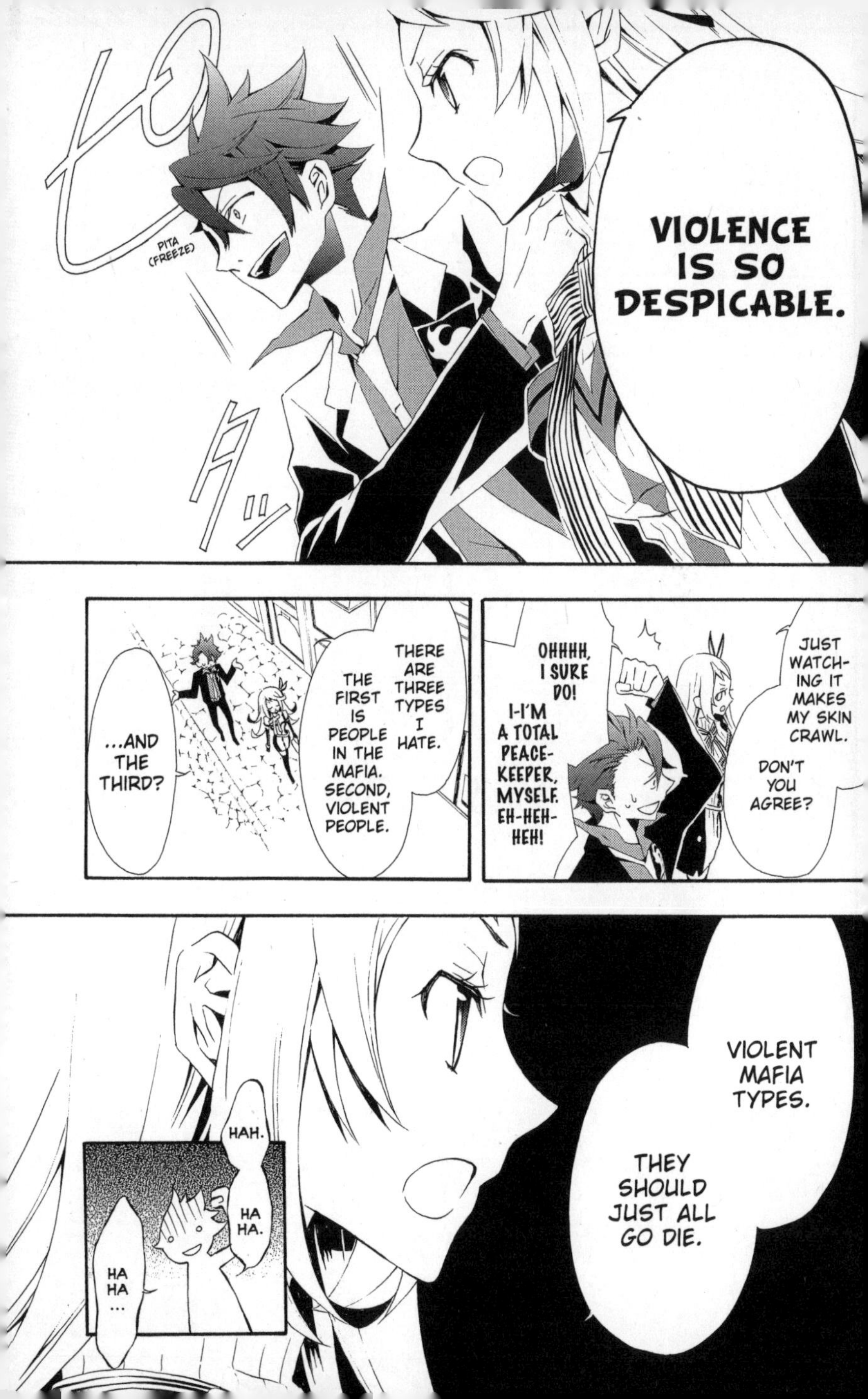
VIOLENCE IS SO DESPICABLE.
PITA (FREEZE)
JUST WATCHING IT MAKES MY SKIN CRAWL.
DON'T YOU AGREE?
OHHHH, I SURE DO!
I-I'M A TOTAL PEACEKEEPER, MYSELF. EH-HEH-HEH!
THERE ARE THREE TYPES I HATE.
THE FIRST IS PEOPLE IN THE MAFIA. SECOND, VIOLENT PEOPLE.
...AND THE THIRD?
VIOLENT MAFIA TYPES.
THEY SHOULD JUST ALL GO DIE.
HAH.
HA HA.
HA HA ...

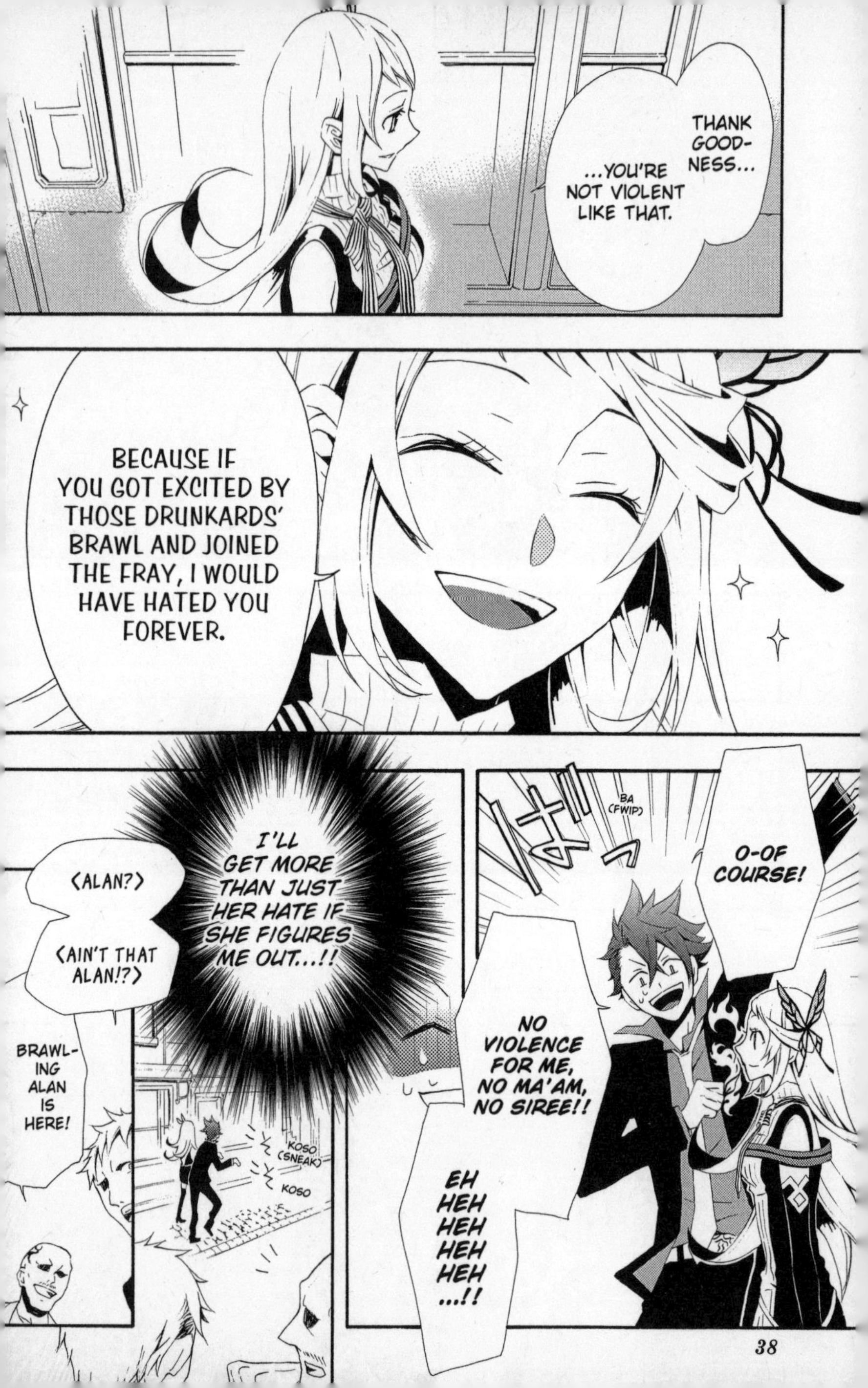
THANK GOODNESS...
...YOU'RE NOT VIOLENT LIKE THAT.
BECAUSE IF YOU GOT EXCITED BY THOSE DRUNKARDS' BRAWL AND JOINED THE FRAY, I WOULD HAVE HATED YOU FOREVER.
O-OF COURSE!
BA (FWIP)
NO VIOLENCE FOR ME, NO MA'AM, NO SIREE!!
EH HEH HEH HEH HEH ...!!
I'LL GET MORE THAN JUST HER HATE IF SHE FIGURES ME OUT...!!
<ALAN?>
<AIN'T THAT ALAN!?>
BRAWLING ALAN IS HERE!
KOSO (SNEAK)
KOSO

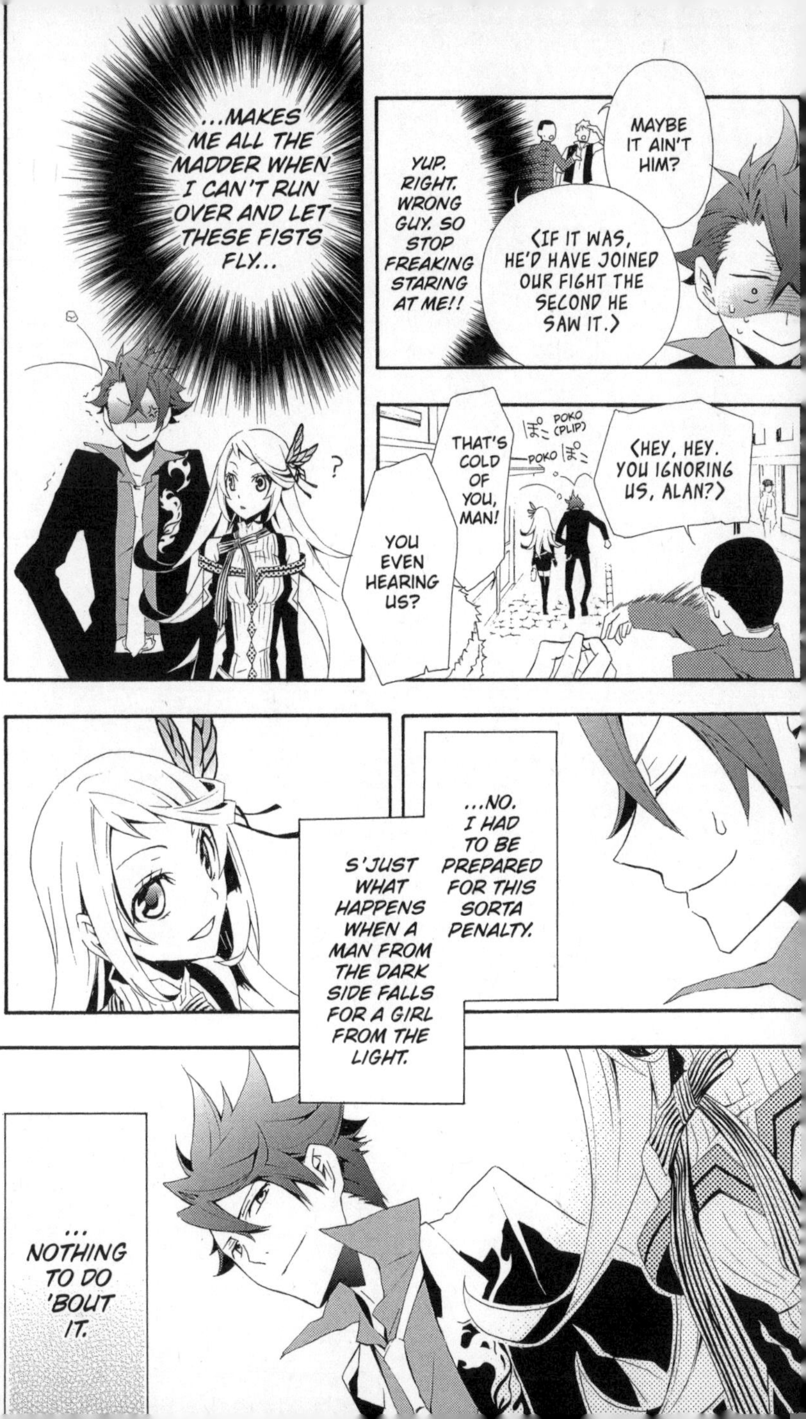
MAYBE IT AIN'T HIM?
<IF IT WAS, HE'D HAVE JOINED OUR FIGHT THE SECOND HE SAW IT.>
YUP. RIGHT. WRONG GUY. SO STOP FREAKING STARING AT ME!!
<HEY, HEY. YOU IGNORING US, ALAN?>
ぽこ POKO (PLIP)
POKO ぽこ
THAT'S COLD OF YOU, MAN!
YOU EVEN HEARING US?
...MAKES ME ALL THE MADDER WHEN I CAN'T RUN OVER AND LET THESE FISTS FLY...
?
...NO. I HAD TO BE PREPARED FOR THIS SORTA PENALTY.
S'JUST WHAT HAPPENS WHEN A MAN FROM THE DARK SIDE FALLS FOR A GIRL FROM THE LIGHT.
... NOTHING TO DO 'BOUT IT.

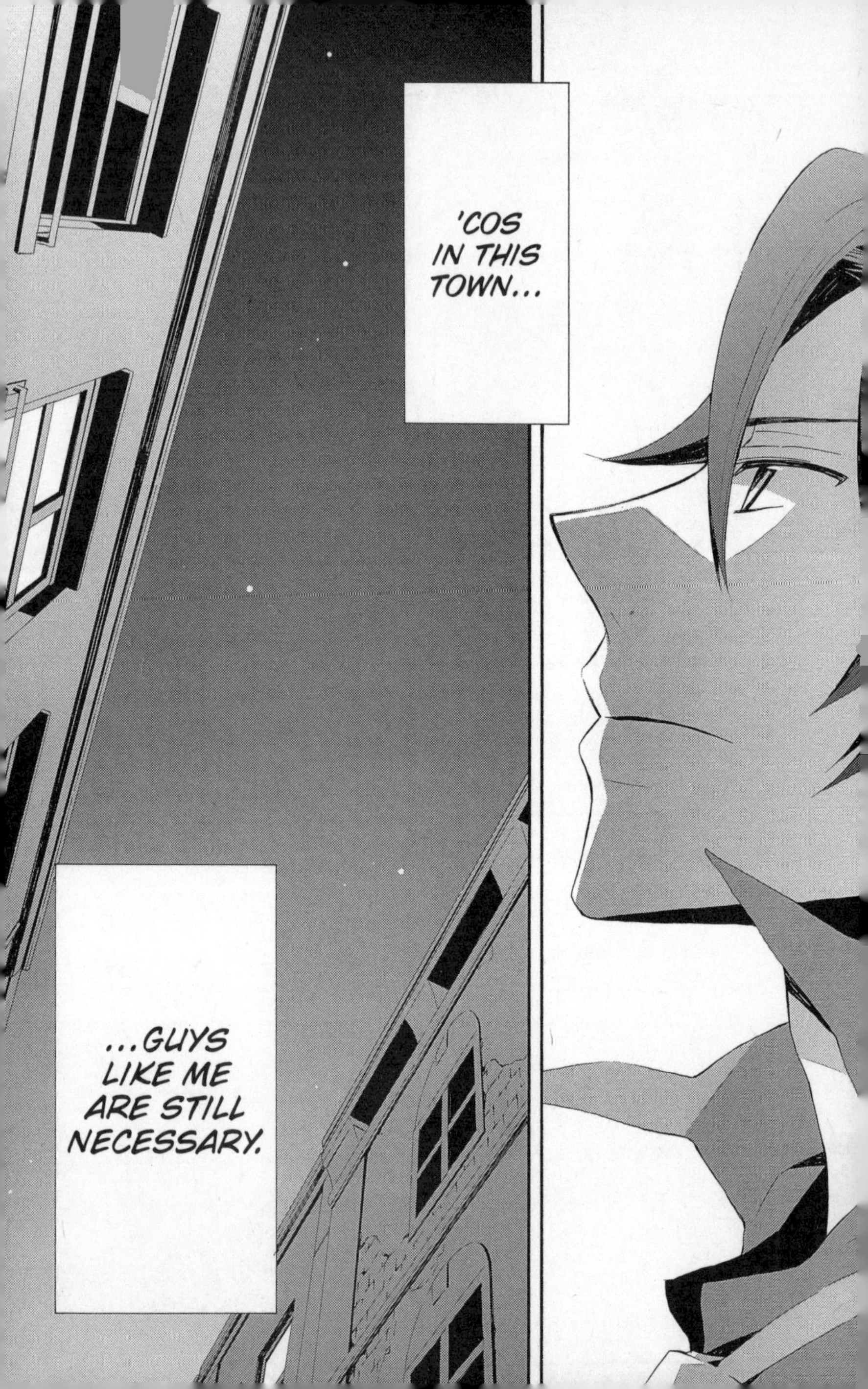
'COS IN THIS TOWN...
...GUYS LIKE ME ARE STILL NECESSARY.

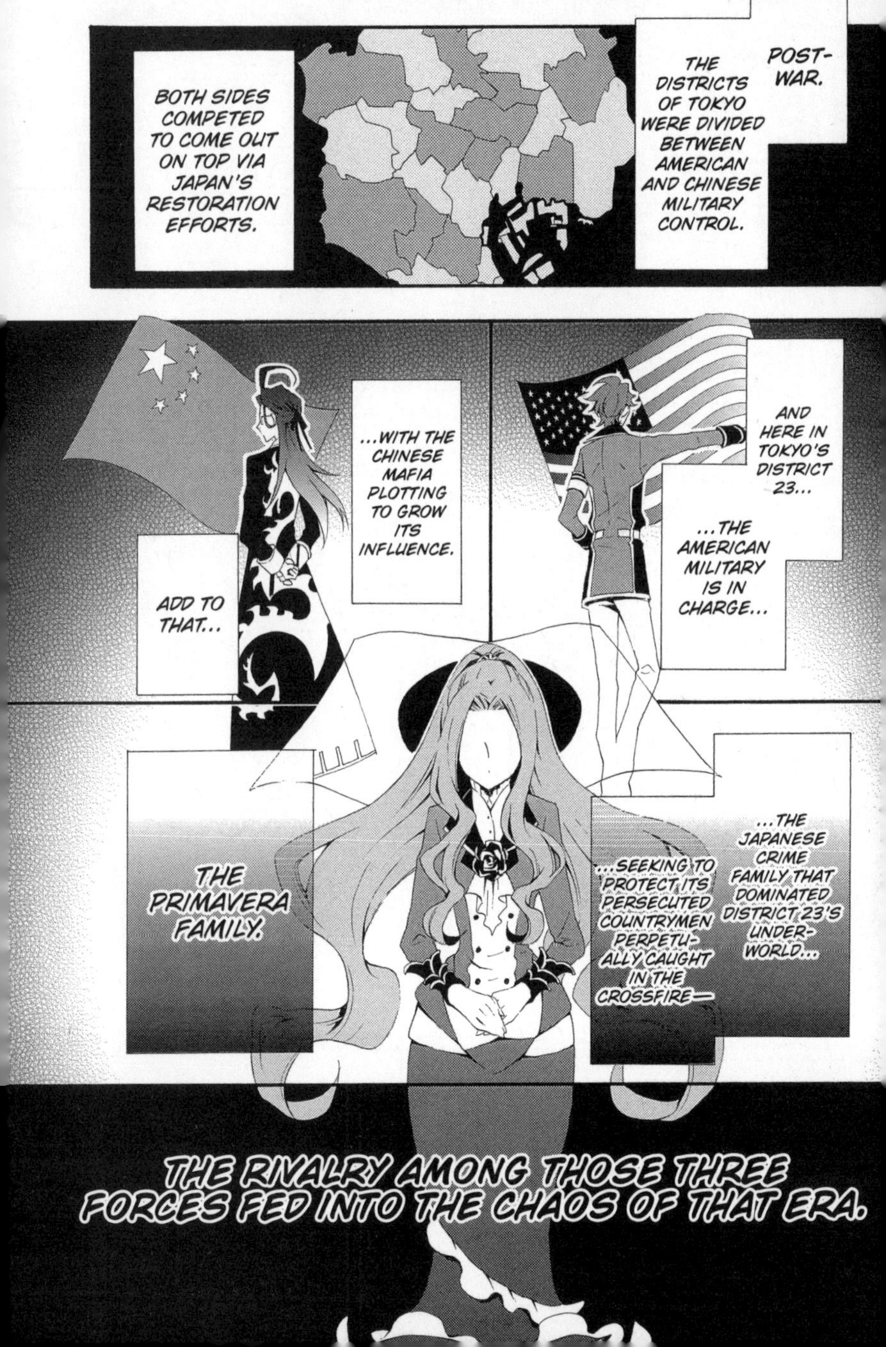
POST-WAR.
THE DISTRICTS OF TOKYO WERE DIVIDED BETWEEN AMERICAN AND CHINESE MILITARY CONTROL.
BOTH SIDES COMPETED TO COME OUT ON TOP VIA JAPAN'S RESTORATION EFFORTS.
AND HERE IN TOKYO'S DISTRICT 23...
...THE AMERICAN MILITARY IS IN CHARGE...
...WITH THE CHINESE MAFIA PLOTTING TO GROW ITS INFLUENCE.
ADD TO THAT...
...THE JAPANESE CRIME FAMILY THAT DOMINATED DISTRICT 23'S UNDER-WORLD...
...SEEKING TO PROTECT ITS PERSECUTED COUNTRYMEN PERPETU-ALLY CAUGHT IN THE CROSSFIRE—
THE PRIMAVERA FAMILY.
THE RIVALRY AMONG THOSE THREE FORCES FED INTO THE CHAOS OF THAT ERA.

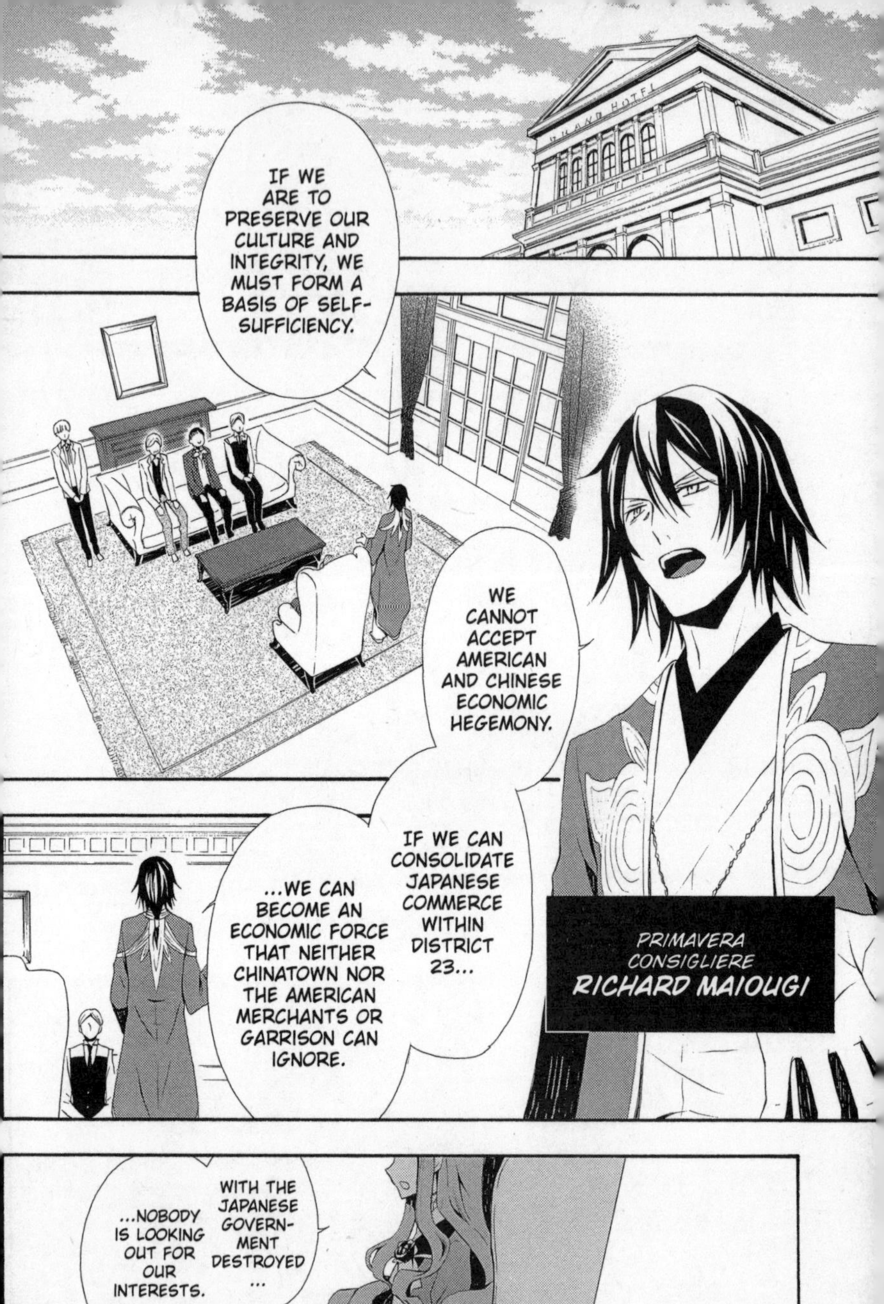
IF WE ARE TO PRESERVE OUR CULTURE AND INTEGRITY, WE MUST FORM A BASIS OF SELF-SUFFICIENCY.
WE CANNOT ACCEPT AMERICAN AND CHINESE ECONOMIC HEGEMONY.
PRIMAVERA CONSIGLIERE RICHARD MAIOUGI
IF WE CAN CONSOLIDATE JAPANESE COMMERCE WITHIN DISTRICT 23...
...WE CAN BECOME AN ECONOMIC FORCE THAT NEITHER CHINATOWN NOR THE AMERICAN MERCHANTS OR GARRISON CAN IGNORE.
WITH THE JAPANESE GOVERNMENT DESTROYED...
...NOBODY IS LOOKING OUT FOR OUR INTERESTS.

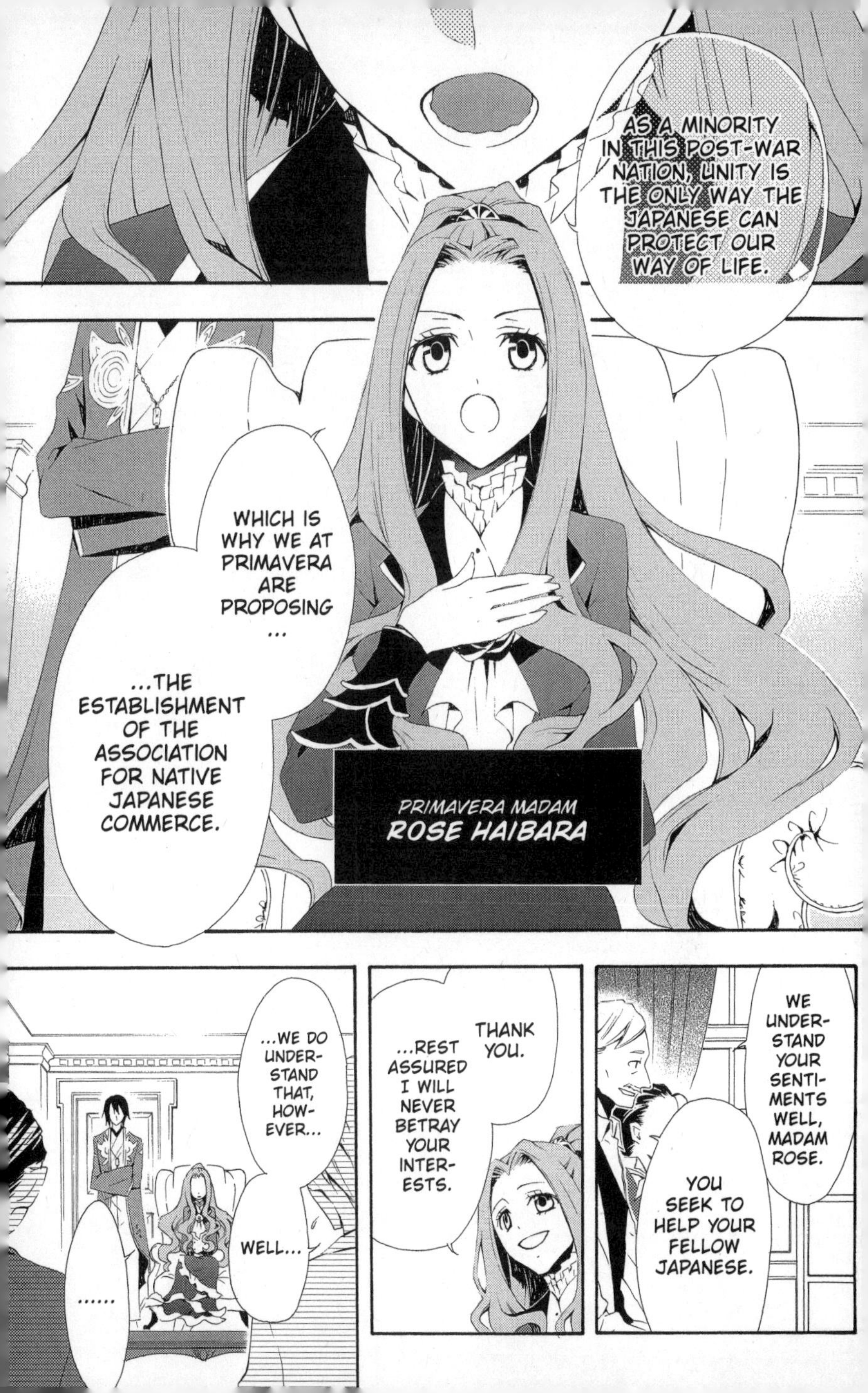
AS A MINORITY IN THIS POST-WAR NATION, UNITY IS THE ONLY WAY THE JAPANESE CAN PROTECT OUR WAY OF LIFE.
WHICH IS WHY WE AT PRIMAVERA ARE PROPOSING...
...THE ESTABLISHMENT OF THE ASSOCIATION FOR NATIVE JAPANESE COMMERCE.
PRIMAVERA MADAM
ROSE HAIBARA
WE UNDER-STAND YOUR SENTI-MENTS WELL, MADAM ROSE.
YOU SEEK TO HELP YOUR FELLOW JAPANESE.
THANK YOU.
...REST ASSURED I WILL NEVER BETRAY YOUR INTER-ESTS.
...WE DO UNDER-STAND THAT, HOW-EVER...
WELL...
......

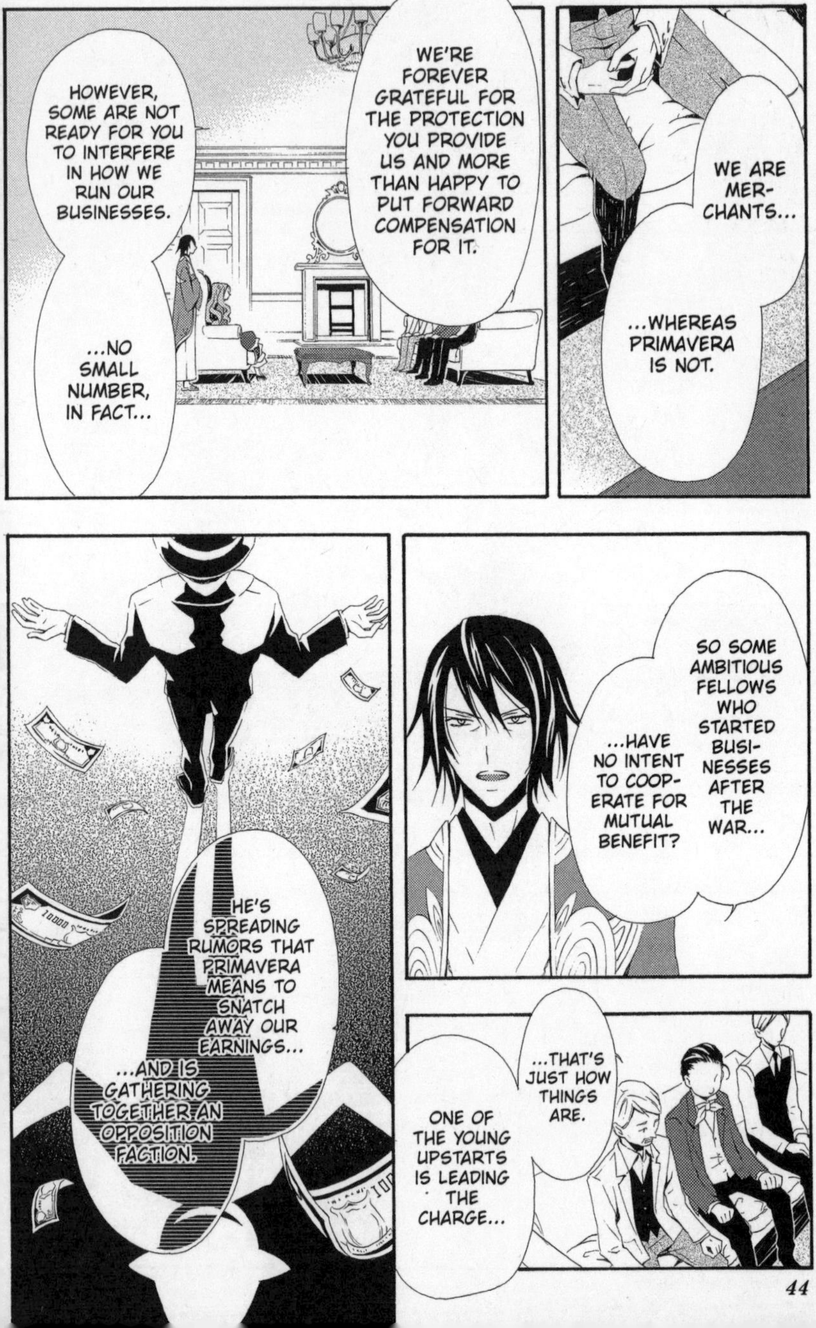
WE ARE MERCHANTS...
...WHEREAS PRIMAVERA IS NOT.
WE'RE FOREVER GRATEFUL FOR THE PROTECTION YOU PROVIDE US AND MORE THAN HAPPY TO PUT FORWARD COMPENSATION FOR IT.
HOWEVER, SOME ARE NOT READY FOR YOU TO INTERFERE IN HOW WE RUN OUR BUSINESSES.
...NO SMALL NUMBER, IN FACT...
SO SOME AMBITIOUS FELLOWS WHO STARTED BUSINESSES AFTER THE WAR...
...HAVE NO INTENT TO COOPERATE FOR MUTUAL BENEFIT?
...THAT'S JUST HOW THINGS ARE.
ONE OF THE YOUNG UPSTARTS IS LEADING THE CHARGE...
HE'S SPREADING RUMORS THAT PRIMAVERA MEANS TO SNATCH AWAY OUR EARNINGS...
...AND IS GATHERING TOGETHER AN OPPOSITION FACTION.

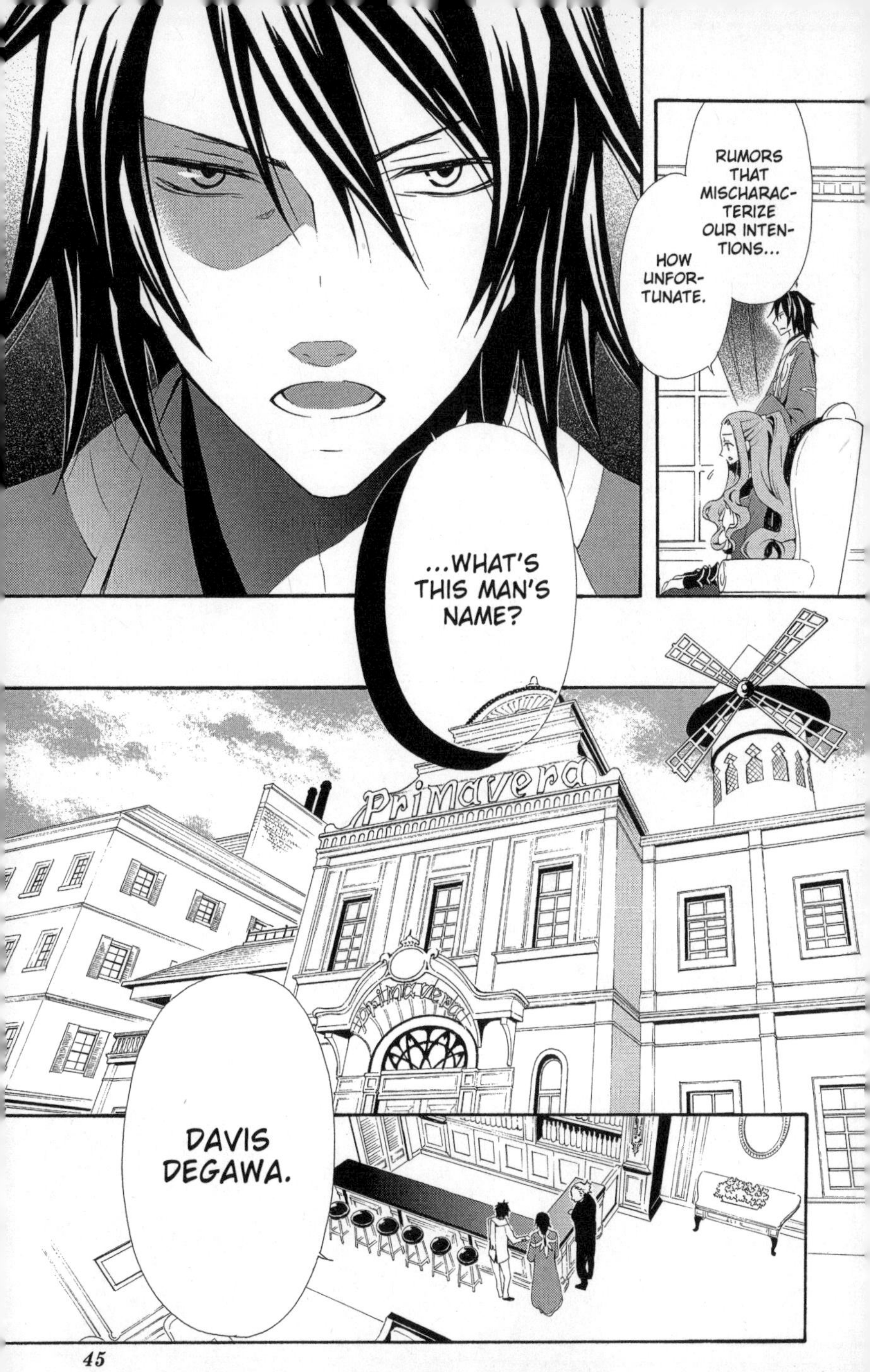
RUMORS THAT MISCHARAC-TERIZE OUR INTEN-TIONS...
HOW UNFOR-TUNATE.
...WHAT'S THIS MAN'S NAME?
Primavera
DAVIS DEGAWA.

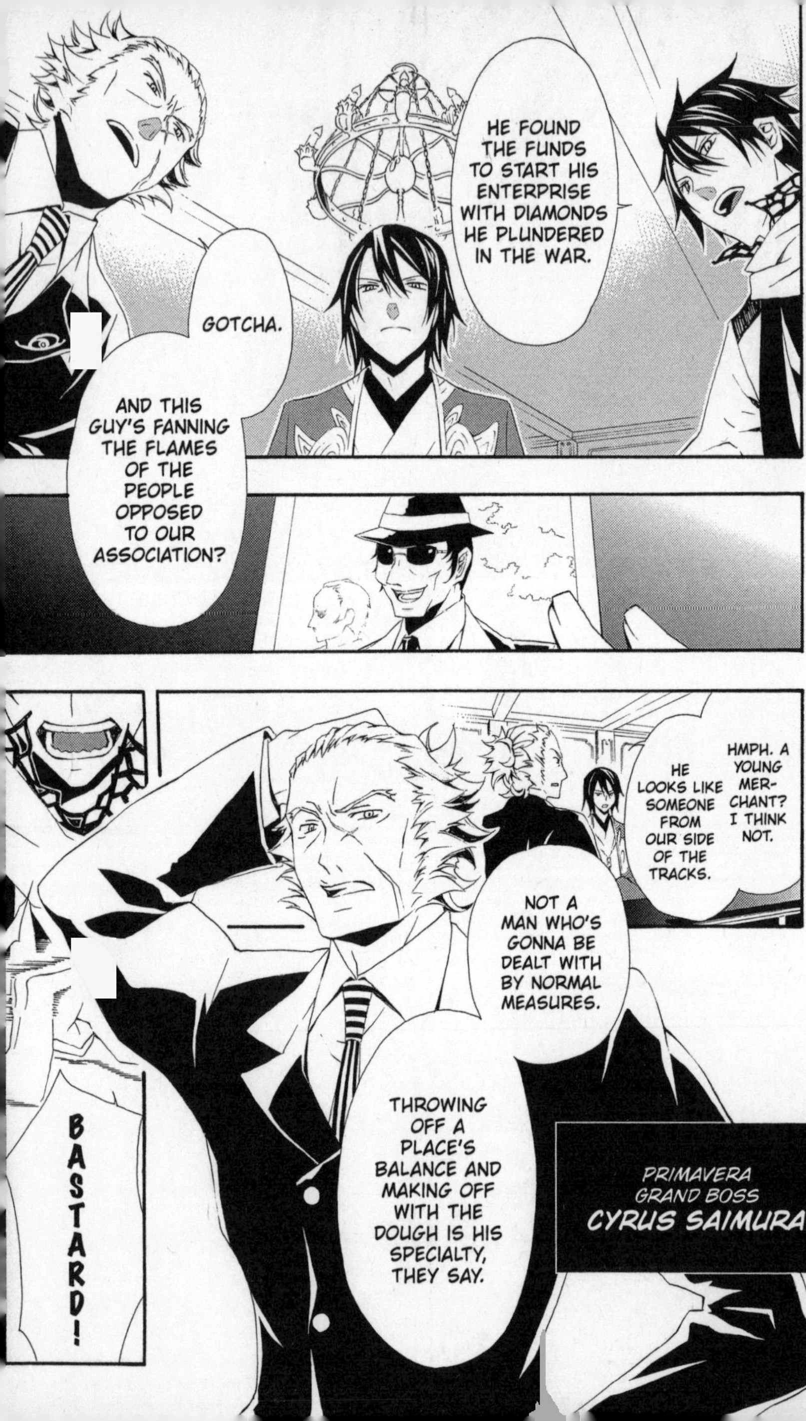
HE FOUND THE FUNDS TO START HIS ENTERPRISE WITH DIAMONDS HE PLUNDERED IN THE WAR.
GOTCHA.
AND THIS GUY'S FANNING THE FLAMES OF THE PEOPLE OPPOSED TO OUR ASSOCIATION?
HMPH. A YOUNG MER-CHANT? I THINK NOT.
HE LOOKS LIKE SOMEONE FROM OUR SIDE OF THE TRACKS.
NOT A MAN WHO'S GONNA BE DEALT WITH BY NORMAL MEASURES.
THROWING OFF A PLACE'S BALANCE AND MAKING OFF WITH THE DOUGH IS HIS SPECIALTY, THEY SAY.
PRIMAVERA GRAND BOSS CYRUS SAIMURA
BASTARD!

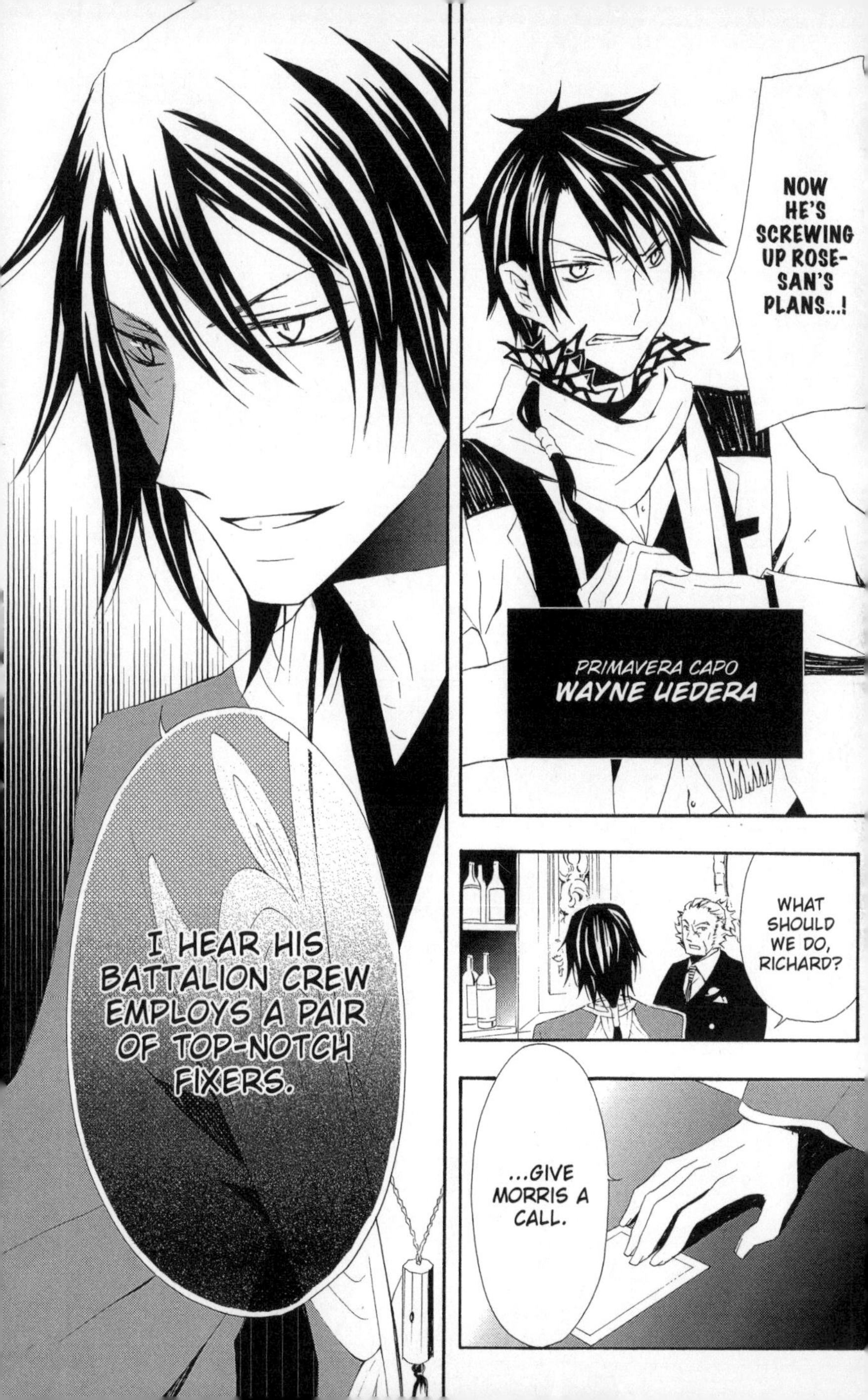
NOW HE'S SCREWING UP ROSE-SAN'S PLANS...!
PRIMAVERA CAPO
WAYNE UEDERA
WHAT SHOULD WE DO, RICHARD?
...GIVE MORRIS A CALL.
I HEAR HIS BATTALION CREW EMPLOYS A PAIR OF TOP-NOTCH FIXERS.

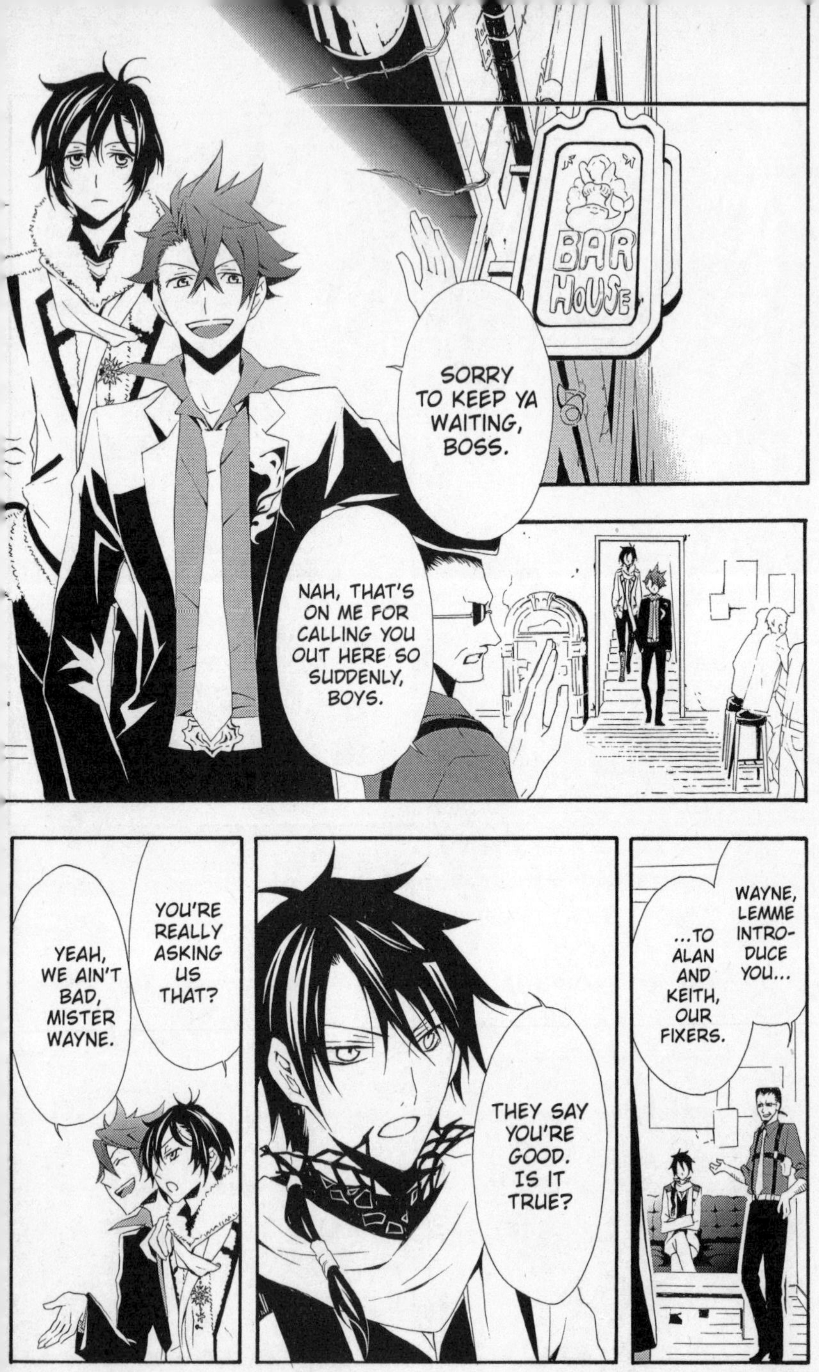
BAR HOUSE
SORRY TO KEEP YA WAITING, BOSS.
NAH, THAT'S ON ME FOR CALLING YOU OUT HERE SO SUDDENLY, BOYS.
WAYNE, LEMME INTRODUCE YOU...
...TO ALAN AND KEITH, OUR FIXERS.
THEY SAY YOU'RE GOOD. IS IT TRUE?
YOU'RE REALLY ASKING US THAT?
YEAH, WE AIN'T BAD, MISTER WAYNE.

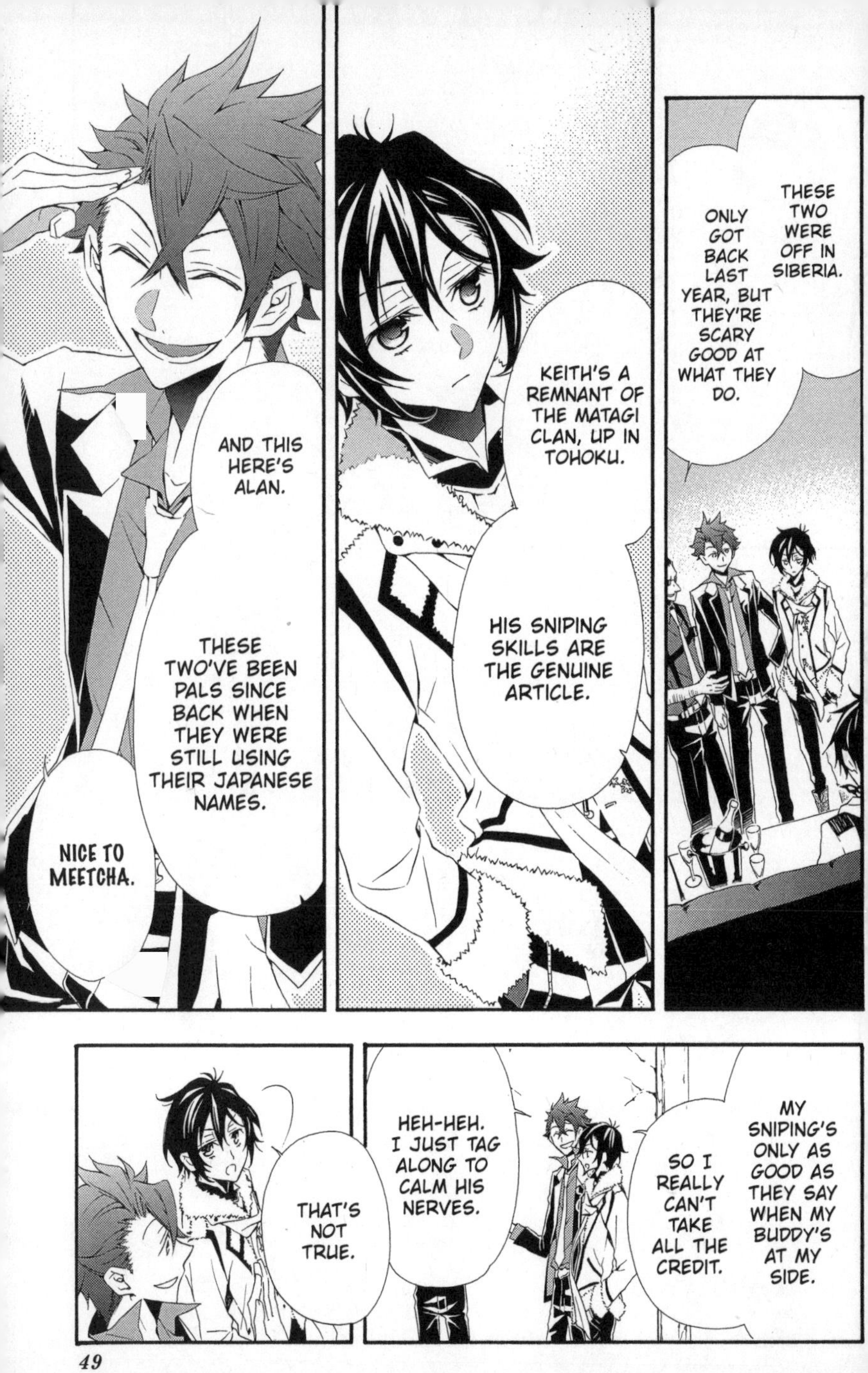
THESE TWO WERE OFF IN SIBERIA.
ONLY GOT BACK LAST YEAR, BUT THEY'RE SCARY GOOD AT WHAT THEY DO.
KEITH'S A REMNANT OF THE MATAGI CLAN, UP IN TOHOKU.
HIS SNIPING SKILLS ARE THE GENUINE ARTICLE.
AND THIS HERE'S ALAN.
THESE TWO'VE BEEN PALS SINCE BACK WHEN THEY WERE STILL USING THEIR JAPANESE NAMES.
NICE TO MEETCHA.
MY SNIPING'S ONLY AS GOOD AS THEY SAY WHEN MY BUDDY'S AT MY SIDE.
SO I REALLY CAN'T TAKE ALL THE CREDIT.
HEH-HEH. I JUST TAG ALONG TO CALM HIS NERVES.
THAT'S NOT TRUE.

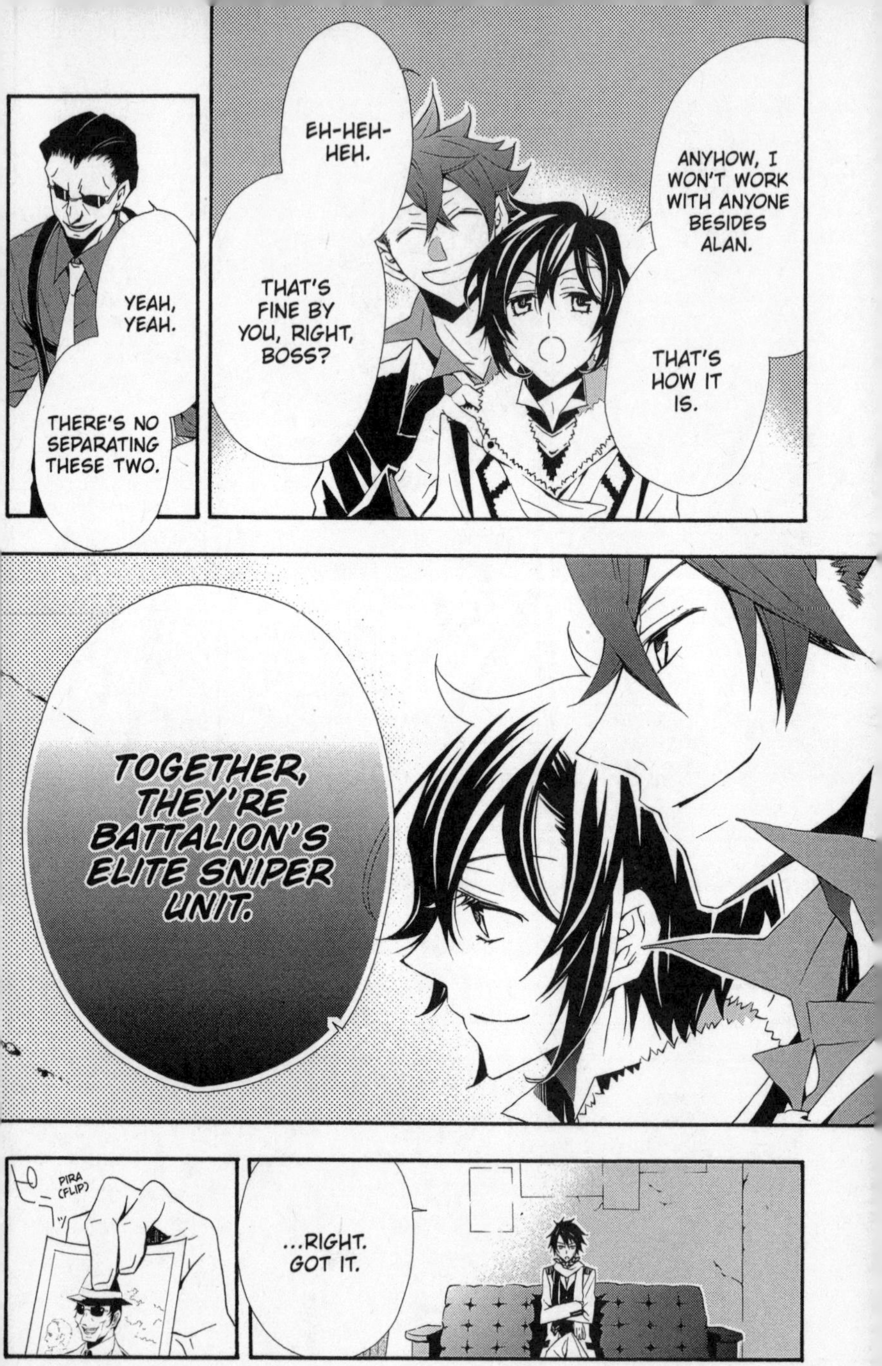
ANYHOW, I WON'T WORK WITH ANYONE BESIDES ALAN.
THAT'S HOW IT IS.
EH-HEH-HEH.
THAT'S FINE BY YOU, RIGHT, BOSS?
YEAH, YEAH.
THERE'S NO SEPARATING THESE TWO.
TOGETHER, THEY'RE BATTALION'S ELITE SNIPER UNIT.
...RIGHT. GOT IT.
PIRA (FLIP)

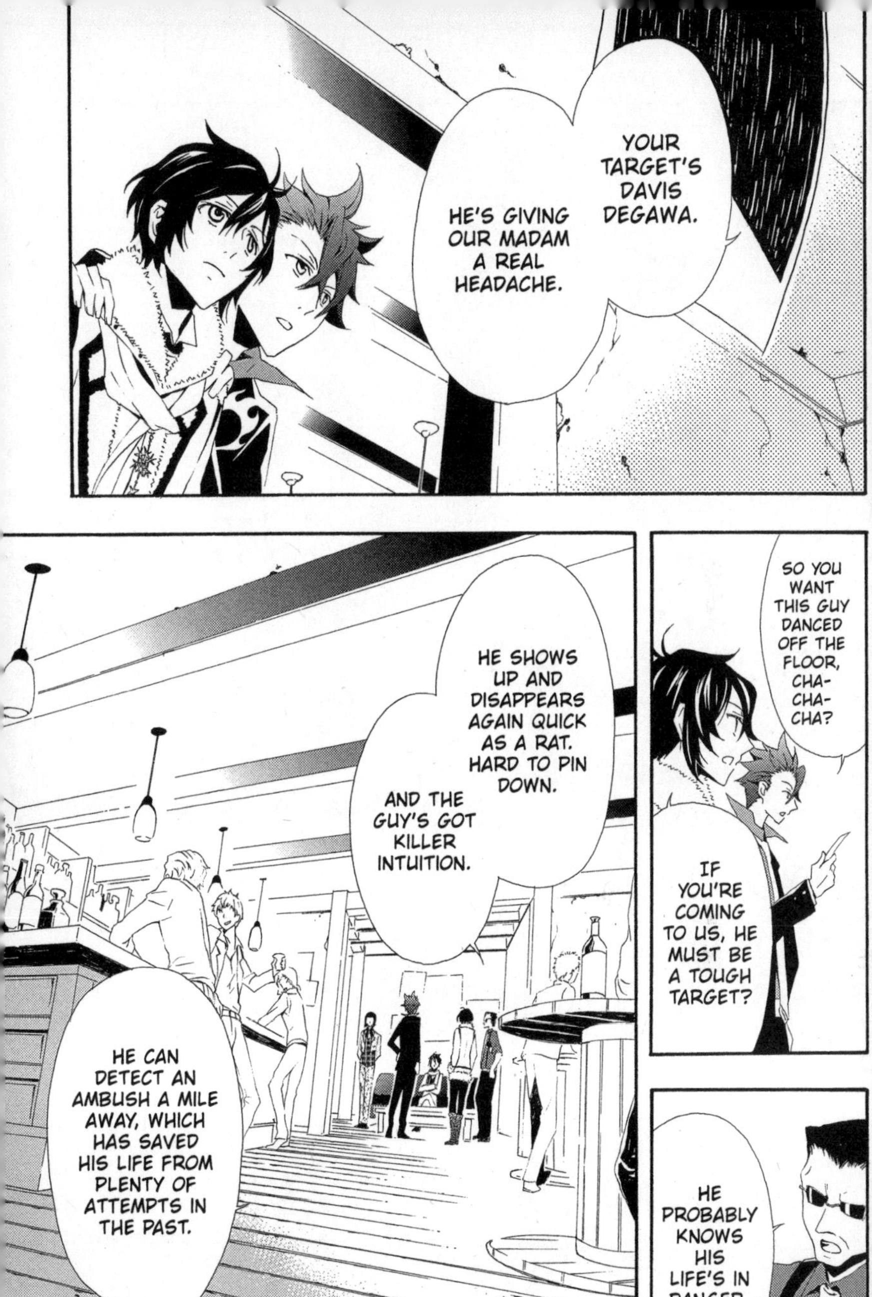
YOUR TARGET'S DAVIS DEGAWA.
HE'S GIVING OUR MADAM A REAL HEADACHE.
SO YOU WANT THIS GUY DANCED OFF THE FLOOR, CHA-CHA-CHA?
IF YOU'RE COMING TO US, HE MUST BE A TOUGH TARGET?
HE PROBABLY KNOWS HIS LIFE'S IN DANGER.
HE SHOWS UP AND DISAPPEARS AGAIN QUICK AS A RAT. HARD TO PIN DOWN.
AND THE GUY'S GOT KILLER INTUITION.
HE CAN DETECT AN AMBUSH A MILE AWAY, WHICH HAS SAVED HIS LIFE FROM PLENTY OF ATTEMPTS IN THE PAST.

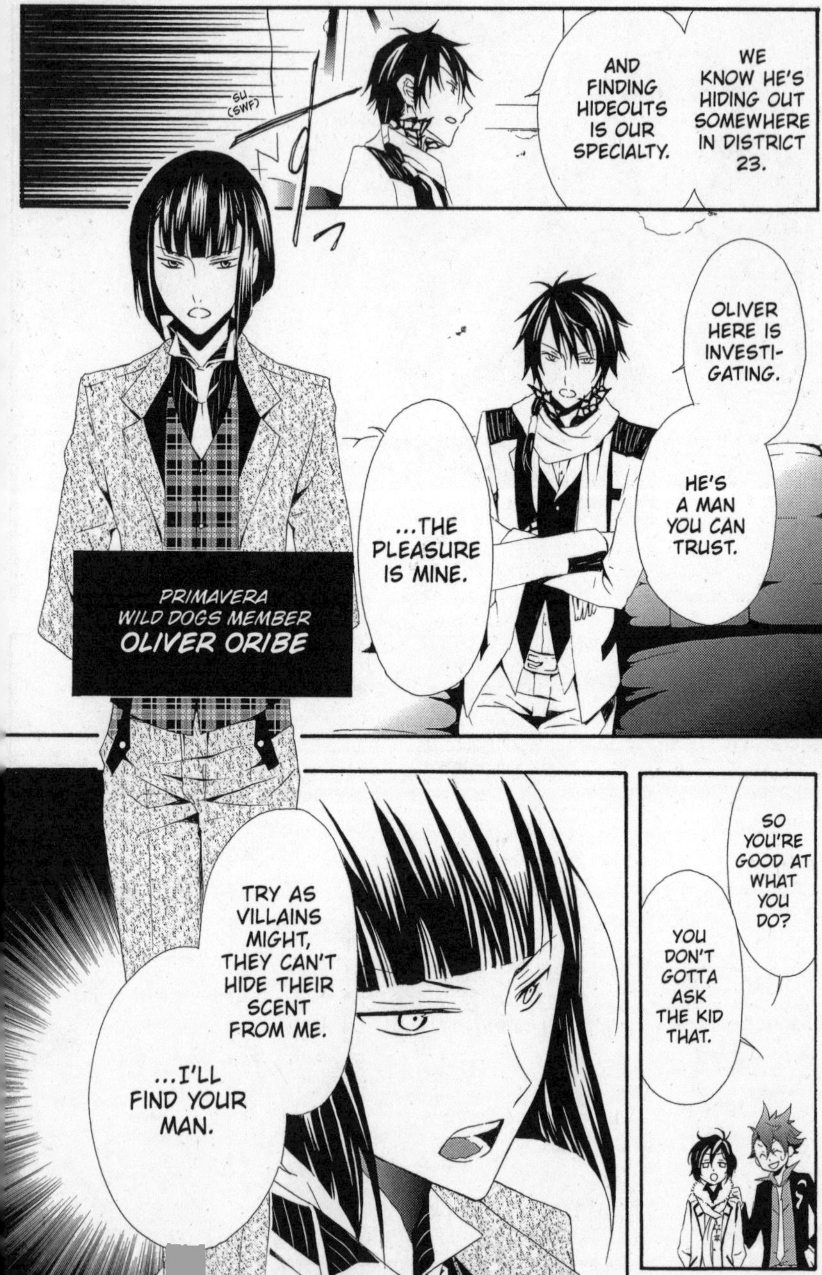
WE KNOW HE'S HIDING OUT SOMEWHERE IN DISTRICT 23.
AND FINDING HIDEOUTS IS OUR SPECIALTY.
SU (SWF)
OLIVER HERE IS INVESTI-GATING.
HE'S A MAN YOU CAN TRUST.
...THE PLEASURE IS MINE.
PRIMAVERA WILD DOGS MEMBER OLIVER ORIBE
SO YOU'RE GOOD AT WHAT YOU DO?
YOU DON'T GOTTA ASK THE KID THAT.
TRY AS VILLAINS MIGHT, THEY CAN'T HIDE THEIR SCENT FROM ME.
...I'LL FIND YOUR MAN.

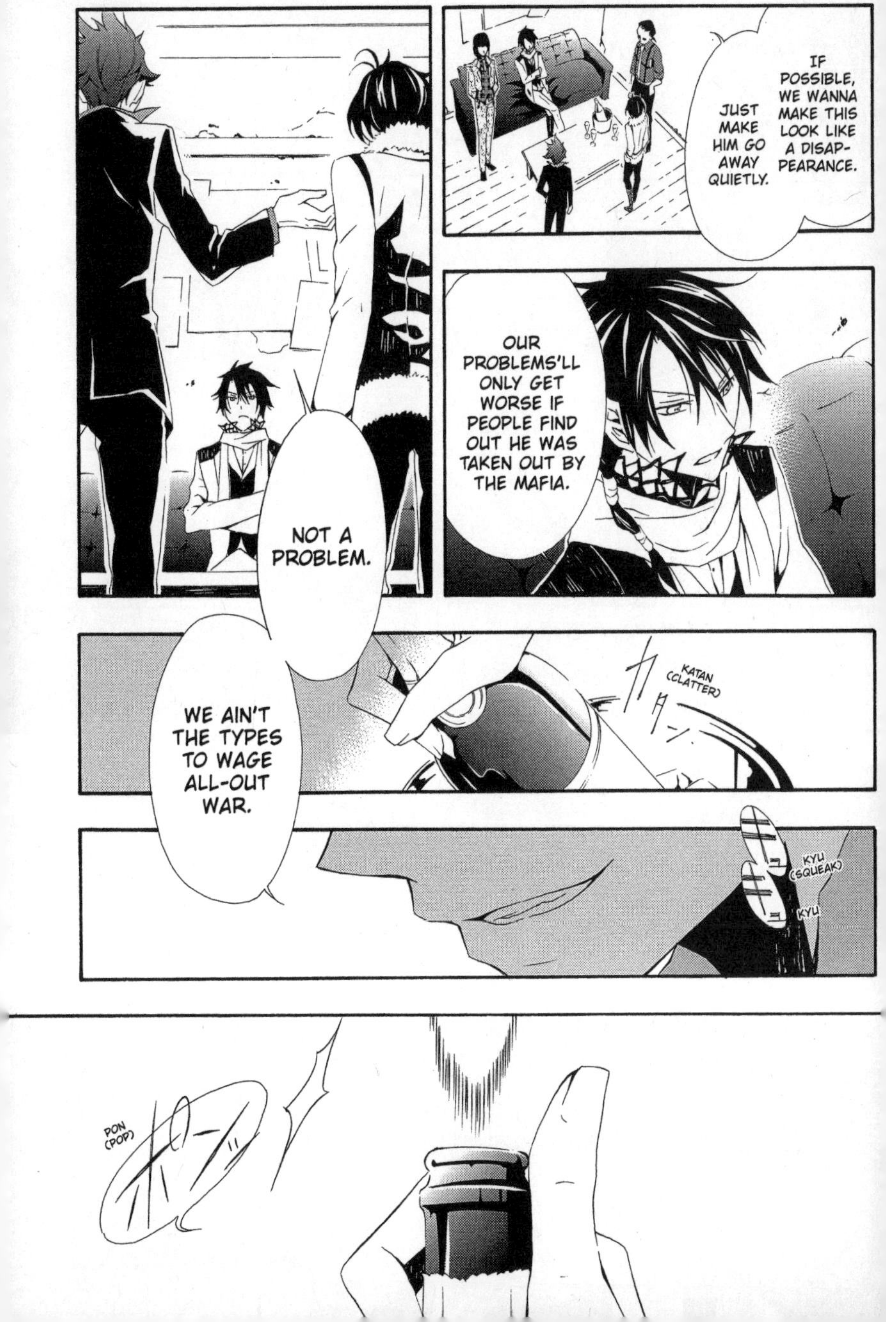
IF POSSIBLE, WE WANNA MAKE THIS LOOK LIKE A DISAPPEARANCE.
JUST MAKE HIM GO AWAY QUIETLY.
OUR PROBLEMS'LL ONLY GET WORSE IF PEOPLE FIND OUT HE WAS TAKEN OUT BY THE MAFIA.
NOT A PROBLEM.
KATAN (CLATTER)
WE AIN'T THE TYPES TO WAGE ALL-OUT WAR.
KYU (SQUEAK)
KYU
PON (POP)

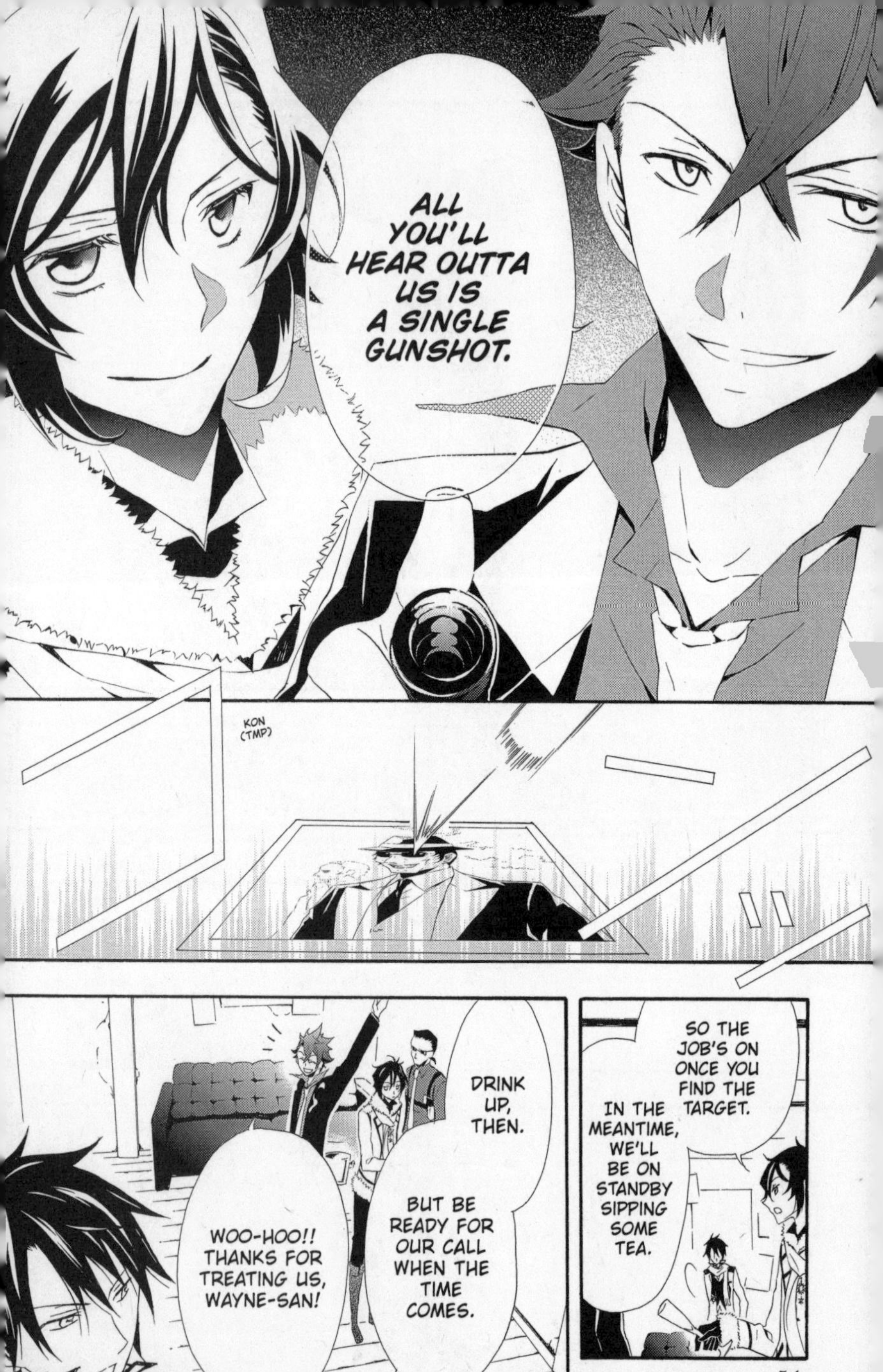
ALL YOU'LL HEAR OUTTA US IS A SINGLE GUNSHOT.
KON (TMP)
SO THE JOB'S ON ONCE YOU FIND THE TARGET.
IN THE MEANTIME, WE'LL BE ON STANDBY SIPPING SOME TEA.
DRINK UP, THEN.
BUT BE READY FOR OUR CALL WHEN THE TIME COMES.
WOO-HOO!! THANKS FOR TREATING US, WAYNE-SAN!

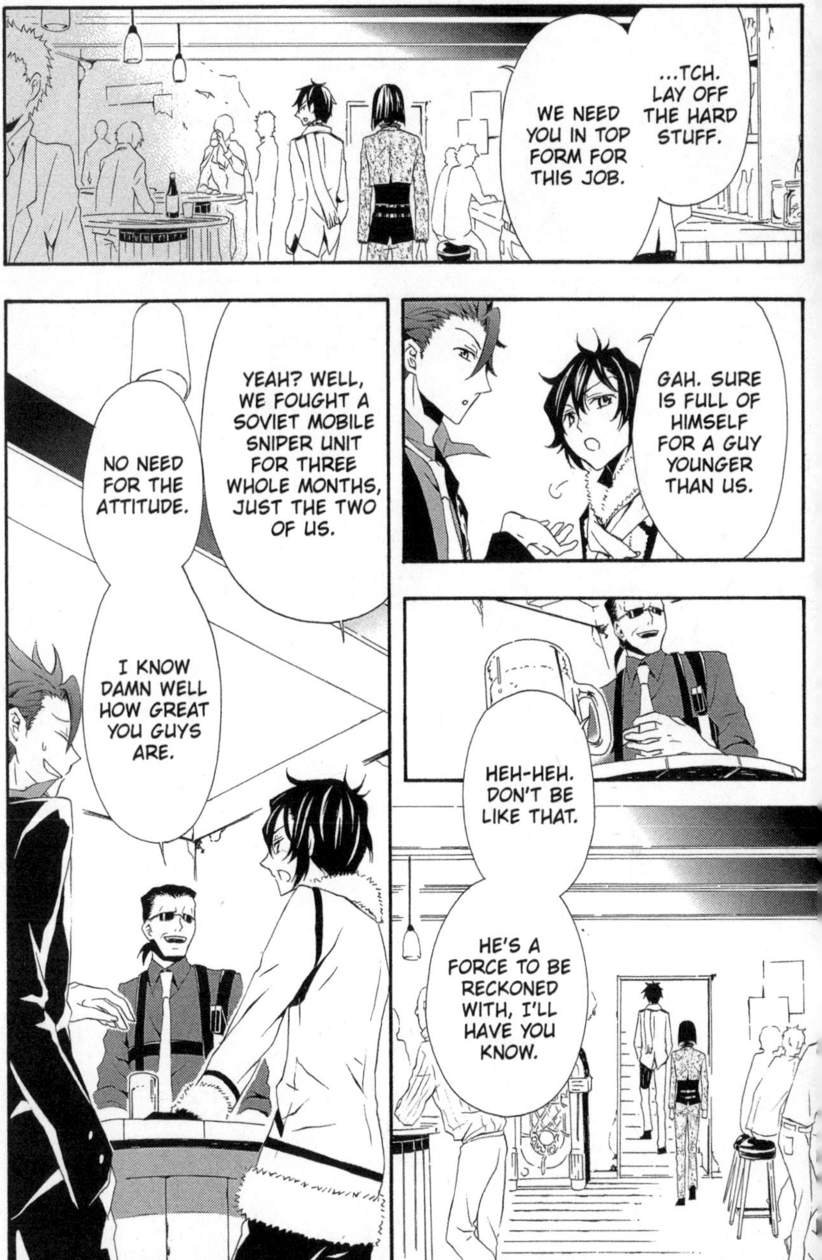
...TCH. LAY OFF THE HARD STUFF.
WE NEED YOU IN TOP FORM FOR THIS JOB.
GAH. SURE IS FULL OF HIMSELF FOR A GUY YOUNGER THAN US.
HEH-HEH. DON'T BE LIKE THAT.
HE'S A FORCE TO BE RECKONED WITH, I'LL HAVE YOU KNOW.
YEAH? WELL, WE FOUGHT A SOVIET MOBILE SNIPER UNIT FOR THREE WHOLE MONTHS, JUST THE TWO OF US.
NO NEED FOR THE ATTITUDE.
I KNOW DAMN WELL HOW GREAT YOU GUYS ARE.

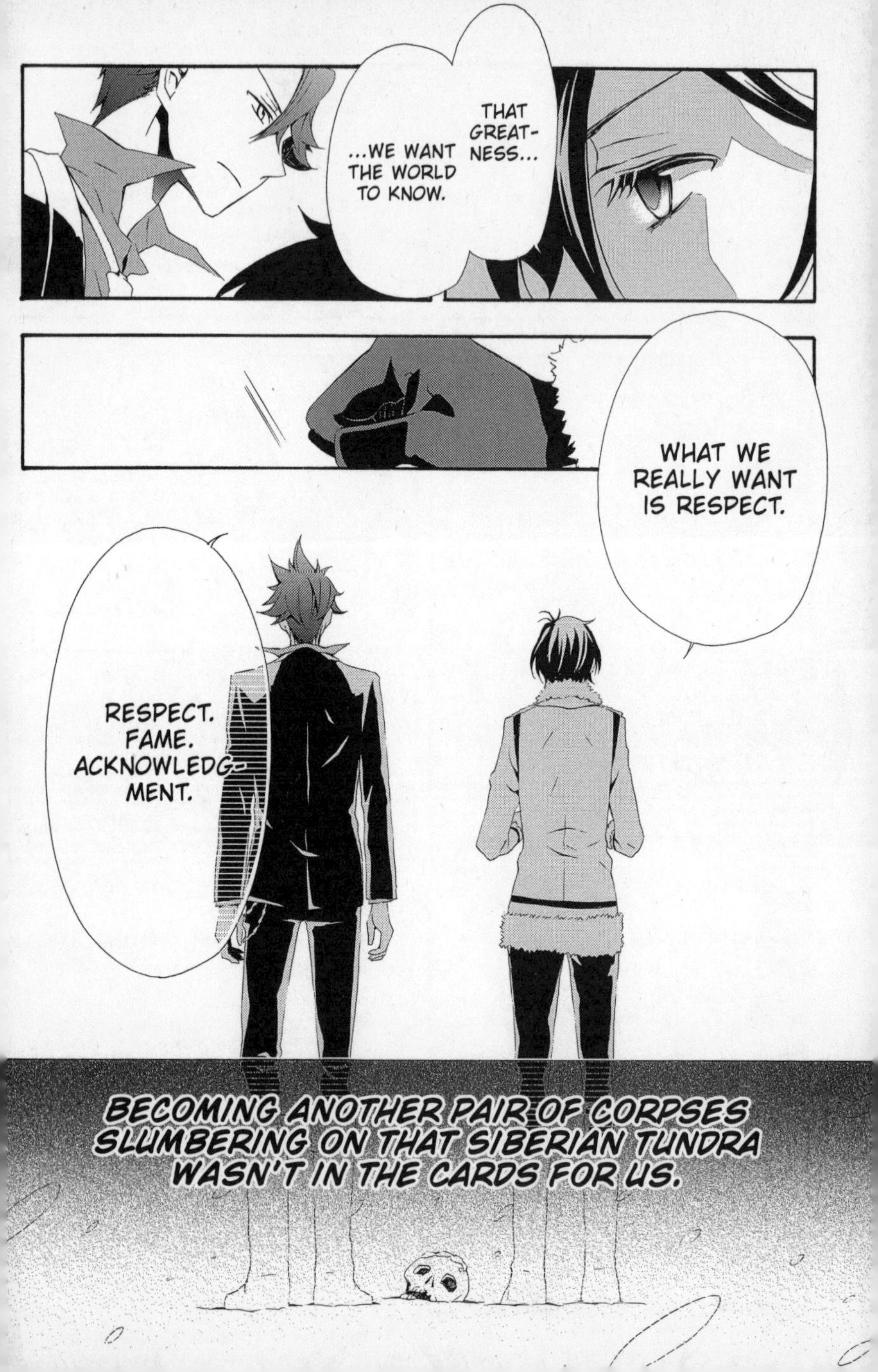
THAT GREAT-NESS... ...WE WANT THE WORLD TO KNOW.
WHAT WE REALLY WANT IS RESPECT.
RESPECT. FAME. ACKNOWLEDG-MENT.
BECOMING ANOTHER PAIR OF CORPSES SLUMBERING ON THAT SIBERIAN TUNDRA WASN'T IN THE CARDS FOR US.

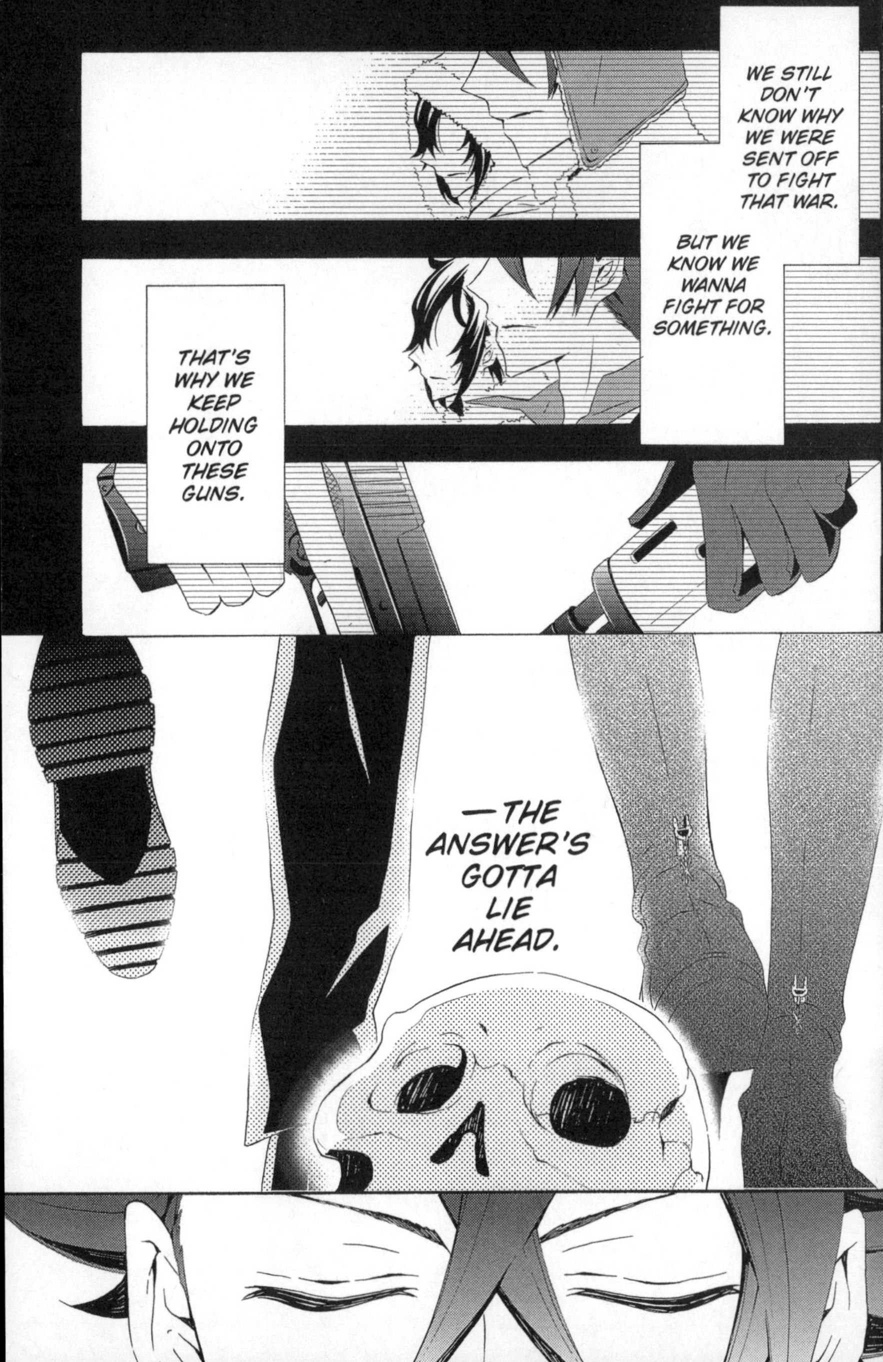
WE STILL DON'T KNOW WHY WE WERE SENT OFF TO FIGHT THAT WAR.
BUT WE KNOW WE WANNA FIGHT FOR SOMETHING.
THAT'S WHY WE KEEP HOLDING ONTO THESE GUNS.
—THE ANSWER'S GOTTA LIE AHEAD.

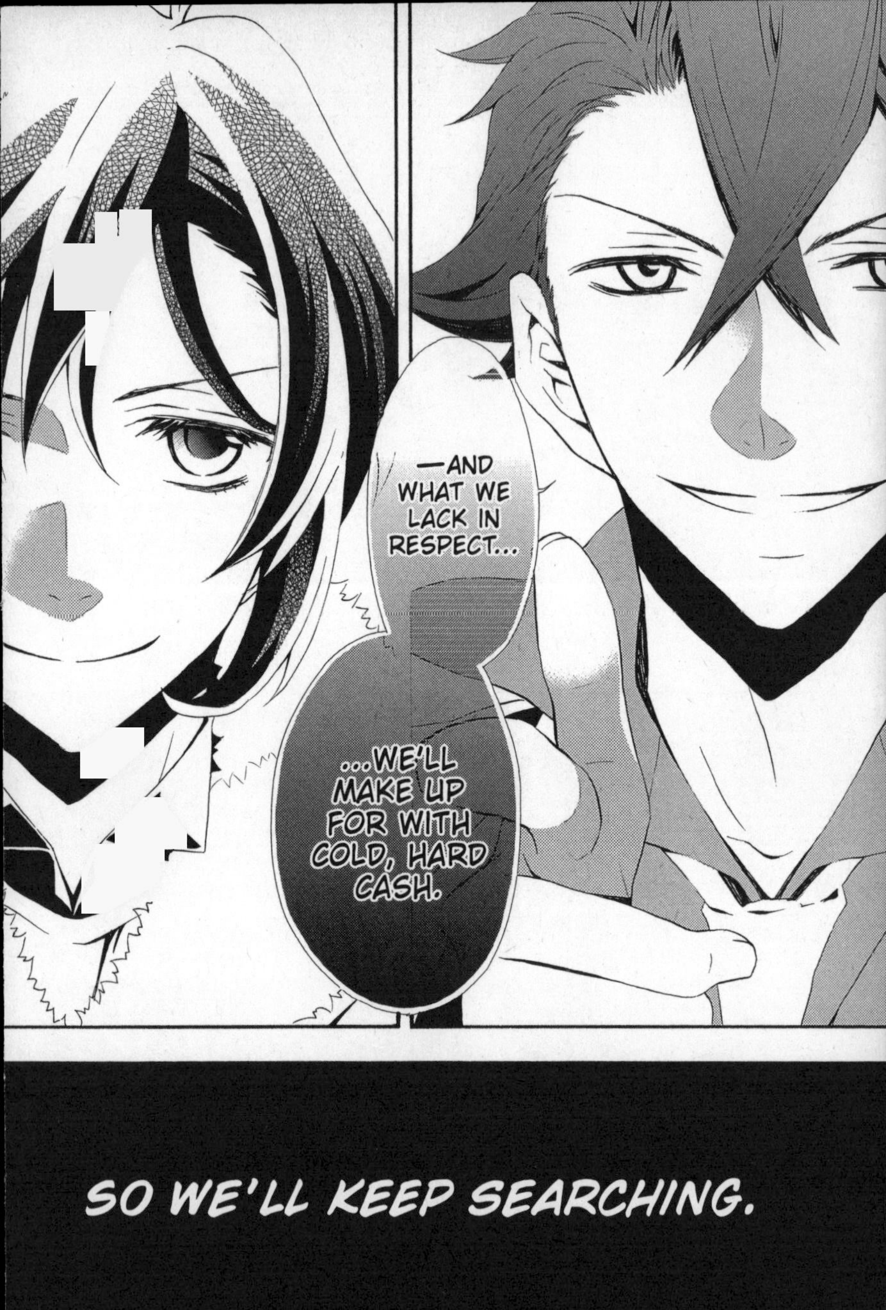
—AND WHAT WE LACK IN RESPECT...
...WE'LL MAKE UP FOR WITH COLD, HARD CASH.
SO WE'LL KEEP SEARCHING.

ROSE GUNS DAYS

Season 3

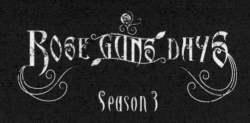

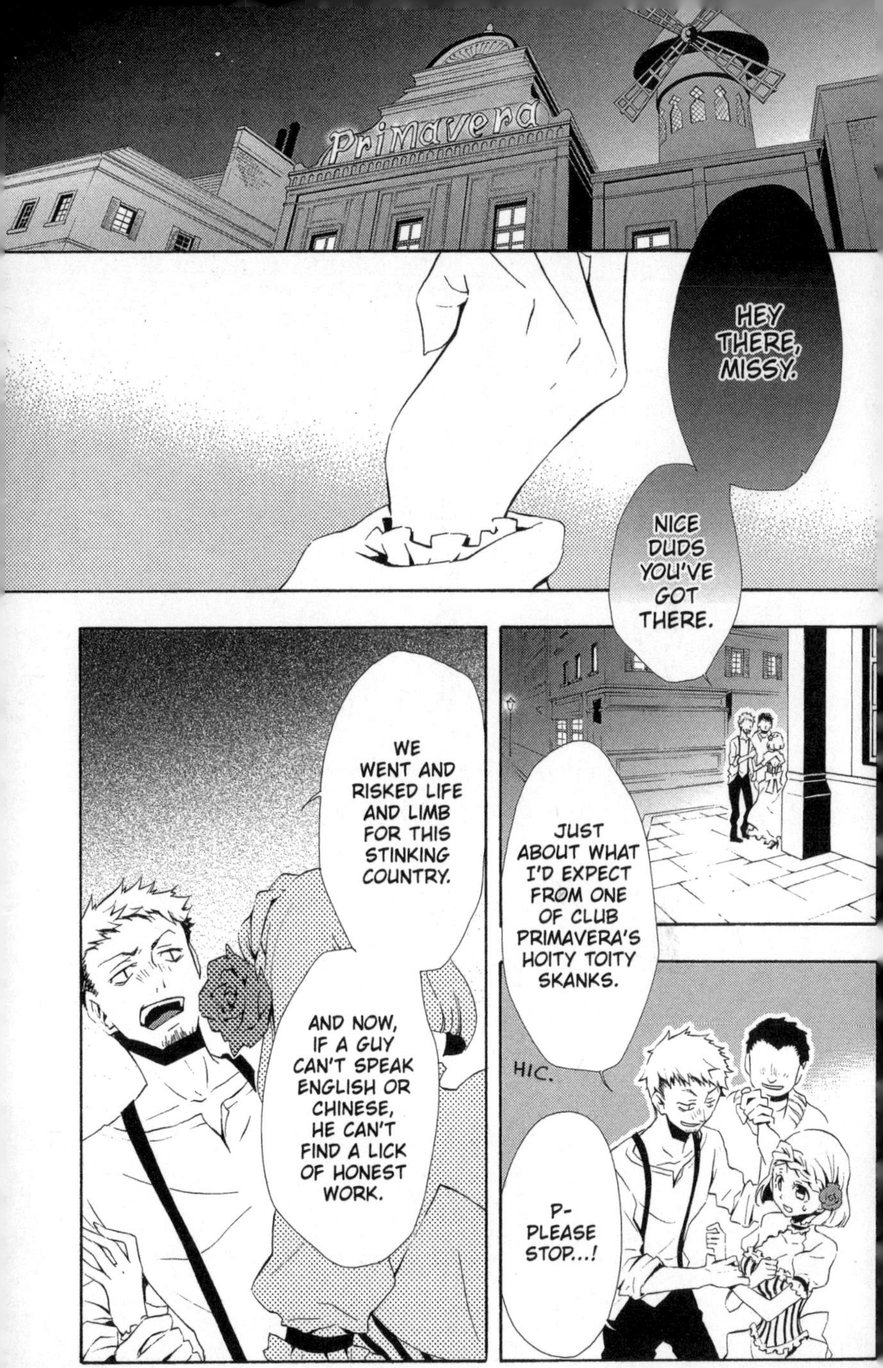
Primavera
HEY THERE, MISSY.
NICE DUDS YOU'VE GOT THERE.
JUST ABOUT WHAT I'D EXPECT FROM ONE OF CLUB PRIMAVERA'S HOITY TOITY SKANKS.
HIC.
P-PLEASE STOP...!
WE WENT AND RISKED LIFE AND LIMB FOR THIS STINKING COUNTRY.
AND NOW, IF A GUY CAN'T SPEAK ENGLISH OR CHINESE, HE CAN'T FIND A LICK OF HONEST WORK.

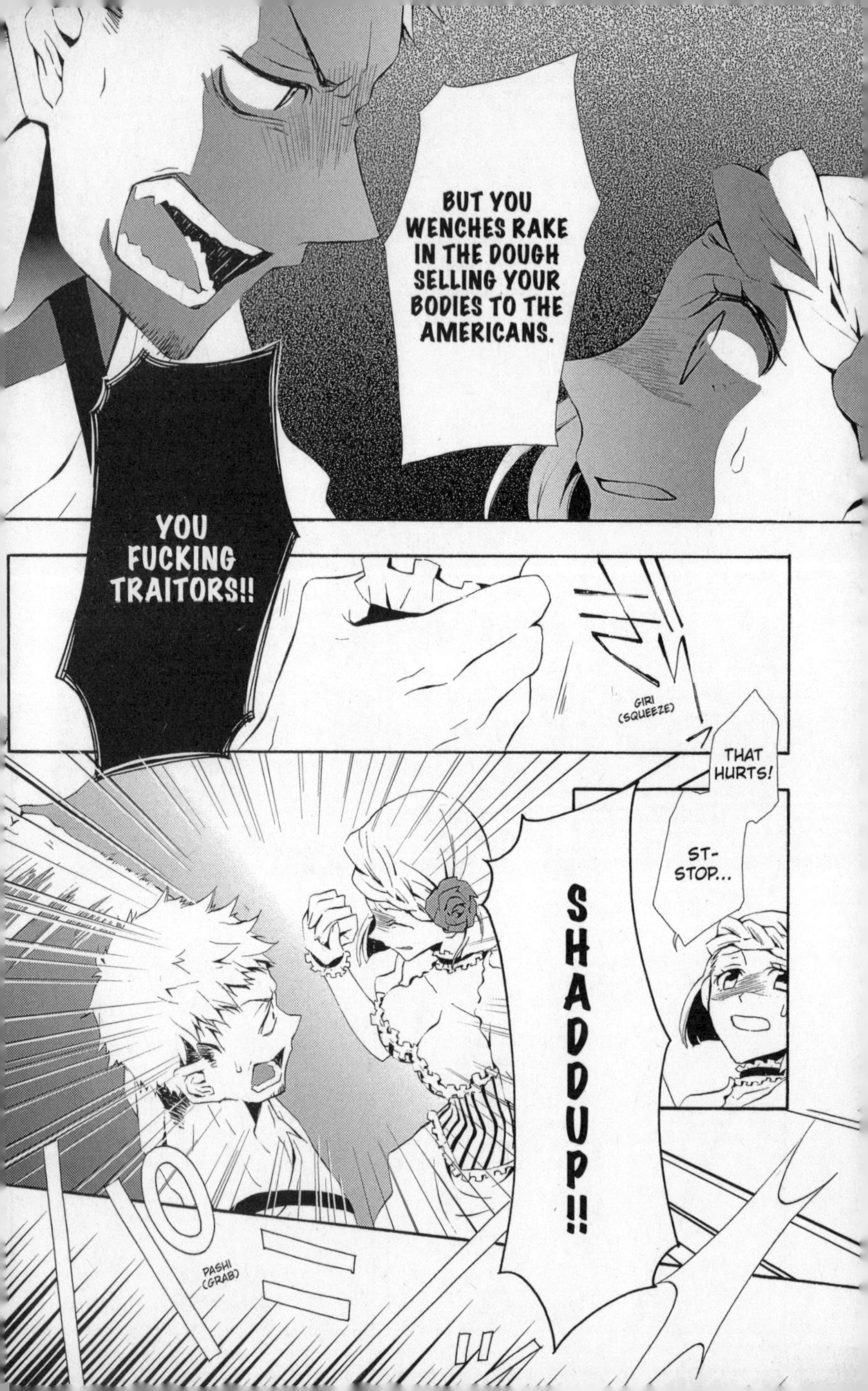
BUT YOU WENCHES RAKE IN THE DOUGH SELLING YOUR BODIES TO THE AMERICANS.
YOU FUCKING TRAITORS!!
THAT HURTS!
GIRI (SQUEEZE)
ST- STOP...
SHADDUP!!
PASHI (GRAB)

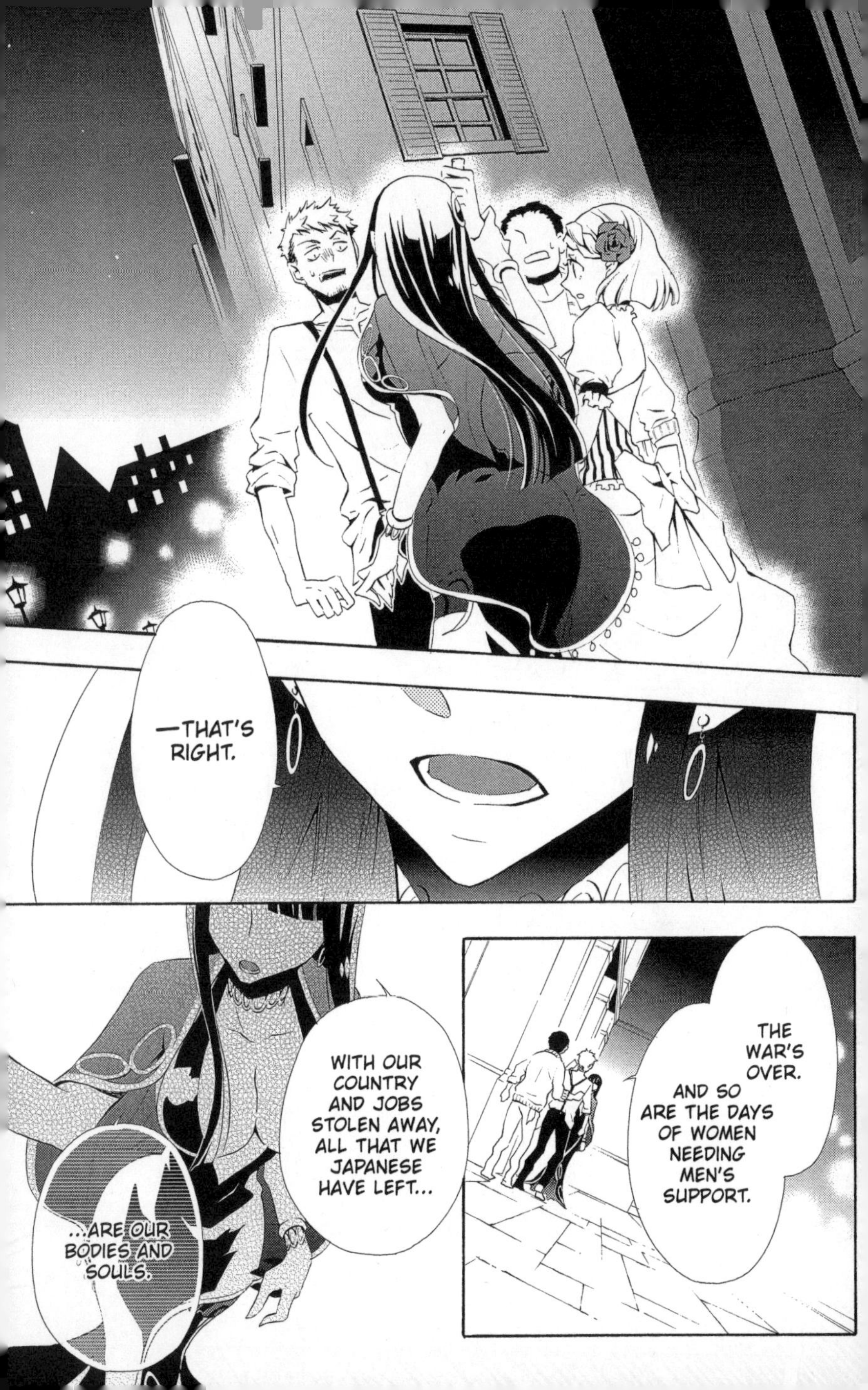
—THAT'S RIGHT.
THE WAR'S OVER.
AND SO ARE THE DAYS OF WOMEN NEEDING MEN'S SUPPORT.
WITH OUR COUNTRY AND JOBS STOLEN AWAY, ALL THAT WE JAPANESE HAVE LEFT...
...ARE OUR BODIES AND SOULS.

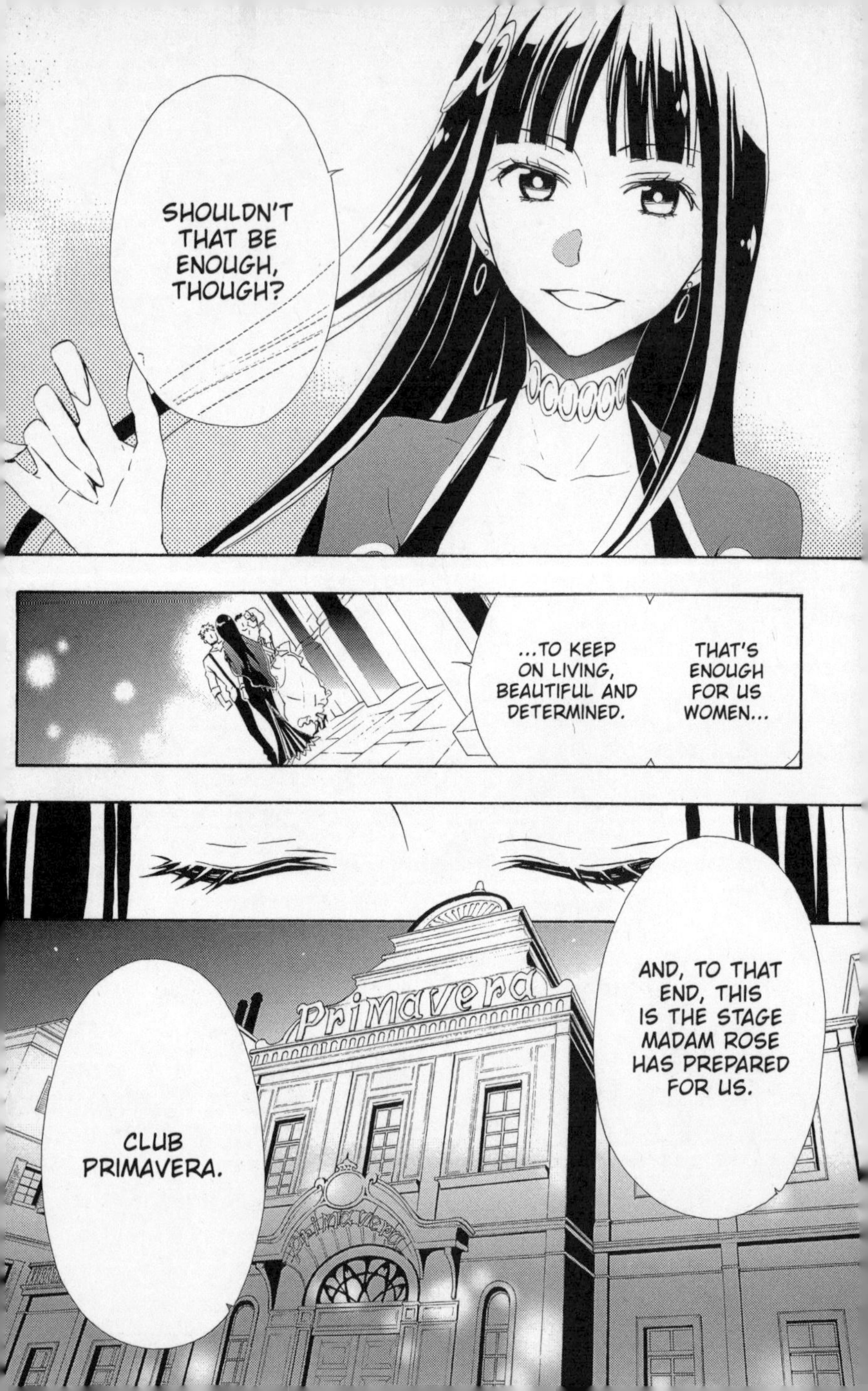
SHOULDN'T THAT BE ENOUGH, THOUGH?
THAT'S ENOUGH FOR US WOMEN...
...TO KEEP ON LIVING, BEAUTIFUL AND DETERMINED.
AND, TO THAT END, THIS IS THE STAGE MADAM ROSE HAS PREPARED FOR US.
Primavera
CLUB PRIMAVERA.

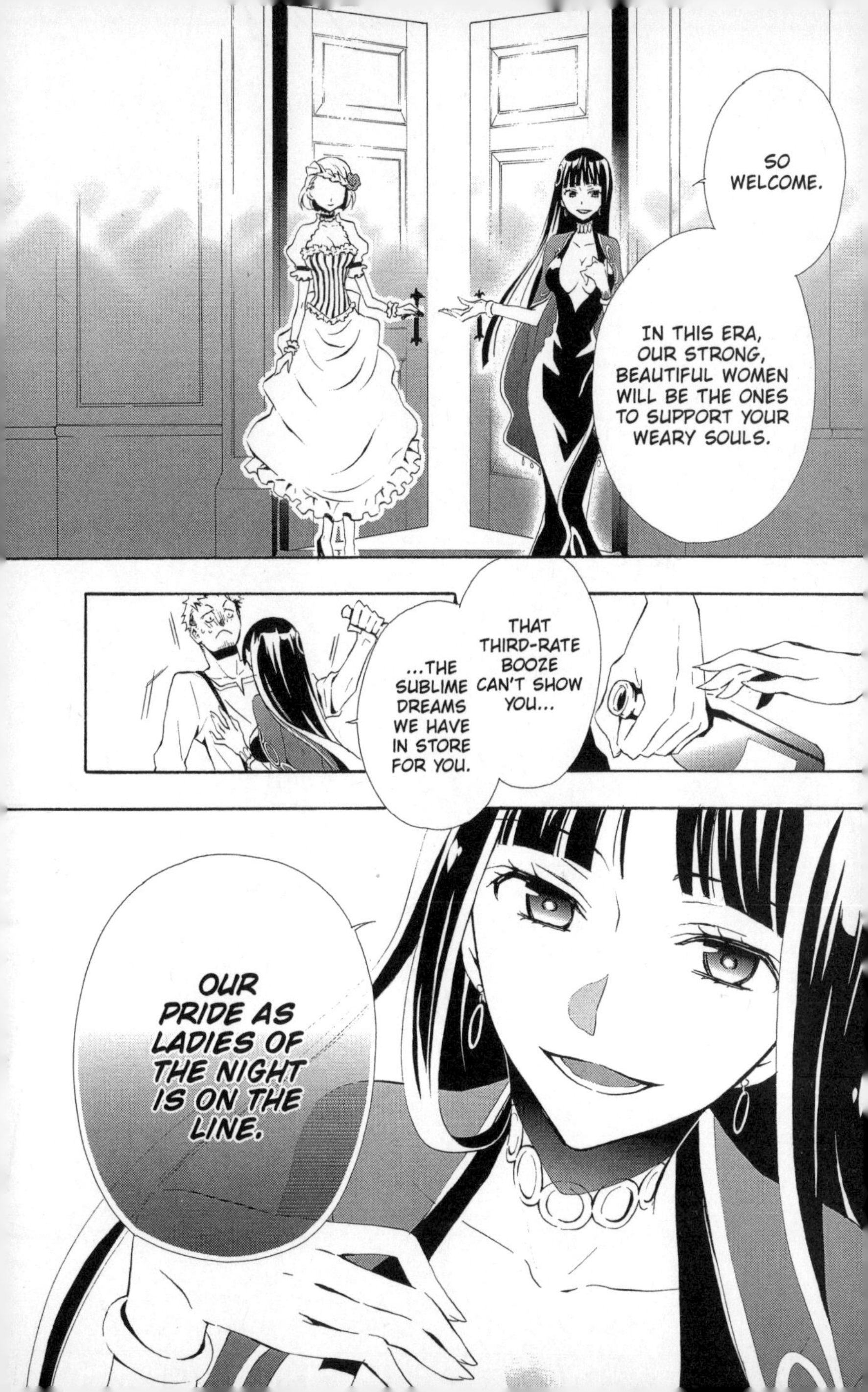
SO WELCOME.
IN THIS ERA, OUR STRONG, BEAUTIFUL WOMEN WILL BE THE ONES TO SUPPORT YOUR WEARY SOULS.
THAT THIRD-RATE BOOZE CAN'T SHOW YOU...
...THE SUBLIME DREAMS WE HAVE IN STORE FOR YOU.
OUR PRIDE AS LADIES OF THE NIGHT IS ON THE LINE.

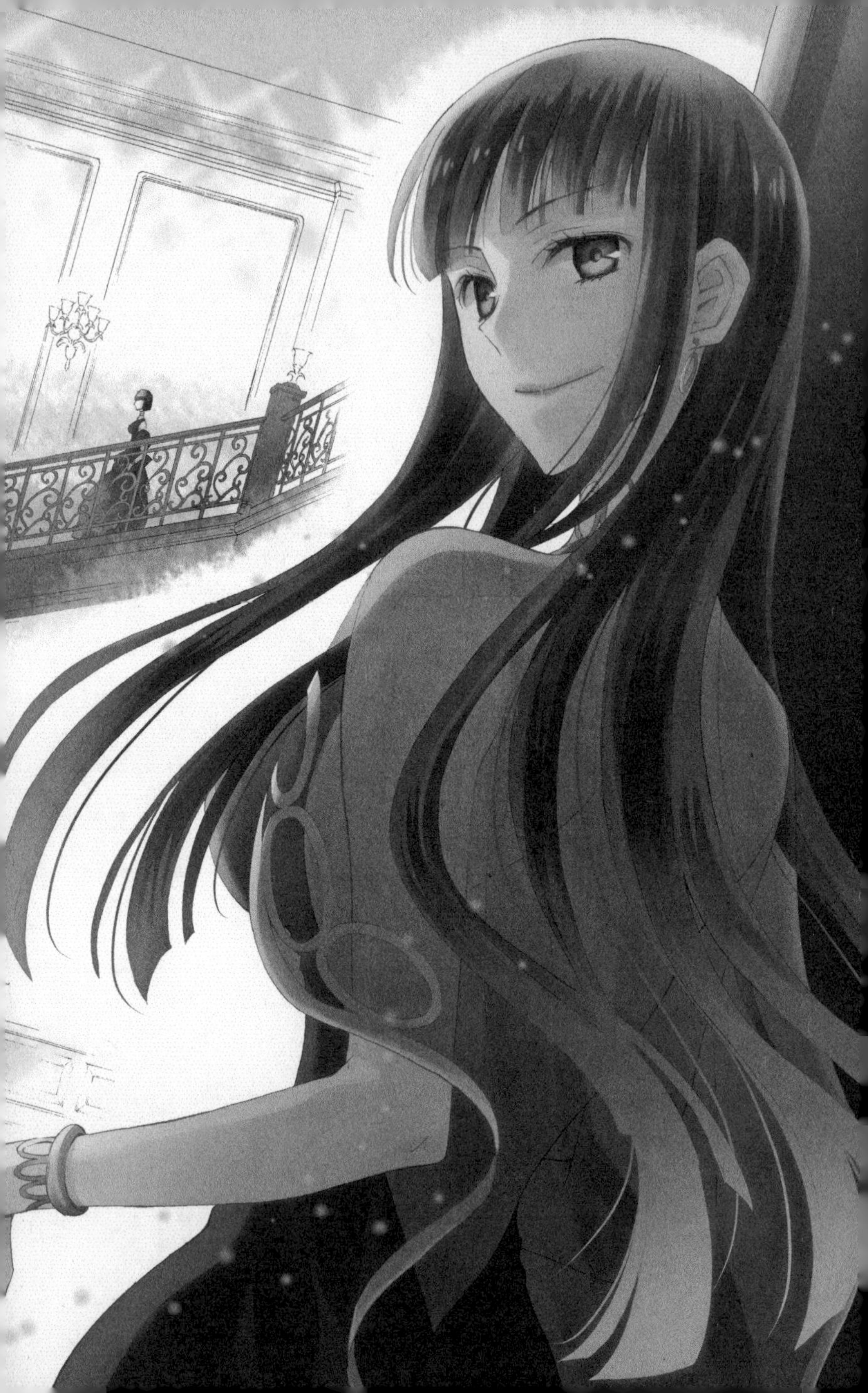

REASON 2: Power for the Future

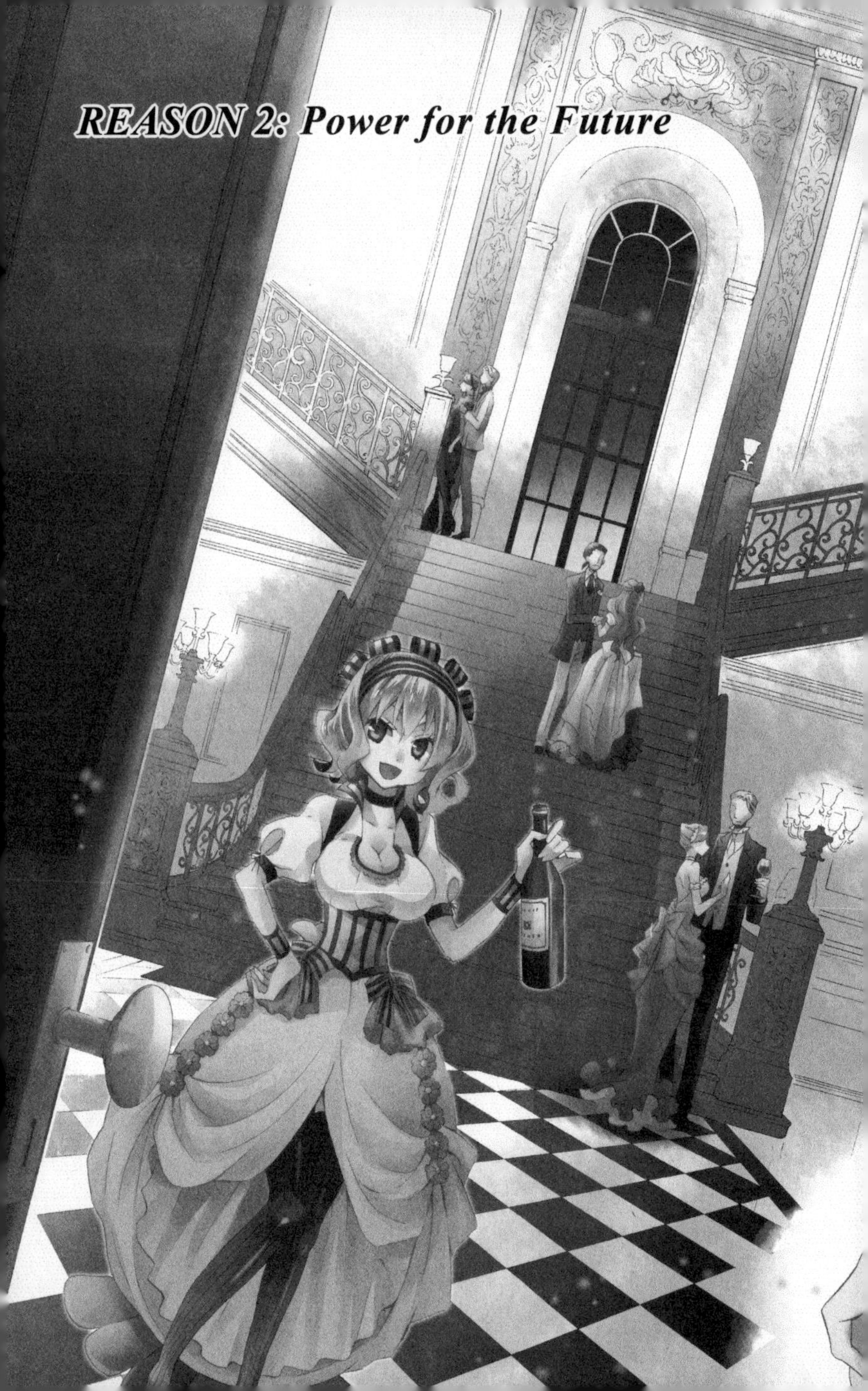

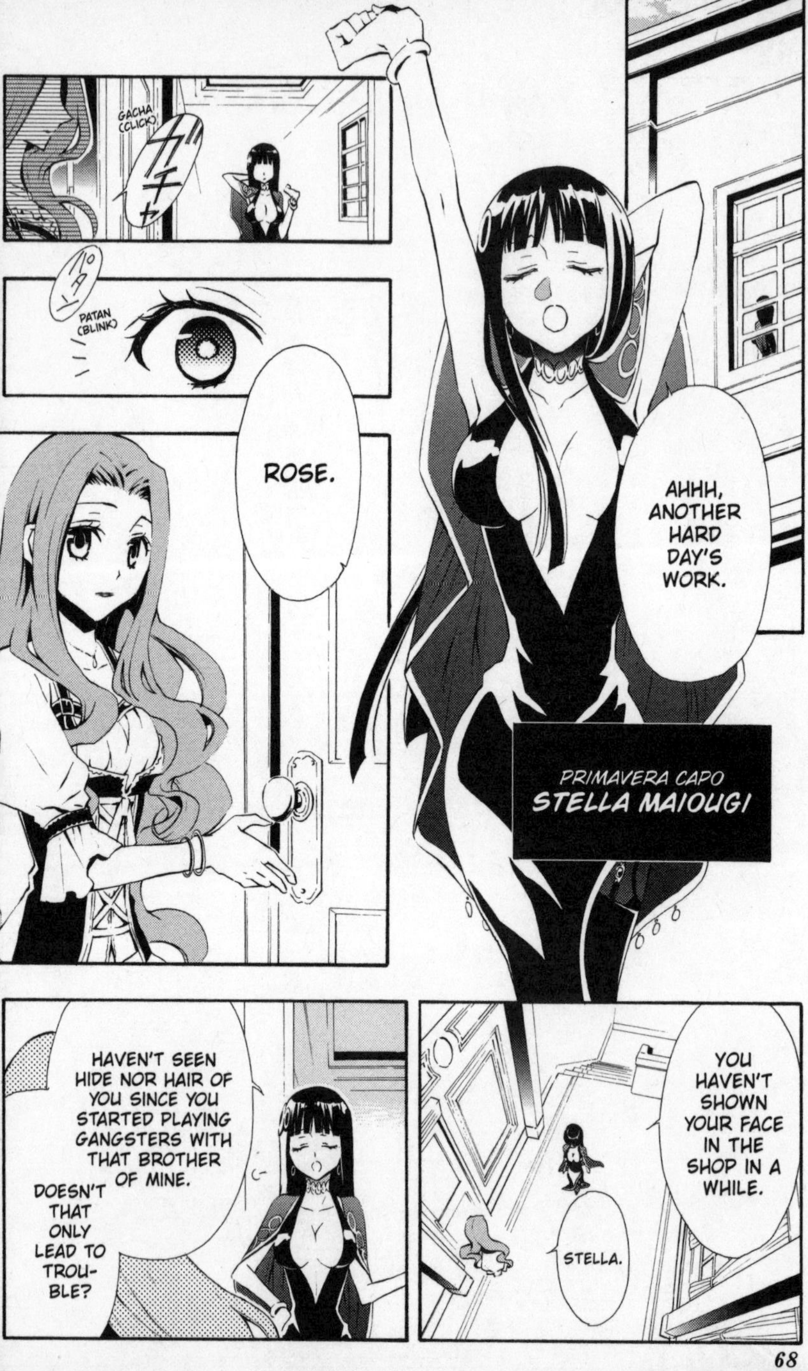
AHHH, ANOTHER HARD DAY'S WORK.
PRIMAVERA CAPO
STELLA MAIOUGI
カチャ
GACHA (CLICK)
パタン
PATAN (BLINK)
ROSE.
YOU HAVEN'T SHOWN YOUR FACE IN THE SHOP IN A WHILE.
STELLA.
HAVEN'T SEEN HIDE NOR HAIR OF YOU SINCE YOU STARTED PLAYING GANGSTERS WITH THAT BROTHER OF MINE.
DOESN'T THAT ONLY LEAD TO TROU-BLE?

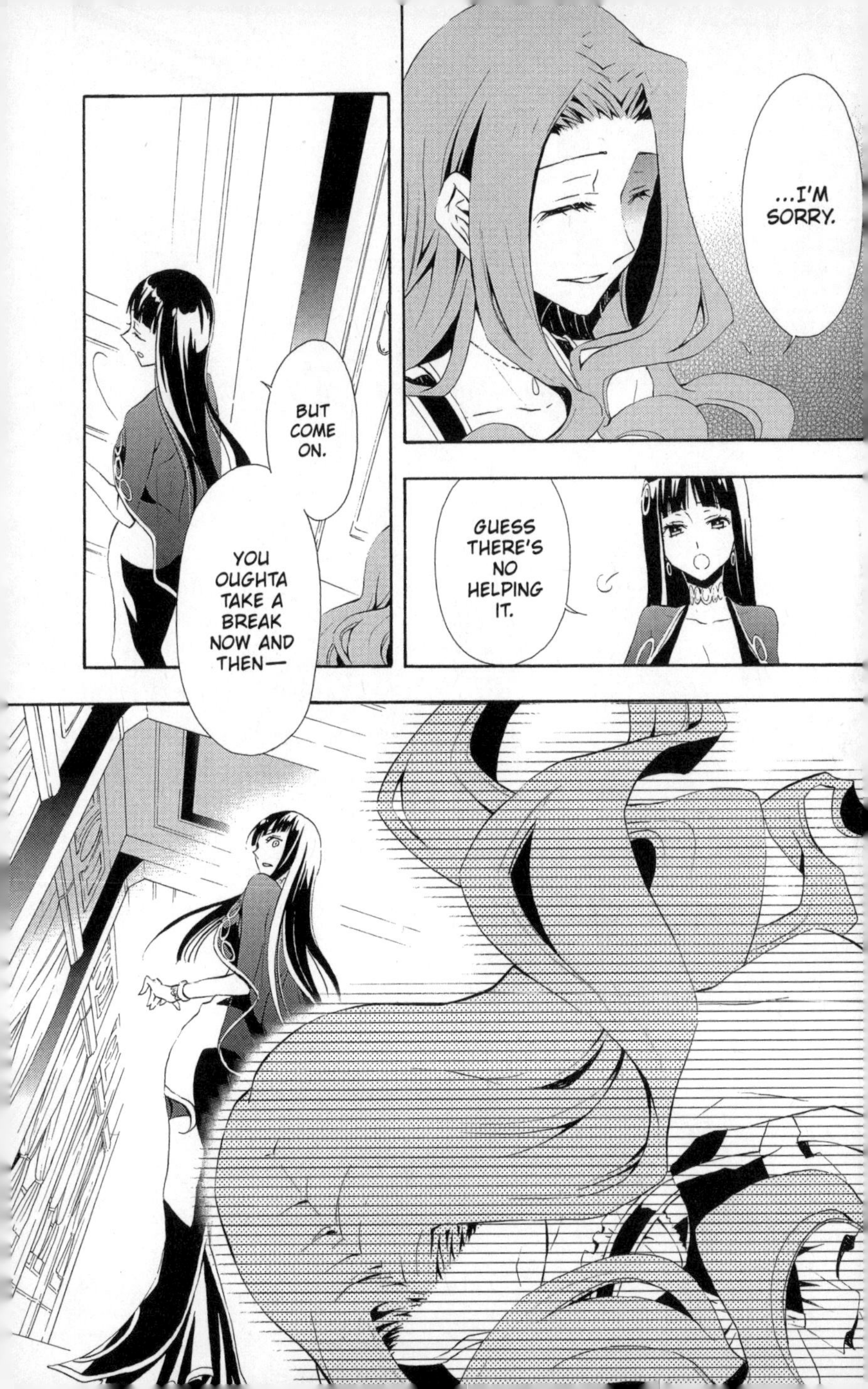
...I'M SORRY.
GUESS THERE'S NO HELPING IT.
BUT COME ON.
YOU OUGHTA TAKE A BREAK NOW AND THEN—

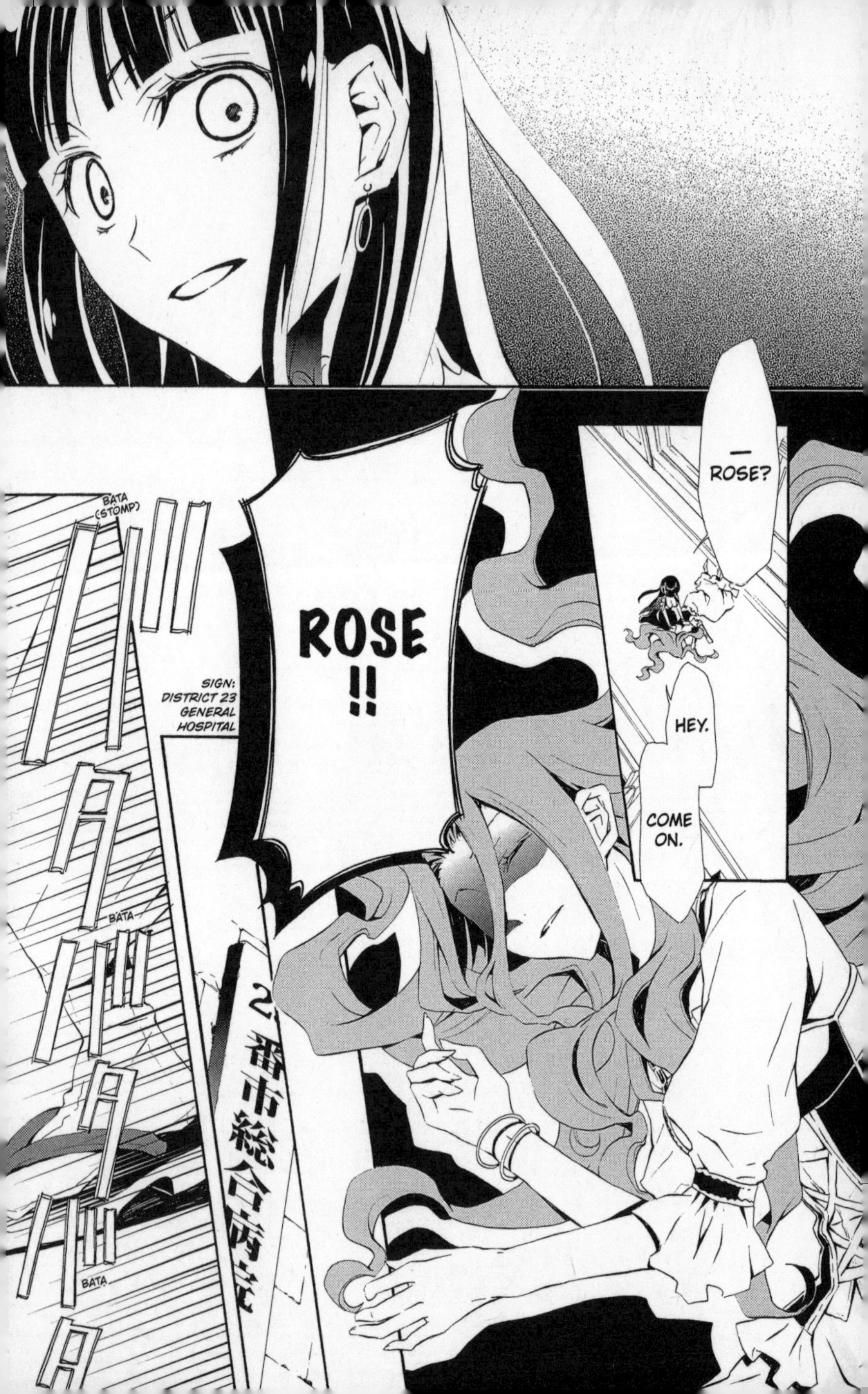
—ROSE?
HEY.
COME ON.
ROSE !!
BATA (STOMP)
SIGN: DISTRICT 23 GENERAL HOSPITAL
BATA
BATA

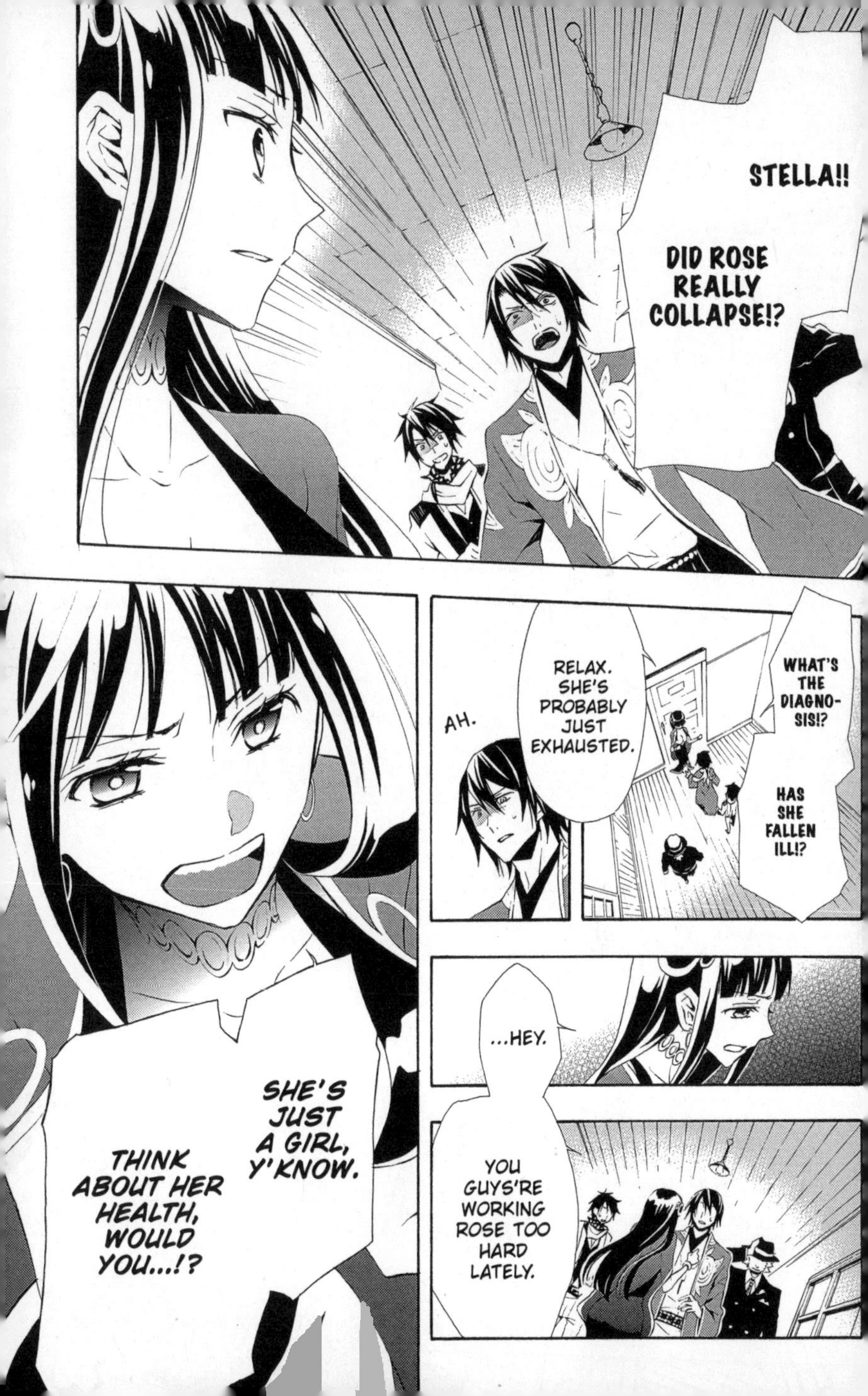
STELLA!!
DID ROSE REALLY COLLAPSE!?
WHAT'S THE DIAGNO-SIS!?
HAS SHE FALLEN ILL!?
RELAX. SHE'S PROBABLY JUST EXHAUSTED.
AH.
...HEY.
YOU GUYS'RE WORKING ROSE TOO HARD LATELY.
SHE'S JUST A GIRL, Y'KNOW.
THINK ABOUT HER HEALTH, WOULD YOU...!?

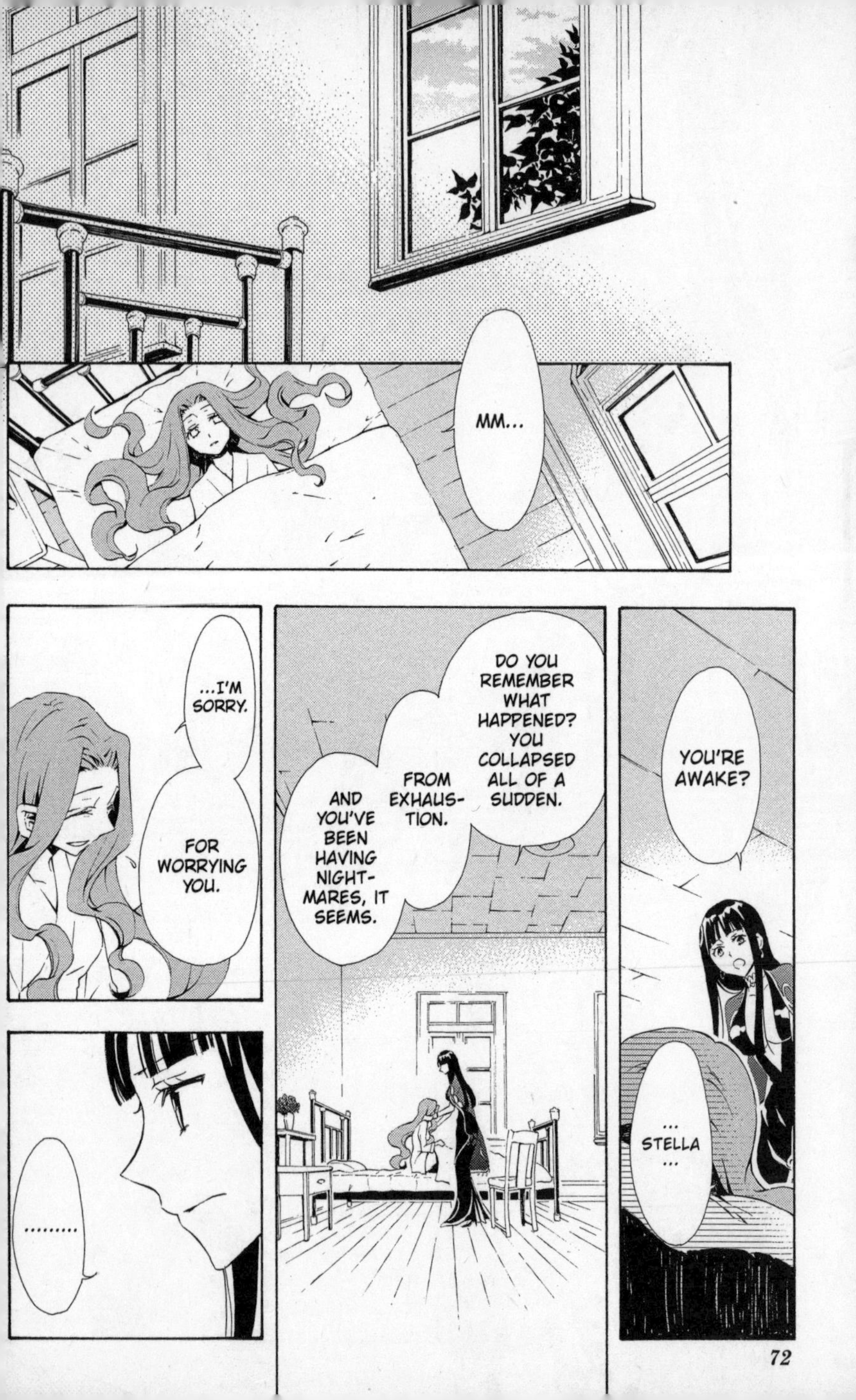
MM...
YOU'RE AWAKE?
... STELLA ...
DO YOU REMEMBER WHAT HAPPENED? YOU COLLAPSED ALL OF A SUDDEN.
FROM EXHAUSTION.
AND YOU'VE BEEN HAVING NIGHTMARES, IT SEEMS.
...I'M SORRY.
FOR WORRYING YOU.
....

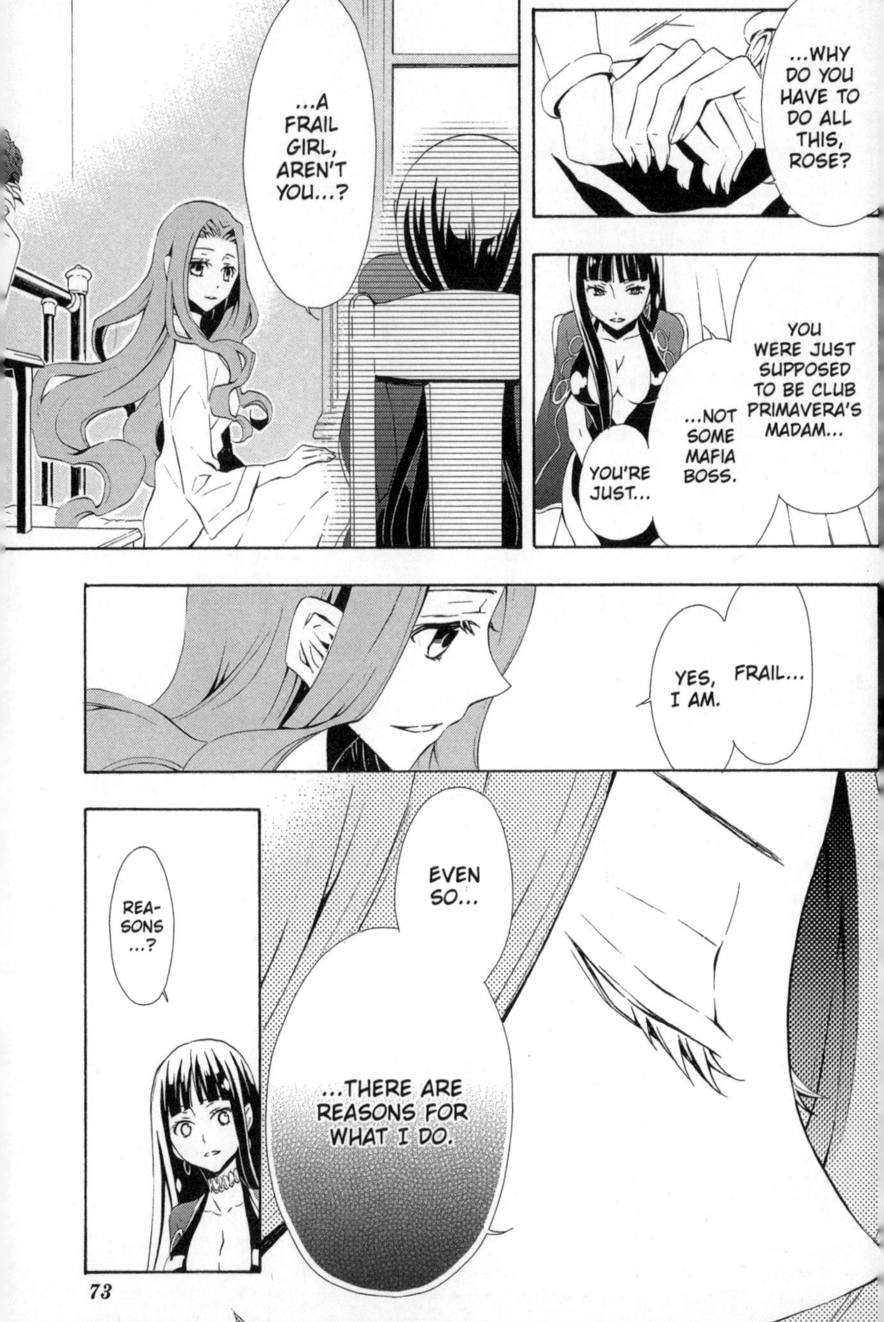
...WHY DO YOU HAVE TO DO ALL THIS, ROSE?
YOU WERE JUST SUPPOSED TO BE CLUB PRIMAVERA'S MADAM...
...NOT SOME MAFIA BOSS.
YOU'RE JUST...
...A FRAIL GIRL, AREN'T YOU...?
FRAIL...
YES, I AM.
EVEN SO...
...THERE ARE REASONS FOR WHAT I DO.
REA-SONS...?

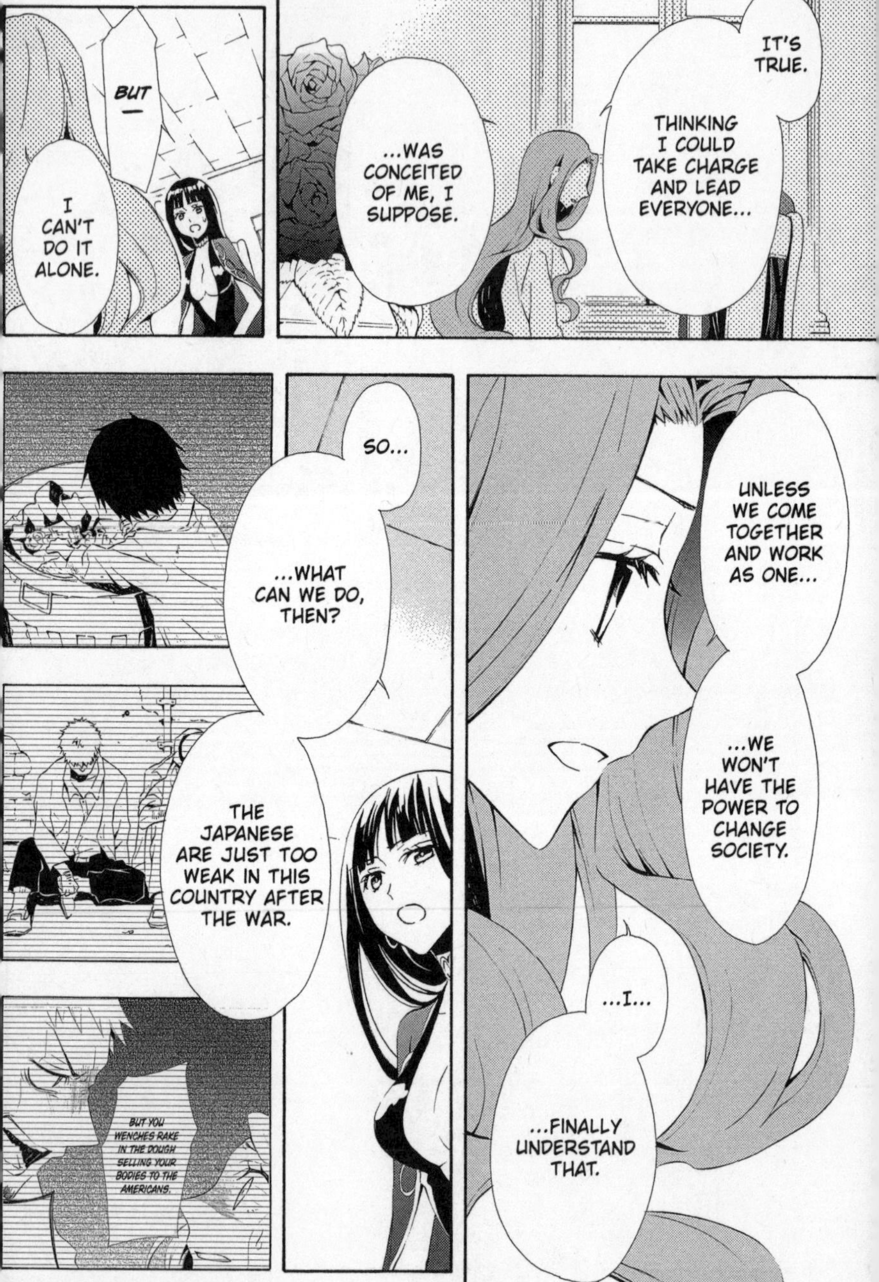
IT'S TRUE.
THINKING I COULD TAKE CHARGE AND LEAD EVERYONE...
...WAS CONCEITED OF ME, I SUPPOSE.
BUT—
I CAN'T DO IT ALONE.
UNLESS WE COME TOGETHER AND WORK AS ONE...
...WE WON'T HAVE THE POWER TO CHANGE SOCIETY.
...I...
...FINALLY UNDERSTAND THAT.
SO...
...WHAT CAN WE DO, THEN?
THE JAPANESE ARE JUST TOO WEAK IN THIS COUNTRY AFTER THE WAR.
BUT YOU WENCHES RAKE IN THE DOUGH SELLING YOUR BODIES TO THE AMERICANS.

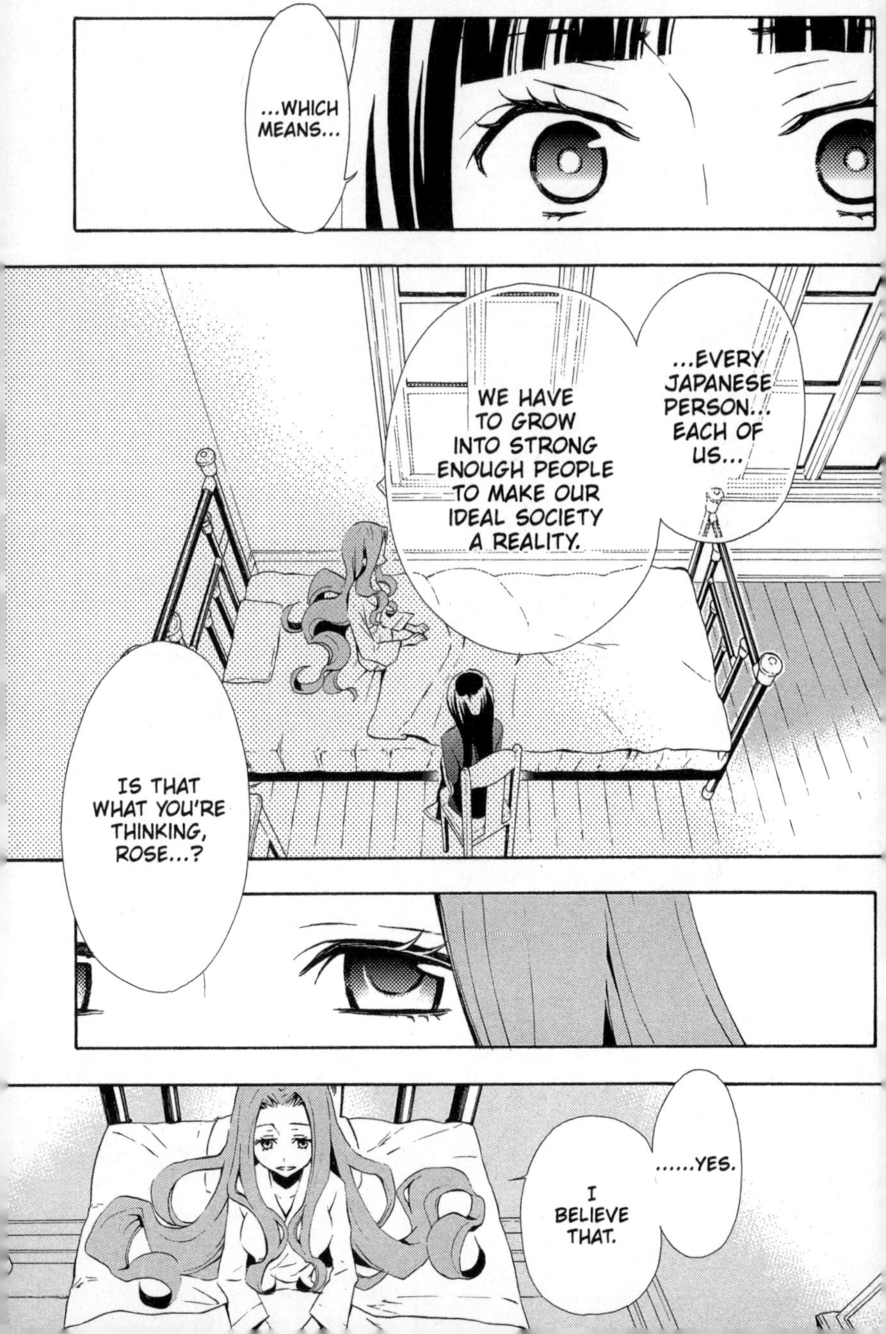
...WHICH MEANS...
...EVERY JAPANESE PERSON... EACH OF US...
WE HAVE TO GROW INTO STRONG ENOUGH PEOPLE TO MAKE OUR IDEAL SOCIETY A REALITY.
IS THAT WHAT YOU'RE THINKING, ROSE...?
......YES.
I BELIEVE THAT.

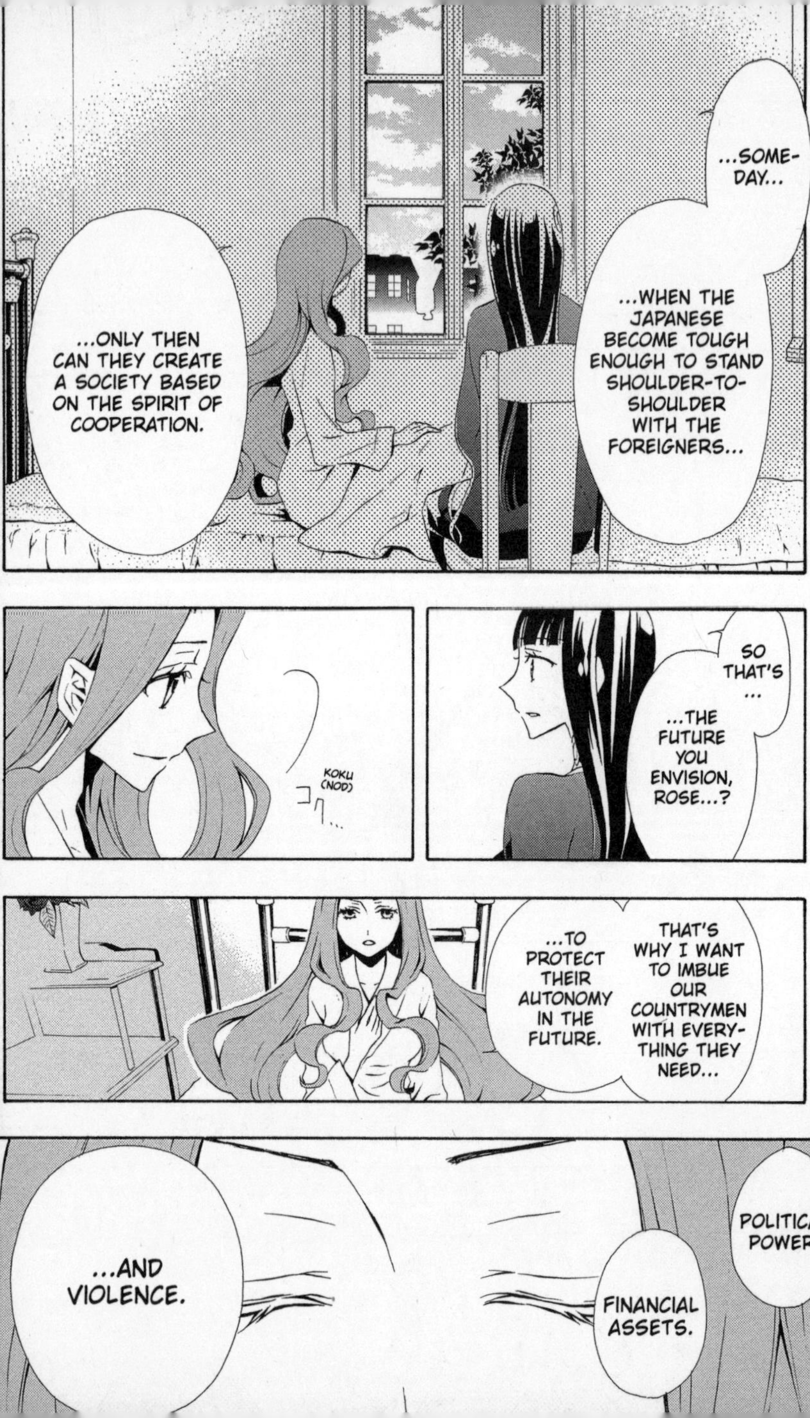
...SOME-DAY...
...WHEN THE JAPANESE BECOME TOUGH ENOUGH TO STAND SHOULDER-TO-SHOULDER WITH THE FOREIGNERS...
...ONLY THEN CAN THEY CREATE A SOCIETY BASED ON THE SPIRIT OF COOPERATION.
SO THAT'S...
...THE FUTURE YOU ENVISION, ROSE...?
KOKU (NOD)
コク...
THAT'S WHY I WANT TO IMBUE OUR COUNTRYMEN WITH EVERY-THING THEY NEED...
...TO PROTECT THEIR AUTONOMY IN THE FUTURE.
POLITICAL POWER.
FINANCIAL ASSETS.
...AND VIOLENCE.

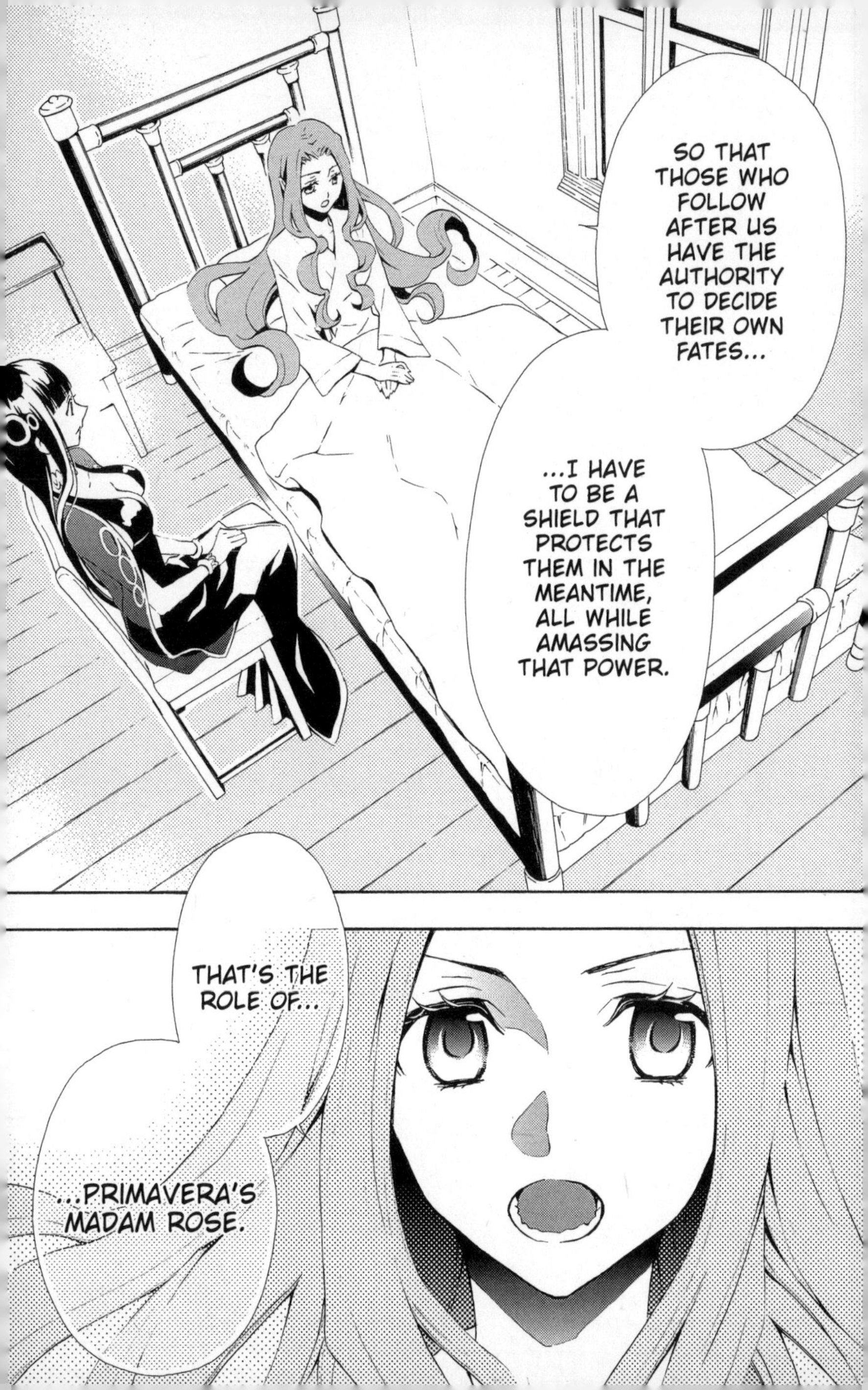
SO THAT THOSE WHO FOLLOW AFTER US HAVE THE AUTHORITY TO DECIDE THEIR OWN FATES...
...I HAVE TO BE A SHIELD THAT PROTECTS THEM IN THE MEANTIME, ALL WHILE AMASSING THAT POWER.
THAT'S THE ROLE OF...
...PRIMAVERA'S MADAM ROSE.

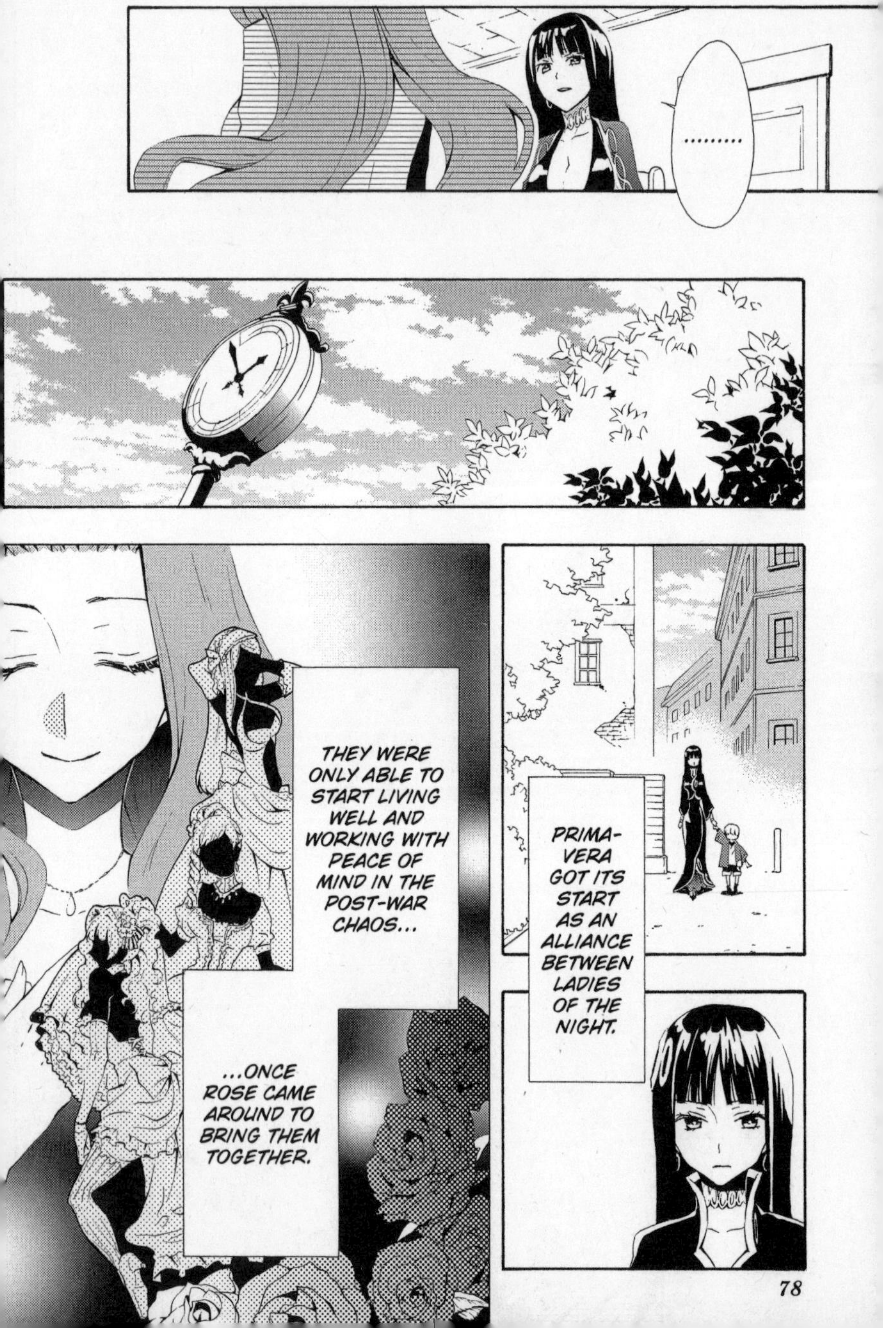
....
PRIMA-VERA GOT ITS START AS AN ALLIANCE BETWEEN LADIES OF THE NIGHT.
THEY WERE ONLY ABLE TO START LIVING WELL AND WORKING WITH PEACE OF MIND IN THE POST-WAR CHAOS...
...ONCE ROSE CAME AROUND TO BRING THEM TOGETHER.

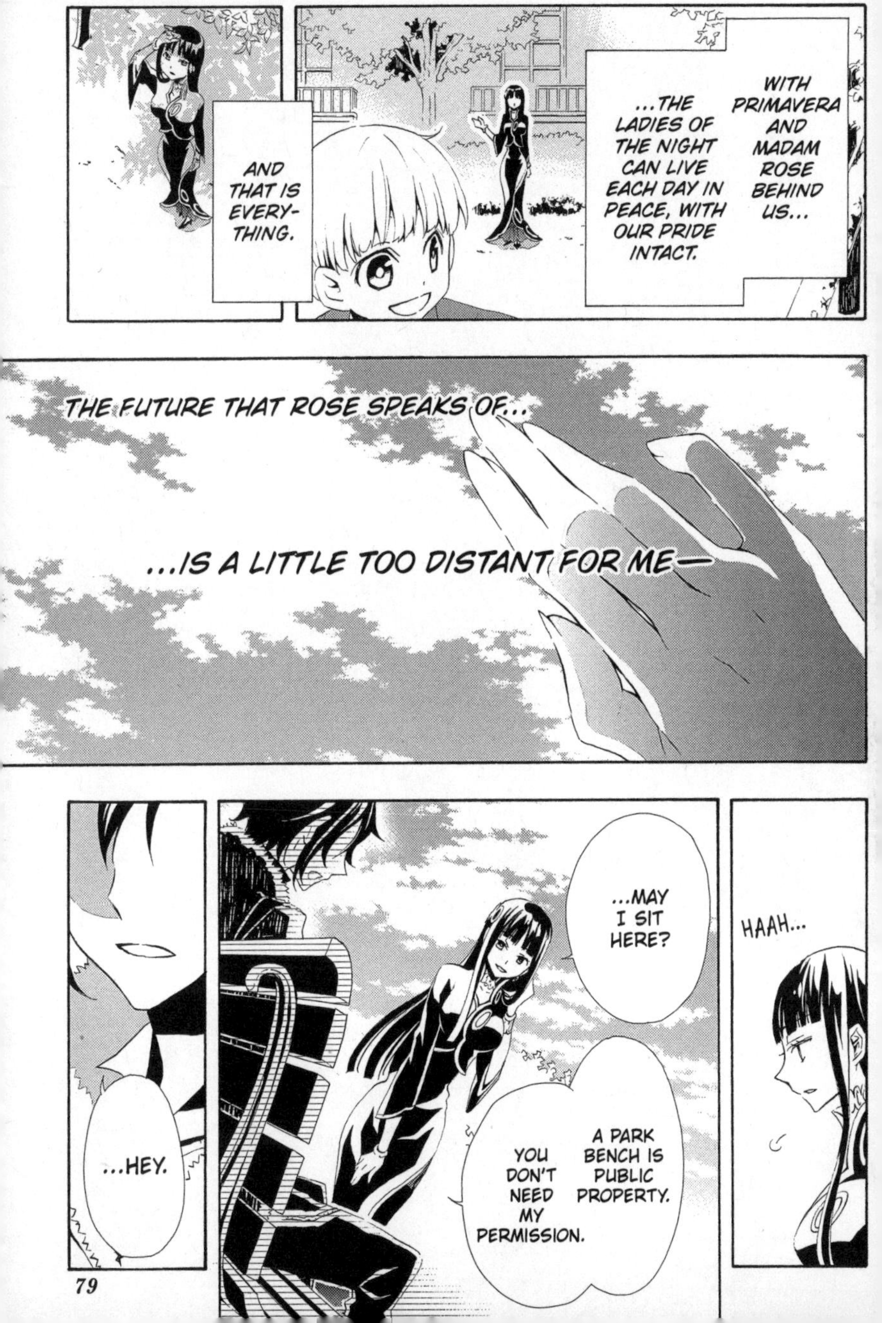
WITH PRIMAVERA AND MADAM ROSE BEHIND US...
...THE LADIES OF THE NIGHT CAN LIVE EACH DAY IN PEACE, WITH OUR PRIDE INTACT.
AND THAT IS EVERY-THING.
THE FUTURE THAT ROSE SPEAKS OF...
...IS A LITTLE TOO DISTANT FOR ME—
HAAH...
...MAY I SIT HERE?
A PARK BENCH IS PUBLIC PROPERTY.
YOU DON'T NEED MY PERMISSION.
...HEY.

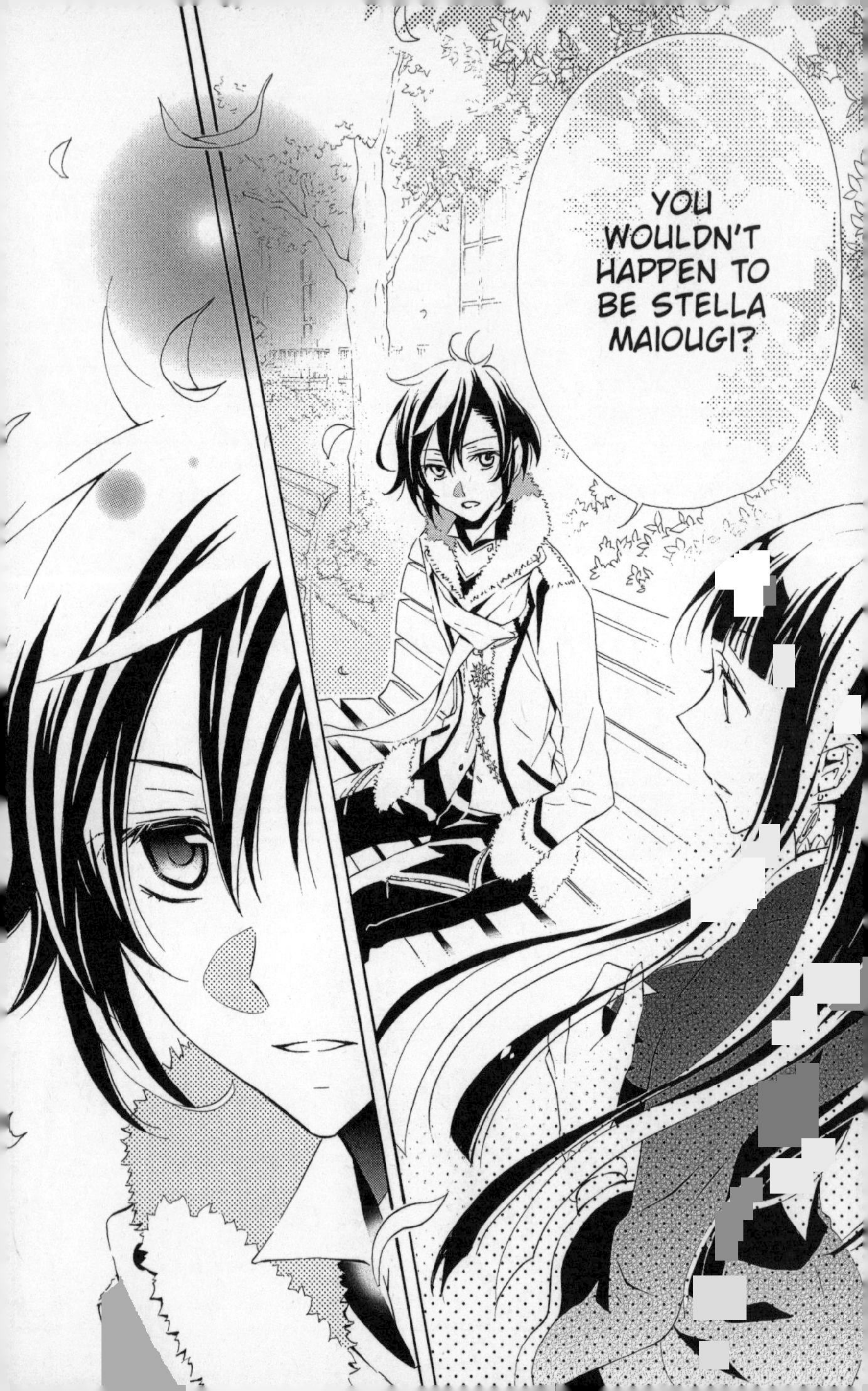
YOU WOULDN'T HAPPEN TO BE STELLA MAIOUGI?

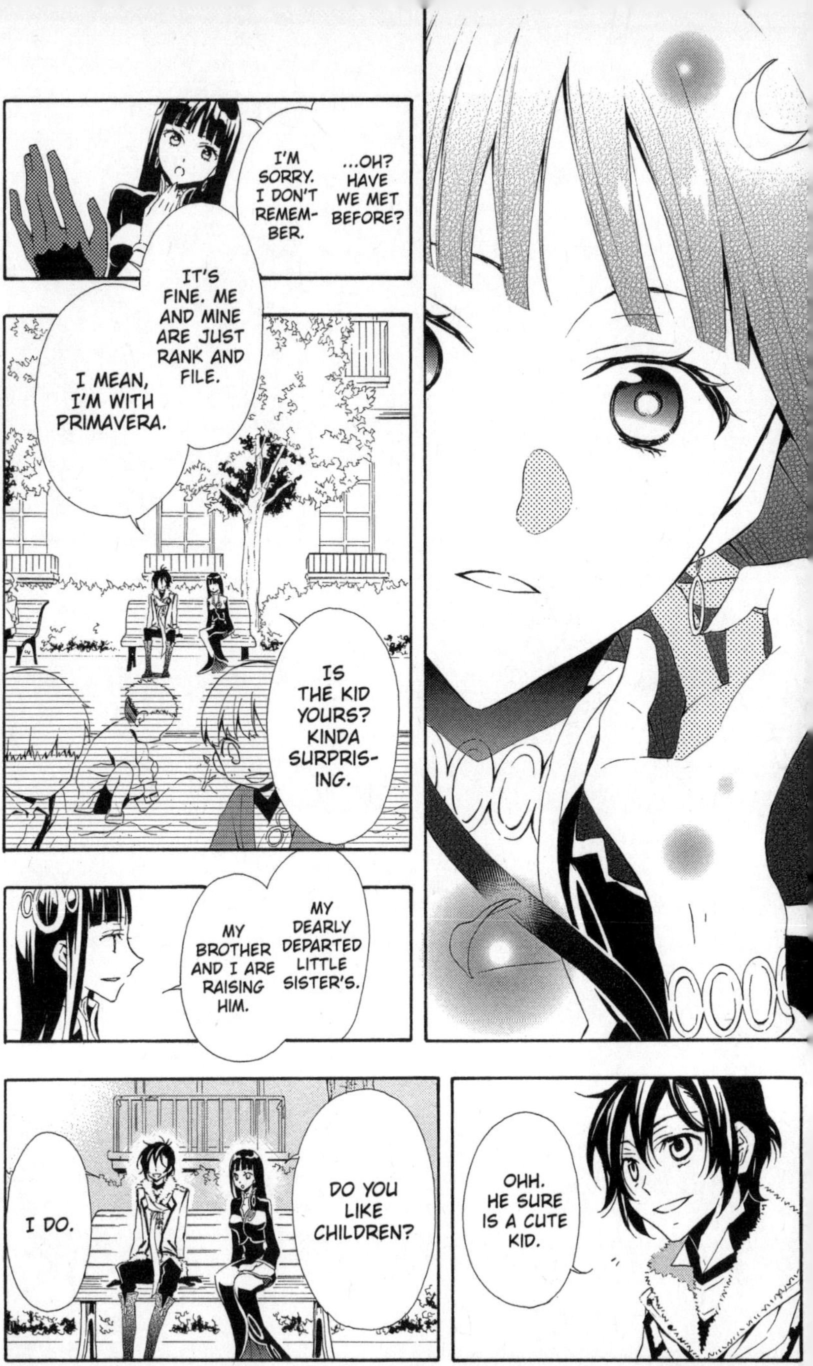
...OH? HAVE WE MET BEFORE?
I'M SORRY. I DON'T REMEMBER.
IT'S FINE. ME AND MINE ARE JUST RANK AND FILE.
I MEAN, I'M WITH PRIMAVERA.
IS THE KID YOURS? KINDA SURPRISING.
MY DEARLY DEPARTED LITTLE SISTER'S.
MY BROTHER AND I ARE RAISING HIM.
OHH. HE SURE IS A CUTE KID.
DO YOU LIKE CHILDREN?
I DO.

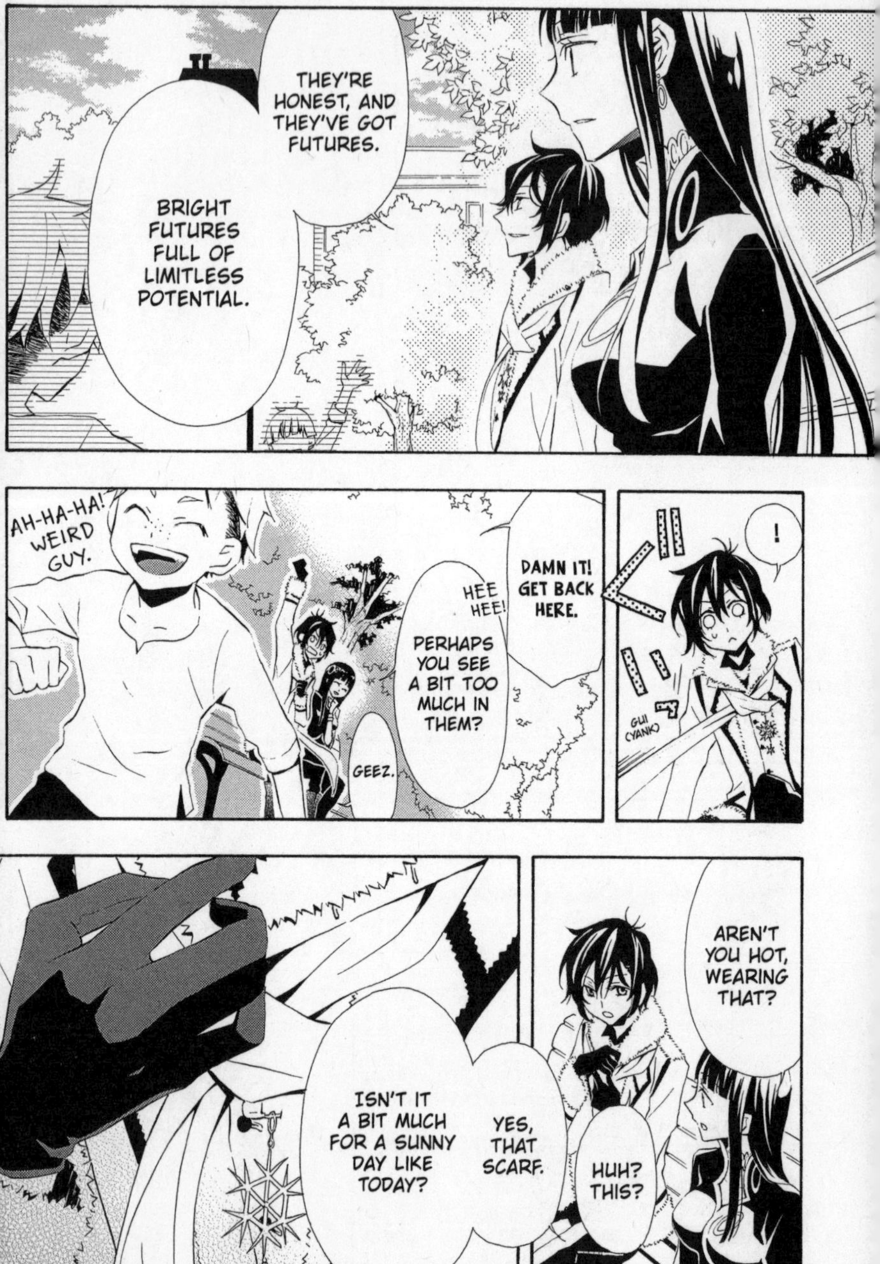
THEY'RE HONEST, AND THEY'VE GOT FUTURES.
BRIGHT FUTURES FULL OF LIMITLESS POTENTIAL.
!
GUI (YANK)
DAMN IT! GET BACK HERE.
HEE HEE!
PERHAPS YOU SEE A BIT TOO MUCH IN THEM?
GEEZ.
AH-HA-HA! WEIRD GUY.
AREN'T YOU HOT, WEARING THAT?
HUH? THIS?
YES, THAT SCARF.
ISN'T IT A BIT MUCH FOR A SUNNY DAY LIKE TODAY?

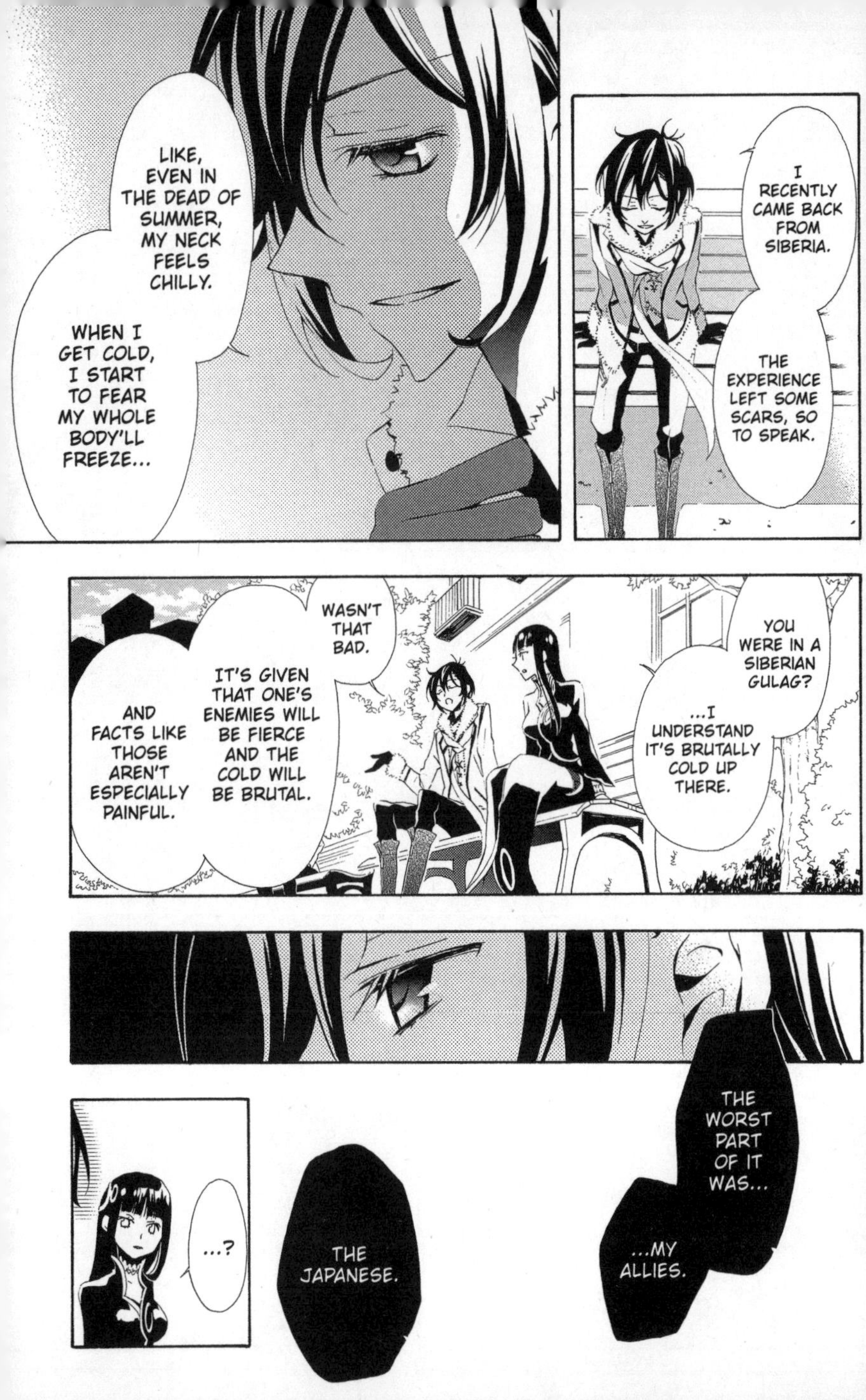
I RECENTLY CAME BACK FROM SIBERIA.
THE EXPERIENCE LEFT SOME SCARS, SO TO SPEAK.
LIKE, EVEN IN THE DEAD OF SUMMER, MY NECK FEELS CHILLY.
WHEN I GET COLD, I START TO FEAR MY WHOLE BODY'LL FREEZE...
YOU WERE IN A SIBERIAN GULAG?
...I UNDERSTAND IT'S BRUTALLY COLD UP THERE.
WASN'T THAT BAD.
IT'S GIVEN THAT ONE'S ENEMIES WILL BE FIERCE AND THE COLD WILL BE BRUTAL.
AND FACTS LIKE THOSE AREN'T ESPECIALLY PAINFUL.
THE WORST PART OF IT WAS...
...MY ALLIES.
THE JAPANESE.
...?

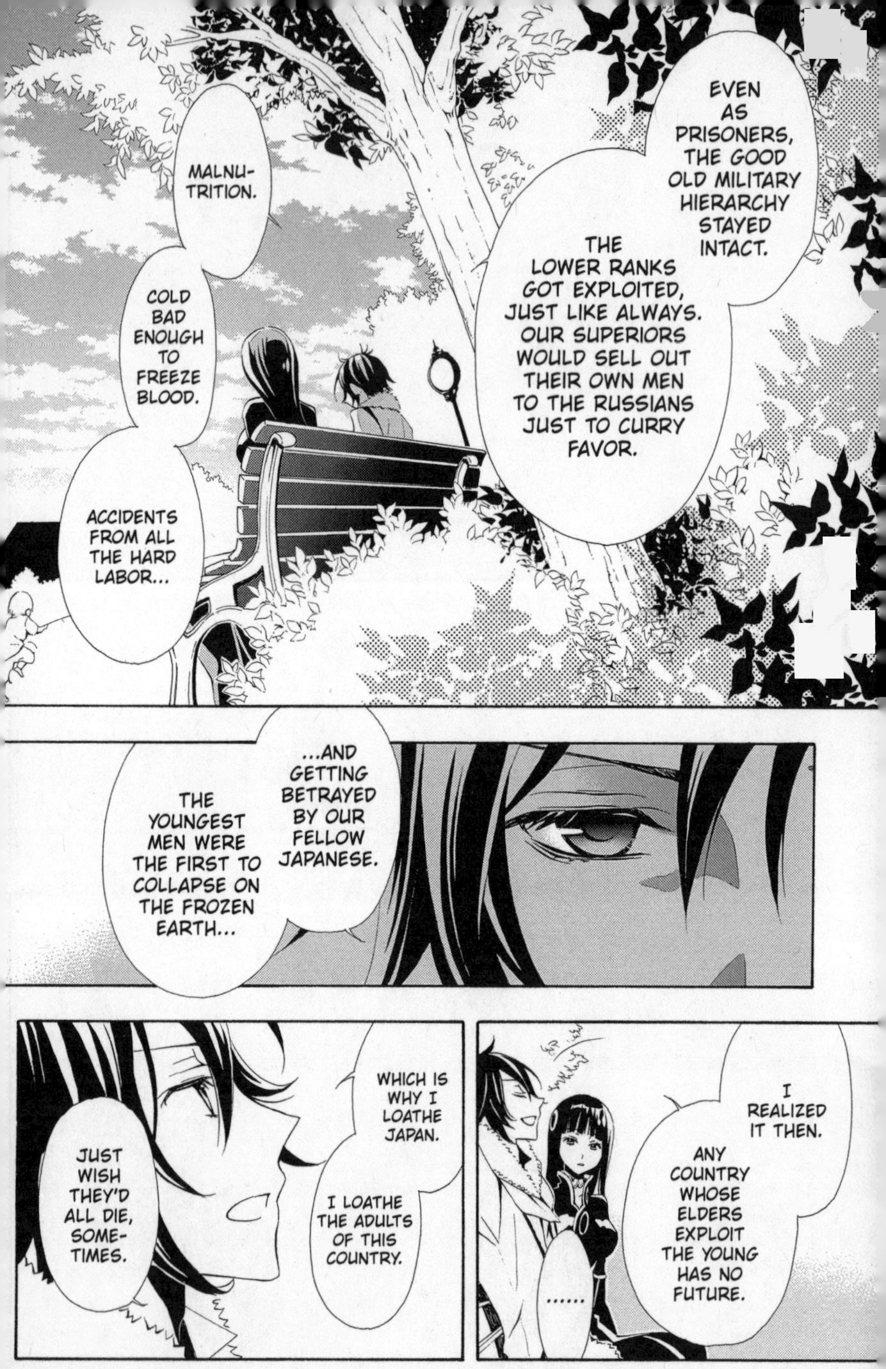
EVEN AS PRISONERS, THE GOOD OLD MILITARY HIERARCHY STAYED INTACT.
THE LOWER RANKS GOT EXPLOITED, JUST LIKE ALWAYS. OUR SUPERIORS WOULD SELL OUT THEIR OWN MEN TO THE RUSSIANS JUST TO CURRY FAVOR.
MALNU-TRITION.
COLD BAD ENOUGH TO FREEZE BLOOD.
ACCIDENTS FROM ALL THE HARD LABOR...
...AND GETTING BETRAYED BY OUR FELLOW JAPANESE.
THE YOUNGEST MEN WERE THE FIRST TO COLLAPSE ON THE FROZEN EARTH...
I REALIZED IT THEN.
ANY COUNTRY WHOSE ELDERS EXPLOIT THE YOUNG HAS NO FUTURE.
......
WHICH IS WHY I LOATHE JAPAN.
I LOATHE THE ADULTS OF THIS COUNTRY.
JUST WISH THEY'D ALL DIE, SOME-TIMES.

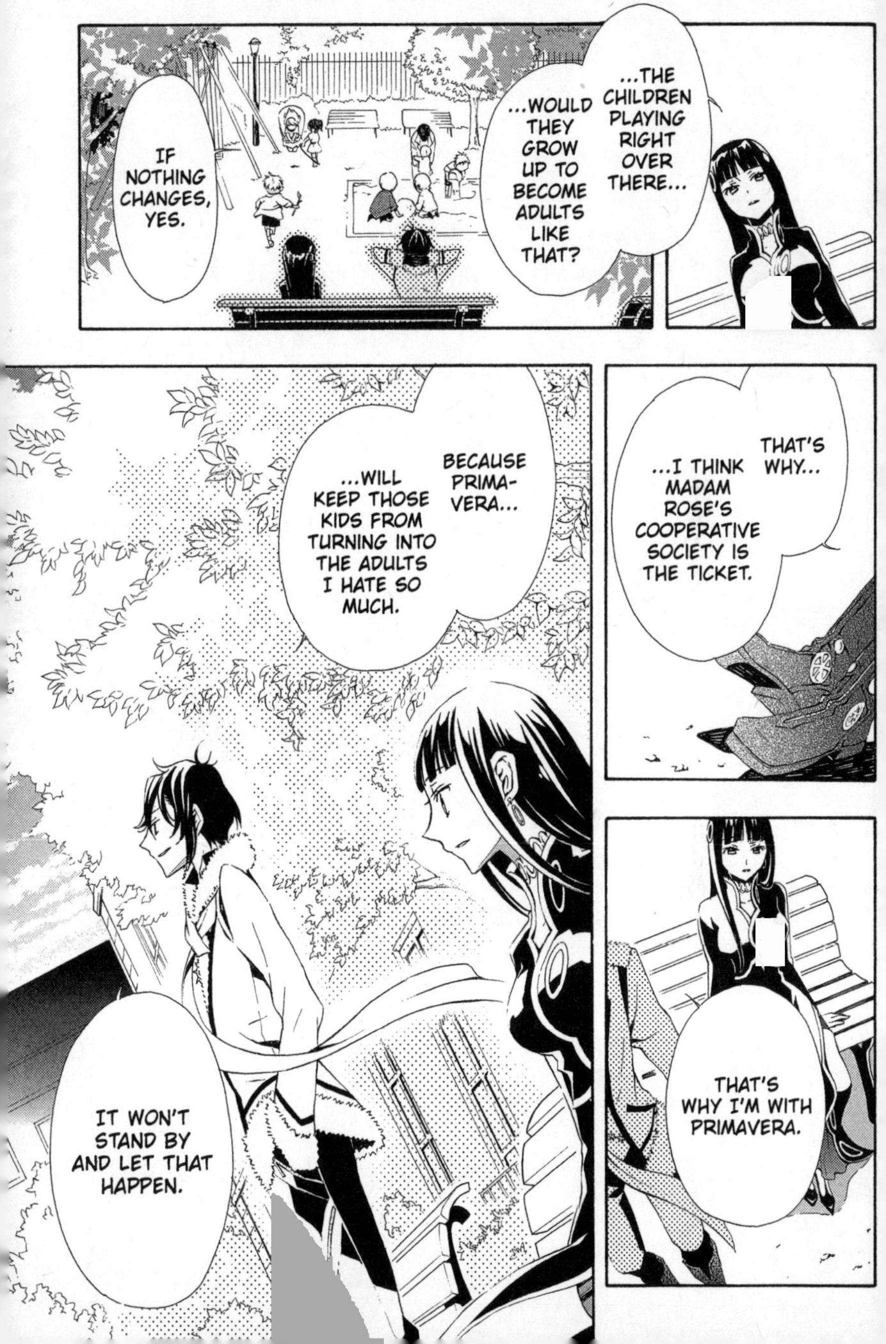
...THE CHILDREN PLAYING RIGHT OVER THERE...
...WOULD THEY GROW UP TO BECOME ADULTS LIKE THAT?
IF NOTHING CHANGES, YES.
THAT'S WHY...
...I THINK MADAM ROSE'S COOPERATIVE SOCIETY IS THE TICKET.
THAT'S WHY I'M WITH PRIMAVERA.
BECAUSE PRIMAVERA...
...WILL KEEP THOSE KIDS FROM TURNING INTO THE ADULTS I HATE SO MUCH.
IT WON'T STAND BY AND LET THAT HAPPEN.

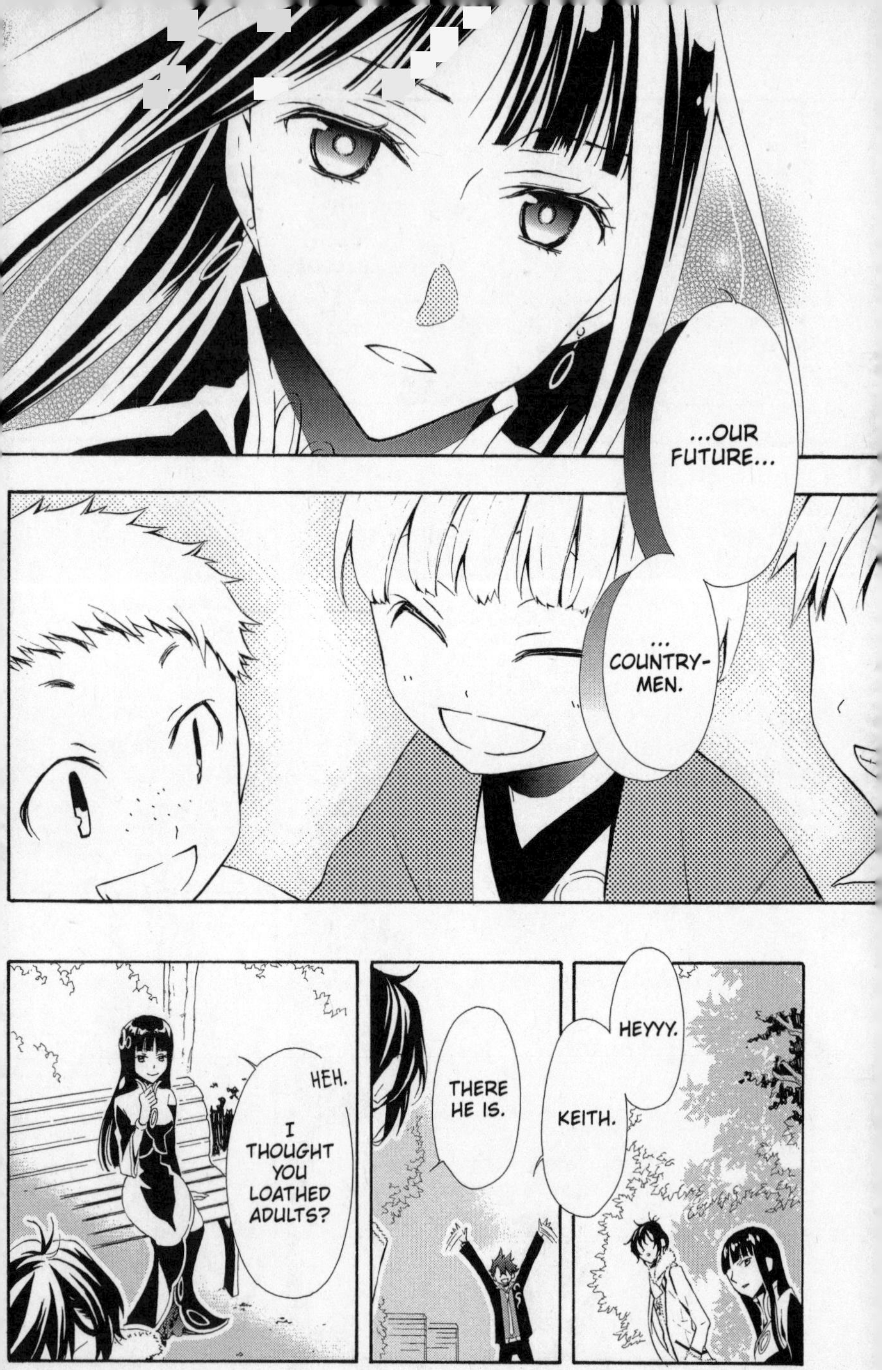
...OUR FUTURE...
... COUNTRY-MEN.
HEYYY.
KEITH.
THERE HE IS.
HEH.
I THOUGHT YOU LOATHED ADULTS?

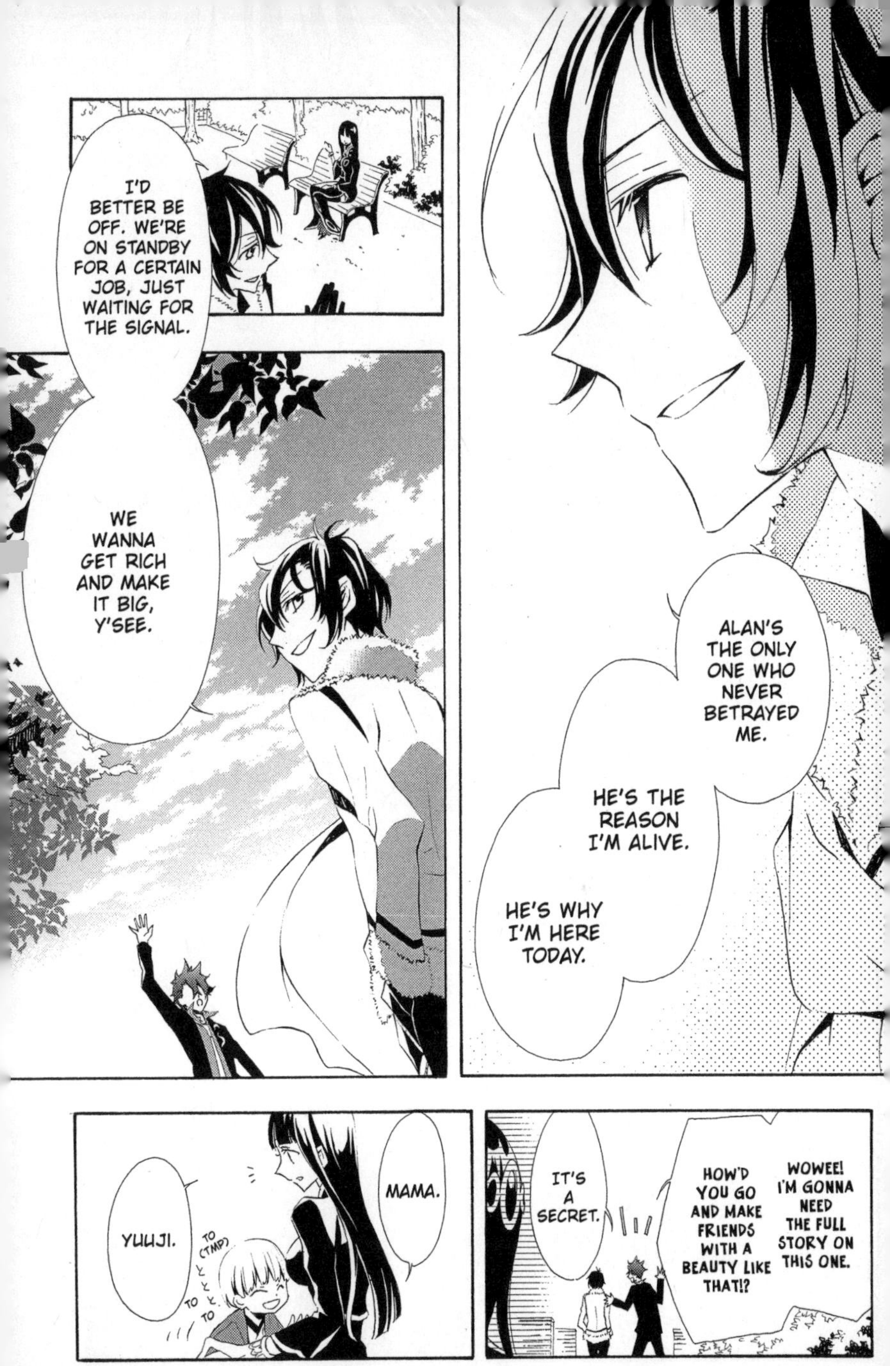
ALAN'S THE ONLY ONE WHO NEVER BETRAYED ME.
HE'S THE REASON I'M ALIVE.
HE'S WHY I'M HERE TODAY.
I'D BETTER BE OFF. WE'RE ON STANDBY FOR A CERTAIN JOB, JUST WAITING FOR THE SIGNAL.
WE WANNA GET RICH AND MAKE IT BIG, Y'SEE.
WOWEE! I'M GONNA NEED THE FULL STORY ON THIS ONE.
HOW'D YOU GO AND MAKE FRIENDS WITH A BEAUTY LIKE THAT!?
IT'S A SECRET.
MAMA.
YUUJI.
TO (TMP)
TO
TO

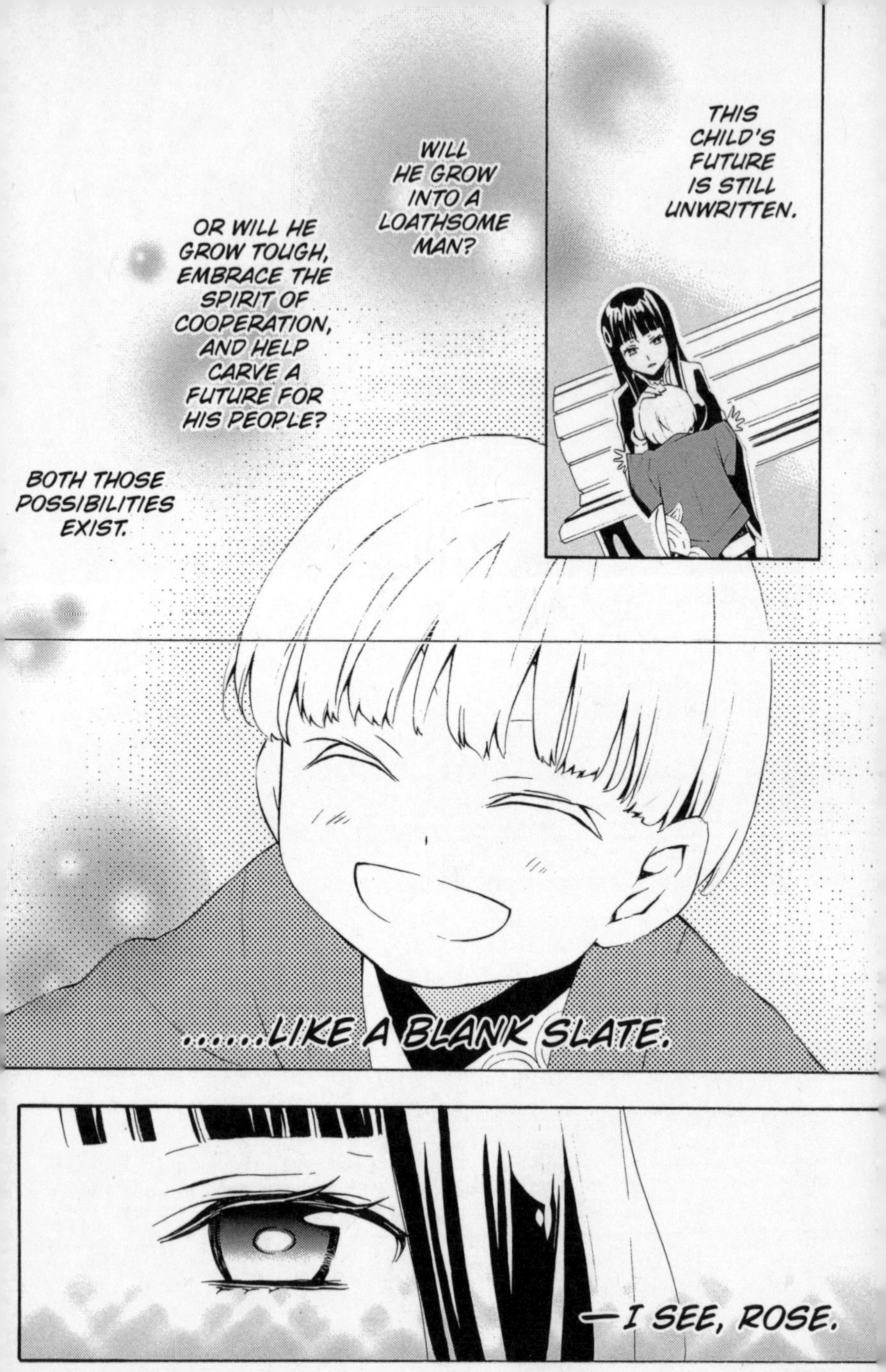
THIS CHILD'S FUTURE IS STILL UNWRITTEN.
WILL HE GROW INTO A LOATHSOME MAN?
OR WILL HE GROW TOUGH, EMBRACE THE SPIRIT OF COOPERATION, AND HELP CARVE A FUTURE FOR HIS PEOPLE?
BOTH THOSE POSSIBILITIES EXIST.
......LIKE A BLANK SLATE.
—I SEE, ROSE.

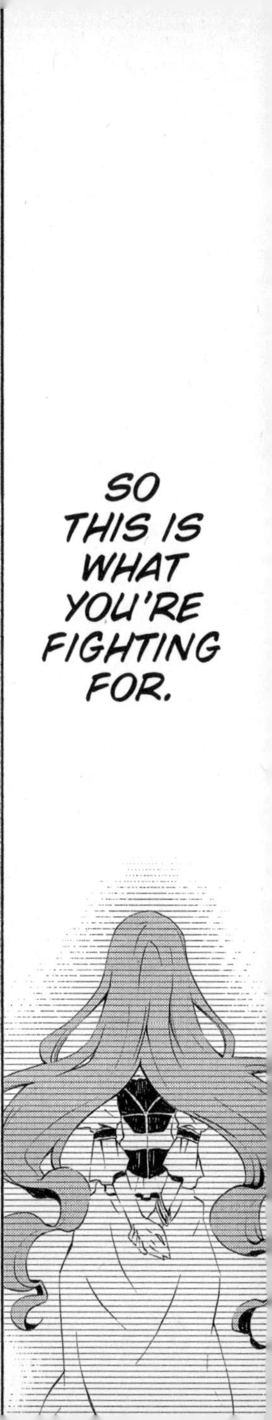
SO THIS IS WHAT YOU'RE FIGHTING FOR.

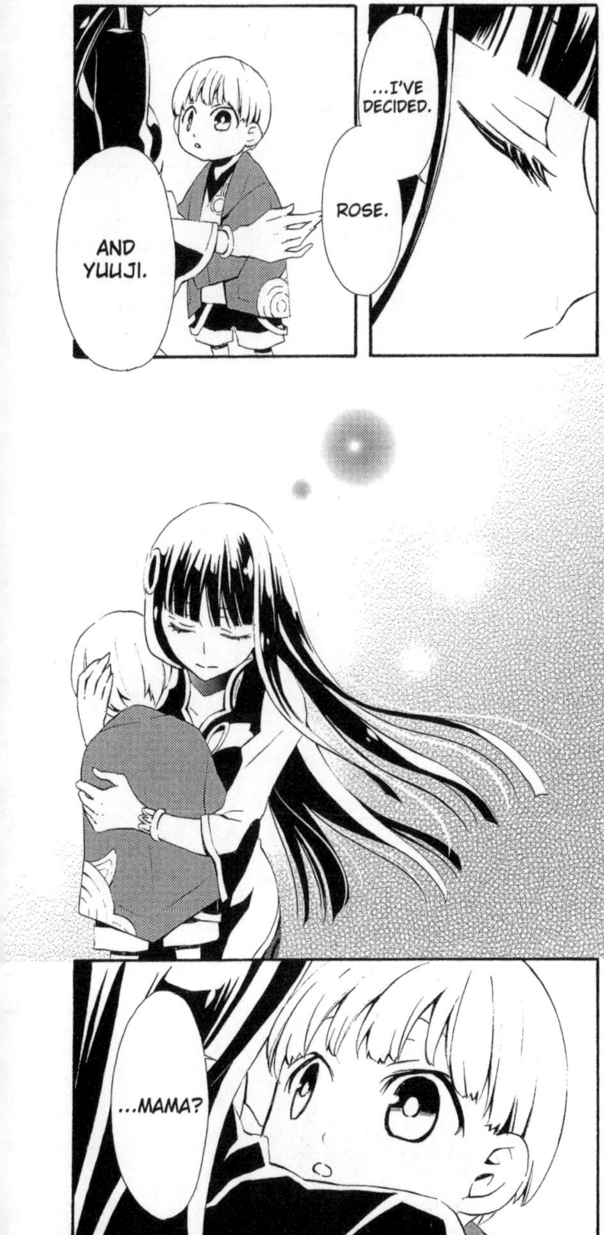
...I'VE DECIDED.
ROSE.
AND YUUJI.
...MAMA?

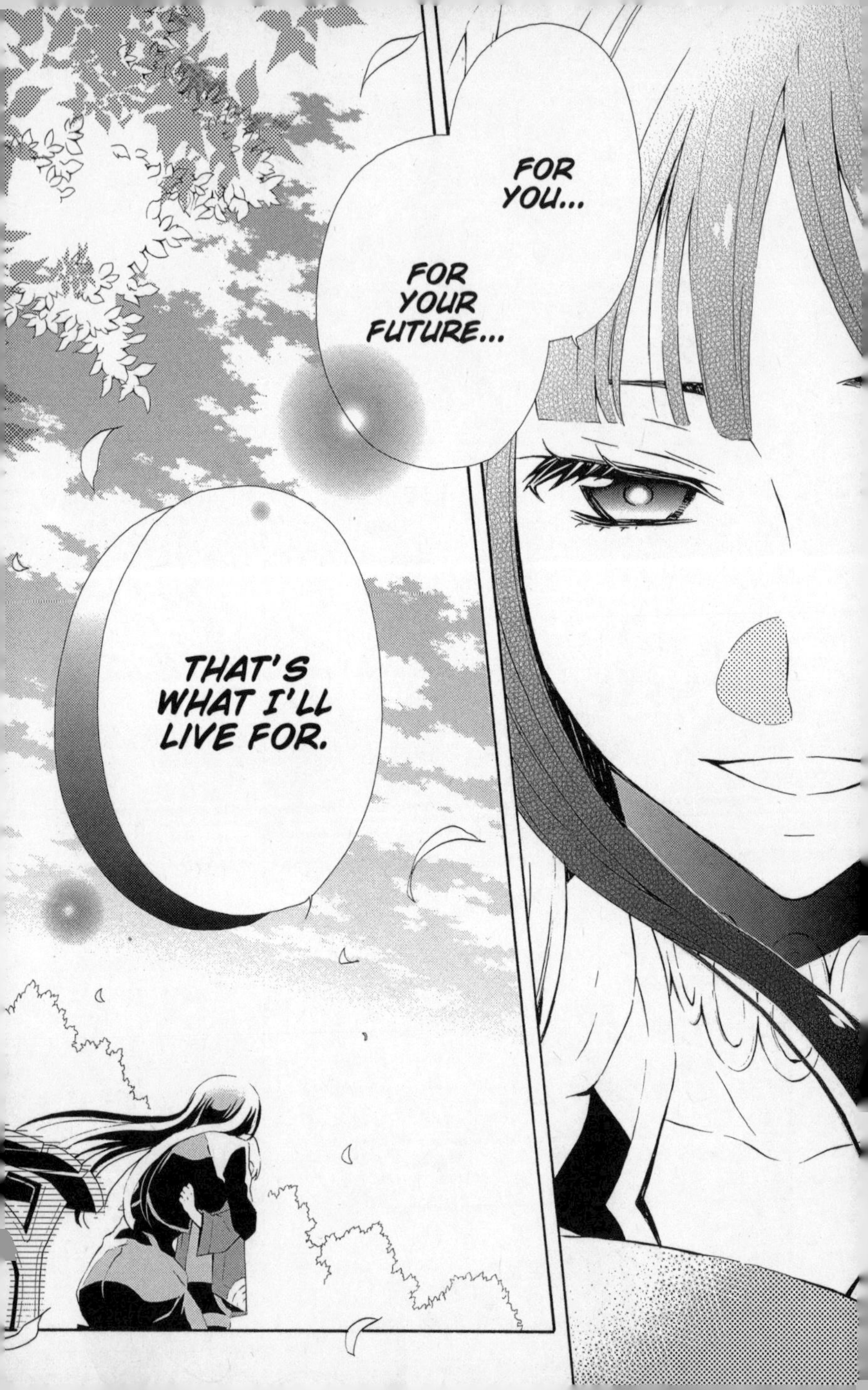
FOR YOU...
FOR YOUR FUTURE...
THAT'S WHAT I'LL LIVE FOR.

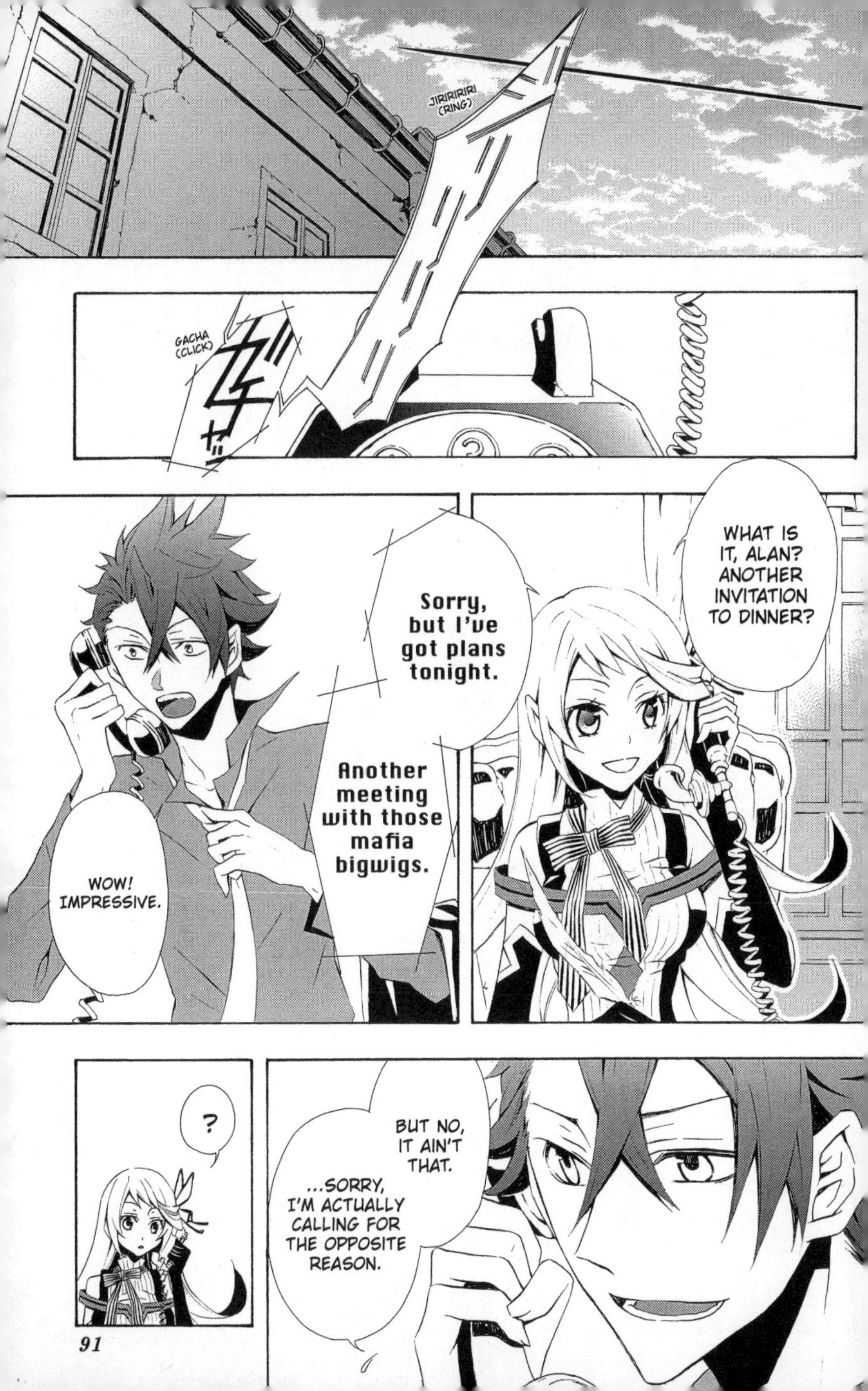
JIRIRIRIRI (RING)
GACHA (CLICK)
WHAT IS IT, ALAN? ANOTHER INVITATION TO DINNER?
Sorry, but I've got plans tonight.
Another meeting with those mafia bigwigs.
WOW! IMPRESSIVE.
BUT NO, IT AIN'T THAT.
...SORRY, I'M ACTUALLY CALLING FOR THE OPPOSITE REASON.
?

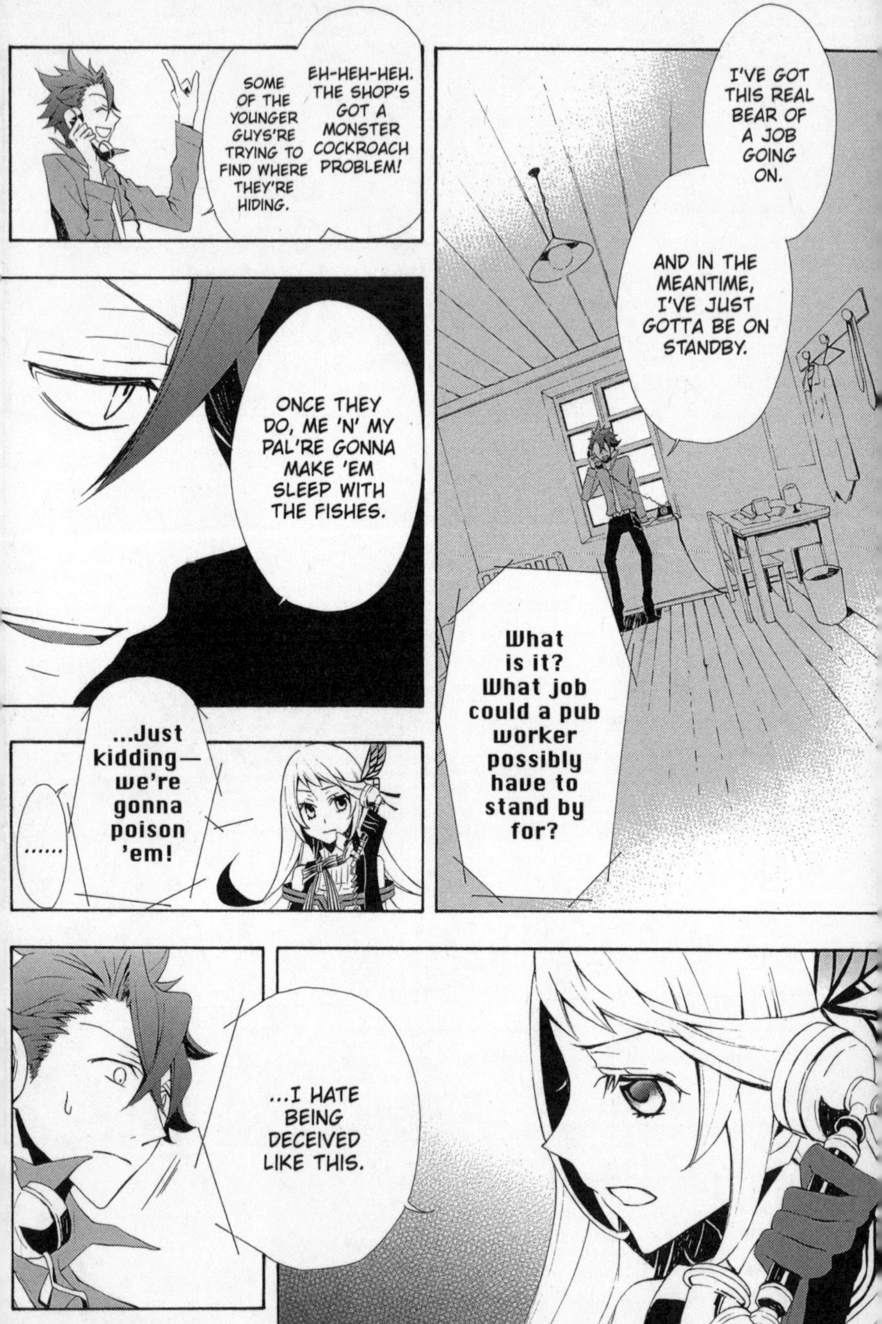
I'VE GOT THIS REAL BEAR OF A JOB GOING ON.
AND IN THE MEANTIME, I'VE JUST GOTTA BE ON STANDBY.
What is it? What job could a pub worker possibly have to stand by for?
EH-HEH-HEH. THE SHOP'S GOT A MONSTER COCKROACH PROBLEM!
SOME OF THE YOUNGER GUYS'RE TRYING TO FIND WHERE THEY'RE HIDING.
ONCE THEY DO, ME 'N' MY PAL'RE GONNA MAKE 'EM SLEEP WITH THE FISHES.
...Just kidding—we're gonna poison 'em!
......
...I HATE BEING DECEIVED LIKE THIS.

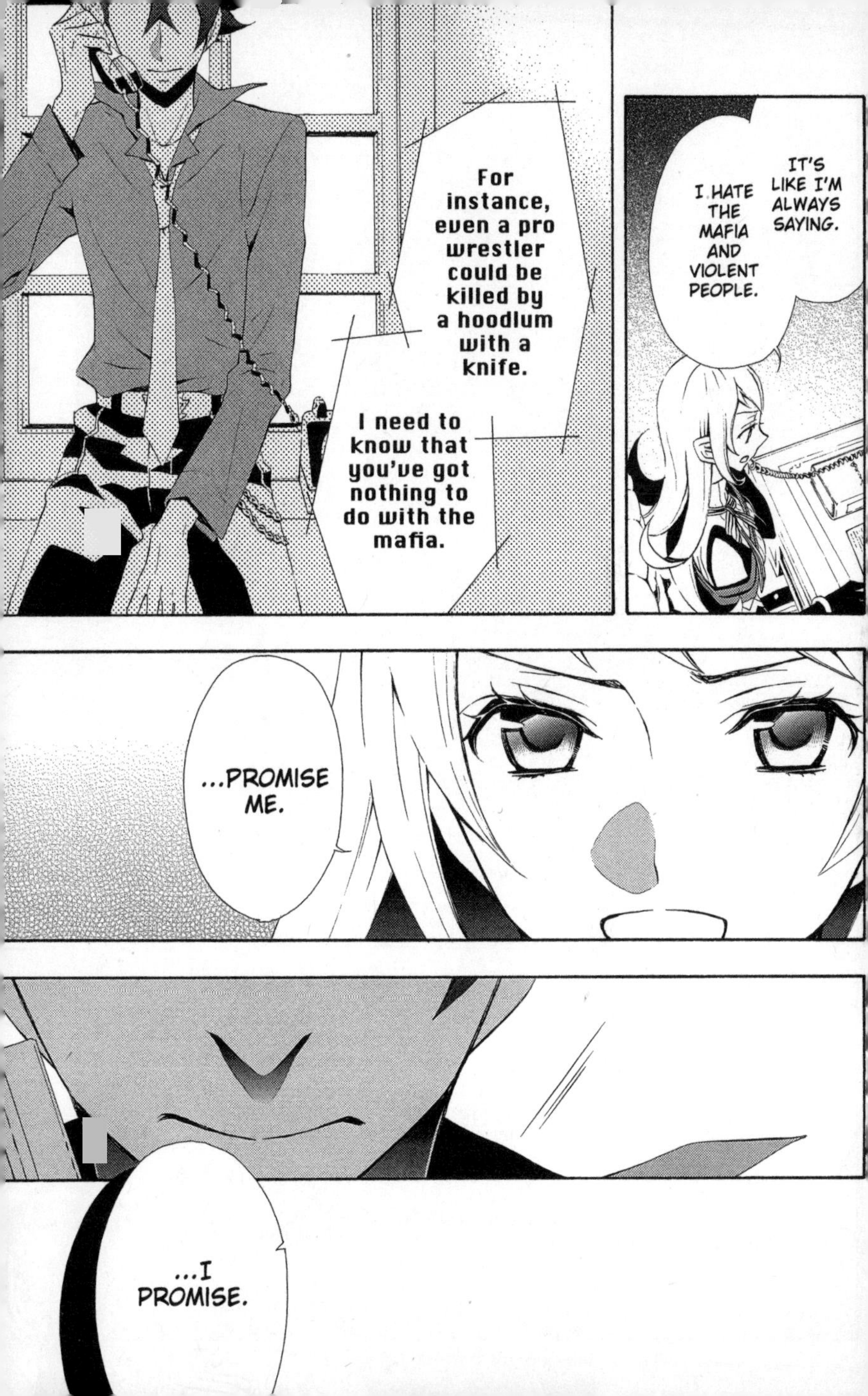
IT'S LIKE I'M ALWAYS SAYING.
I HATE THE MAFIA AND VIOLENT PEOPLE.
For instance, even a pro wrestler could be killed by a hoodlum with a knife.
I need to know that you've got nothing to do with the mafia.
...PROMISE ME.
...I PROMISE.

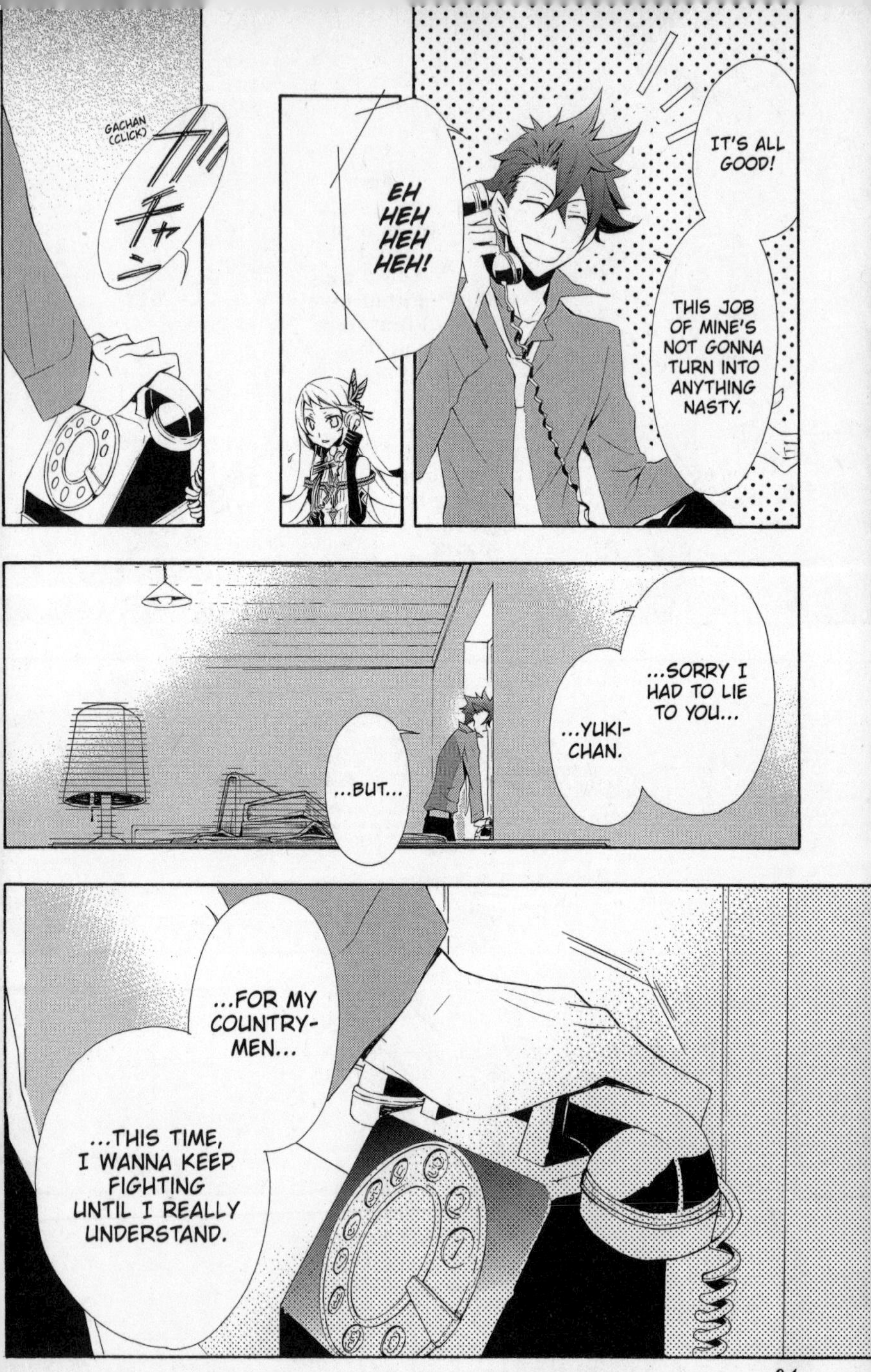
IT'S ALL GOOD!
THIS JOB OF MINE'S NOT GONNA TURN INTO ANYTHING NASTY.
EH HEH HEH HEH!
ガチャン
GACHAN (CLICK)
...SORRY I HAD TO LIE TO YOU...
...YUKI-CHAN.
...BUT...
...FOR MY COUNTRY-MEN...
...THIS TIME, I WANNA KEEP FIGHTING UNTIL I REALLY UNDERSTAND.

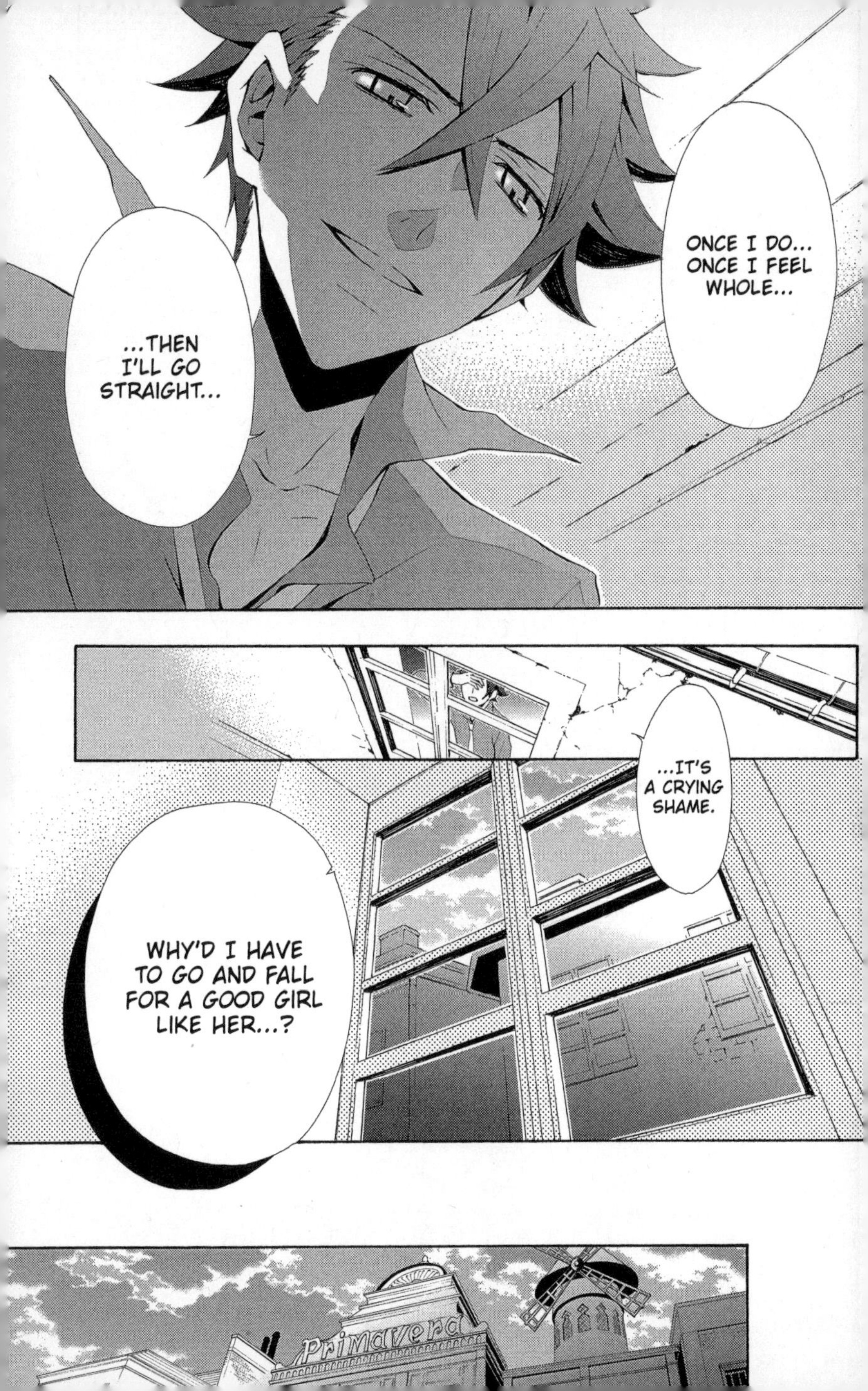
ONCE I DO... ONCE I FEEL WHOLE...
...THEN I'LL GO STRAIGHT...
...IT'S A CRYING SHAME.
WHY'D I HAVE TO GO AND FALL FOR A GOOD GIRL LIKE HER...?
Primavera

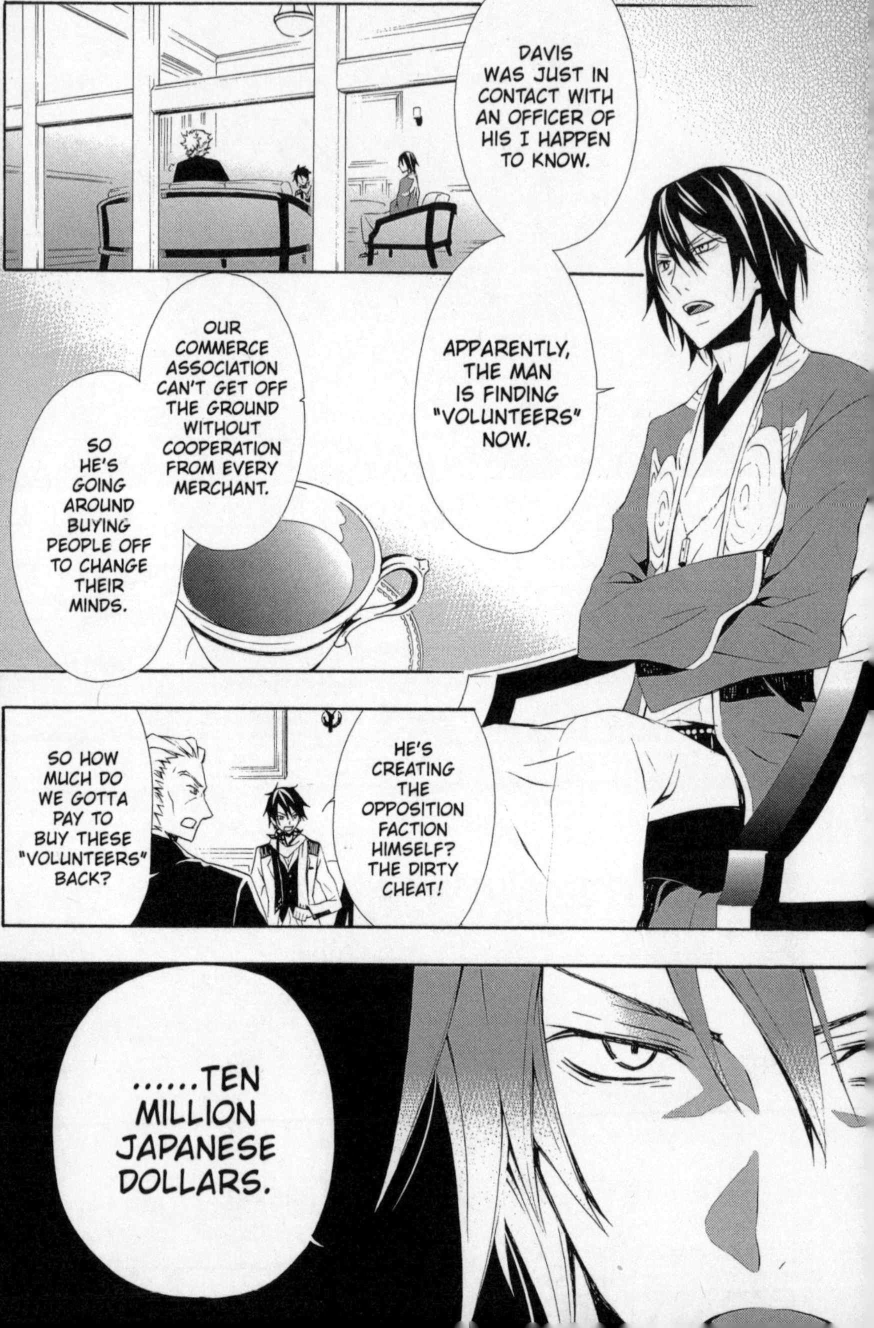
DAVIS WAS JUST IN CONTACT WITH AN OFFICER OF HIS I HAPPEN TO KNOW.
APPARENTLY, THE MAN IS FINDING "VOLUNTEERS" NOW.
OUR COMMERCE ASSOCIATION CAN'T GET OFF THE GROUND WITHOUT COOPERATION FROM EVERY MERCHANT.
SO HE'S GOING AROUND BUYING PEOPLE OFF TO CHANGE THEIR MINDS.
HE'S CREATING THE OPPOSITION FACTION HIMSELF? THE DIRTY CHEAT!
SO HOW MUCH DO WE GOTTA PAY TO BUY THESE "VOLUNTEERS" BACK?
......TEN MILLION JAPANESE DOLLARS.

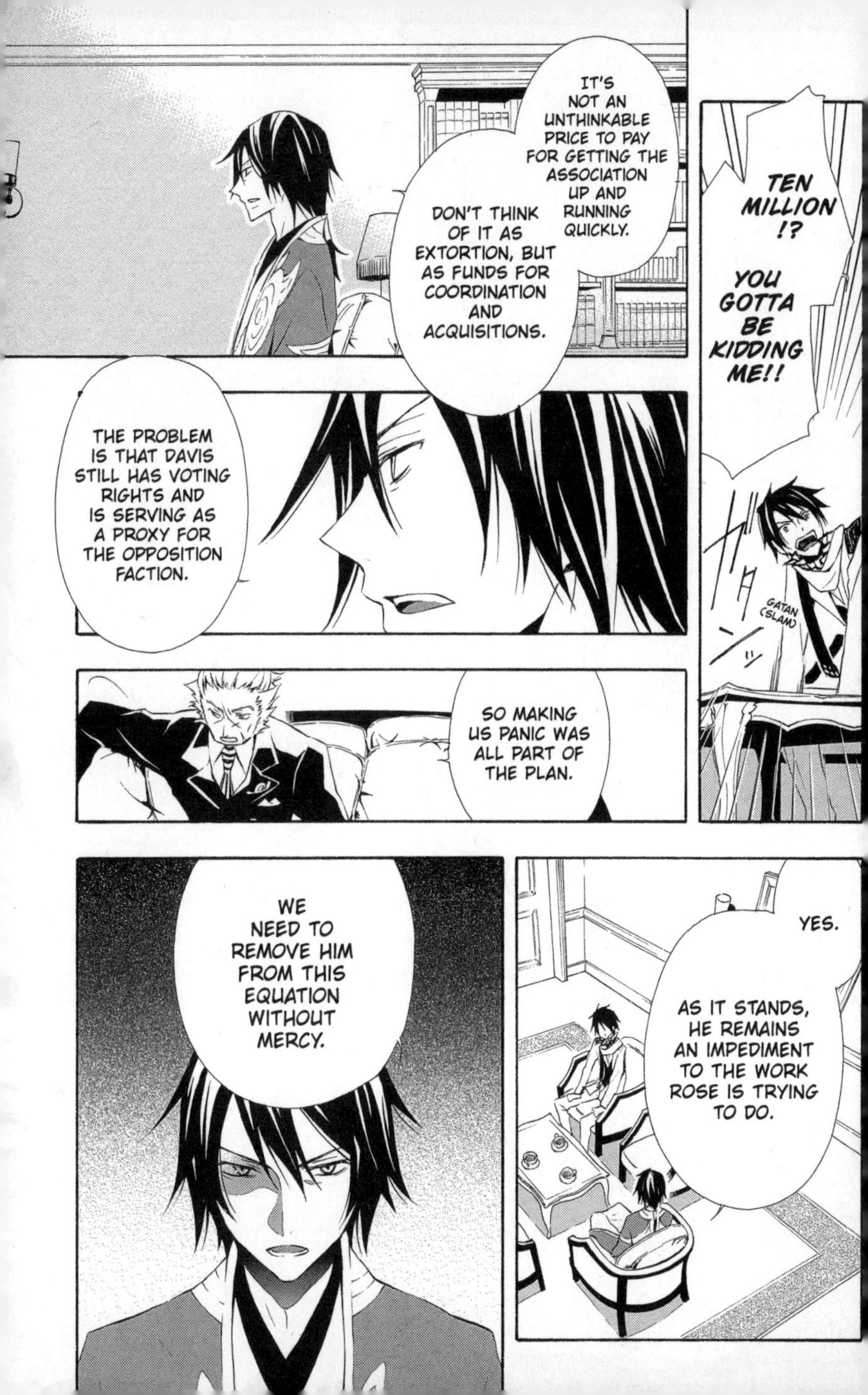
TEN MILLION!? YOU GOTTA BE KIDDING ME!!
GATAN (SLAM)
IT'S NOT AN UNTHINKABLE PRICE TO PAY FOR GETTING THE ASSOCIATION UP AND RUNNING QUICKLY.
DON'T THINK OF IT AS EXTORTION, BUT AS FUNDS FOR COORDINATION AND ACQUISITIONS.
THE PROBLEM IS THAT DAVIS STILL HAS VOTING RIGHTS AND IS SERVING AS A PROXY FOR THE OPPOSITION FACTION.
SO MAKING US PANIC WAS ALL PART OF THE PLAN.
YES.
AS IT STANDS, HE REMAINS AN IMPEDIMENT TO THE WORK ROSE IS TRYING TO DO.
WE NEED TO REMOVE HIM FROM THIS EQUATION WITHOUT MERCY.

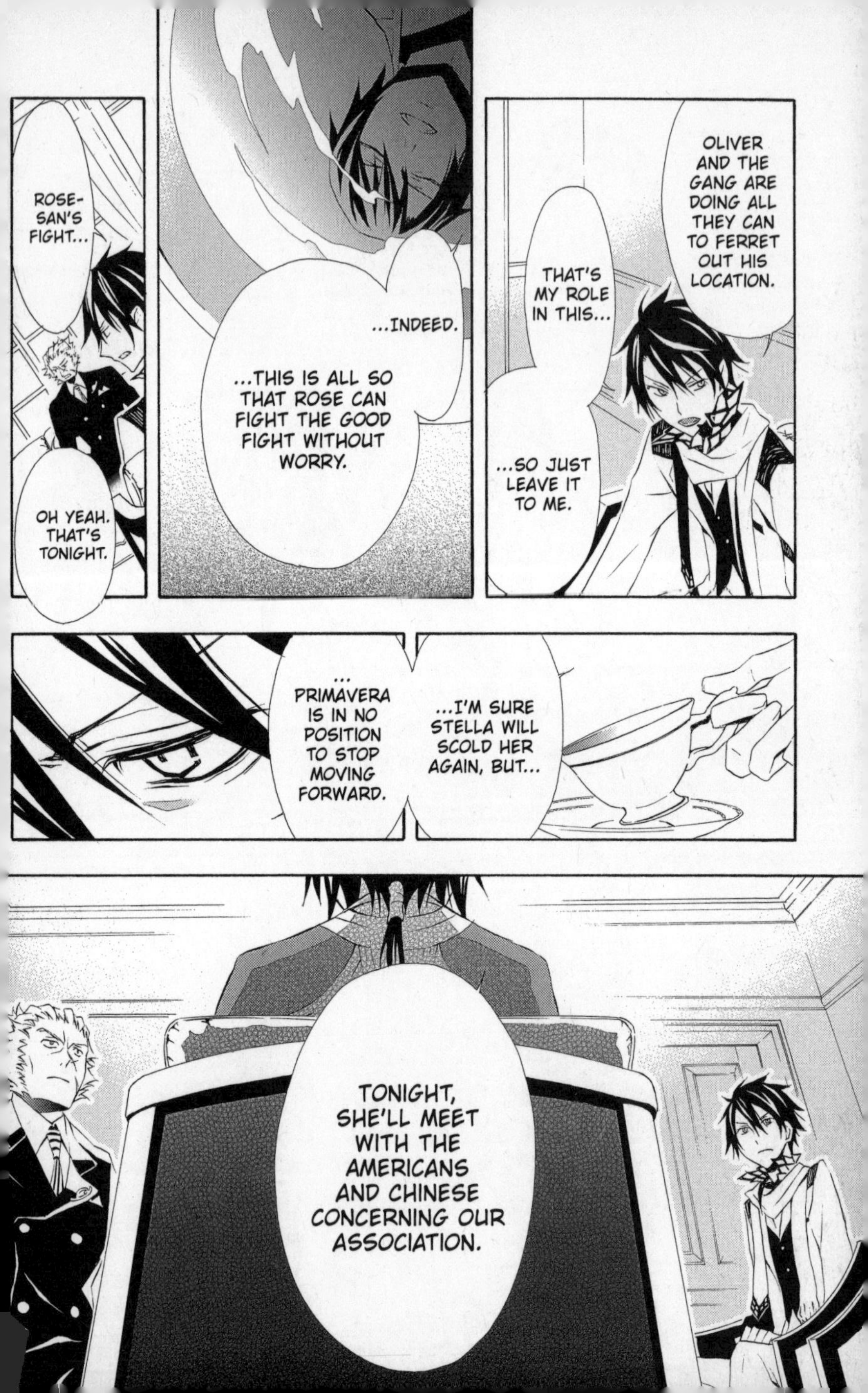
OLIVER AND THE GANG ARE DOING ALL THEY CAN TO FERRET OUT HIS LOCATION.
THAT'S MY ROLE IN THIS...
...SO JUST LEAVE IT TO ME.
...INDEED.
...THIS IS ALL SO THAT ROSE CAN FIGHT THE GOOD FIGHT WITHOUT WORRY.
ROSE-SAN'S FIGHT...
OH YEAH. THAT'S TONIGHT.
...I'M SURE STELLA WILL SCOLD HER AGAIN, BUT...
... PRIMAVERA IS IN NO POSITION TO STOP MOVING FORWARD.
TONIGHT, SHE'LL MEET WITH THE AMERICANS AND CHINESE CONCERNING OUR ASSOCIATION.

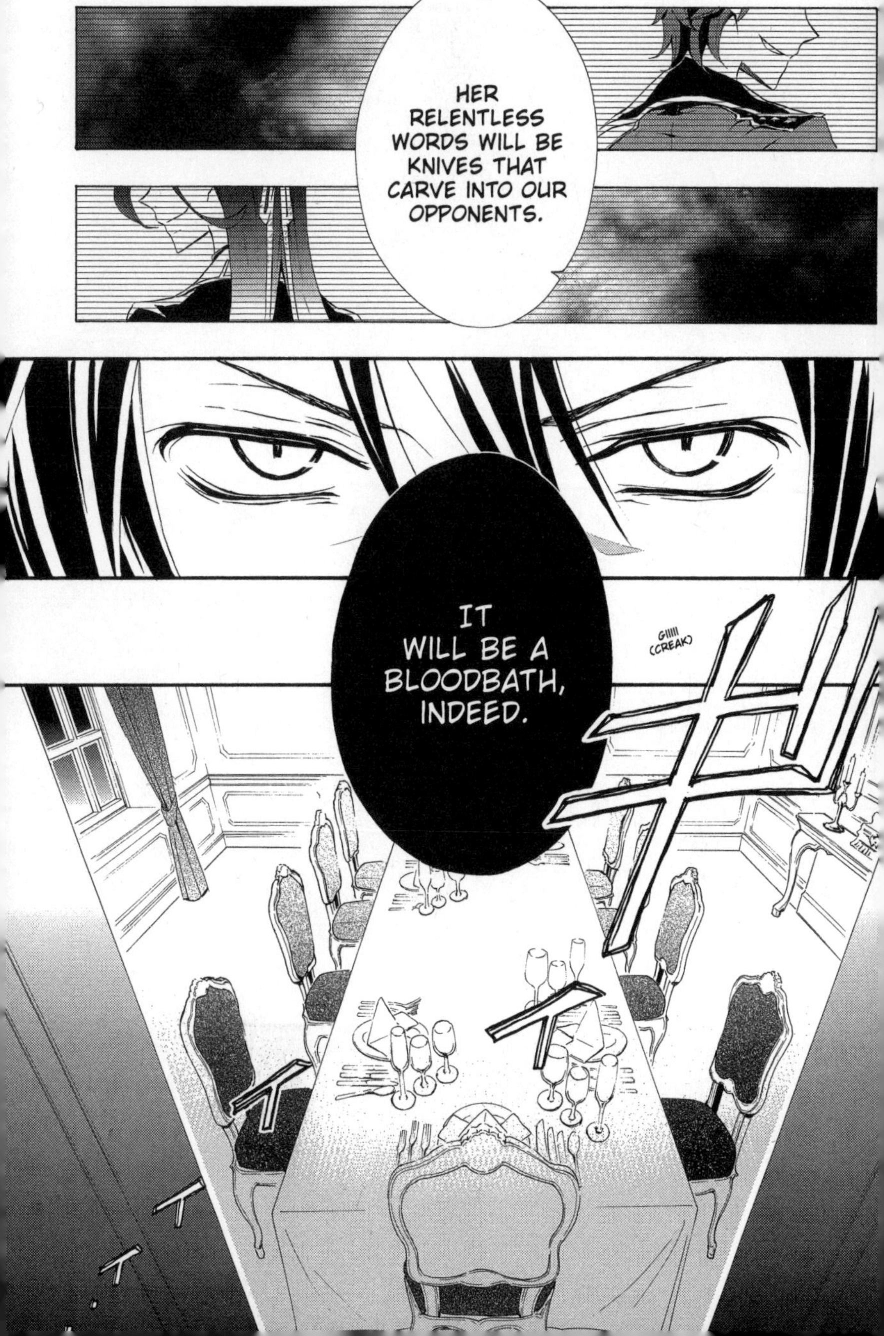
HER RELENTLESS WORDS WILL BE KNIVES THAT CARVE INTO OUR OPPONENTS.
IT WILL BE A BLOODBATH, INDEED.
GIIIII (CREAK)

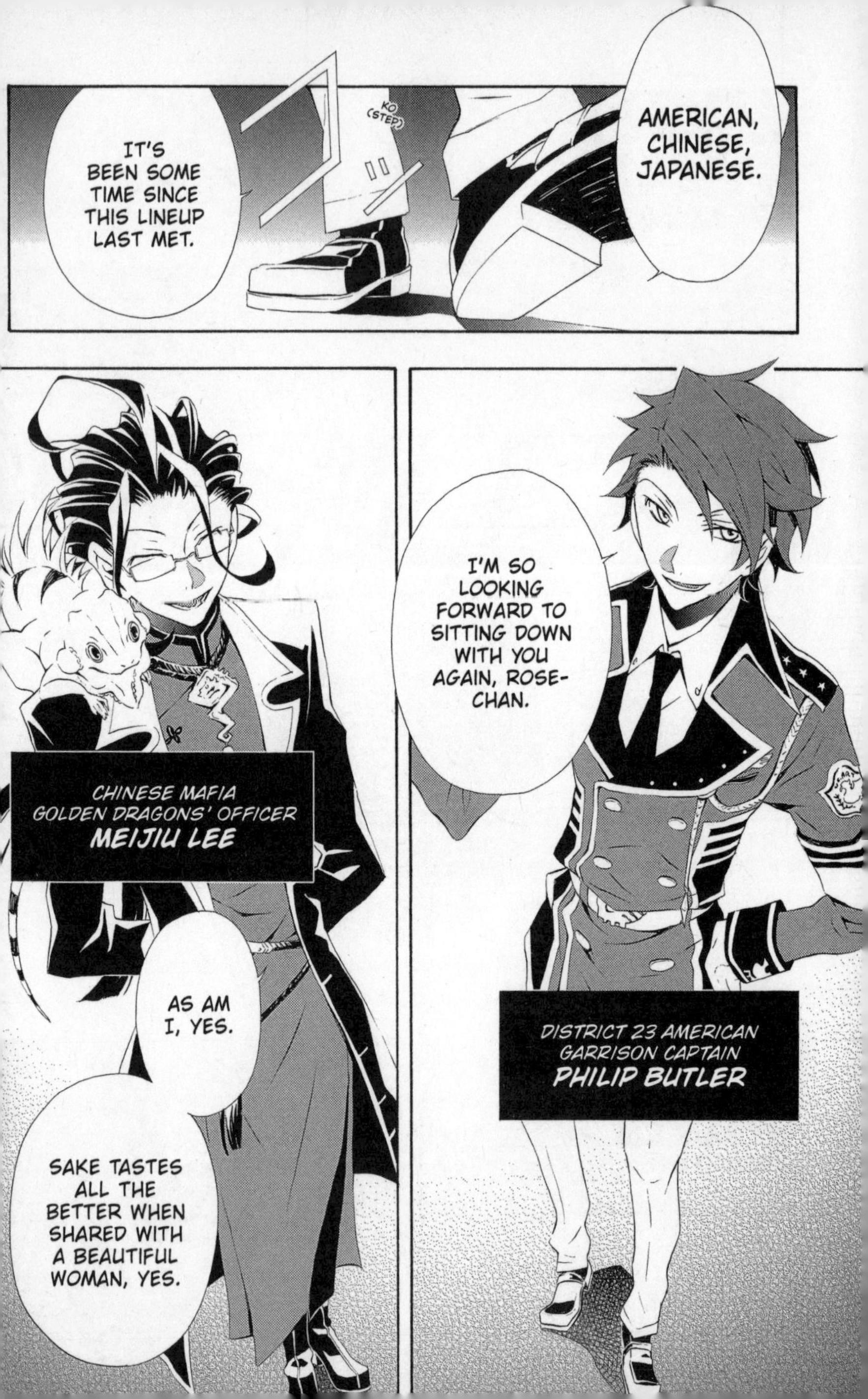
AMERICAN, CHINESE, JAPANESE.
KO (STEP)
IT'S BEEN SOME TIME SINCE THIS LINEUP LAST MET.
I'M SO LOOKING FORWARD TO SITTING DOWN WITH YOU AGAIN, ROSE-CHAN.
DISTRICT 23 AMERICAN GARRISON CAPTAIN
PHILIP BUTLER
CHINESE MAFIA GOLDEN DRAGONS' OFFICER
MEIJIU LEE
AS AM I, YES.
SAKE TASTES ALL THE BETTER WHEN SHARED WITH A BEAUTIFUL WOMAN, YES.

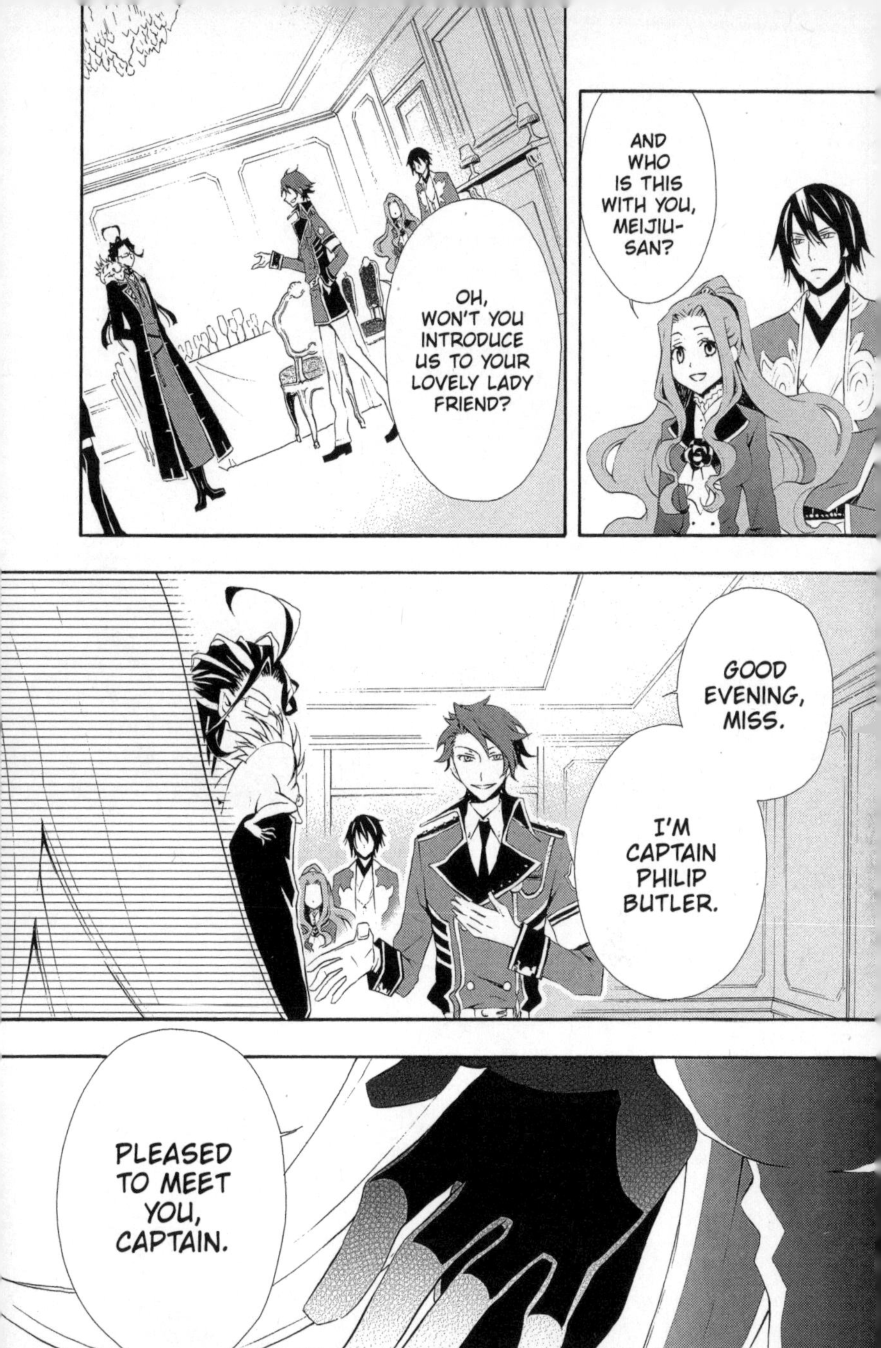
AND WHO IS THIS WITH YOU, MEIJIU-SAN?
OH, WON'T YOU INTRODUCE US TO YOUR LOVELY LADY FRIEND?
GOOD EVENING, MISS.
I'M CAPTAIN PHILIP BUTLER.
PLEASED TO MEET YOU, CAPTAIN.

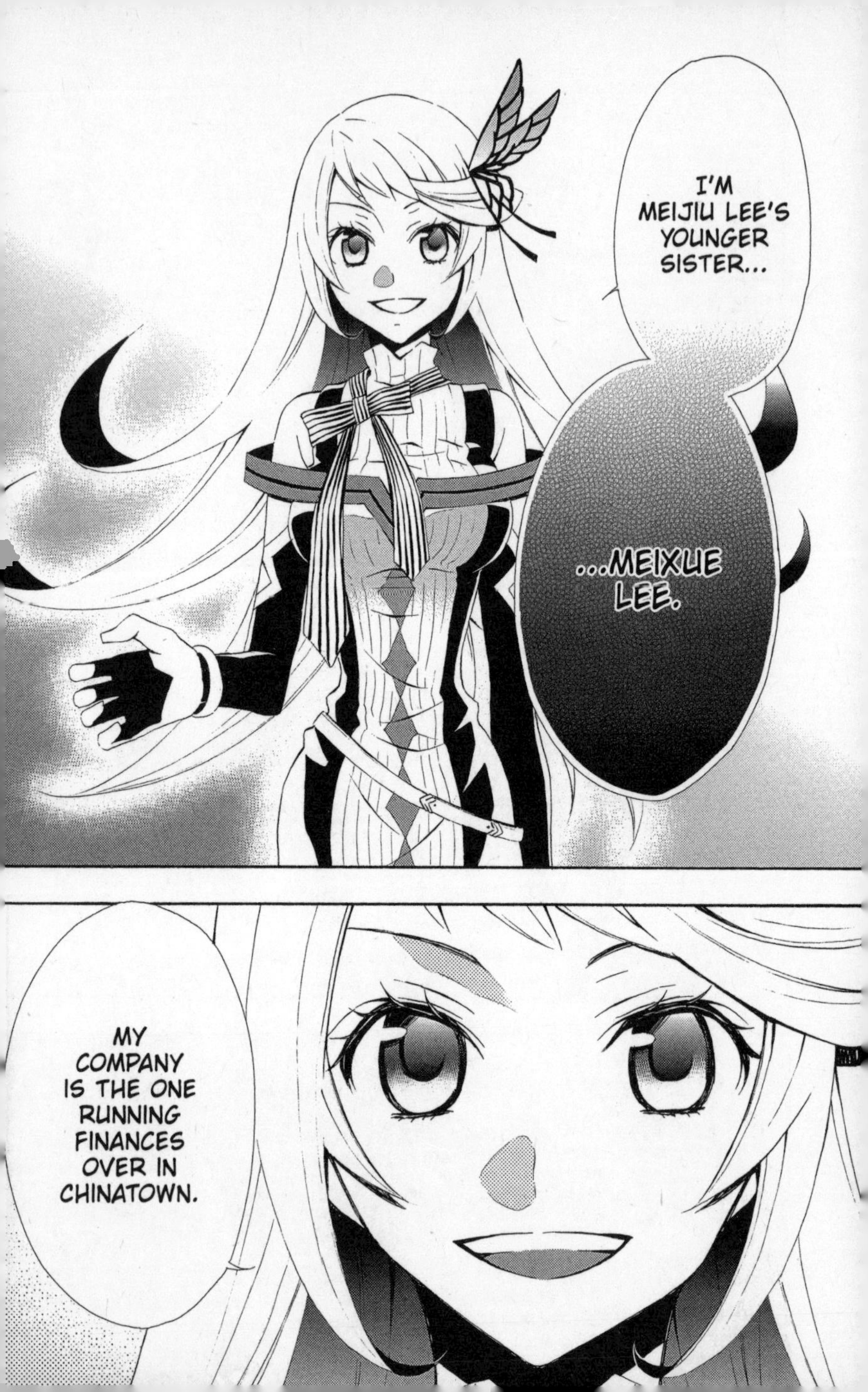
I'M MEIJIU LEE'S YOUNGER SISTER...
...MEIXUE LEE.
MY COMPANY IS THE ONE RUNNING FINANCES OVER IN CHINATOWN.

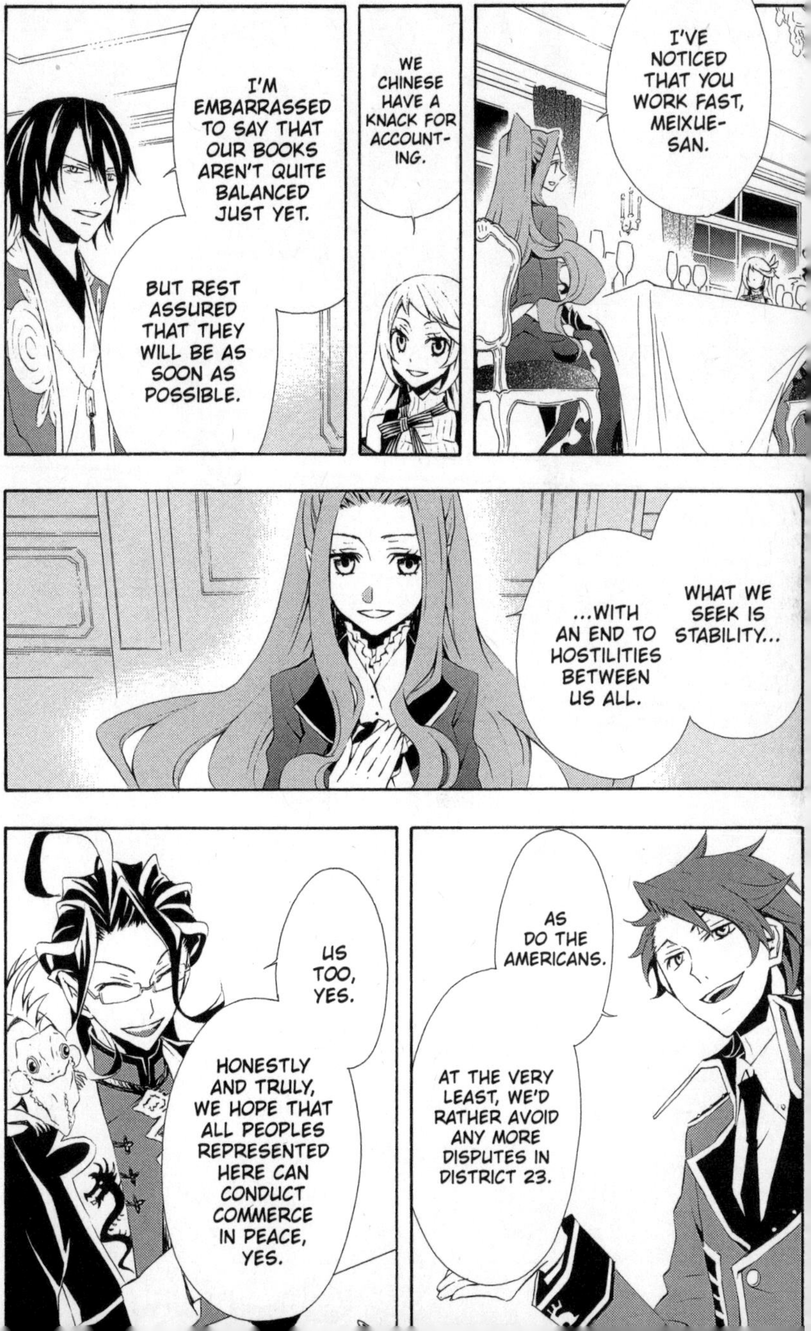
I'VE NOTICED THAT YOU WORK FAST, MEIXUE-SAN.
WE CHINESE HAVE A KNACK FOR ACCOUNT-ING.
I'M EMBARRASSED TO SAY THAT OUR BOOKS AREN'T QUITE BALANCED JUST YET.
BUT REST ASSURED THAT THEY WILL BE AS SOON AS POSSIBLE.
WHAT WE SEEK IS STABILITY...
...WITH AN END TO HOSTILITIES BETWEEN US ALL.
AS DO THE AMERICANS.
AT THE VERY LEAST, WE'D RATHER AVOID ANY MORE DISPUTES IN DISTRICT 23.
US TOO, YES.
HONESTLY AND TRULY, WE HOPE THAT ALL PEOPLES REPRESENTED HERE CAN CONDUCT COMMERCE IN PEACE, YES.

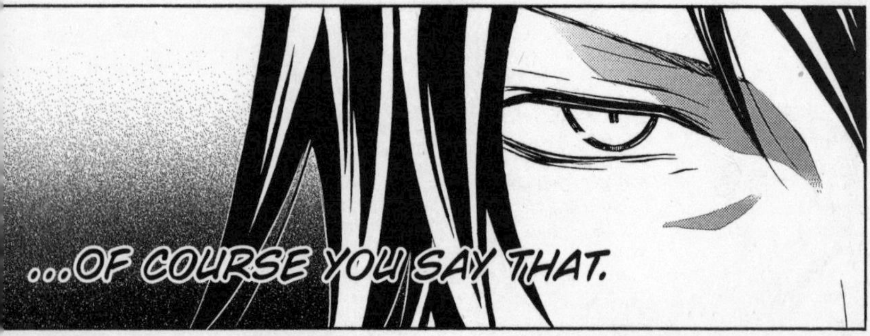
...OF COURSE YOU SAY THAT.

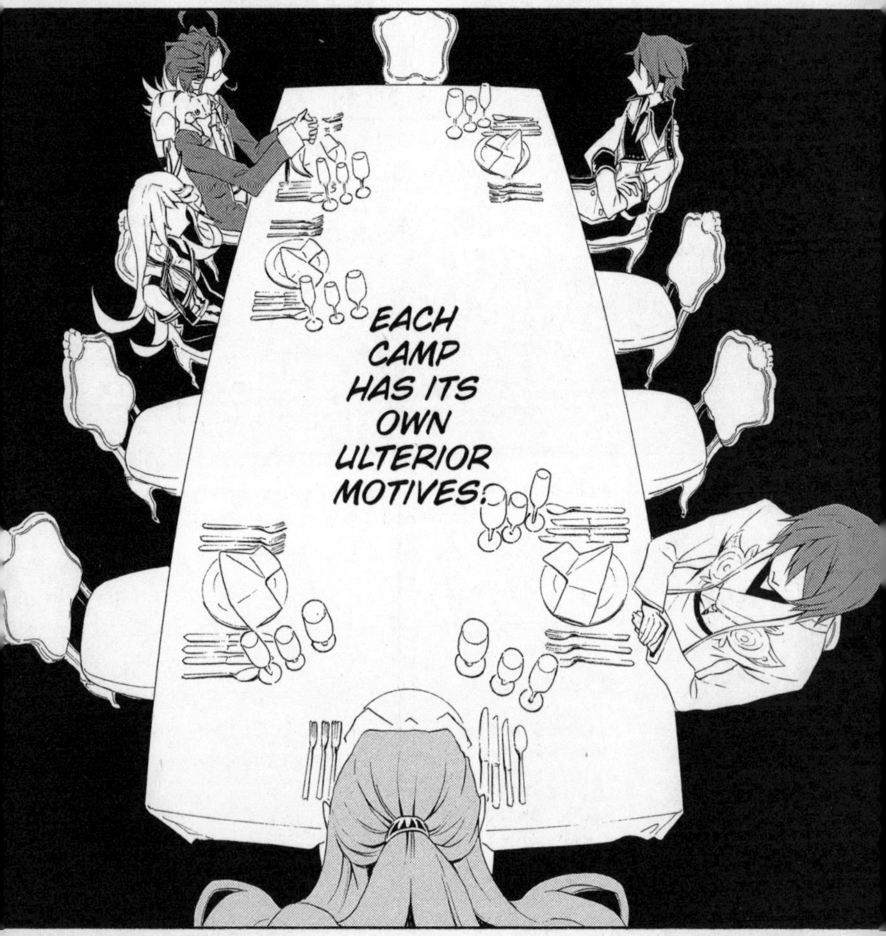
EACH CAMP HAS ITS OWN ULTERIOR MOTIVES.

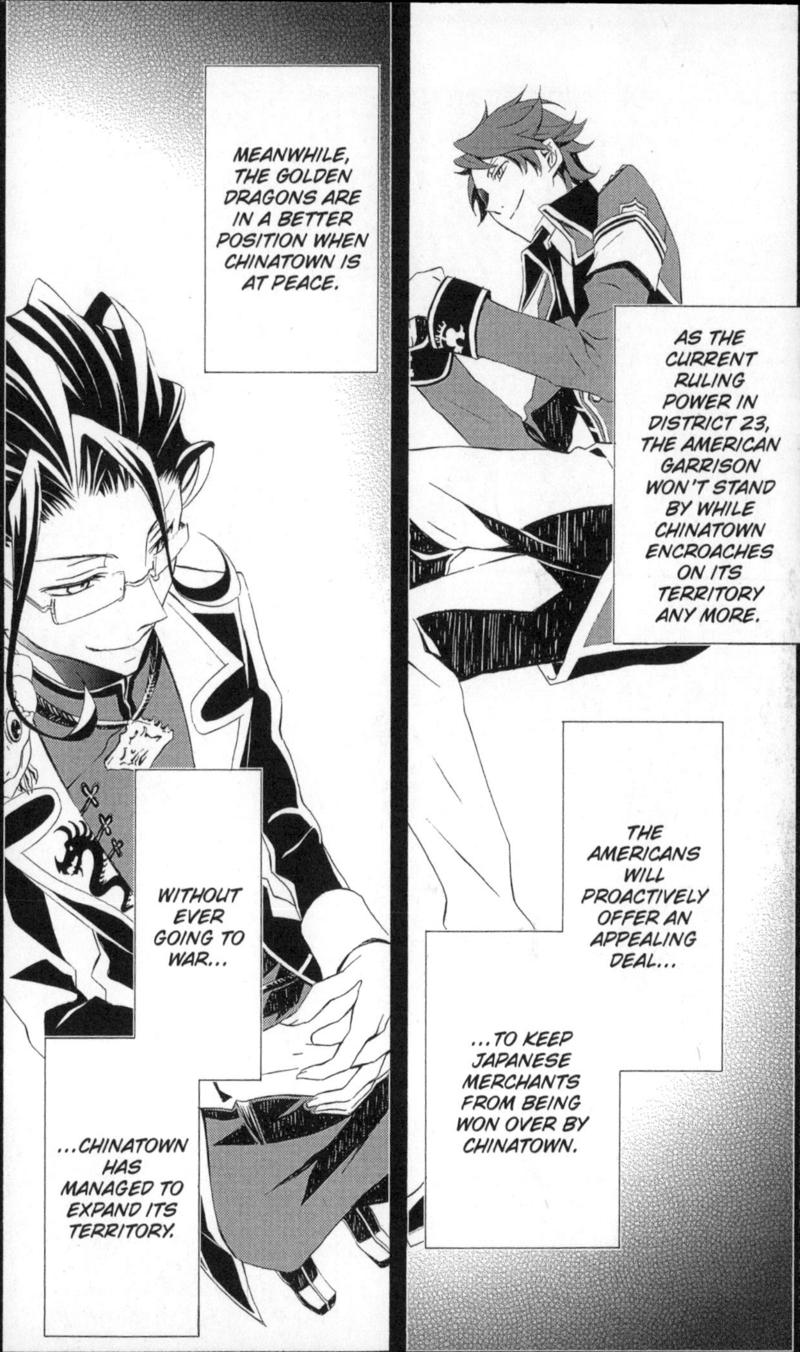
AS THE CURRENT RULING POWER IN DISTRICT 23, THE AMERICAN GARRISON WON'T STAND BY WHILE CHINATOWN ENCROACHES ON ITS TERRITORY ANY MORE.
THE AMERICANS WILL PROACTIVELY OFFER AN APPEALING DEAL...
...TO KEEP JAPANESE MERCHANTS FROM BEING WON OVER BY CHINATOWN.
MEANWHILE, THE GOLDEN DRAGONS ARE IN A BETTER POSITION WHEN CHINATOWN IS AT PEACE.
WITHOUT EVER GOING TO WAR...
...CHINATOWN HAS MANAGED TO EXPAND ITS TERRITORY.

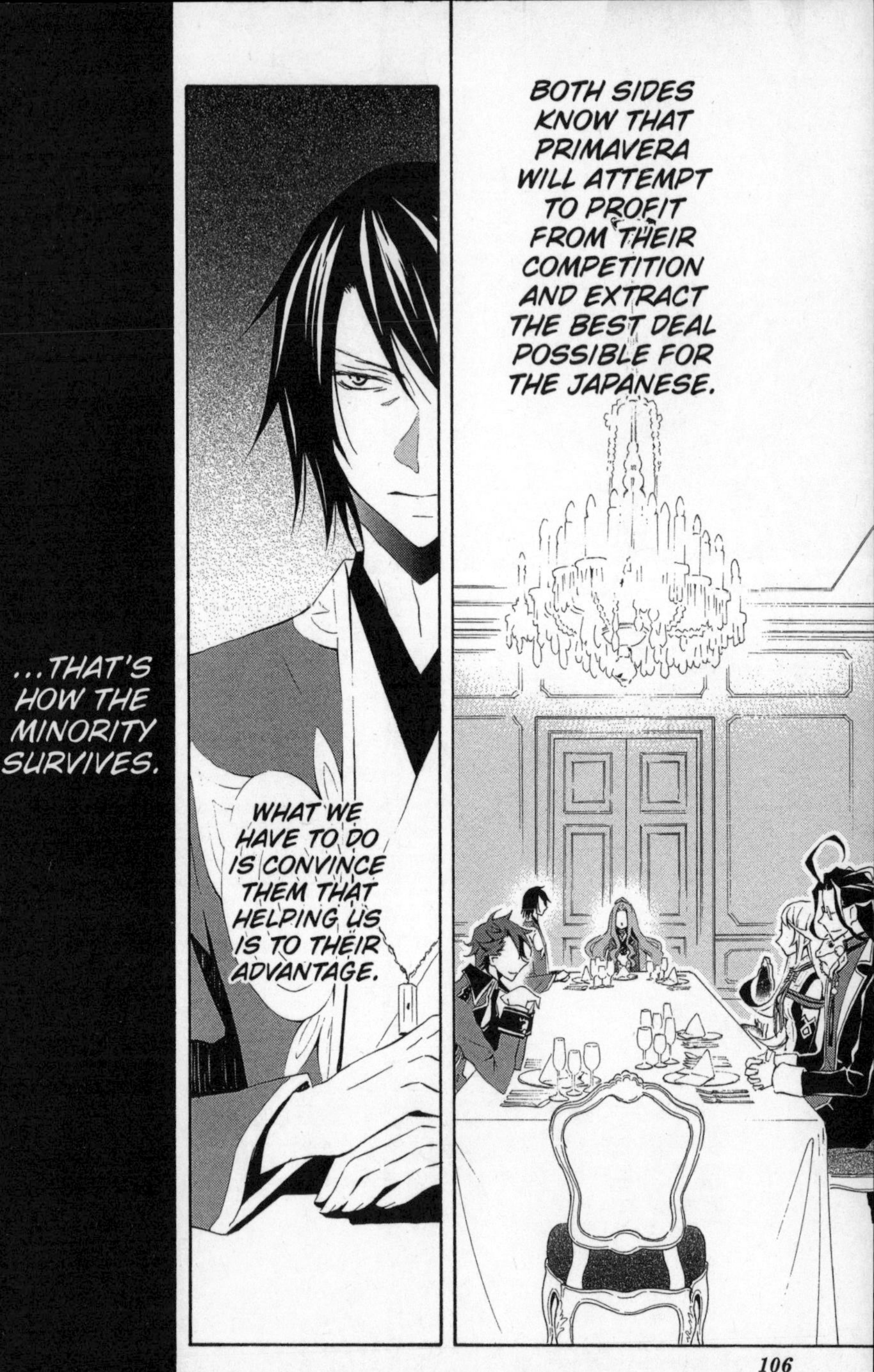
BOTH SIDES KNOW THAT PRIMAVERA WILL ATTEMPT TO PROFIT FROM THEIR COMPETITION AND EXTRACT THE BEST DEAL POSSIBLE FOR THE JAPANESE.
WHAT WE HAVE TO DO IS CONVINCE THEM THAT HELPING US IS TO THEIR ADVANTAGE.
...THAT'S HOW THE MINORITY SURVIVES.

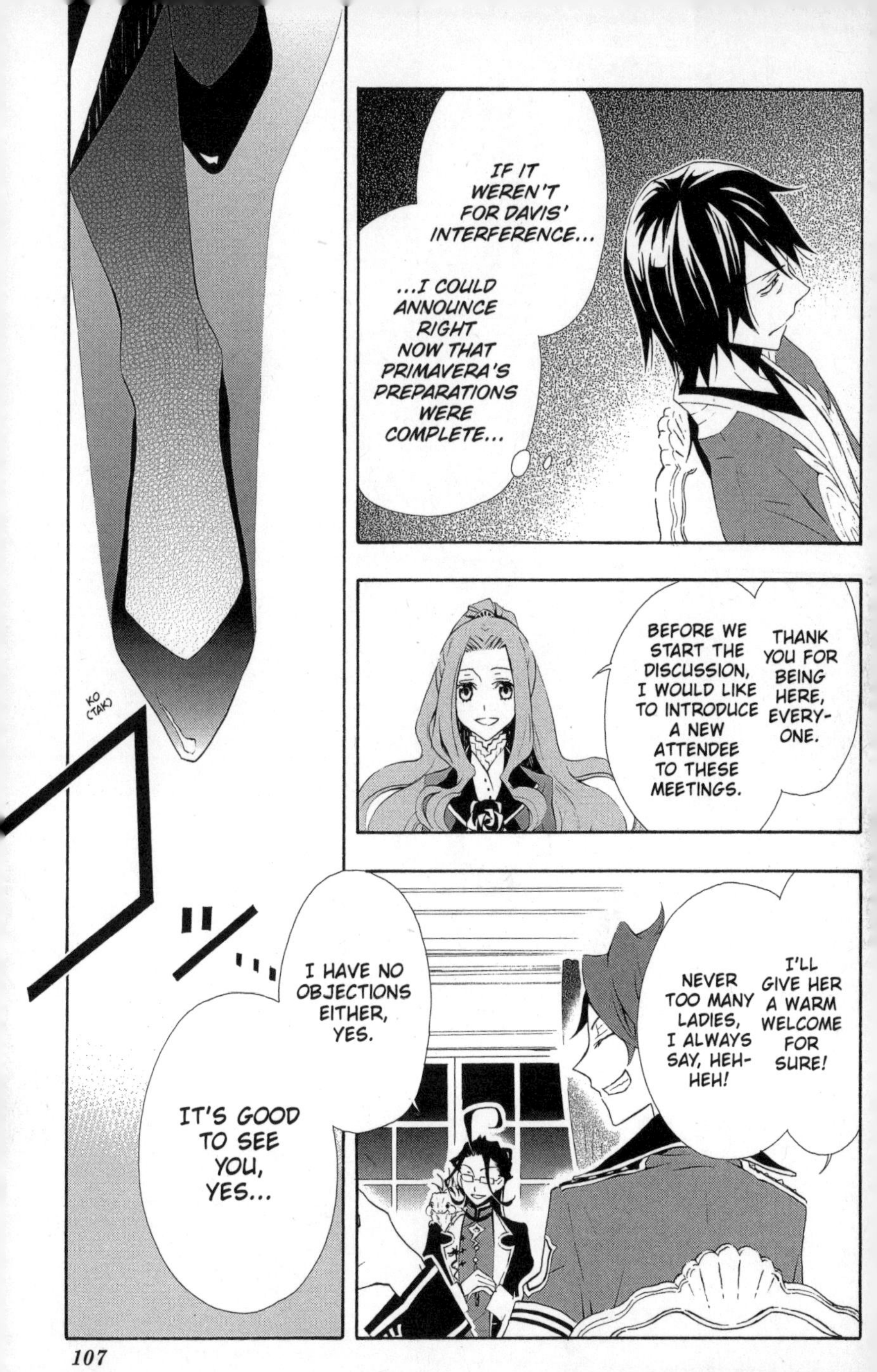
IF IT WEREN'T FOR DAVIS' INTERFERENCE...
...I COULD ANNOUNCE RIGHT NOW THAT PRIMAVERA'S PREPARATIONS WERE COMPLETE...
THANK YOU FOR BEING HERE, EVERY-ONE.
BEFORE WE START THE DISCUSSION, I WOULD LIKE TO INTRODUCE A NEW ATTENDEE TO THESE MEETINGS.
I'LL GIVE HER A WARM WELCOME FOR SURE!
NEVER TOO MANY LADIES, I ALWAYS SAY, HEH-HEH!
I HAVE NO OBJECTIONS EITHER, YES.
IT'S GOOD TO SEE YOU, YES...
KO (TAK)
...

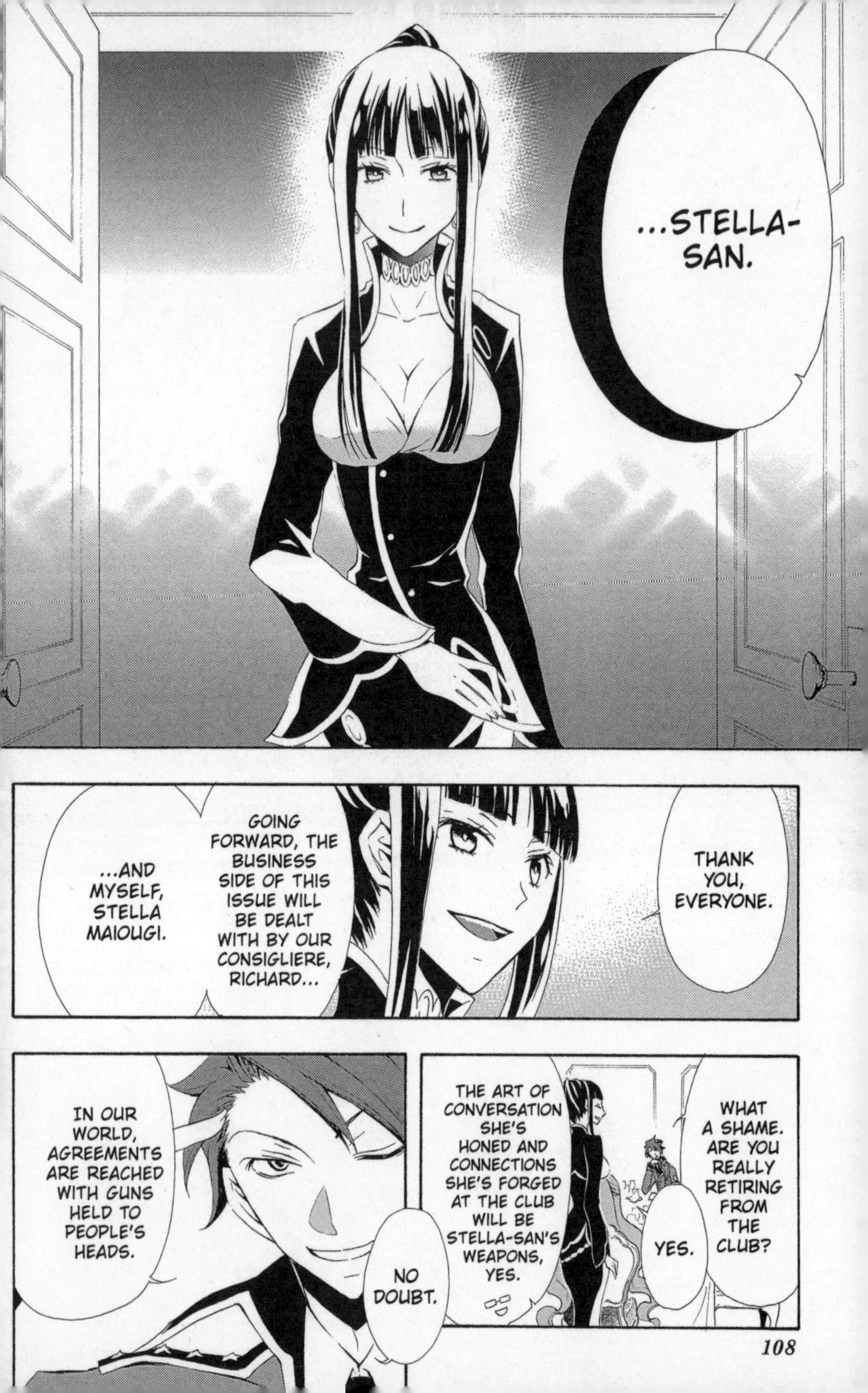
...STELLA-SAN.
THANK YOU, EVERYONE.
GOING FORWARD, THE BUSINESS SIDE OF THIS ISSUE WILL BE DEALT WITH BY OUR CONSIGLIERE, RICHARD...
...AND MYSELF, STELLA MAIOUGI.
WHAT A SHAME. ARE YOU REALLY RETIRING FROM THE CLUB?
YES.
THE ART OF CONVERSATION SHE'S HONED AND CONNECTIONS SHE'S FORGED AT THE CLUB WILL BE STELLA-SAN'S WEAPONS, YES.
IN OUR WORLD, AGREEMENTS ARE REACHED WITH GUNS HELD TO PEOPLE'S HEADS.
NO DOUBT.

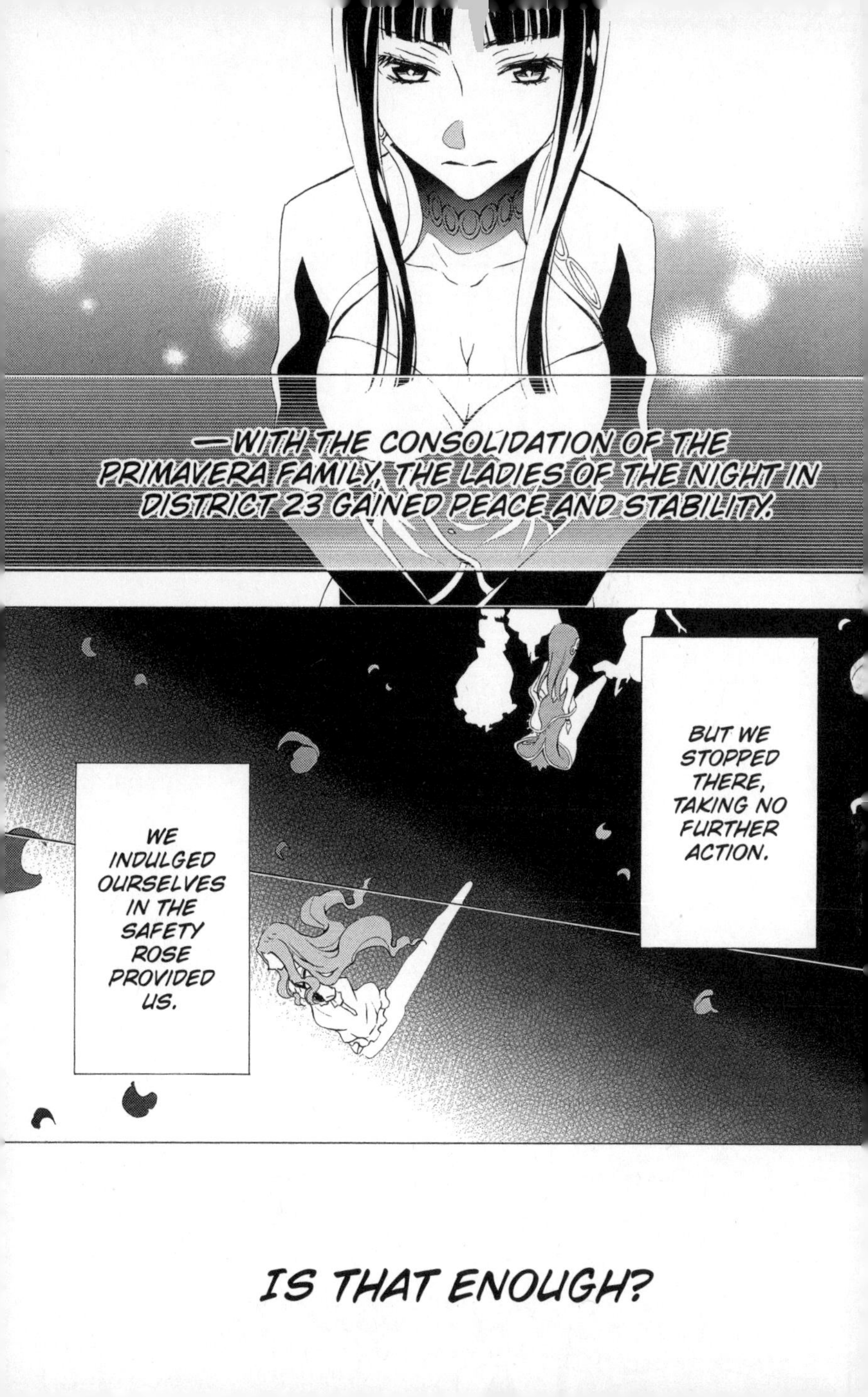
—WITH THE CONSOLIDATION OF THE PRIMAVERA FAMILY, THE LADIES OF THE NIGHT IN DISTRICT 23 GAINED PEACE AND STABILITY.
BUT WE STOPPED THERE, TAKING NO FURTHER ACTION.
WE INDULGED OURSELVES IN THE SAFETY ROSE PROVIDED US.
IS THAT ENOUGH?

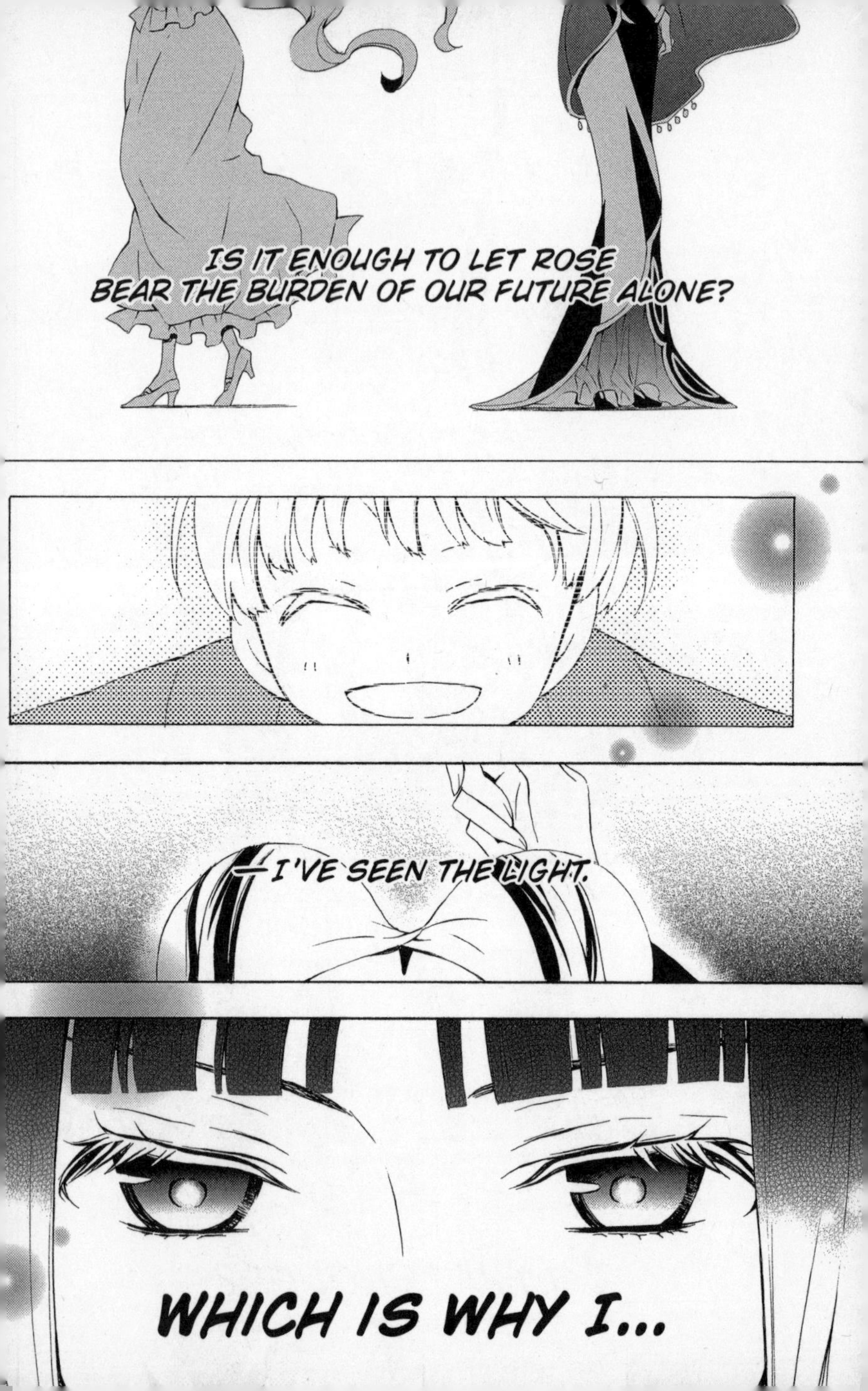
IS IT ENOUGH TO LET ROSE BEAR THE BURDEN OF OUR FUTURE ALONE?
—I'VE SEEN THE LIGHT.
WHICH IS WHY I...

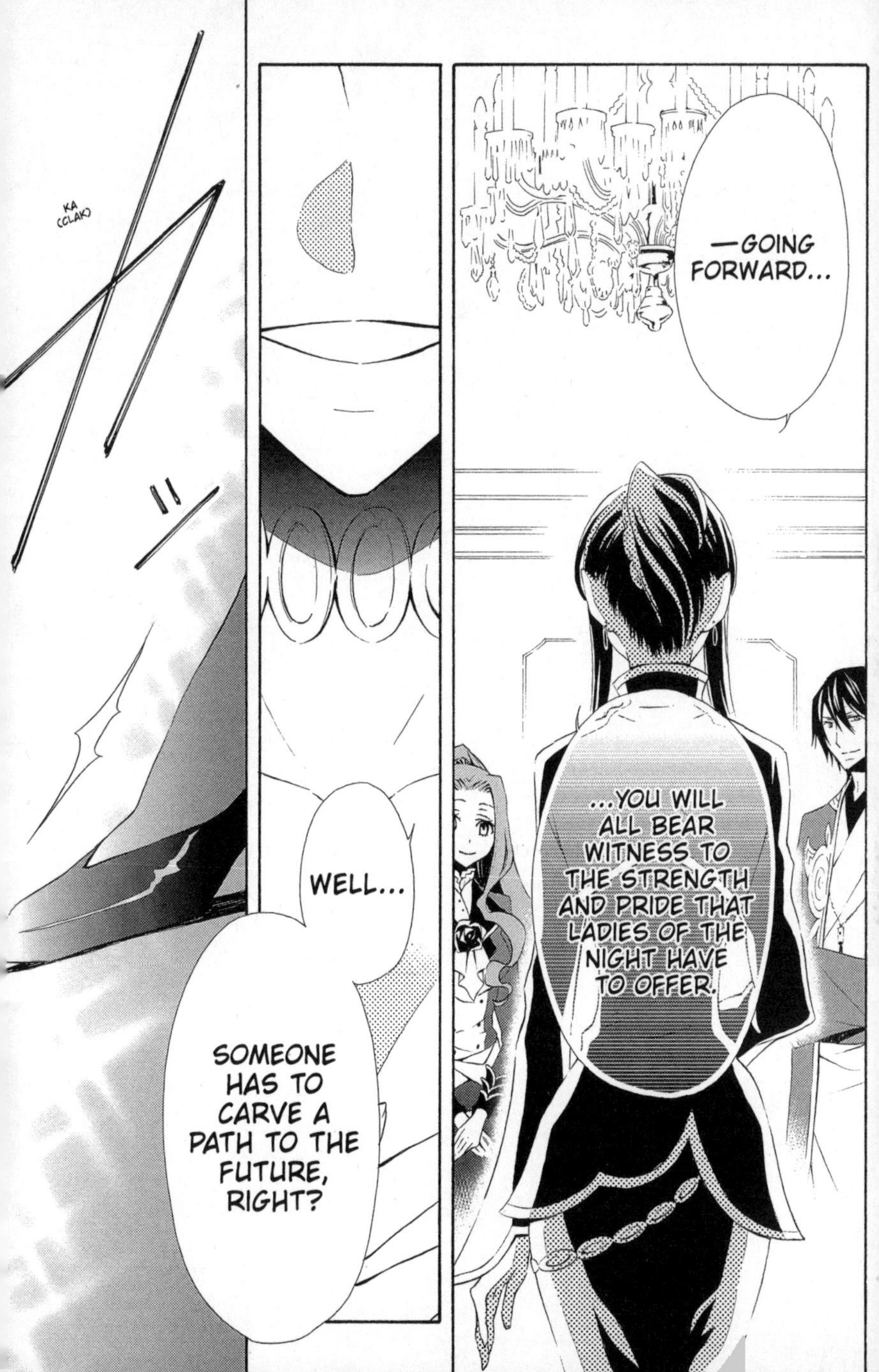
—GOING FORWARD...
...YOU WILL ALL BEAR WITNESS TO THE STRENGTH AND PRIDE THAT LADIES OF THE NIGHT HAVE TO OFFER.
WELL...
SOMEONE HAS TO CARVE A PATH TO THE FUTURE, RIGHT?
KA (CLAK)

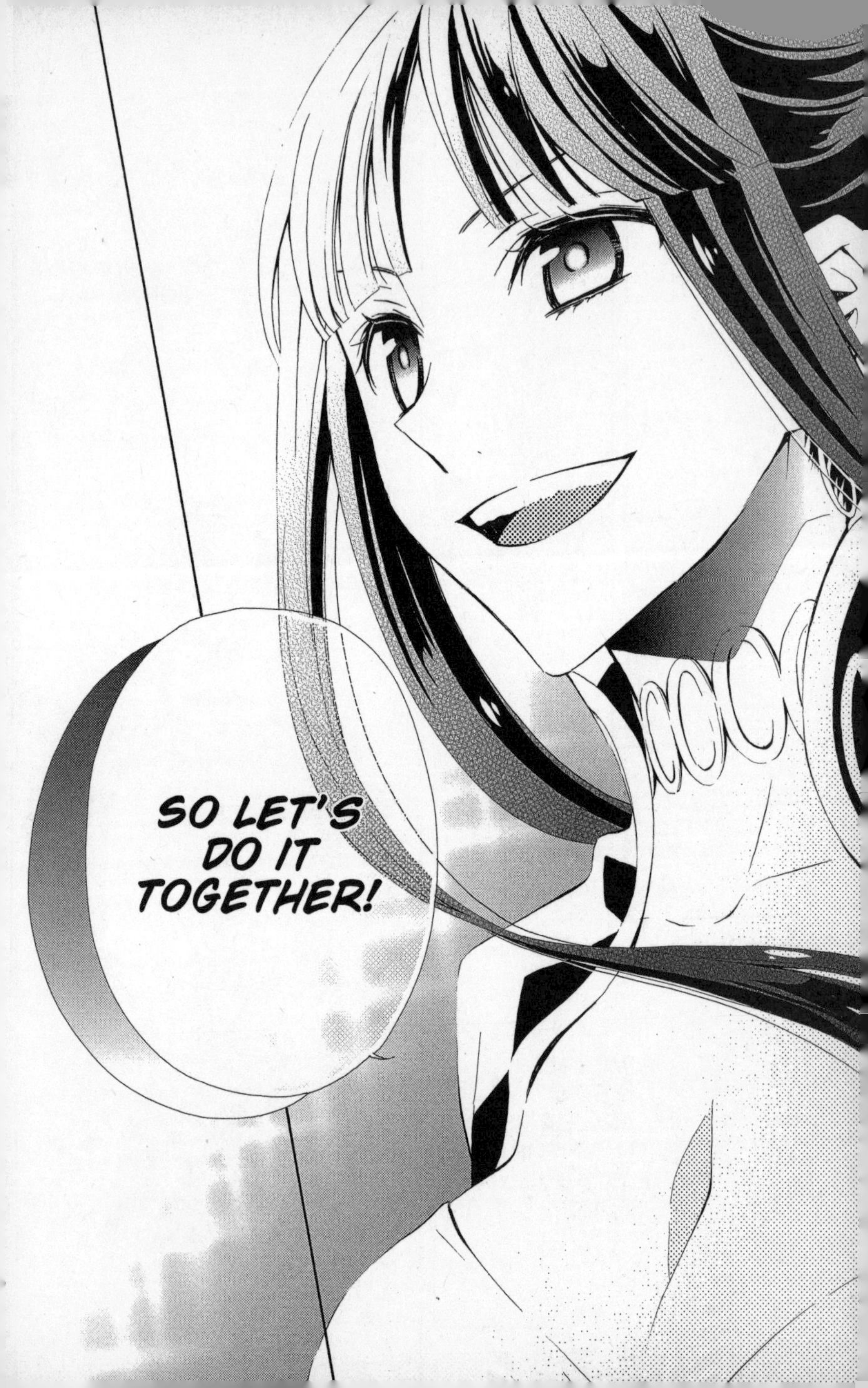
SO LET'S DO IT TOGETHER!

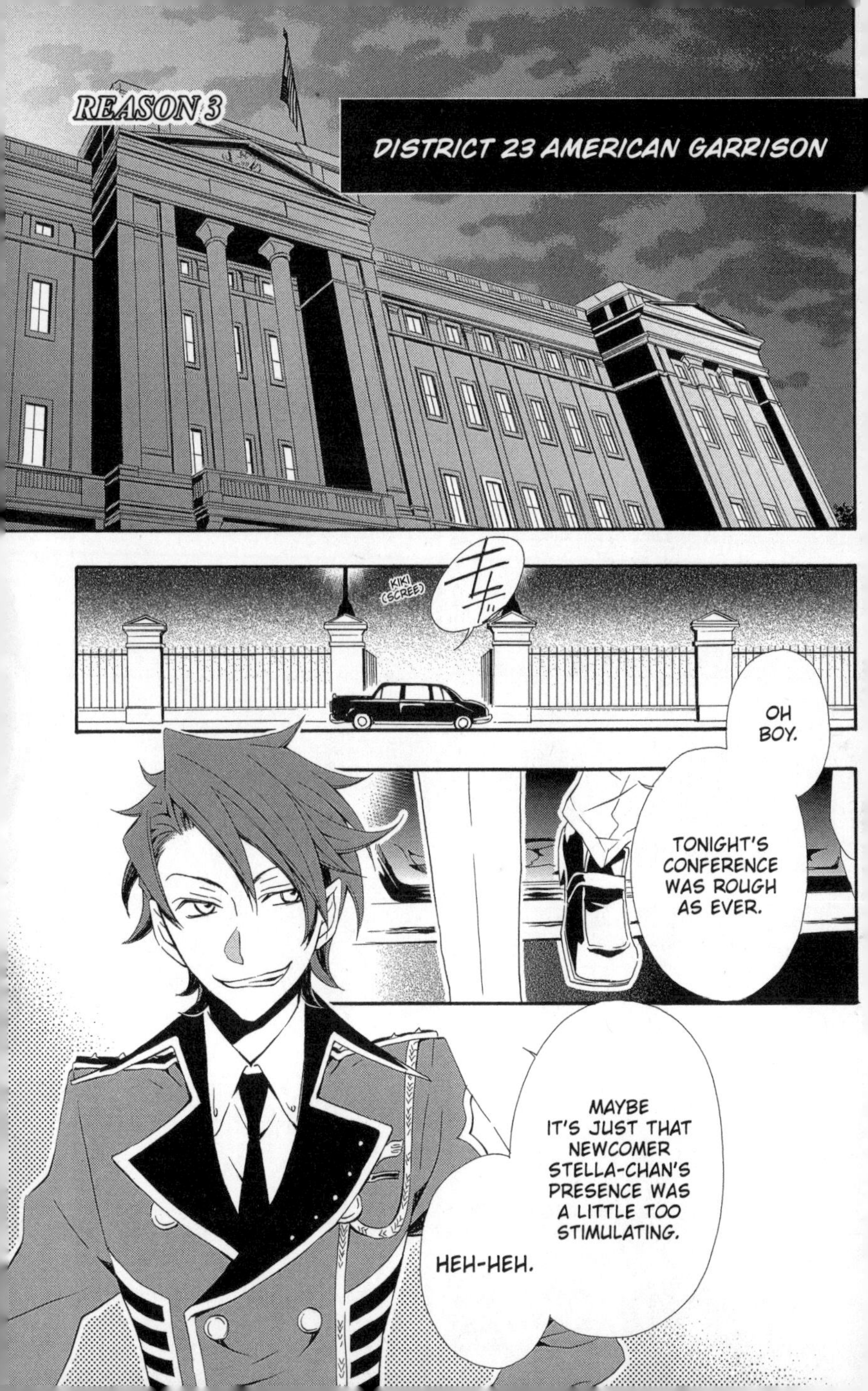
REASON 3
DISTRICT 23 AMERICAN GARRISON
KIKI (SCREE)
OH BOY.
TONIGHT'S CONFERENCE WAS ROUGH AS EVER.
MAYBE IT'S JUST THAT NEWCOMER STELLA-CHAN'S PRESENCE WAS A LITTLE TOO STIMULATING.
HEH-HEH.

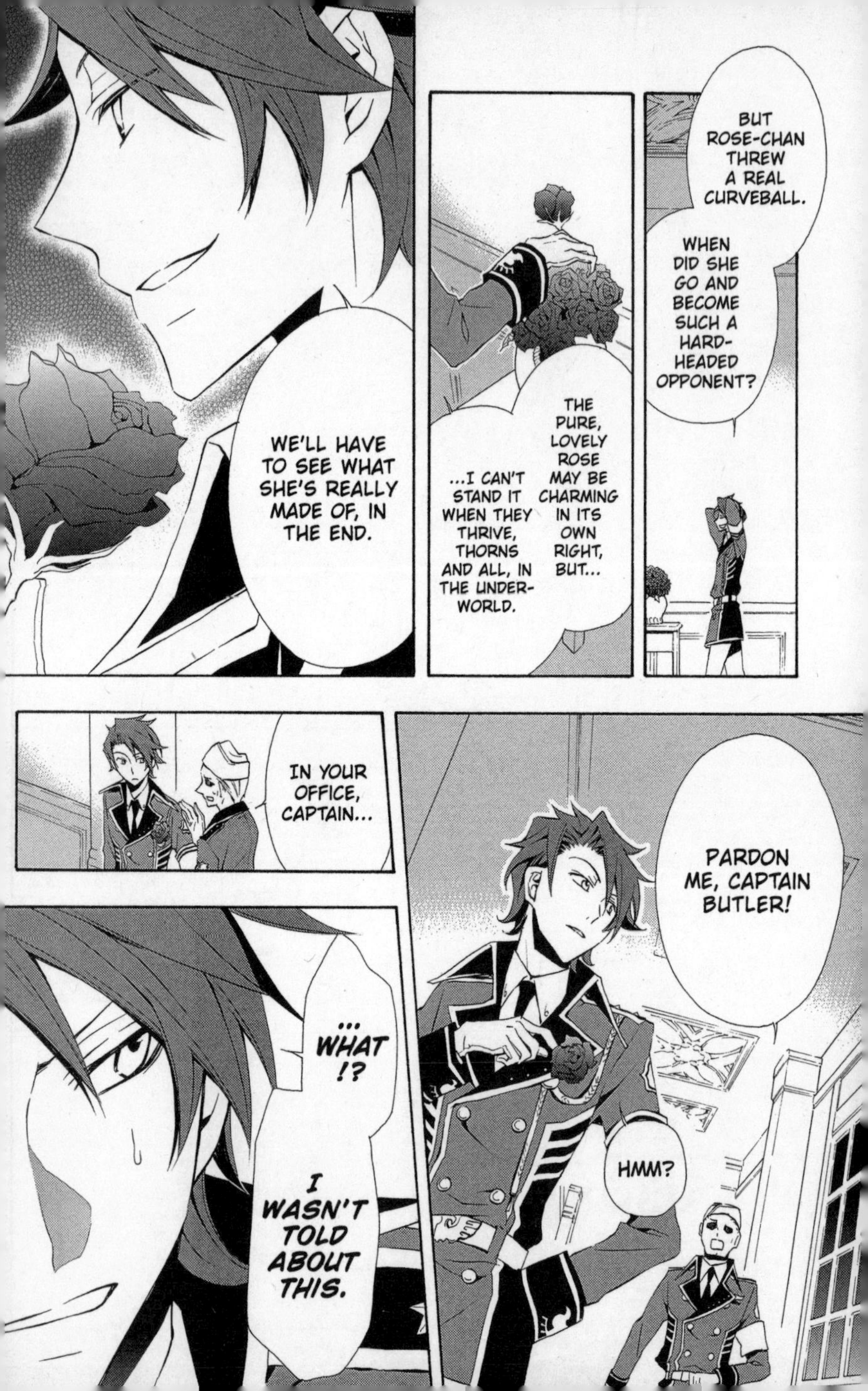
BUT ROSE-CHAN THREW A REAL CURVEBALL.
WHEN DID SHE GO AND BECOME SUCH A HARD-HEADED OPPONENT?
THE PURE, LOVELY ROSE MAY BE CHARMING IN ITS OWN RIGHT, BUT...
...I CAN'T STAND IT WHEN THEY THRIVE, THORNS AND ALL, IN THE UNDER-WORLD.
WE'LL HAVE TO SEE WHAT SHE'S REALLY MADE OF, IN THE END.
PARDON ME, CAPTAIN BUTLER!
HMM?
IN YOUR OFFICE, CAPTAIN...
...WHAT!?
I WASN'T TOLD ABOUT THIS.

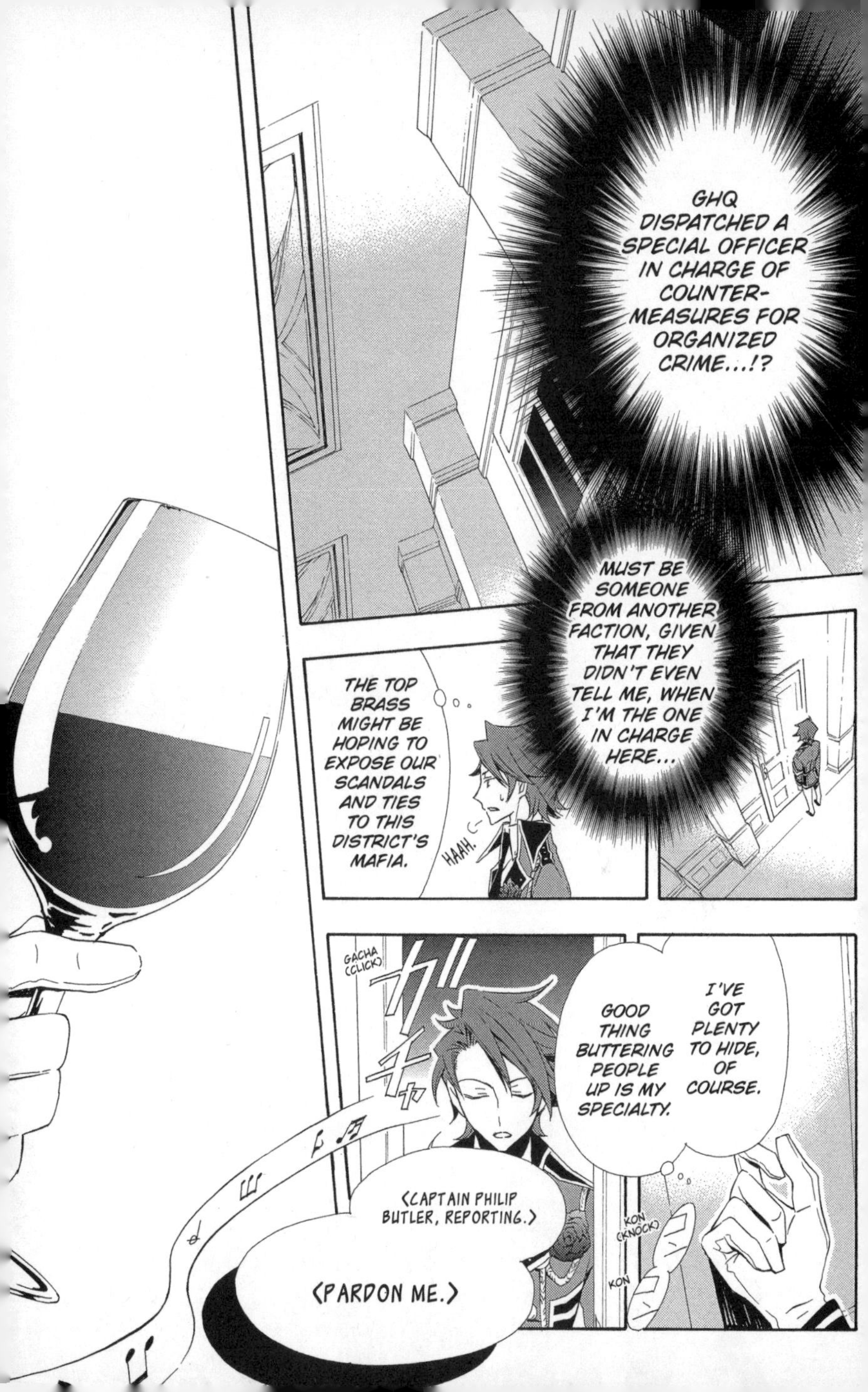
GHQ DISPATCHED A SPECIAL OFFICER IN CHARGE OF COUNTER-MEASURES FOR ORGANIZED CRIME...!?
MUST BE SOMEONE FROM ANOTHER FACTION, GIVEN THAT THEY DIDN'T EVEN TELL ME, WHEN I'M THE ONE IN CHARGE HERE...
THE TOP BRASS MIGHT BE HOPING TO EXPOSE OUR SCANDALS AND TIES TO THIS DISTRICT'S MAFIA.
HAAH.
I'VE GOT PLENTY TO HIDE, OF COURSE.
GOOD THING BUTTERING PEOPLE UP IS MY SPECIALTY.
KON (KNOCK)
KON
GACHA (CLICK)
⟨CAPTAIN PHILIP BUTLER, REPORTING.⟩
⟨PARDON ME.⟩

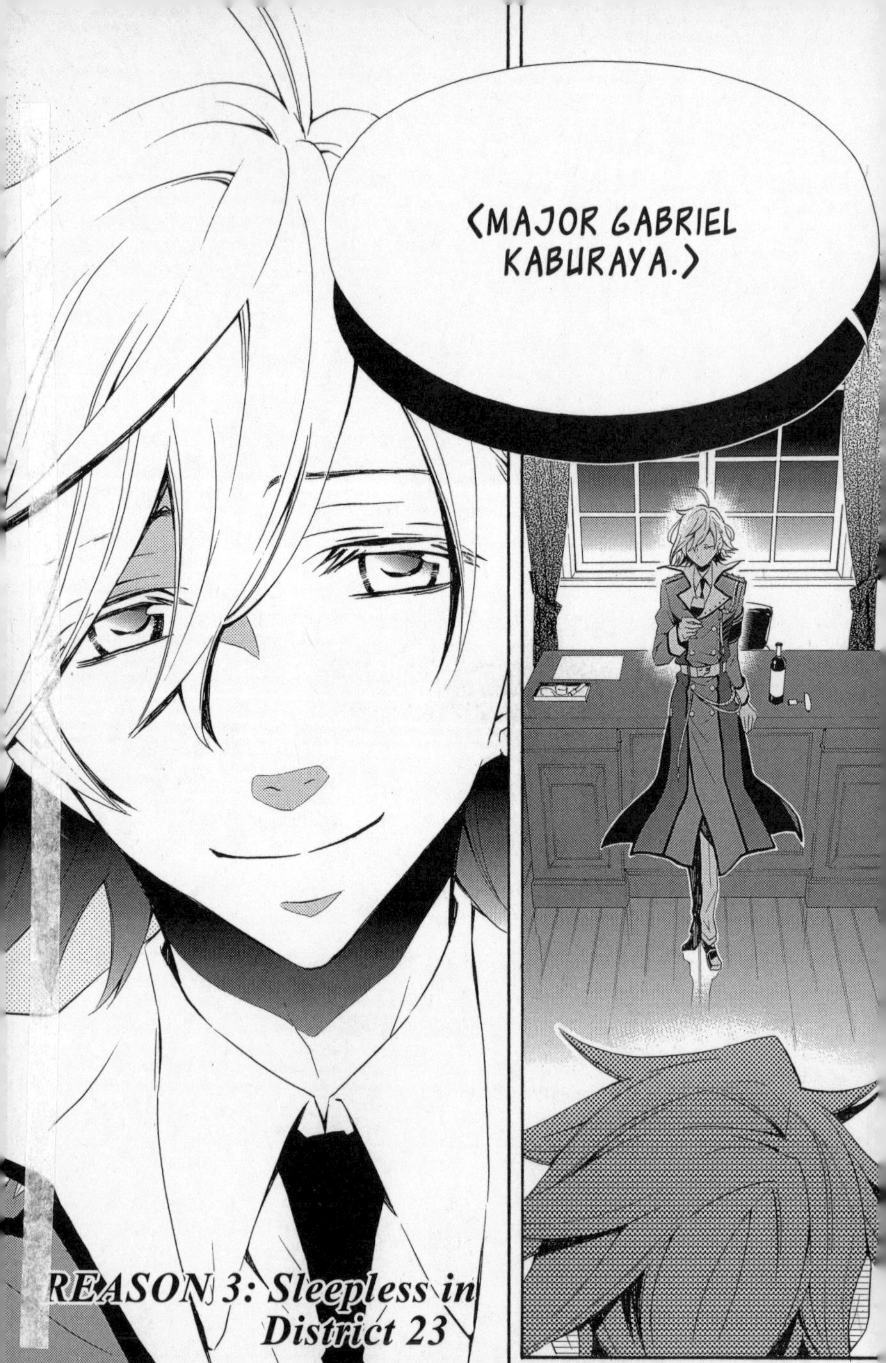

<MAJOR GABRIEL KABURAYA.>
REASON 3: Sleepless in District 23

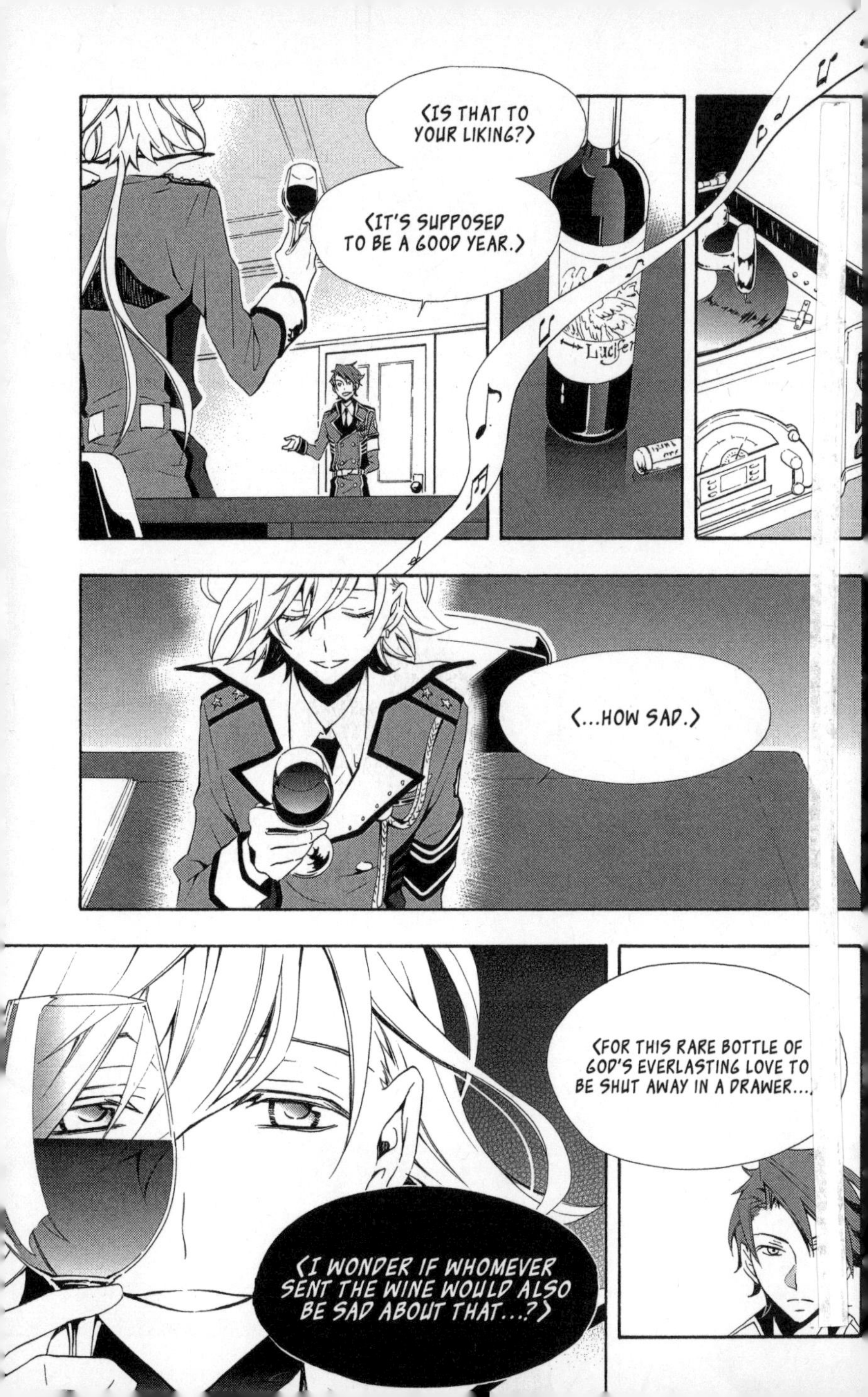
〈IS THAT TO YOUR LIKING?〉
〈IT'S SUPPOSED TO BE A GOOD YEAR.〉
Lucifer
〈...HOW SAD.〉
〈FOR THIS RARE BOTTLE OF GOD'S EVERLASTING LOVE TO BE SHUT AWAY IN A DRAWER...〉
〈I WONDER IF WHOMEVER SENT THE WINE WOULD ALSO BE SAD ABOUT THAT...?〉

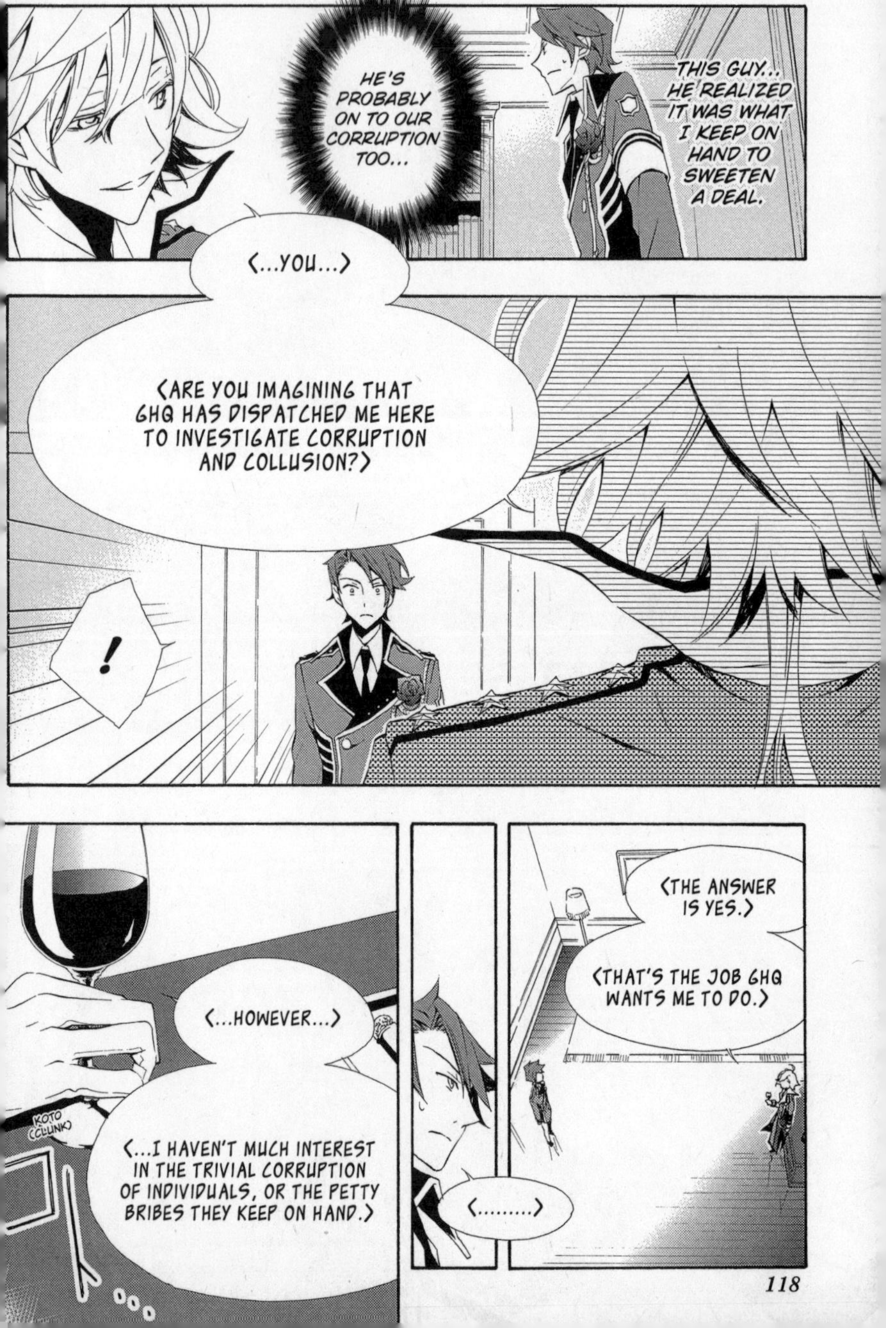
THIS GUY... HE REALIZED IT WAS WHAT I KEEP ON HAND TO SWEETEN A DEAL.
HE'S PROBABLY ON TO OUR CORRUPTION TOO...
<...YOU...>
<ARE YOU IMAGINING THAT GHQ HAS DISPATCHED ME HERE TO INVESTIGATE CORRUPTION AND COLLUSION?>
!
<THE ANSWER IS YES.>
<THAT'S THE JOB GHQ WANTS ME TO DO.>
<.........>
<...HOWEVER...>
<...I HAVEN'T MUCH INTEREST IN THE TRIVIAL CORRUPTION OF INDIVIDUALS, OR THE PETTY BRIBES THEY KEEP ON HAND.>
KOTO (CLUNK)

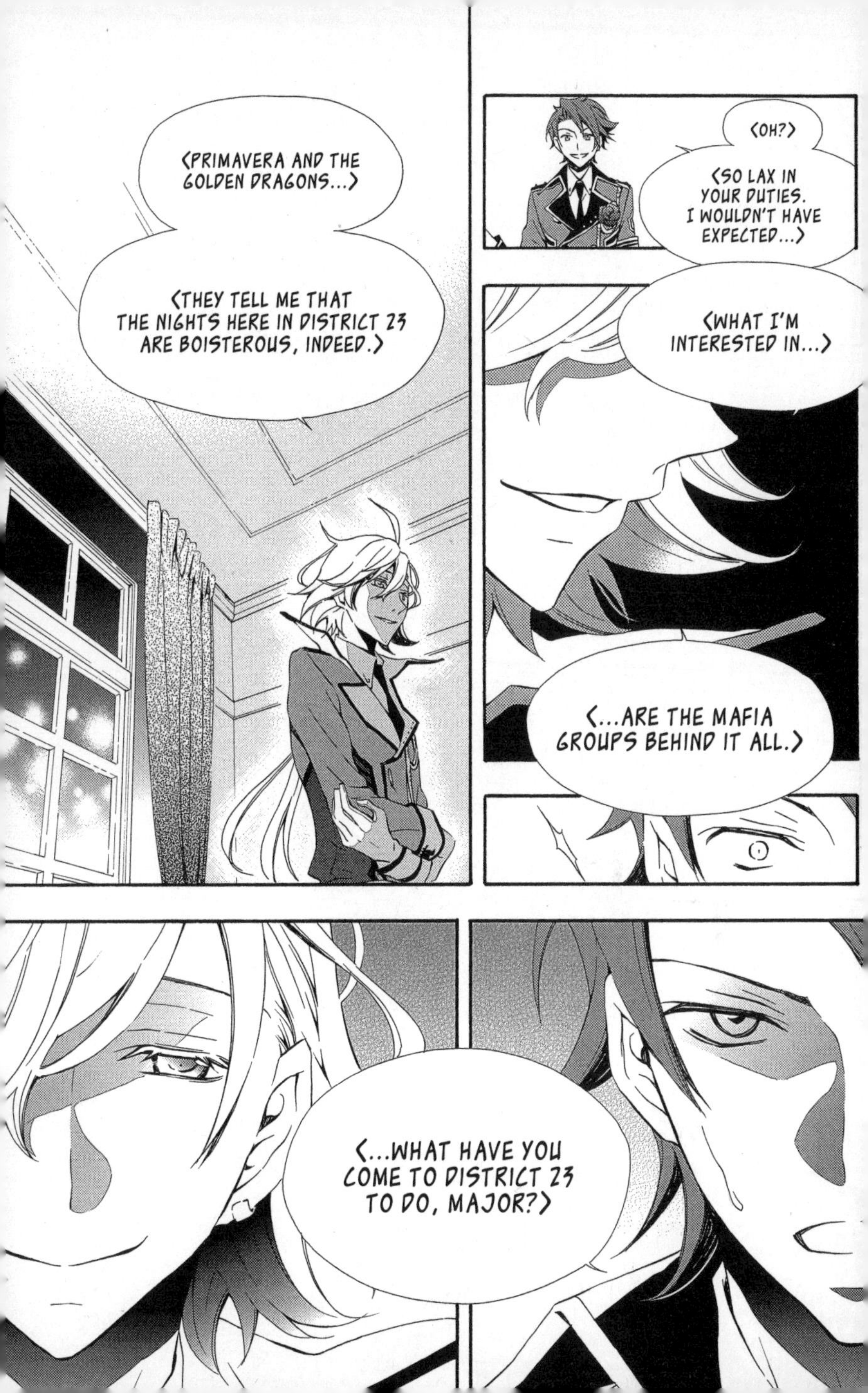

〈OH?〉
〈SO LAX IN YOUR DUTIES. I WOULDN'T HAVE EXPECTED...〉
〈WHAT I'M INTERESTED IN...〉
〈...ARE THE MAFIA GROUPS BEHIND IT ALL.〉
〈PRIMAVERA AND THE GOLDEN DRAGONS...〉
〈THEY TELL ME THAT THE NIGHTS HERE IN DISTRICT 23 ARE BOISTEROUS, INDEED.〉
〈...WHAT HAVE YOU COME TO DISTRICT 23 TO DO, MAJOR?〉

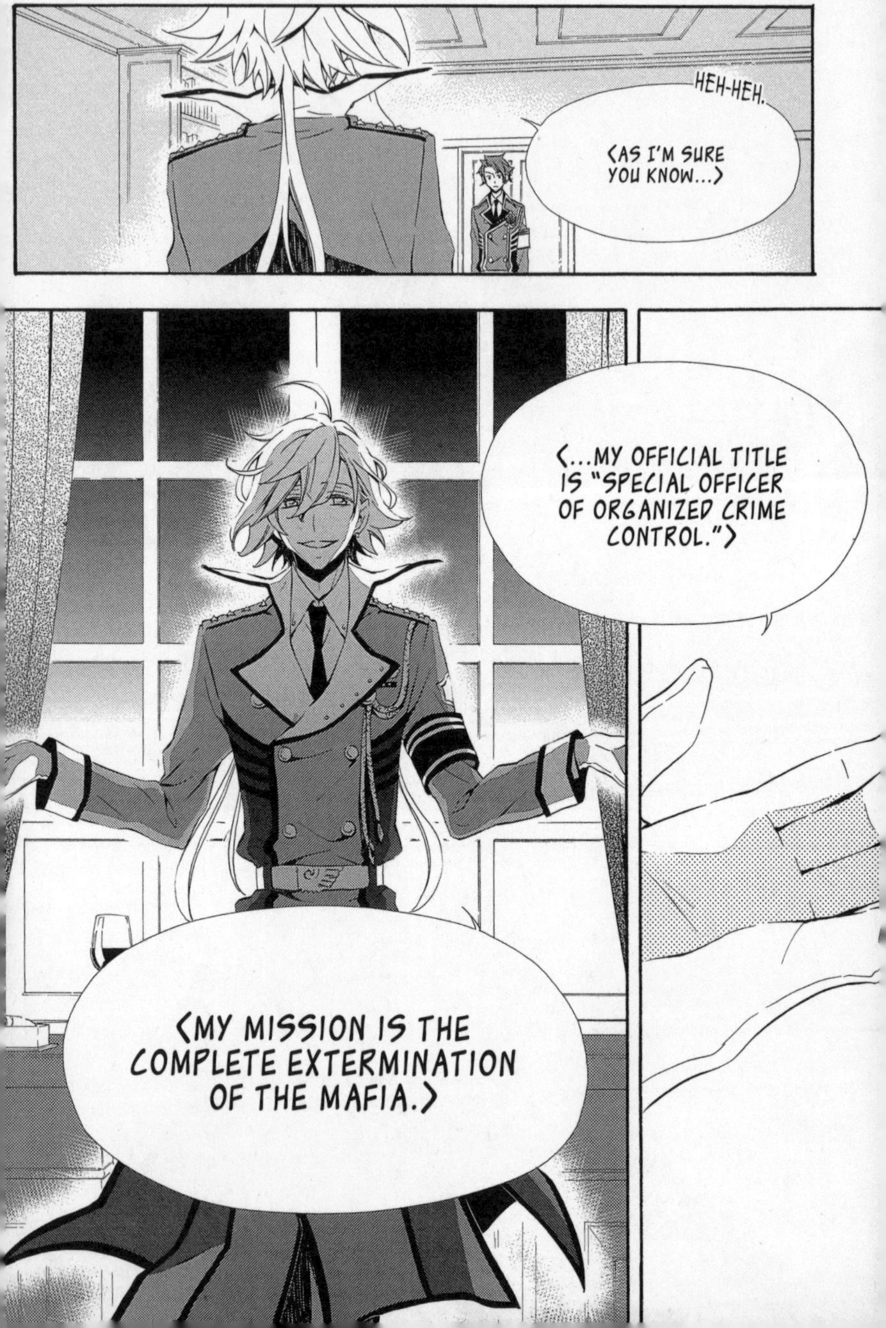
HEH-HEH.
‹AS I'M SURE YOU KNOW...›
‹...MY OFFICIAL TITLE IS "SPECIAL OFFICER OF ORGANIZED CRIME CONTROL."›
‹MY MISSION IS THE COMPLETE EXTERMINATION OF THE MAFIA.›

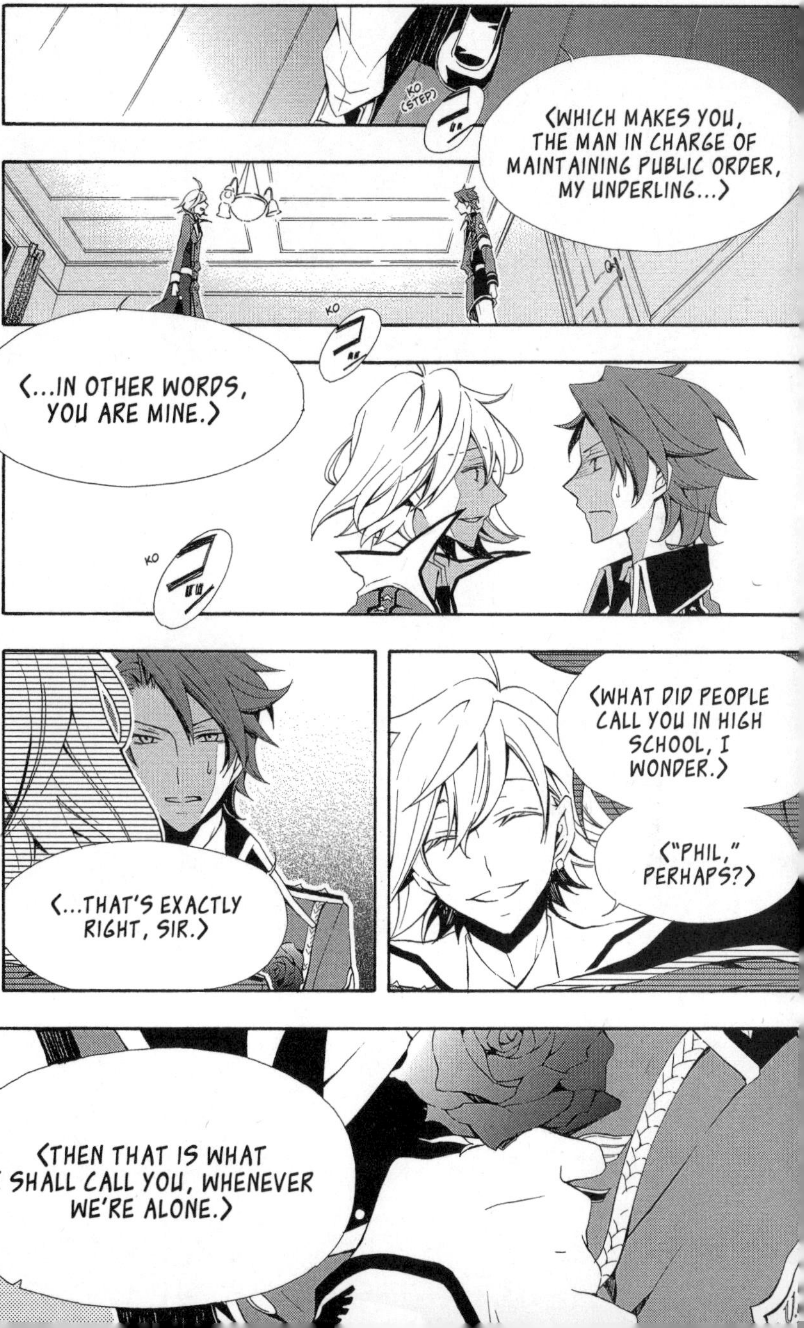
KO (STEP)
‹WHICH MAKES YOU, THE MAN IN CHARGE OF MAINTAINING PUBLIC ORDER, MY UNDERLING...›
KO
‹...IN OTHER WORDS, YOU ARE MINE.›
KO
‹WHAT DID PEOPLE CALL YOU IN HIGH SCHOOL, I WONDER.›
‹"PHIL," PERHAPS?›
‹...THAT'S EXACTLY RIGHT, SIR.›
‹THEN THAT IS WHAT I SHALL CALL YOU, WHENEVER WE'RE ALONE.›

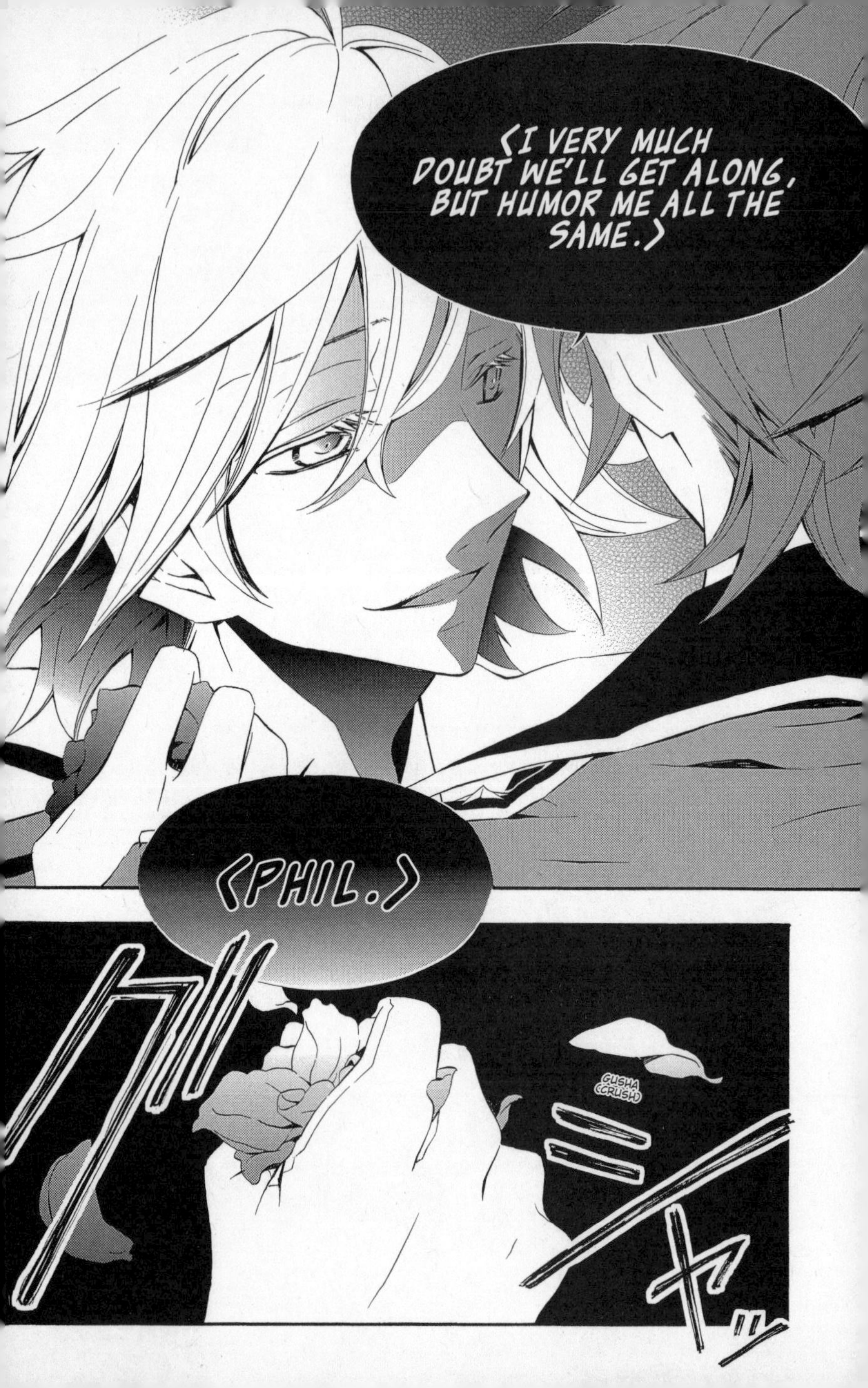
‹I VERY MUCH DOUBT WE'LL GET ALONG, BUT HUMOR ME ALL THE SAME.›
‹PHIL.›
GUSHA (CRUSH)

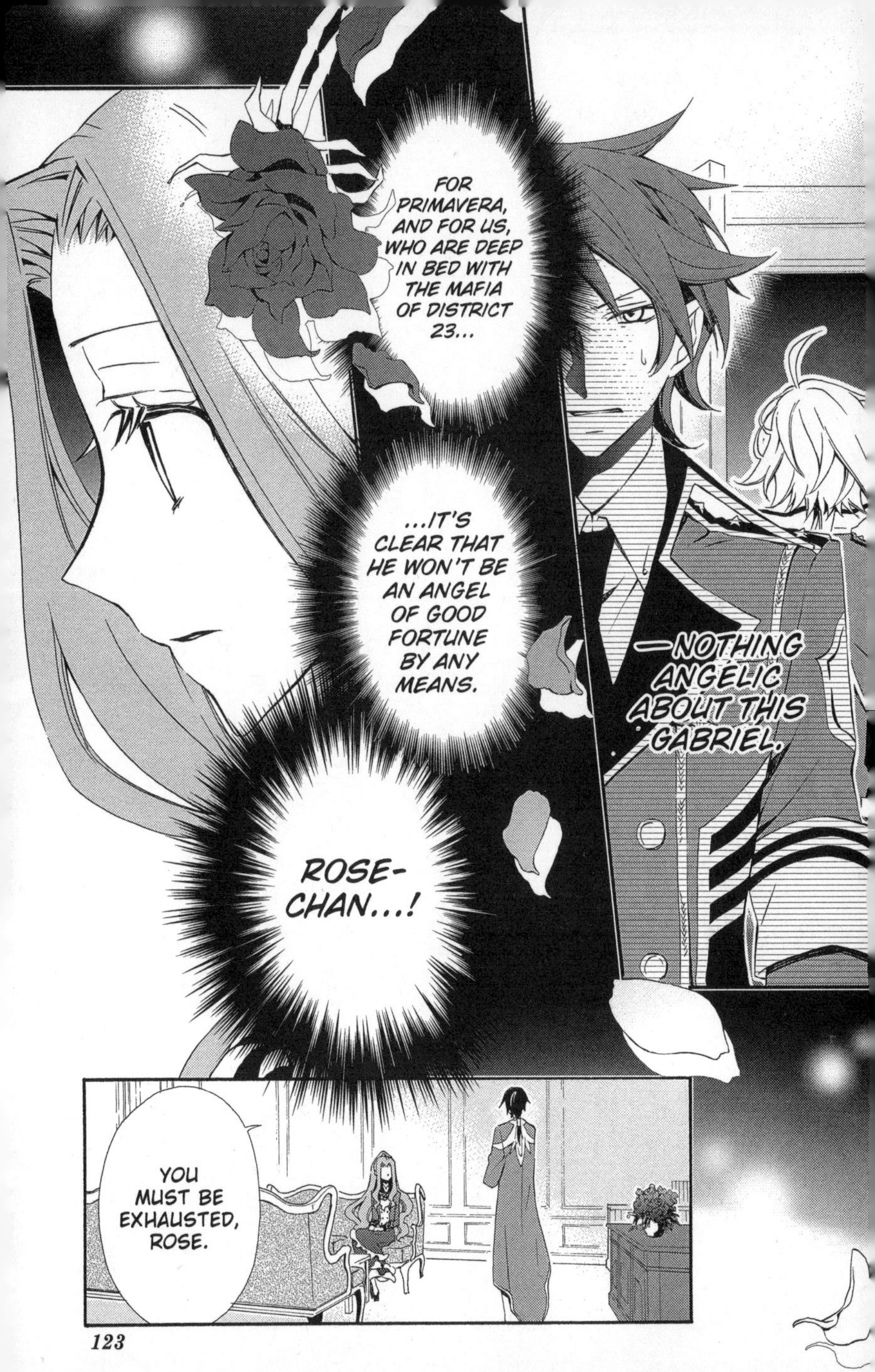
FOR PRIMAVERA, AND FOR US, WHO ARE DEEP IN BED WITH THE MAFIA OF DISTRICT 23...
...IT'S CLEAR THAT HE WON'T BE AN ANGEL OF GOOD FORTUNE BY ANY MEANS.
—NOTHING ANGELIC ABOUT THIS GABRIEL.
ROSE-CHAN...!
YOU MUST BE EXHAUSTED, ROSE.

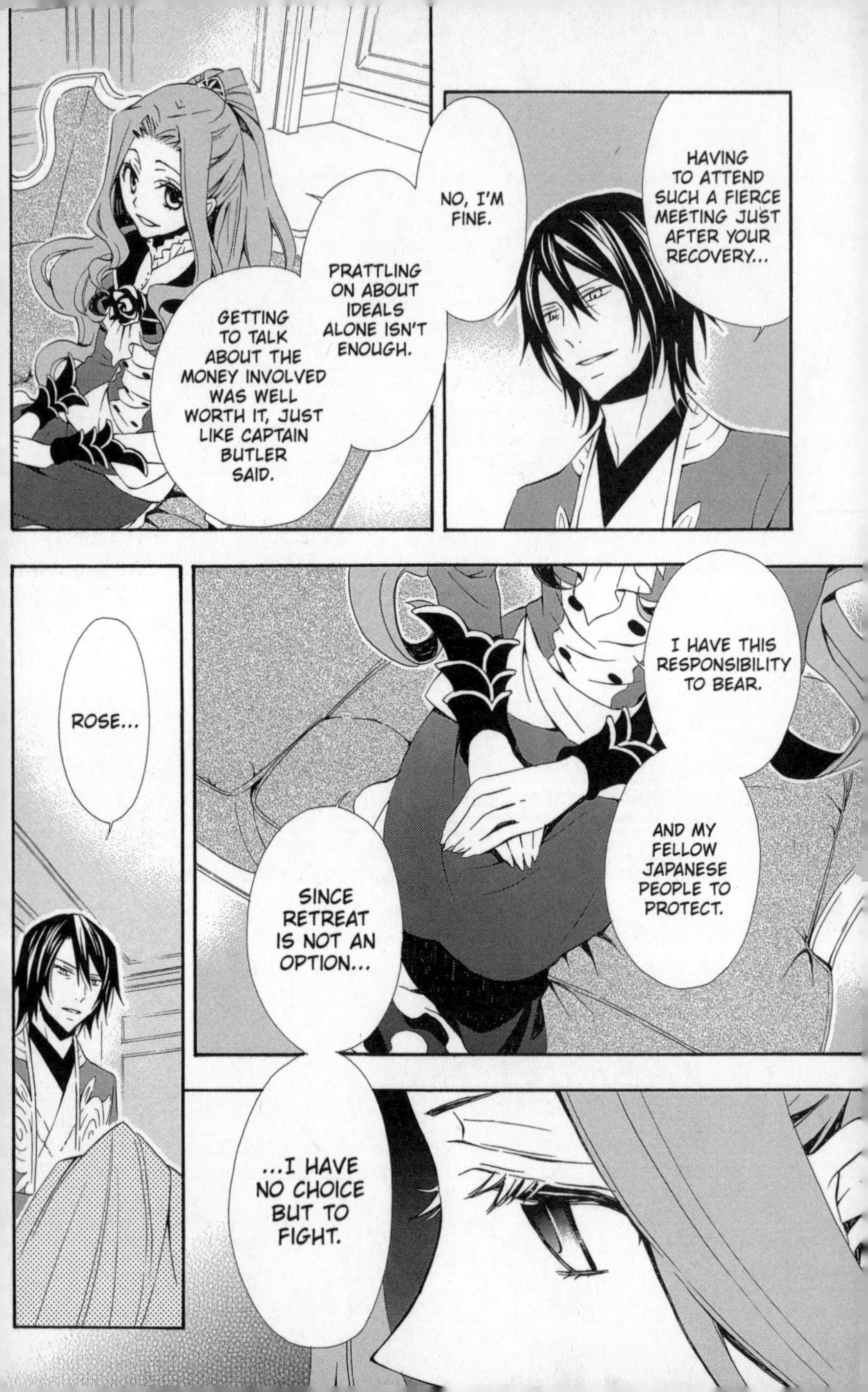
HAVING TO ATTEND SUCH A FIERCE MEETING JUST AFTER YOUR RECOVERY...
NO, I'M FINE.
PRATTLING ON ABOUT IDEALS ALONE ISN'T ENOUGH.
GETTING TO TALK ABOUT THE MONEY INVOLVED WAS WELL WORTH IT, JUST LIKE CAPTAIN BUTLER SAID.
I HAVE THIS RESPONSIBILITY TO BEAR.
AND MY FELLOW JAPANESE PEOPLE TO PROTECT.
SINCE RETREAT IS NOT AN OPTION...
...I HAVE NO CHOICE BUT TO FIGHT.
ROSE...

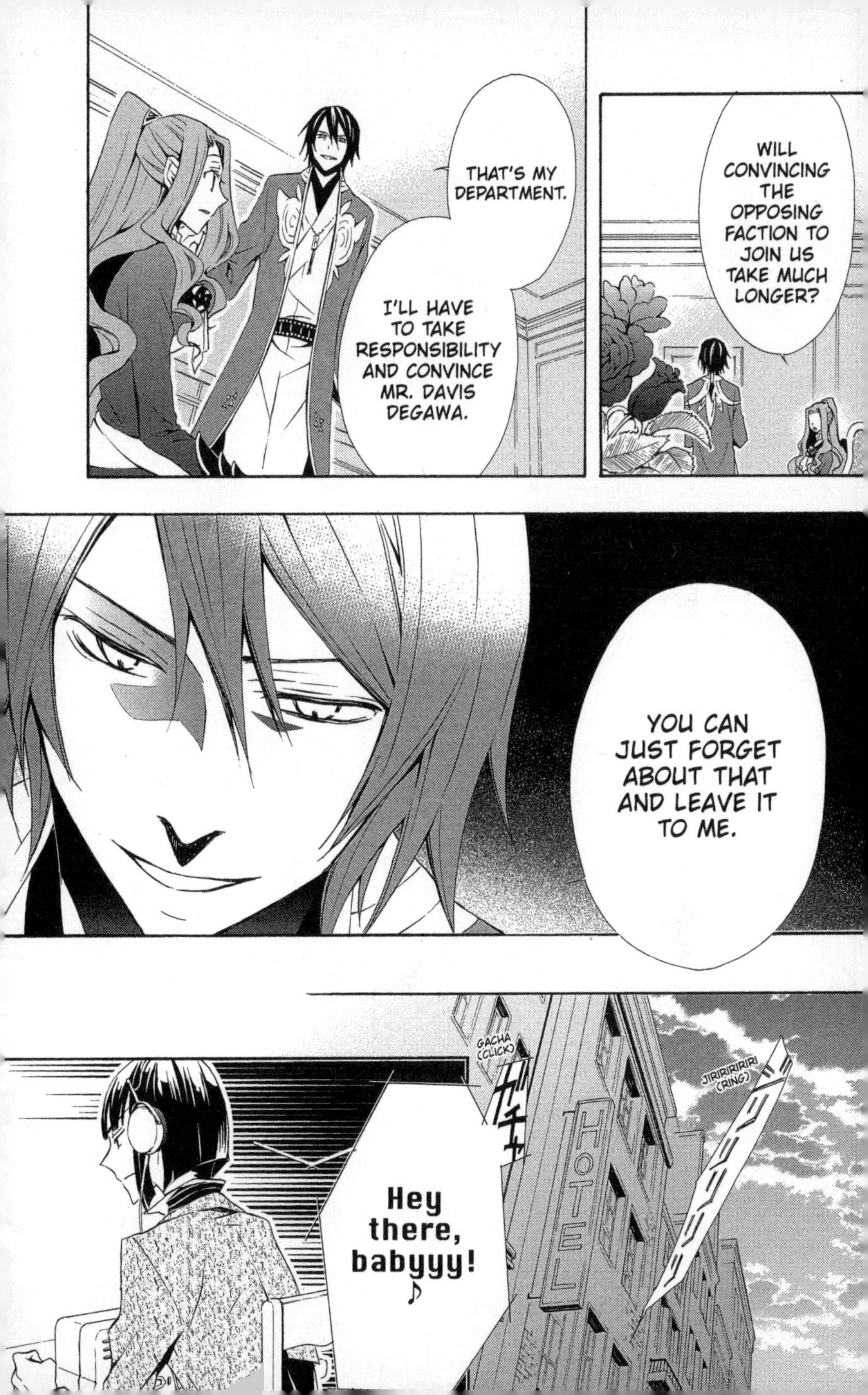
WILL CONVINCING THE OPPOSING FACTION TO JOIN US TAKE MUCH LONGER?
THAT'S MY DEPARTMENT.
I'LL HAVE TO TAKE RESPONSIBILITY AND CONVINCE MR. DAVIS DEGAWA.
YOU CAN JUST FORGET ABOUT THAT AND LEAVE IT TO ME.
JIRIRIRIRIRI (RING)
GACHA (CLICK)
Hey there, babyyy! ♪

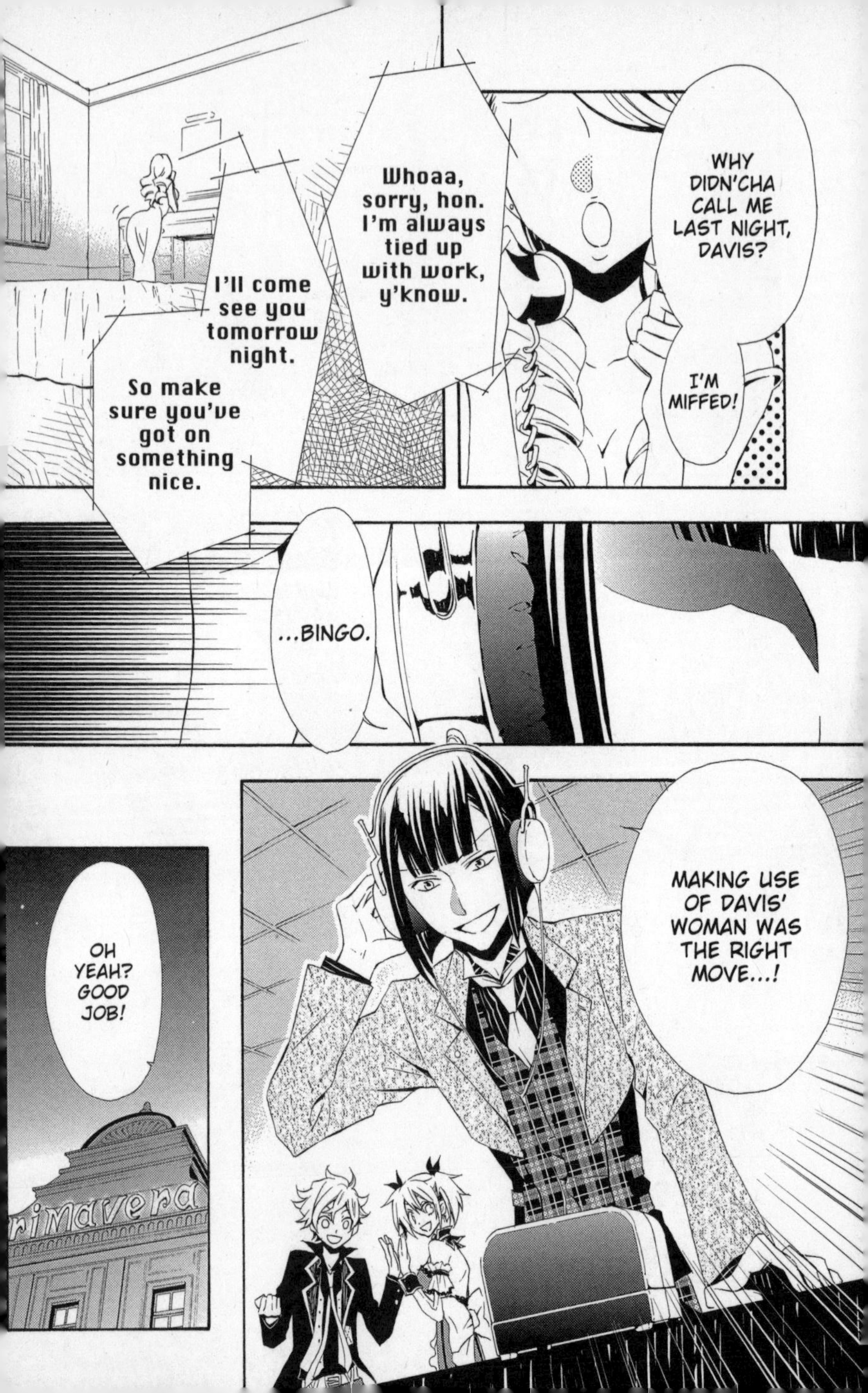
WHY DIDN'CHA CALL ME LAST NIGHT, DAVIS?
I'M MIFFED!
Whoaa, sorry, hon. I'm always tied up with work, y'know.
I'll come see you tomorrow night.
So make sure you've got on something nice.
...BINGO.
MAKING USE OF DAVIS' WOMAN WAS THE RIGHT MOVE...!
OH YEAH? GOOD JOB!

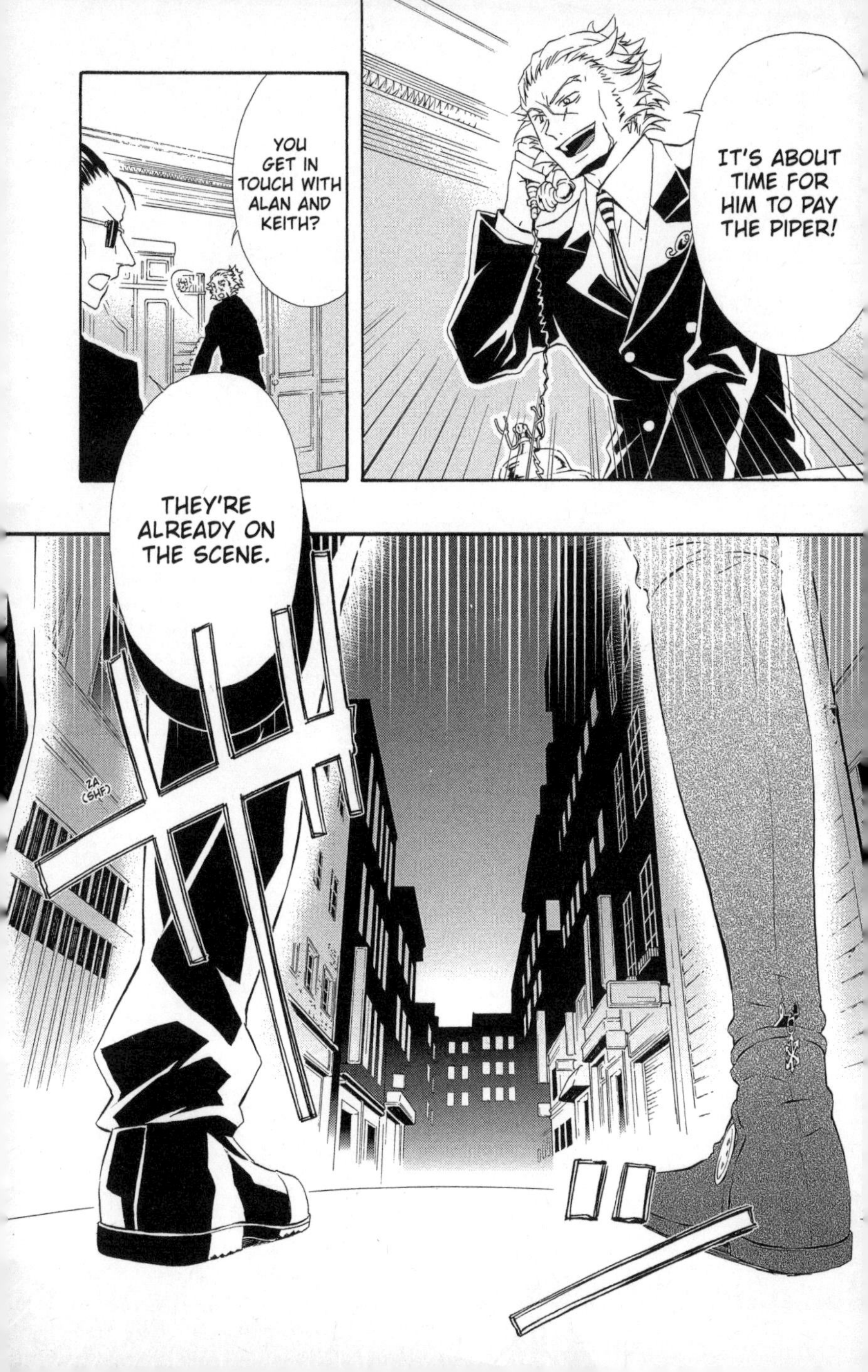
IT'S ABOUT TIME FOR HIM TO PAY THE PIPER!
YOU GET IN TOUCH WITH ALAN AND KEITH?
THEY'RE ALREADY ON THE SCENE.
ZA (SHF)

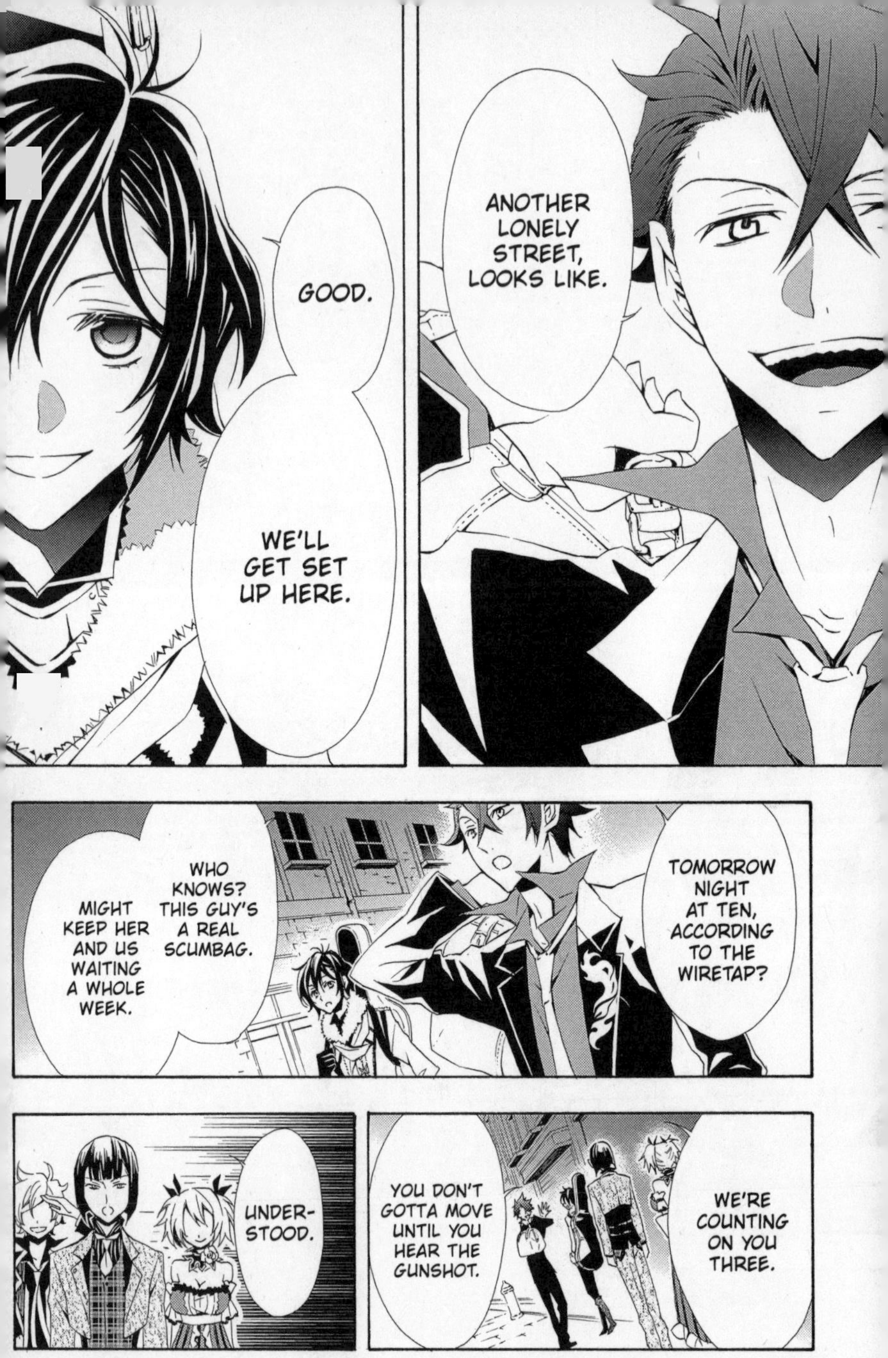
ANOTHER LONELY STREET, LOOKS LIKE.
GOOD.
WE'LL GET SET UP HERE.
TOMORROW NIGHT AT TEN, ACCORDING TO THE WIRETAP?
WHO KNOWS? THIS GUY'S A REAL SCUMBAG.
MIGHT KEEP HER AND US WAITING A WHOLE WEEK.
WE'RE COUNTING ON YOU THREE.
YOU DON'T GOTTA MOVE UNTIL YOU HEAR THE GUNSHOT.
UNDER-STOOD.

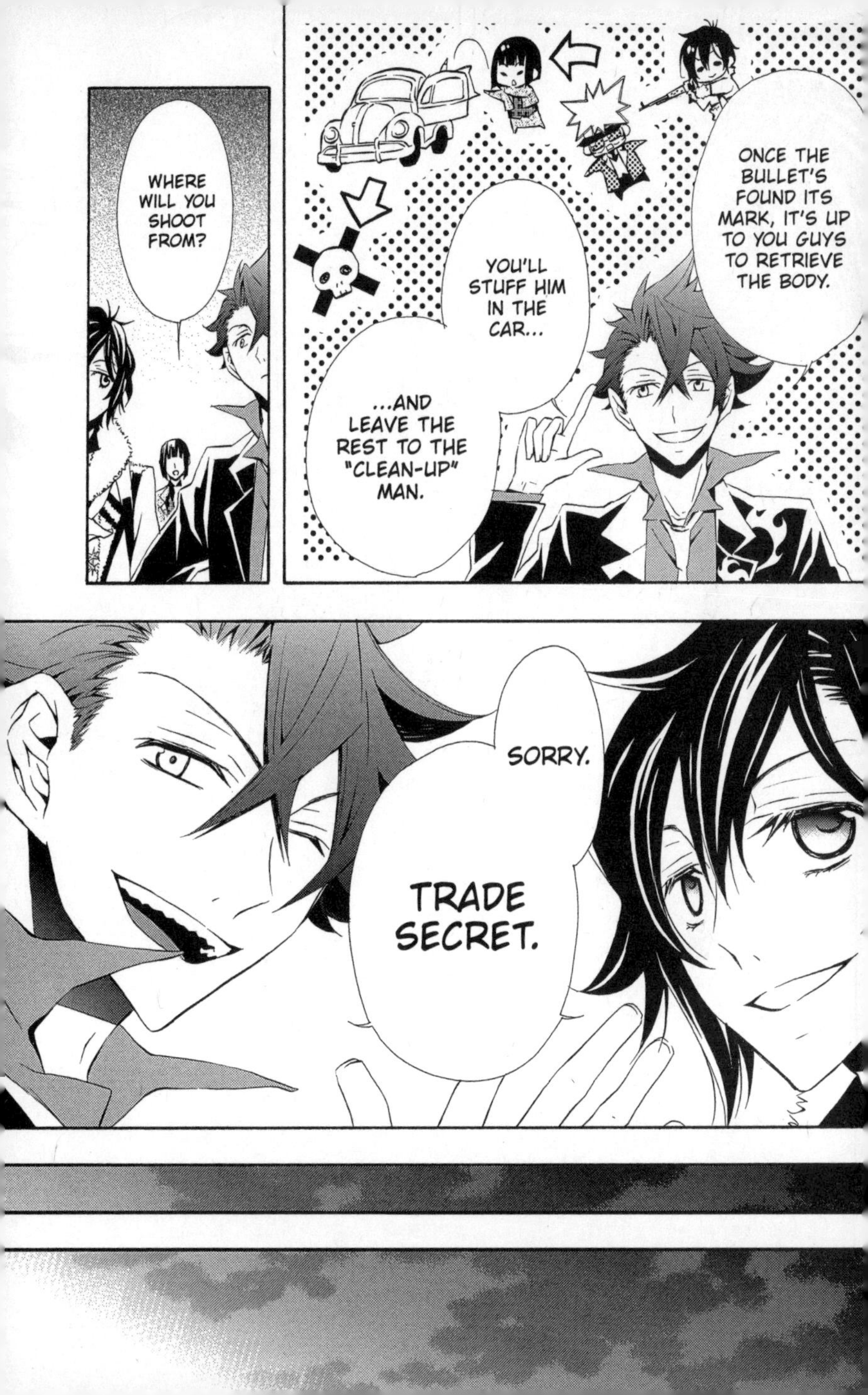
ONCE THE BULLET'S FOUND ITS MARK, IT'S UP TO YOU GUYS TO RETRIEVE THE BODY.
YOU'LL STUFF HIM IN THE CAR...
...AND LEAVE THE REST TO THE "CLEAN-UP" MAN.
WHERE WILL YOU SHOOT FROM?
SORRY.
TRADE SECRET.

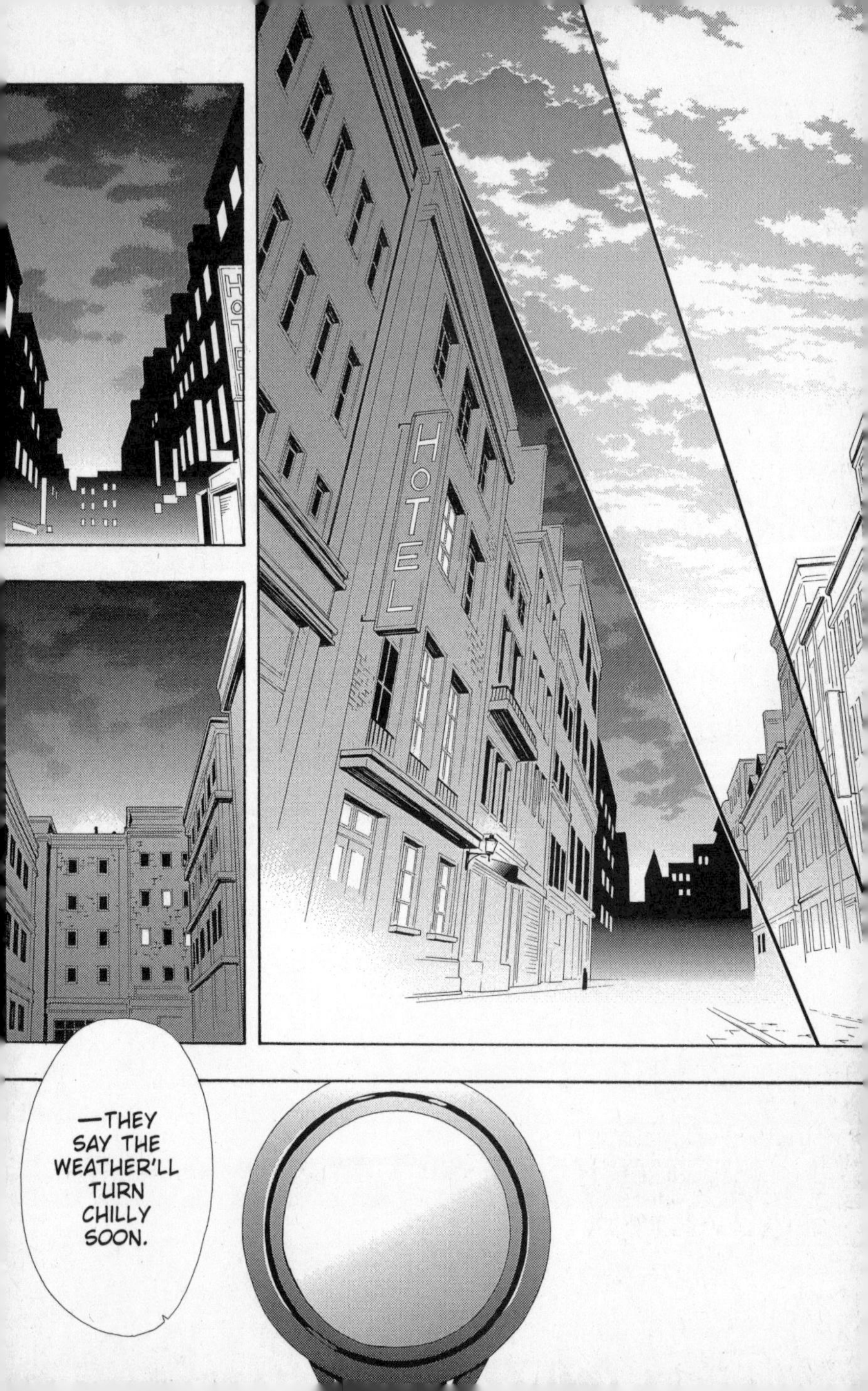
HOTEL
—THEY SAY THE WEATHER'LL TURN CHILLY SOON.

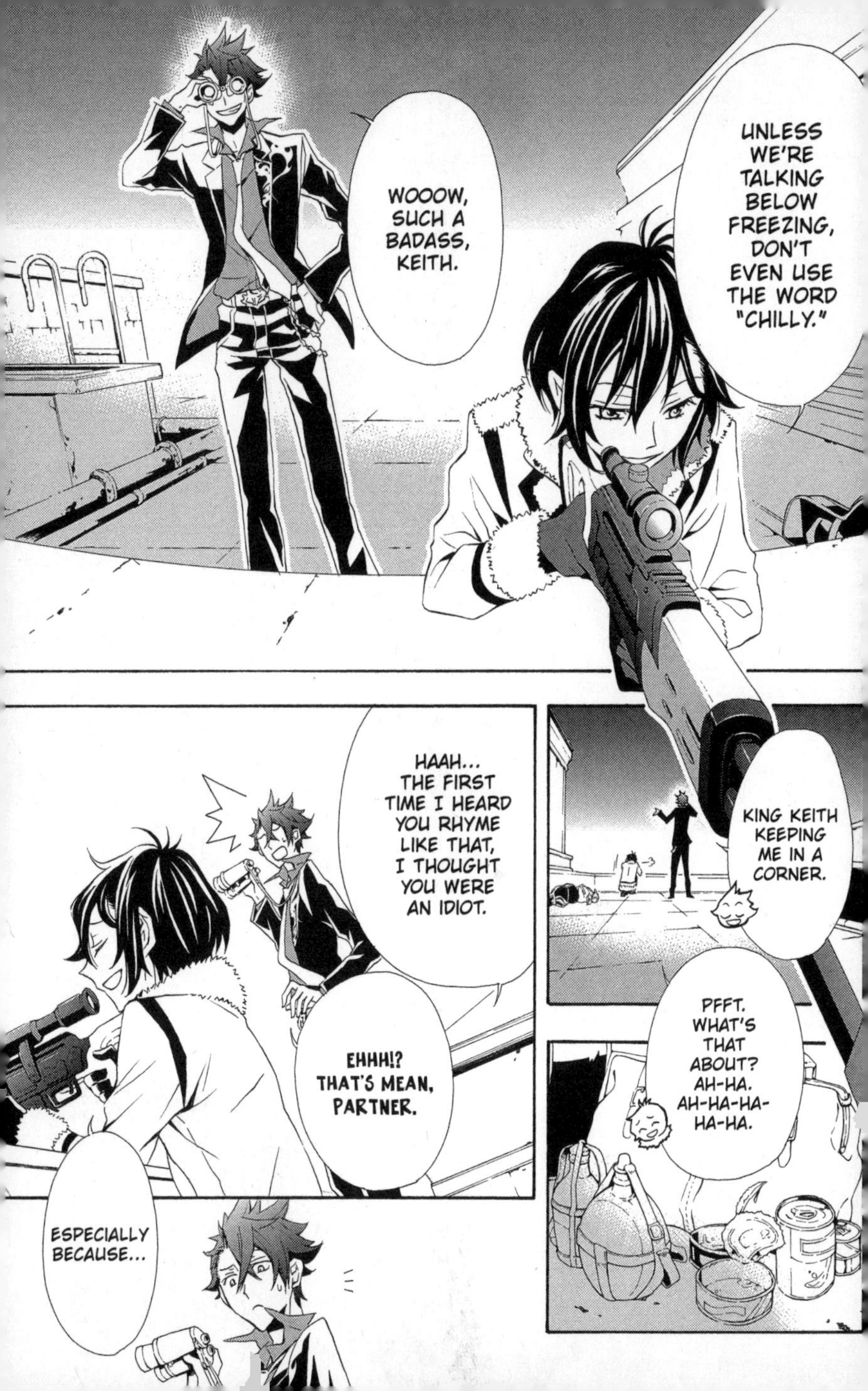
UNLESS WE'RE TALKING BELOW FREEZING, DON'T EVEN USE THE WORD "CHILLY."
WOOOW, SUCH A BADASS, KEITH.
KING KEITH KEEPING ME IN A CORNER.
PFFT. WHAT'S THAT ABOUT? AH-HA. AH-HA-HA-HA-HA.
HAAH... THE FIRST TIME I HEARD YOU RHYME LIKE THAT, I THOUGHT YOU WERE AN IDIOT.
EHHH!? THAT'S MEAN, PARTNER.
ESPECIALLY BECAUSE...

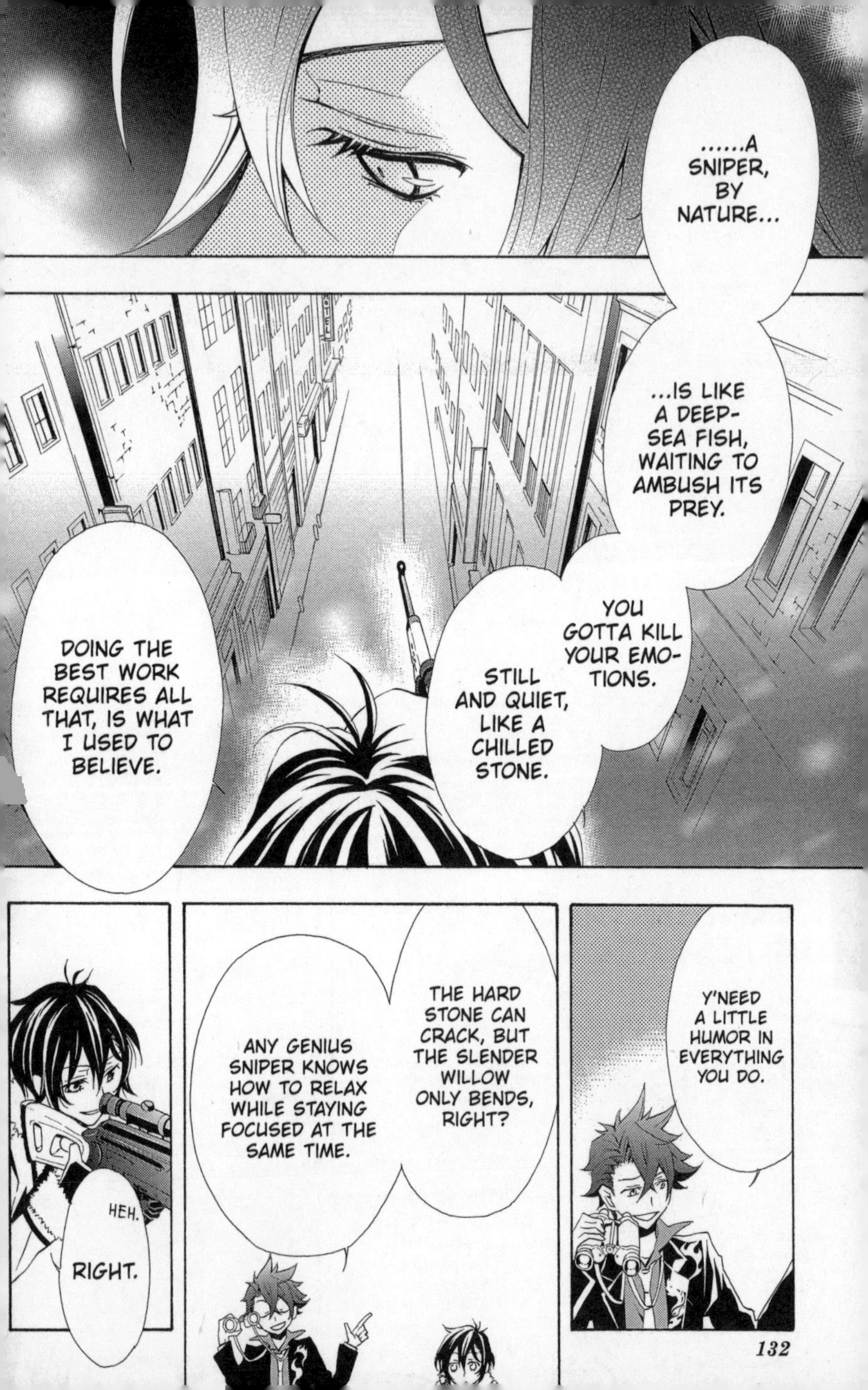
......A SNIPER, BY NATURE...
...IS LIKE A DEEP-SEA FISH, WAITING TO AMBUSH ITS PREY.
YOU GOTTA KILL YOUR EMOTIONS.
STILL AND QUIET, LIKE A CHILLED STONE.
DOING THE BEST WORK REQUIRES ALL THAT, IS WHAT I USED TO BELIEVE.
Y'NEED A LITTLE HUMOR IN EVERYTHING YOU DO.
THE HARD STONE CAN CRACK, BUT THE SLENDER WILLOW ONLY BENDS, RIGHT?
ANY GENIUS SNIPER KNOWS HOW TO RELAX WHILE STAYING FOCUSED AT THE SAME TIME.
HEH.
RIGHT.

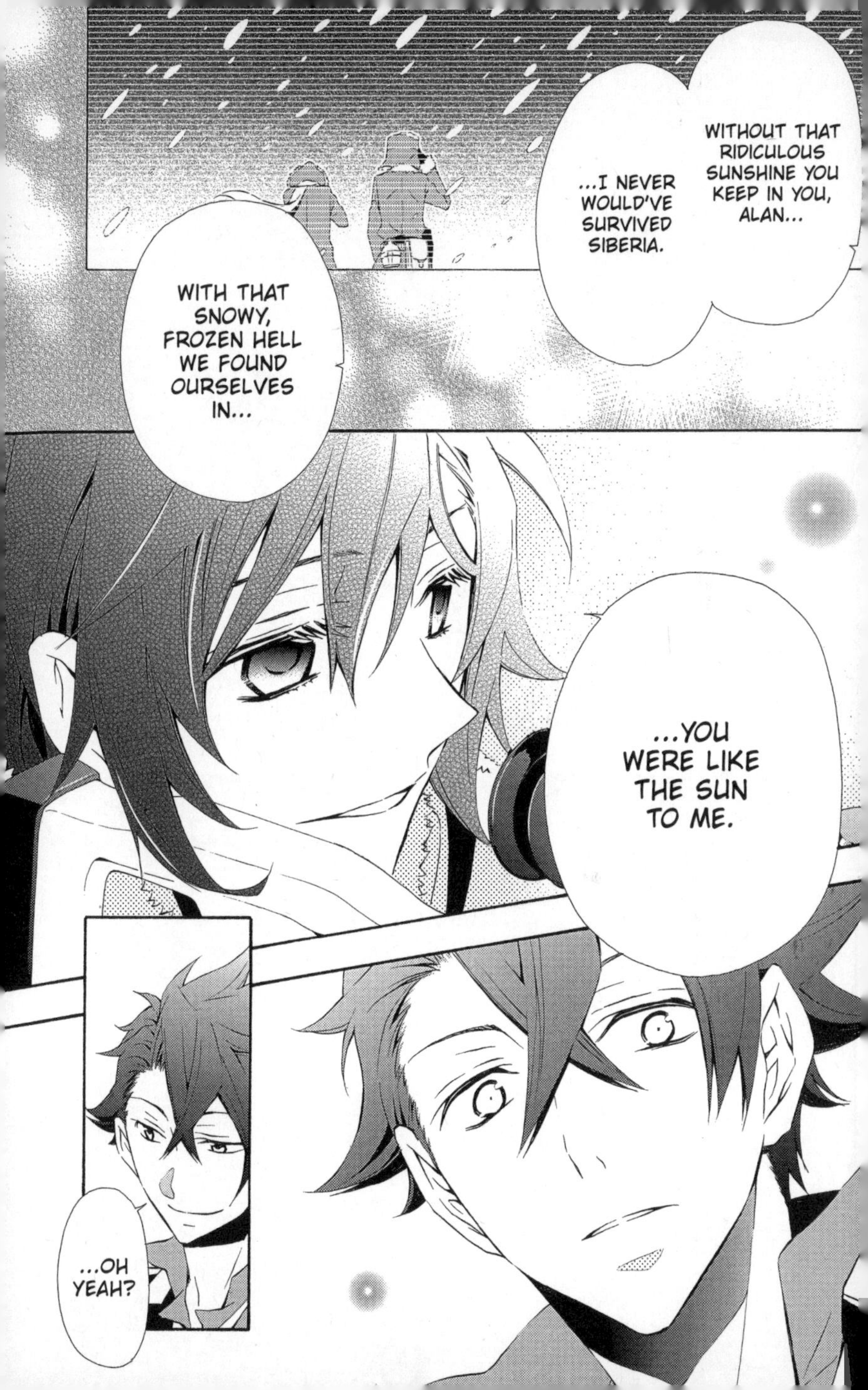
WITHOUT THAT RIDICULOUS SUNSHINE YOU KEEP IN YOU, ALAN...
...I NEVER WOULD'VE SURVIVED SIBERIA.
WITH THAT SNOWY, FROZEN HELL WE FOUND OURSELVES IN...
...YOU WERE LIKE THE SUN TO ME.
...OH YEAH?

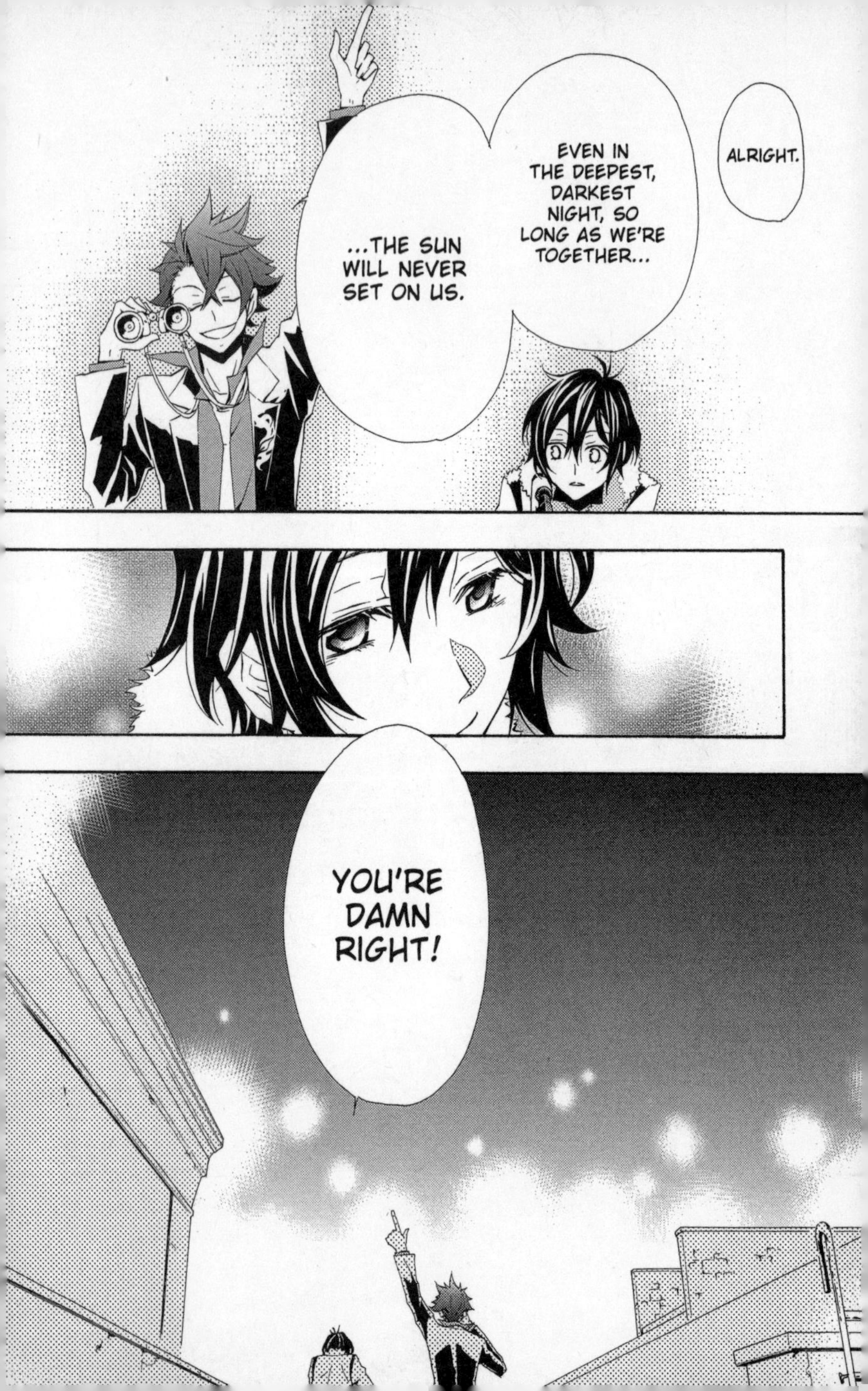
ALRIGHT.
EVEN IN THE DEEPEST, DARKEST NIGHT, SO LONG AS WE'RE TOGETHER...
...THE SUN WILL NEVER SET ON US.
YOU'RE DAMN RIGHT!

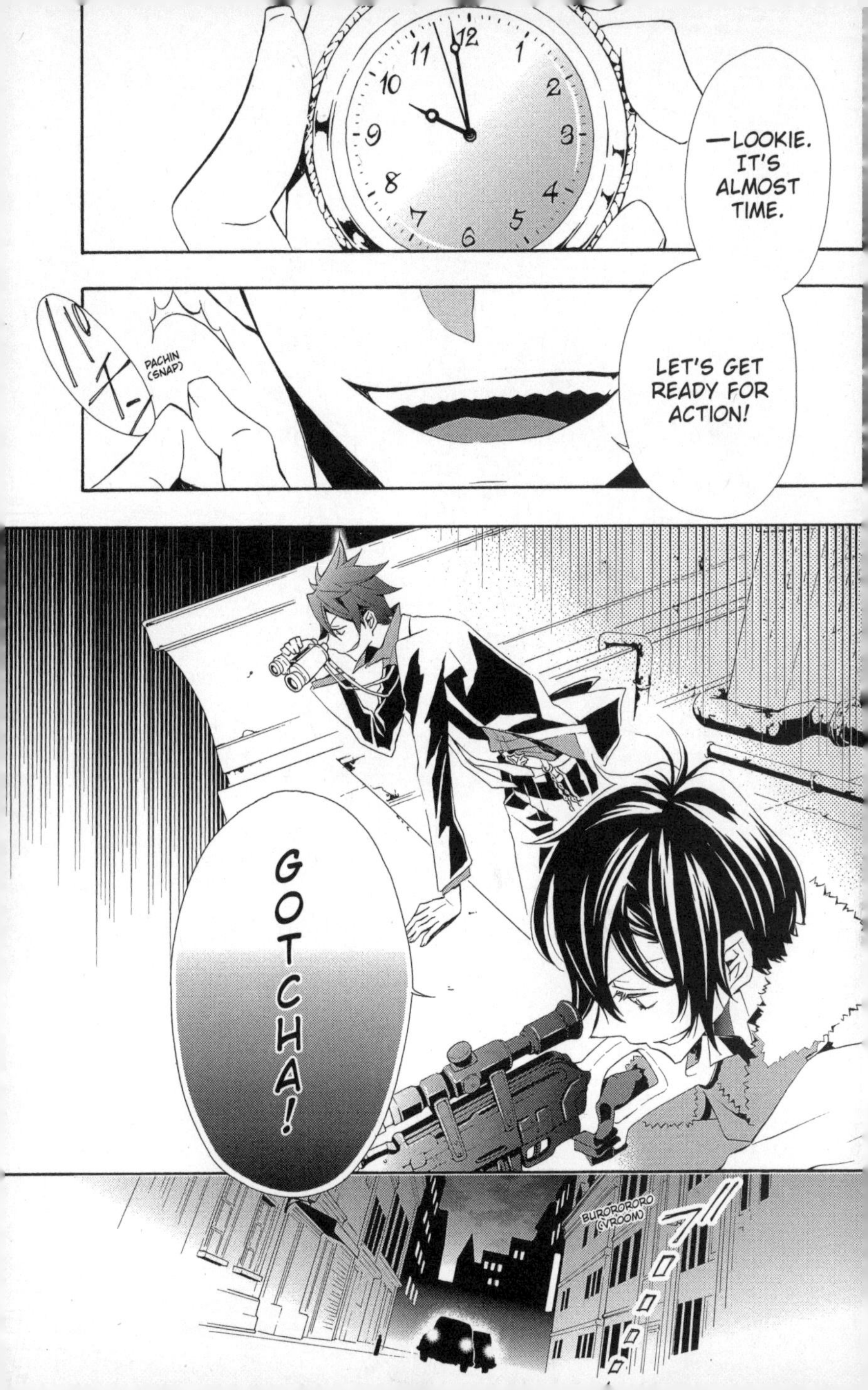
—LOOKIE. IT'S ALMOST TIME.
LET'S GET READY FOR ACTION!
PACHIN (SNAP)
GOTCHA!
BURORORORO (VROOM)

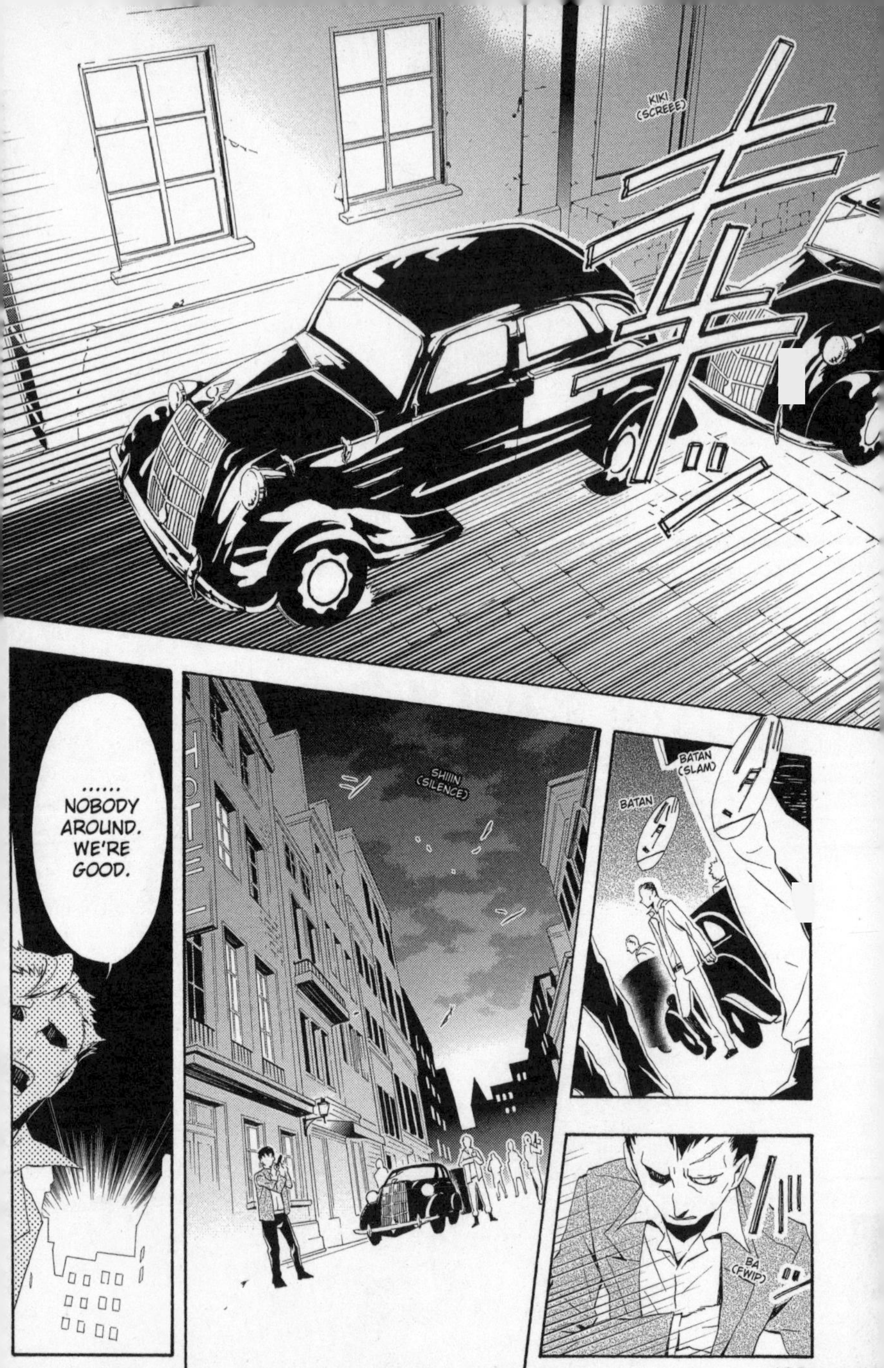
KIKI (SCREEE)
BATAN (SLAM)
BATAN
BA (FWIP)
SHIIIN (SILENCE)
...... NOBODY AROUND. WE'RE GOOD.

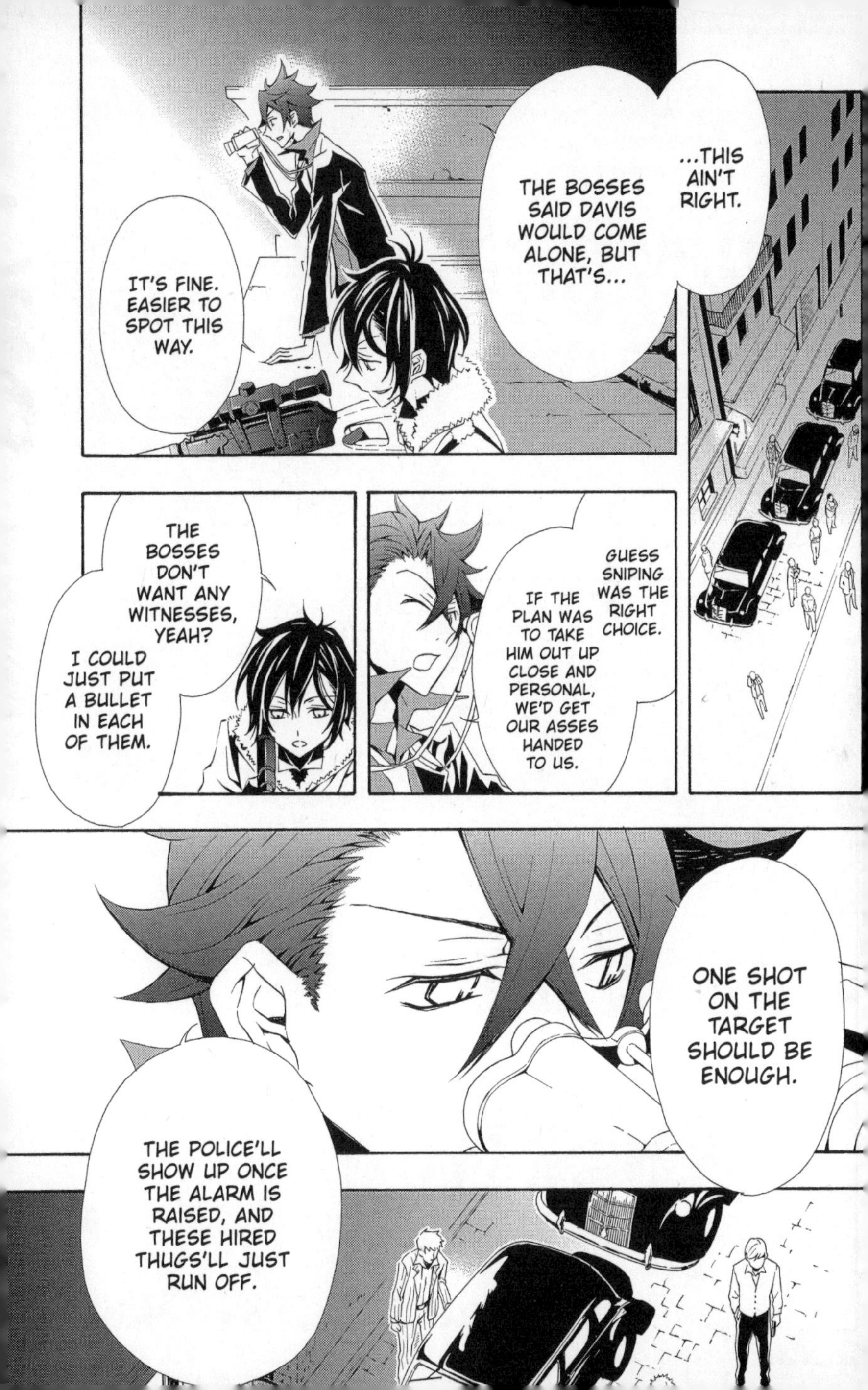
...THIS AIN'T RIGHT.
THE BOSSES SAID DAVIS WOULD COME ALONE, BUT THAT'S...
IT'S FINE. EASIER TO SPOT THIS WAY.
GUESS SNIPING WAS THE RIGHT CHOICE.
IF THE PLAN WAS TO TAKE HIM OUT UP CLOSE AND PERSONAL, WE'D GET OUR ASSES HANDED TO US.
THE BOSSES DON'T WANT ANY WITNESSES, YEAH?
I COULD JUST PUT A BULLET IN EACH OF THEM.
ONE SHOT ON THE TARGET SHOULD BE ENOUGH.
THE POLICE'LL SHOW UP ONCE THE ALARM IS RAISED, AND THESE HIRED THUGS'LL JUST RUN OFF.

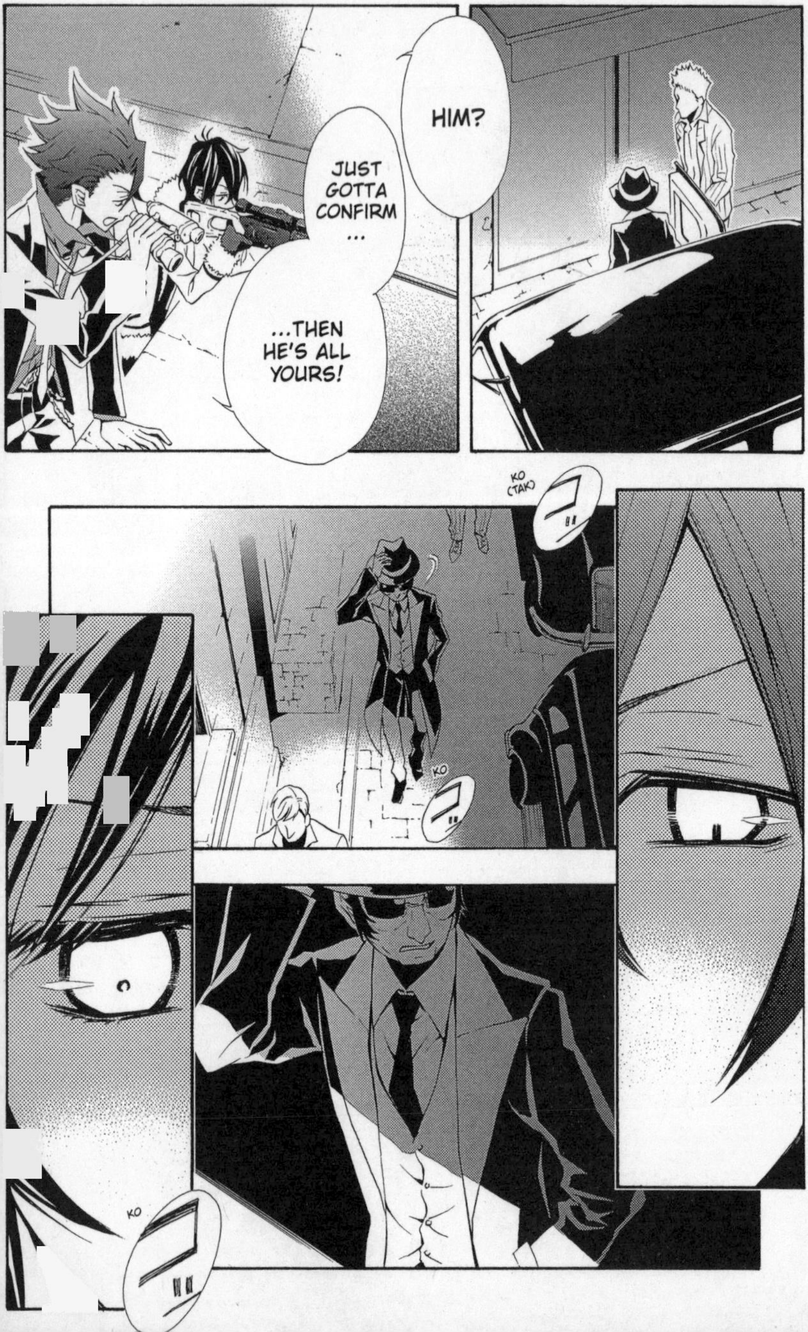
HIM?
JUST GOTTA CONFIRM ...
...THEN HE'S ALL YOURS!
KO (TAK)
KO
KO

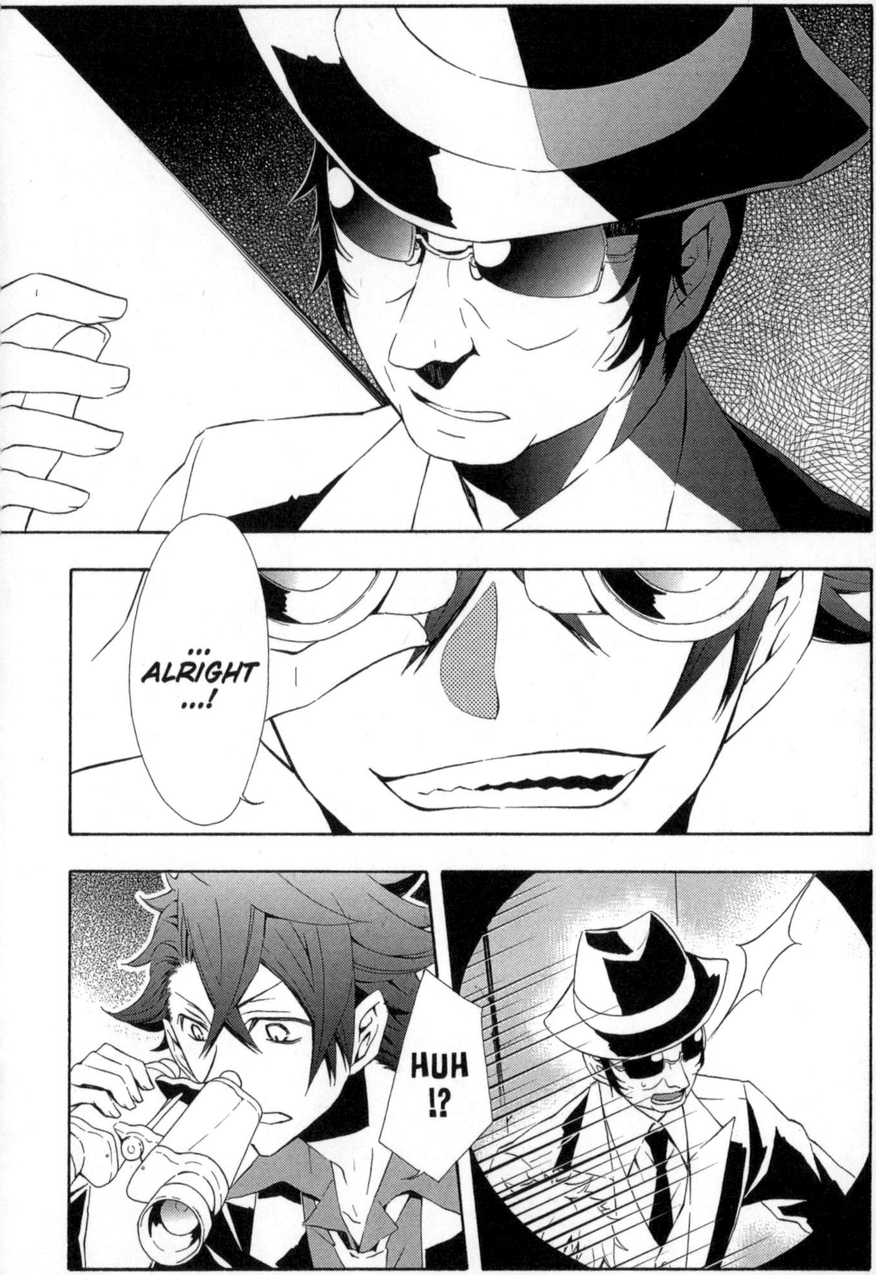
...ALRIGHT ...!
HUH !?

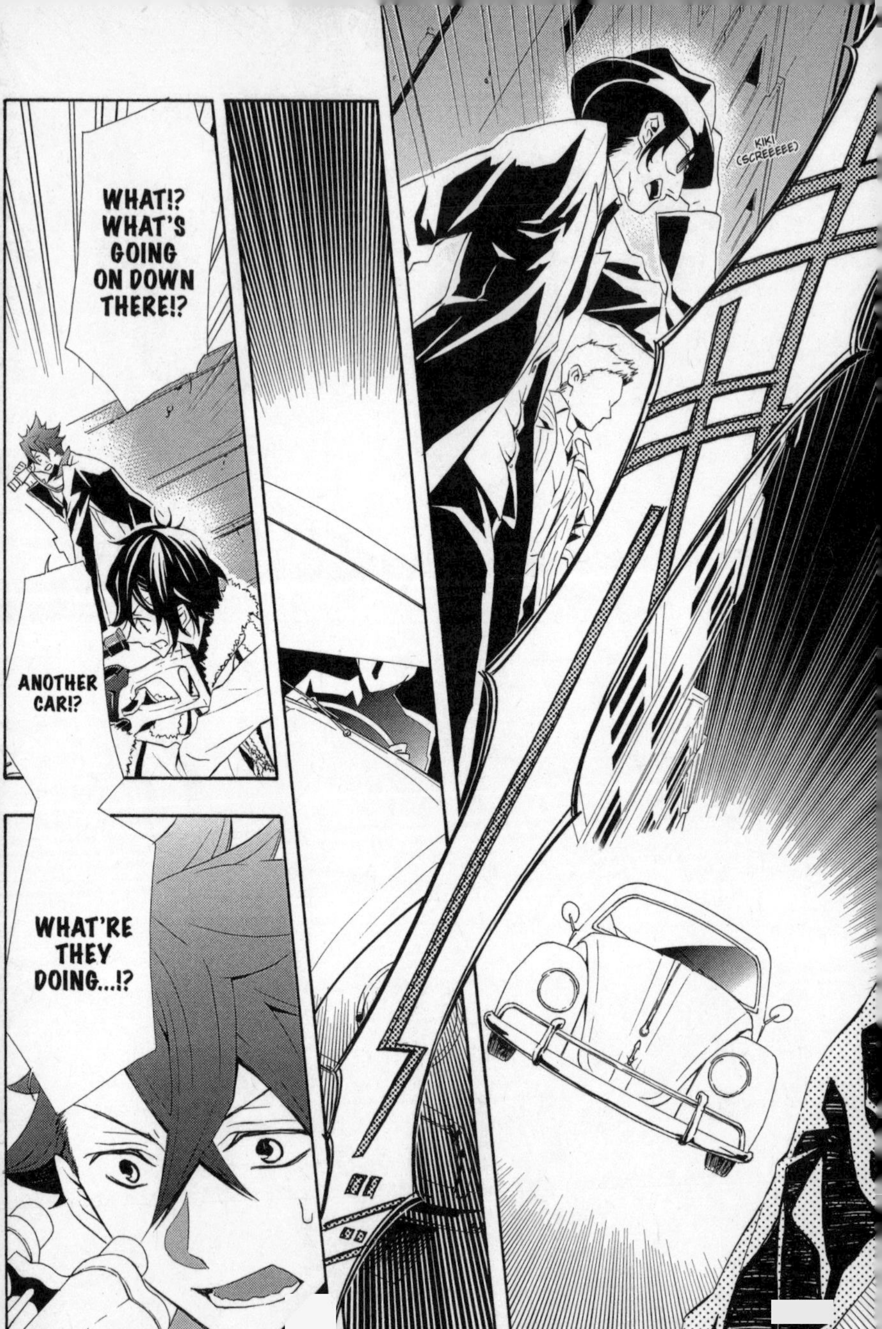
KIKI (SCREEEEE)
WHAT!? WHAT'S GOING ON DOWN THERE!?
ANOTHER CAR!?
WHAT'RE THEY DOING...!?

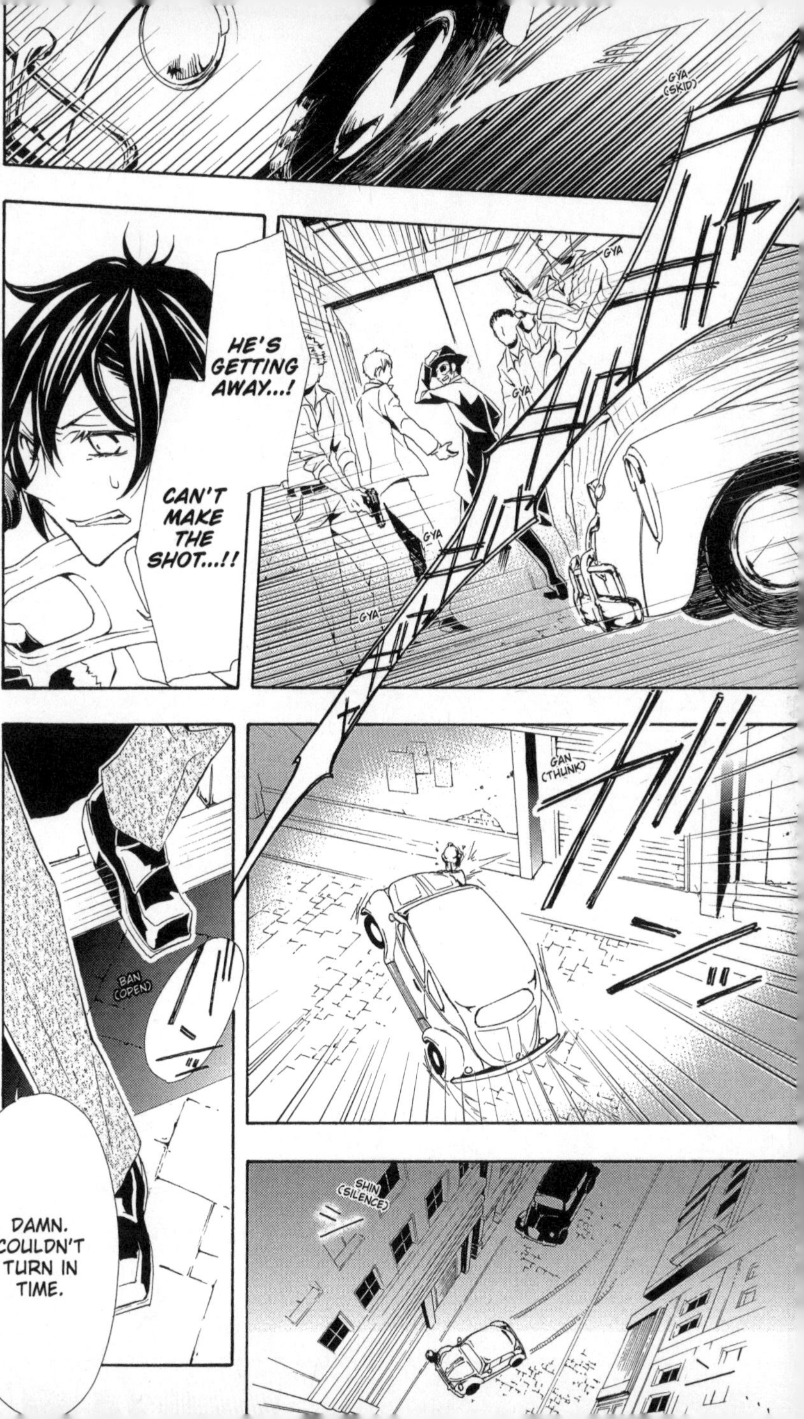
GYA (SKID)
GYA
GYA
GYA
GYA
HE'S GETTING AWAY...!
CAN'T MAKE THE SHOT...!!
GAN (THUNK)
SHIN (SILENCE)
BAN (OPEN)
DAMN. COULDN'T TURN IN TIME.

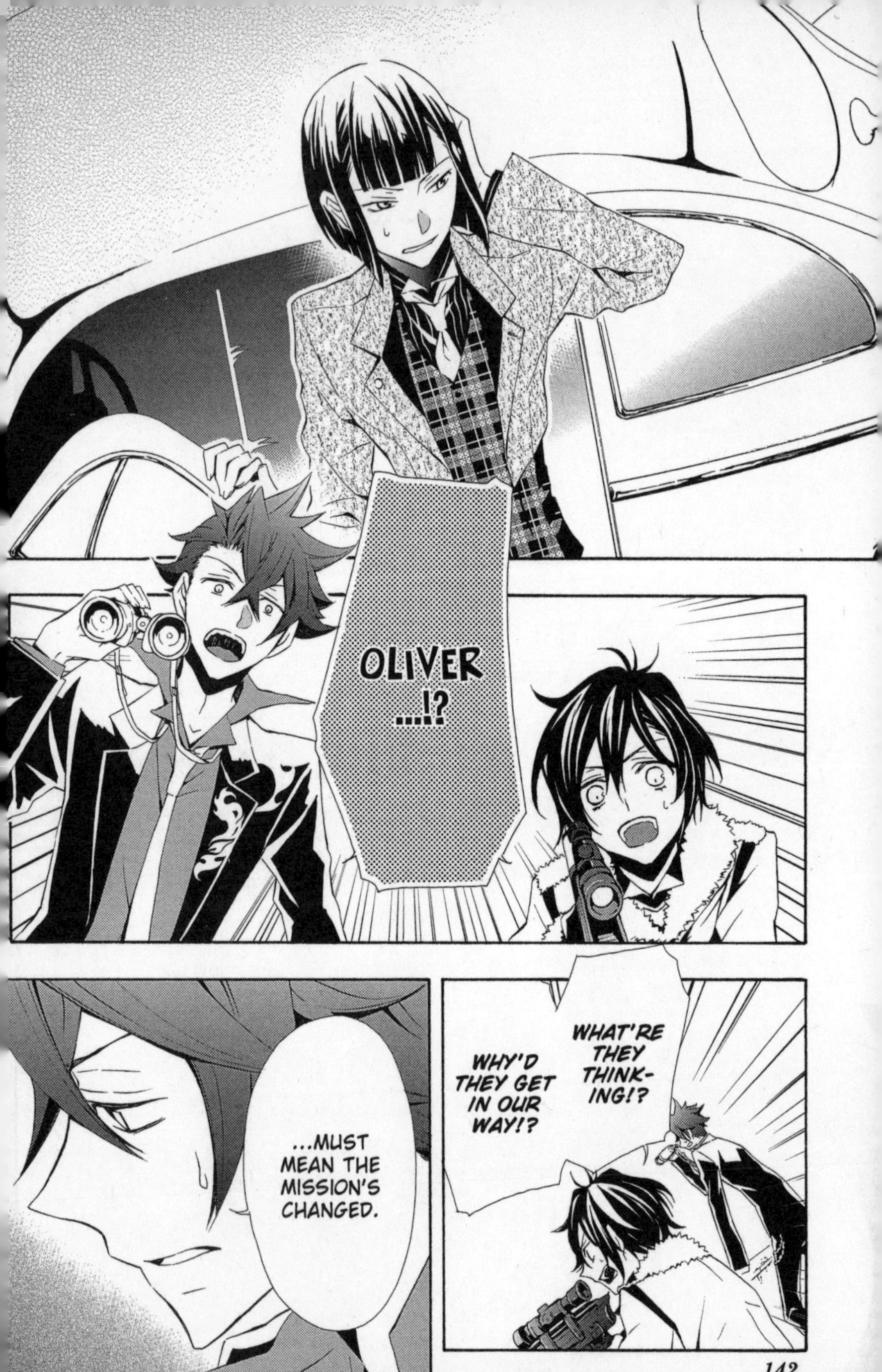
OLIVER ...!?
WHAT'RE THEY THINKING!?
WHY'D THEY GET IN OUR WAY!?
...MUST MEAN THE MISSION'S CHANGED.

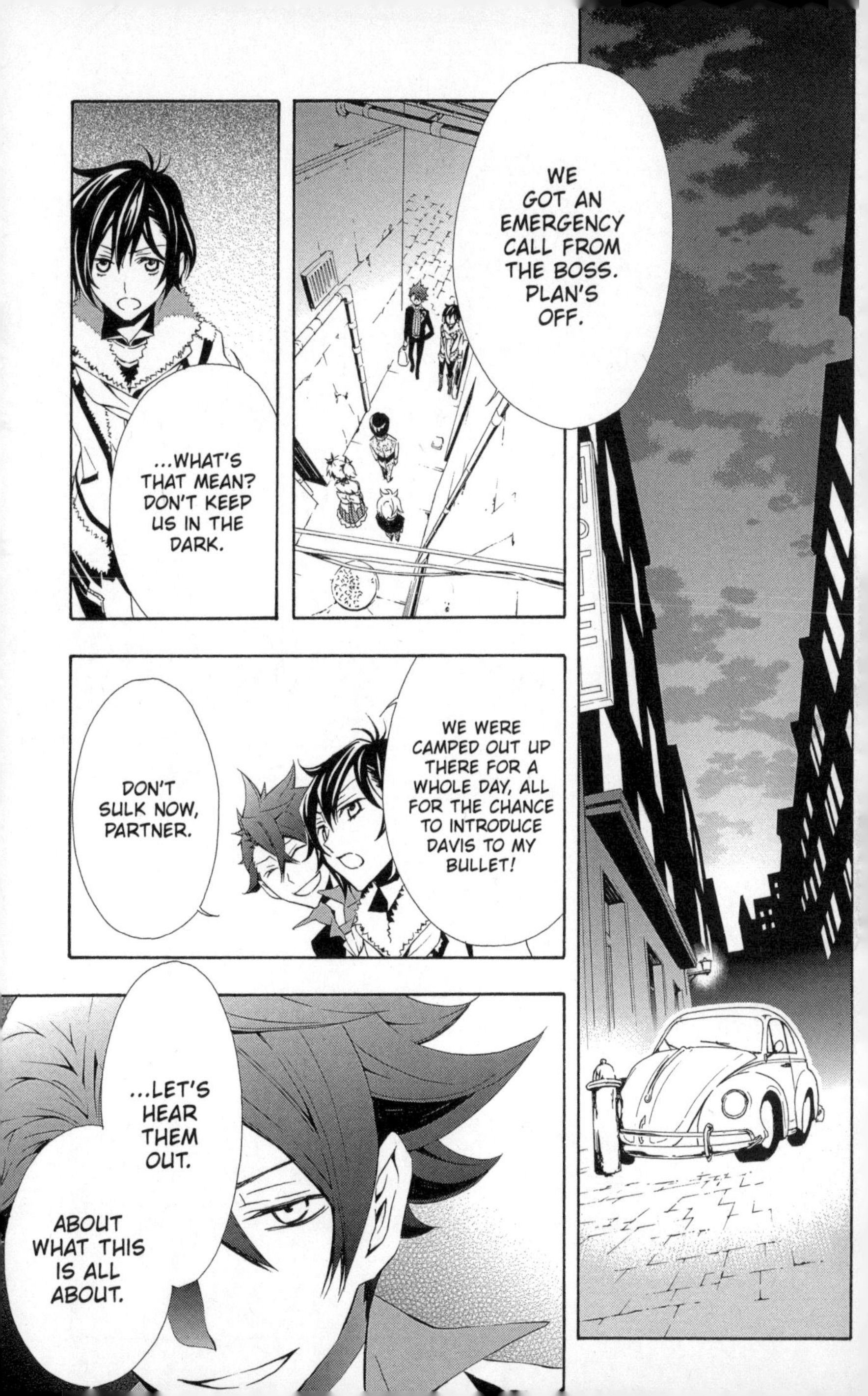
WE GOT AN EMERGENCY CALL FROM THE BOSS. PLAN'S OFF.
...WHAT'S THAT MEAN? DON'T KEEP US IN THE DARK.
WE WERE CAMPED OUT UP THERE FOR A WHOLE DAY, ALL FOR THE CHANCE TO INTRODUCE DAVIS TO MY BULLET!
DON'T SULK NOW, PARTNER.
...LET'S HEAR THEM OUT.
ABOUT WHAT THIS IS ALL ABOUT.

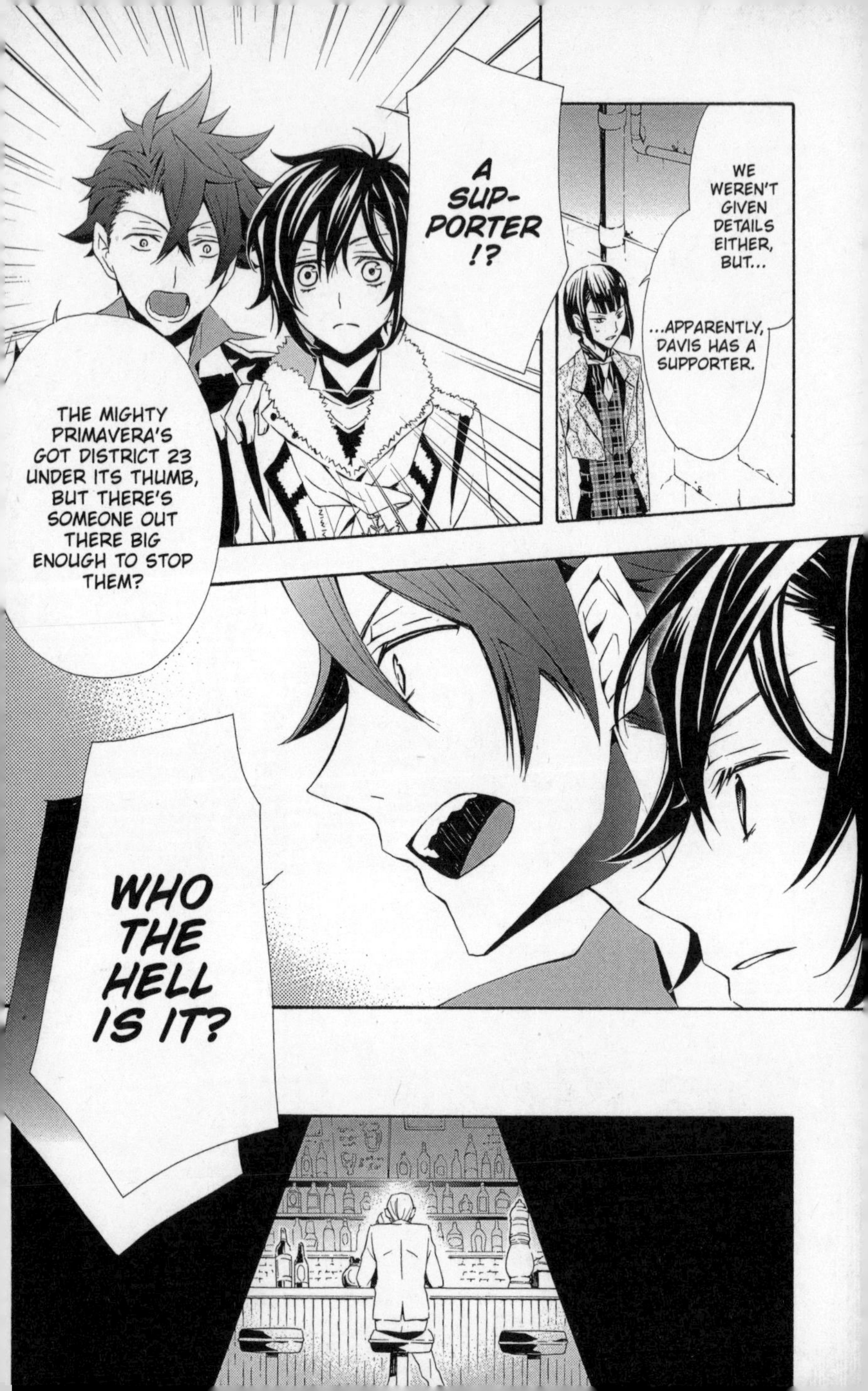
WE WEREN'T GIVEN DETAILS EITHER, BUT...
...APPARENTLY, DAVIS HAS A SUPPORTER.
A SUP-PORTER!?
THE MIGHTY PRIMAVERA'S GOT DISTRICT 23 UNDER ITS THUMB, BUT THERE'S SOMEONE OUT THERE BIG ENOUGH TO STOP THEM?
WHO THE HELL IS IT?

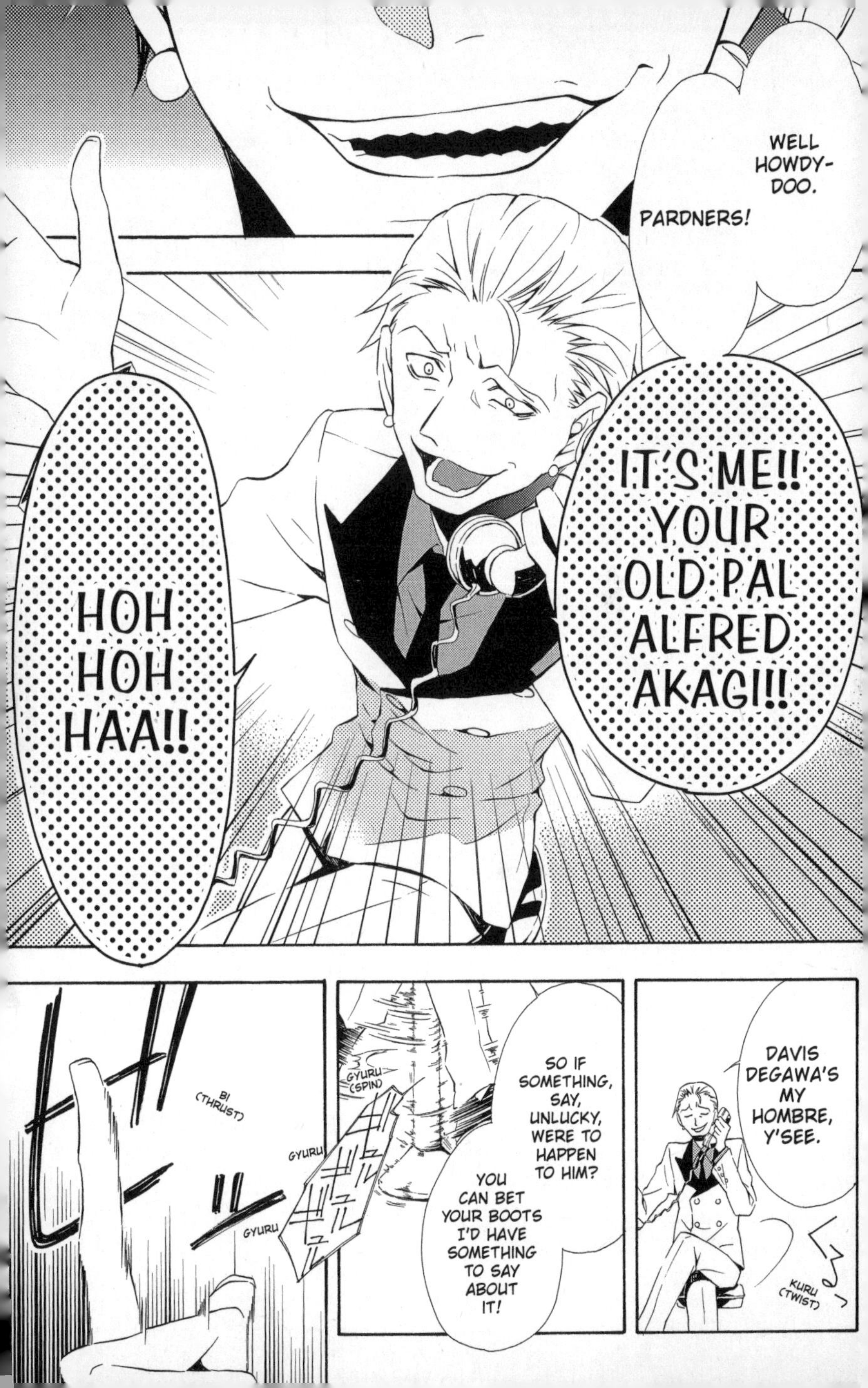
WELL HOWDY-DOO.
PARDNERS!
IT'S ME!! YOUR OLD PAL ALFRED AKAGI!!
HOH HOH HAA!!
DAVIS DEGAWA'S MY HOMBRE, Y'SEE.
KURU (TWIST)
SO IF SOMETHING, SAY, UNLUCKY, WERE TO HAPPEN TO HIM?
YOU CAN BET YOUR BOOTS I'D HAVE SOMETHING TO SAY ABOUT IT!
GYURU (SPIN)
GYURU
GYURU
BI (THRUST)

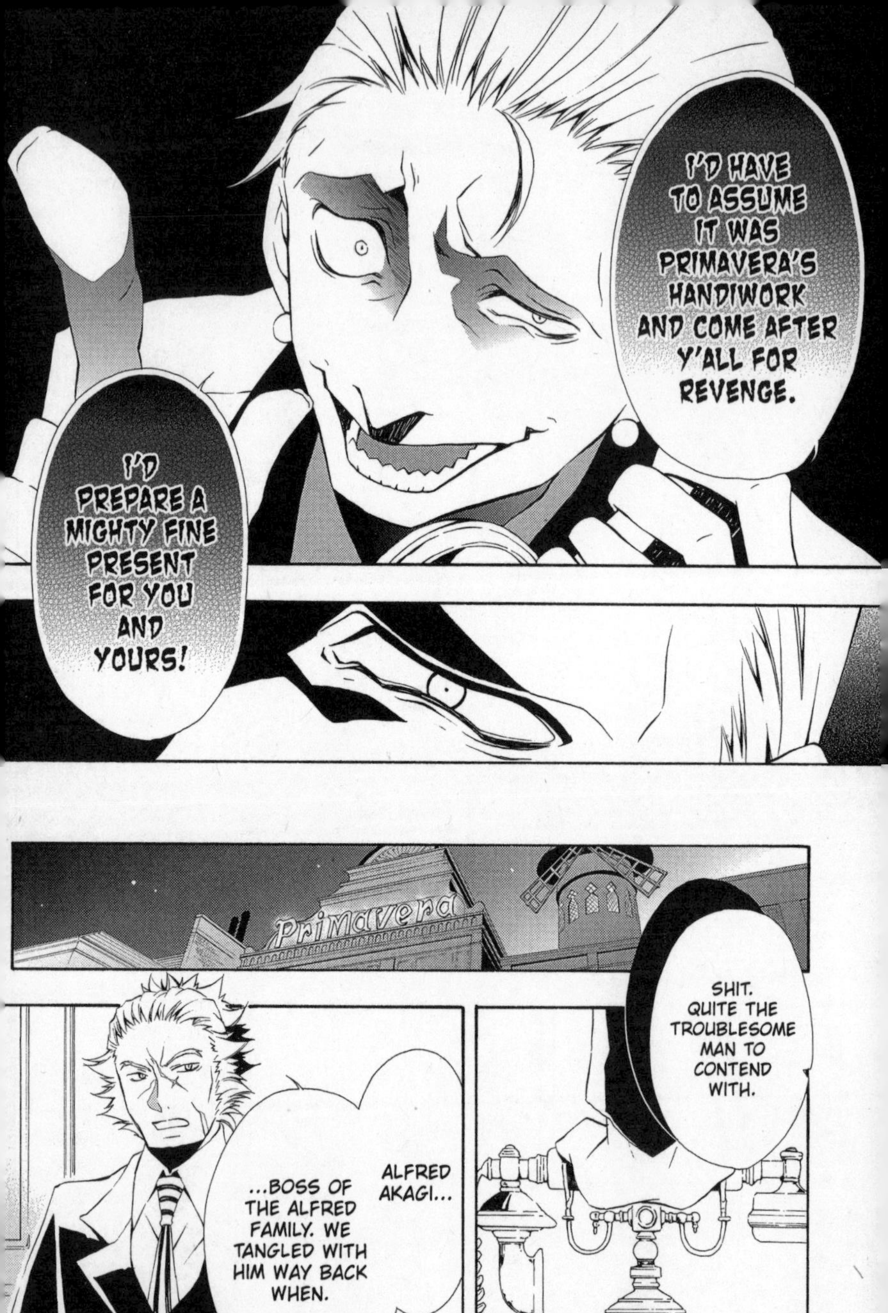
I'D HAVE TO ASSUME IT WAS PRIMAVERA'S HANDIWORK AND COME AFTER Y'ALL FOR REVENGE.
I'D PREPARE A MIGHTY FINE PRESENT FOR YOU AND YOURS!
Primavera
SHIT. QUITE THE TROUBLESOME MAN TO CONTEND WITH.
ALFRED AKAGI...
...BOSS OF THE ALFRED FAMILY. WE TANGLED WITH HIM WAY BACK WHEN.

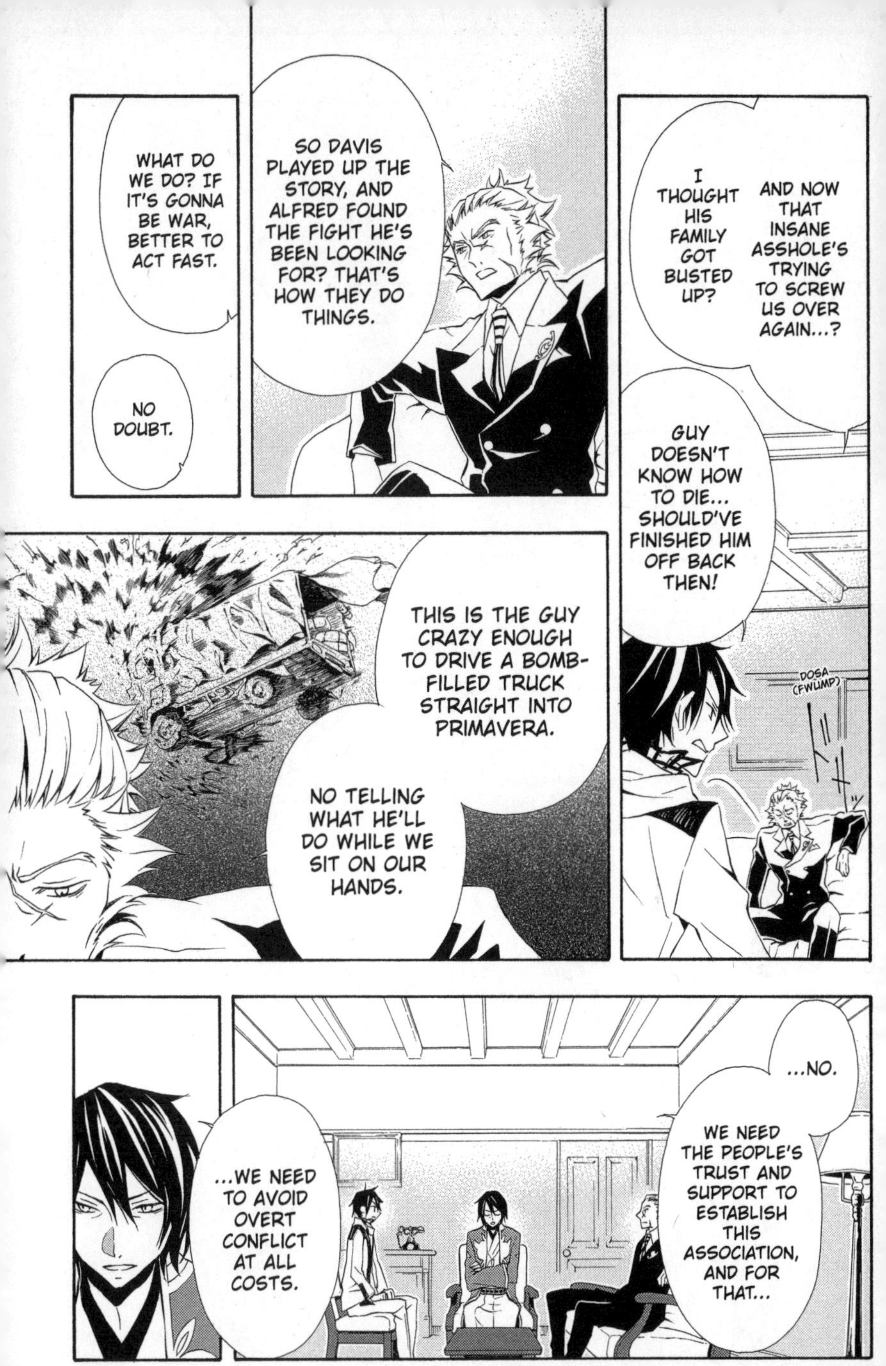

I THOUGHT HIS FAMILY GOT BUSTED UP? AND NOW THAT INSANE ASSHOLE'S TRYING TO SCREW US OVER AGAIN...?
GUY DOESN'T KNOW HOW TO DIE... SHOULD'VE FINISHED HIM OFF BACK THEN!
DOSA (FWUMP)
SO DAVIS PLAYED UP THE STORY, AND ALFRED FOUND THE FIGHT HE'S BEEN LOOKING FOR? THAT'S HOW THEY DO THINGS.
WHAT DO WE DO? IF IT'S GONNA BE WAR, BETTER TO ACT FAST.
NO DOUBT.
THIS IS THE GUY CRAZY ENOUGH TO DRIVE A BOMB-FILLED TRUCK STRAIGHT INTO PRIMAVERA.
NO TELLING WHAT HE'LL DO WHILE WE SIT ON OUR HANDS.
...NO.
WE NEED THE PEOPLE'S TRUST AND SUPPORT TO ESTABLISH THIS ASSOCIATION, AND FOR THAT...
...WE NEED TO AVOID OVERT CONFLICT AT ALL COSTS.

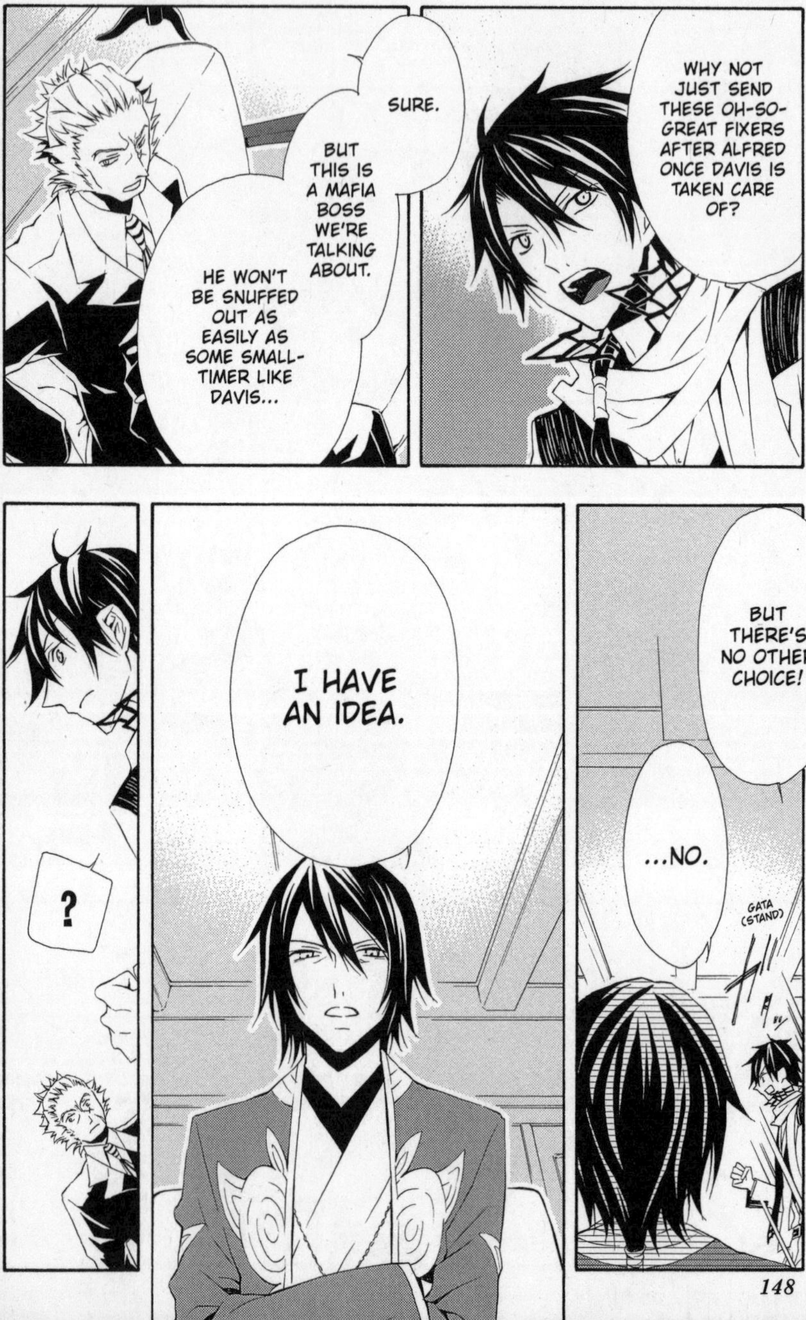
WHY NOT JUST SEND THESE OH-SO-GREAT FIXERS AFTER ALFRED ONCE DAVIS IS TAKEN CARE OF?
SURE.
BUT THIS IS A MAFIA BOSS WE'RE TALKING ABOUT.
HE WON'T BE SNUFFED OUT AS EASILY AS SOME SMALL-TIMER LIKE DAVIS...
BUT THERE'S NO OTHER CHOICE!
...NO.
GATA (STAND)
I HAVE AN IDEA.
?

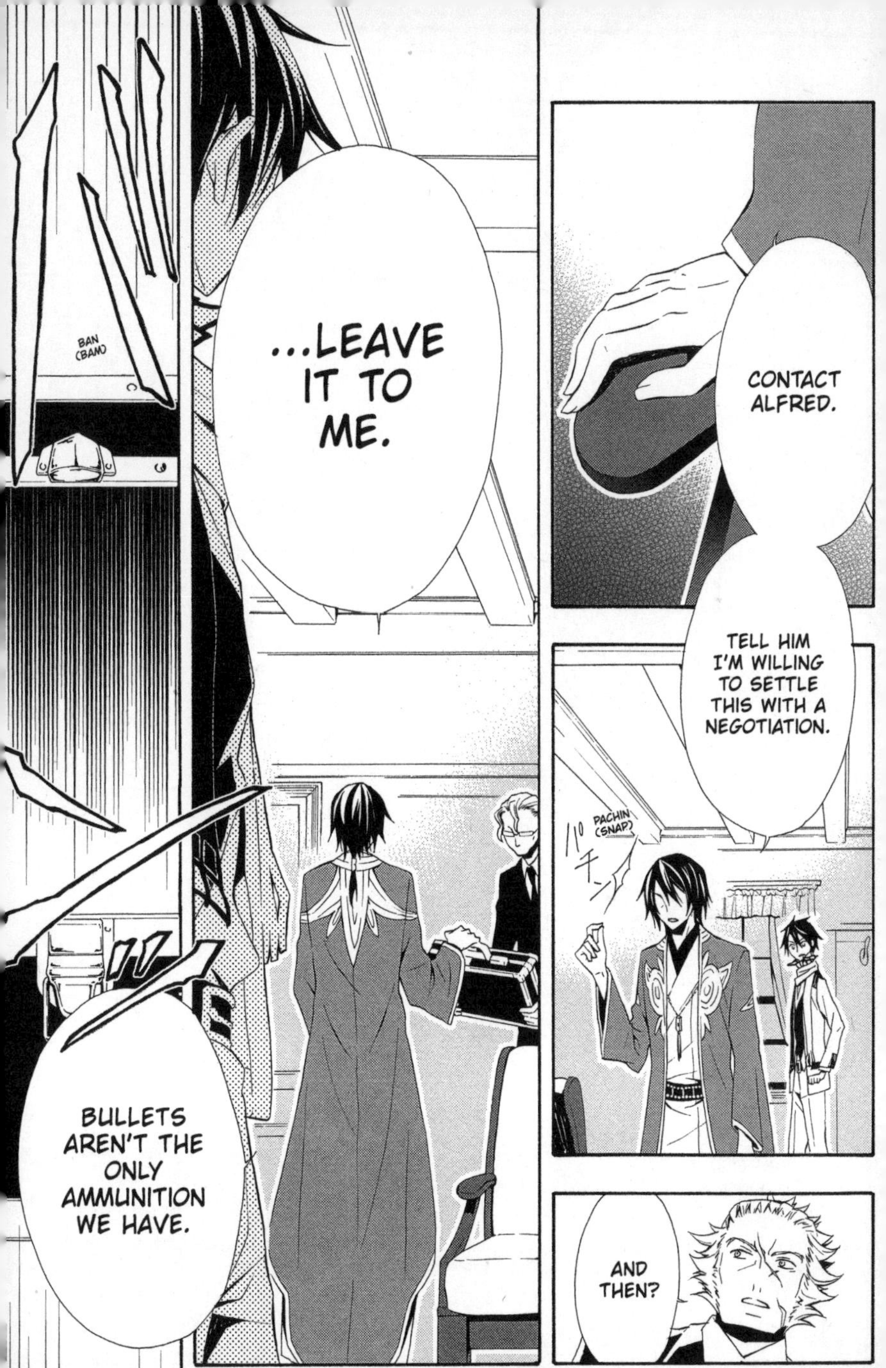

CONTACT ALFRED.
TELL HIM I'M WILLING TO SETTLE THIS WITH A NEGOTIATION.
PACHIN (SNAP)
AND THEN?
BAN (BAM)
...LEAVE IT TO ME.
BULLETS AREN'T THE ONLY AMMUNITION WE HAVE.

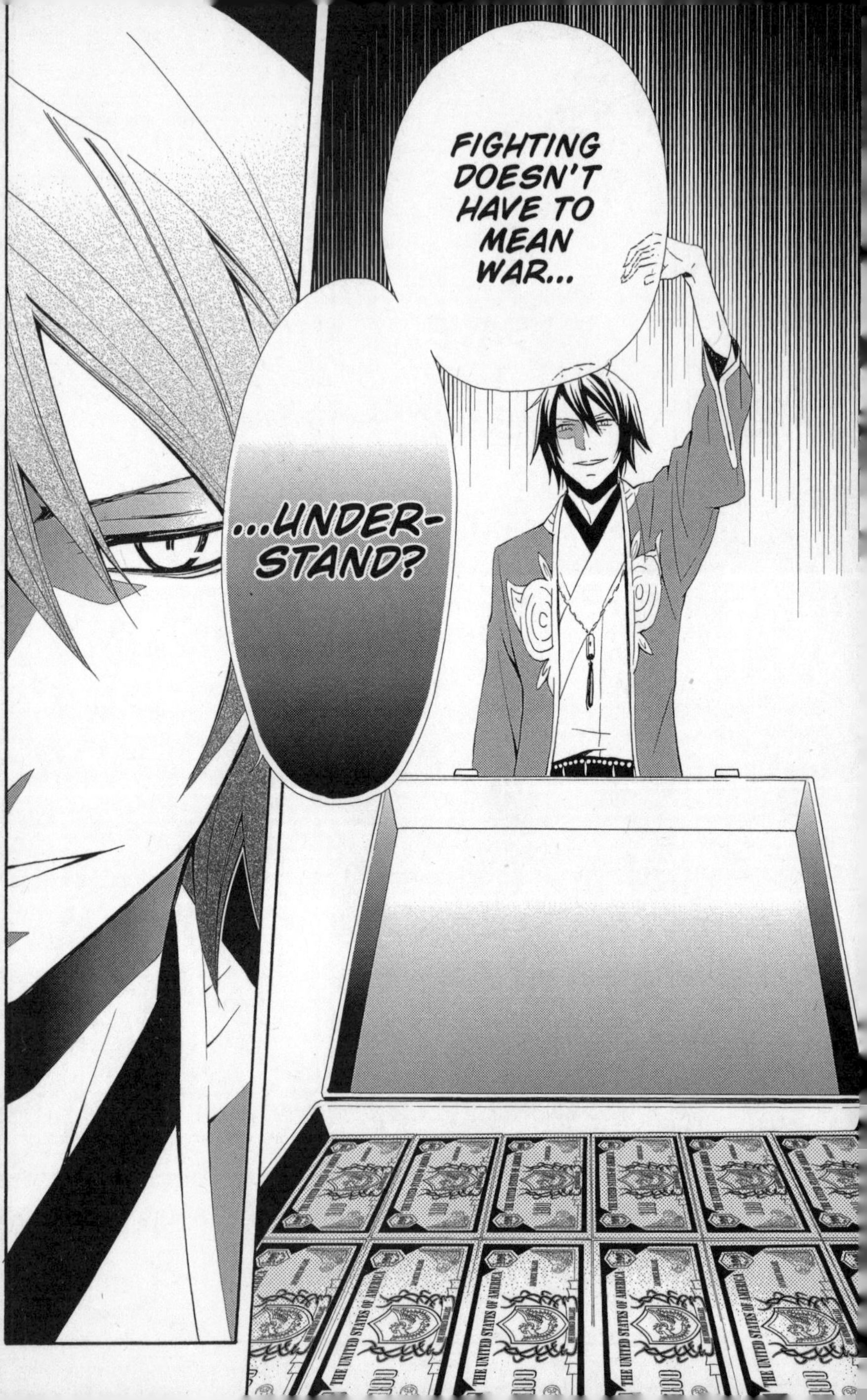
FIGHTING DOESN'T HAVE TO MEAN WAR...
...UNDER-STAND?

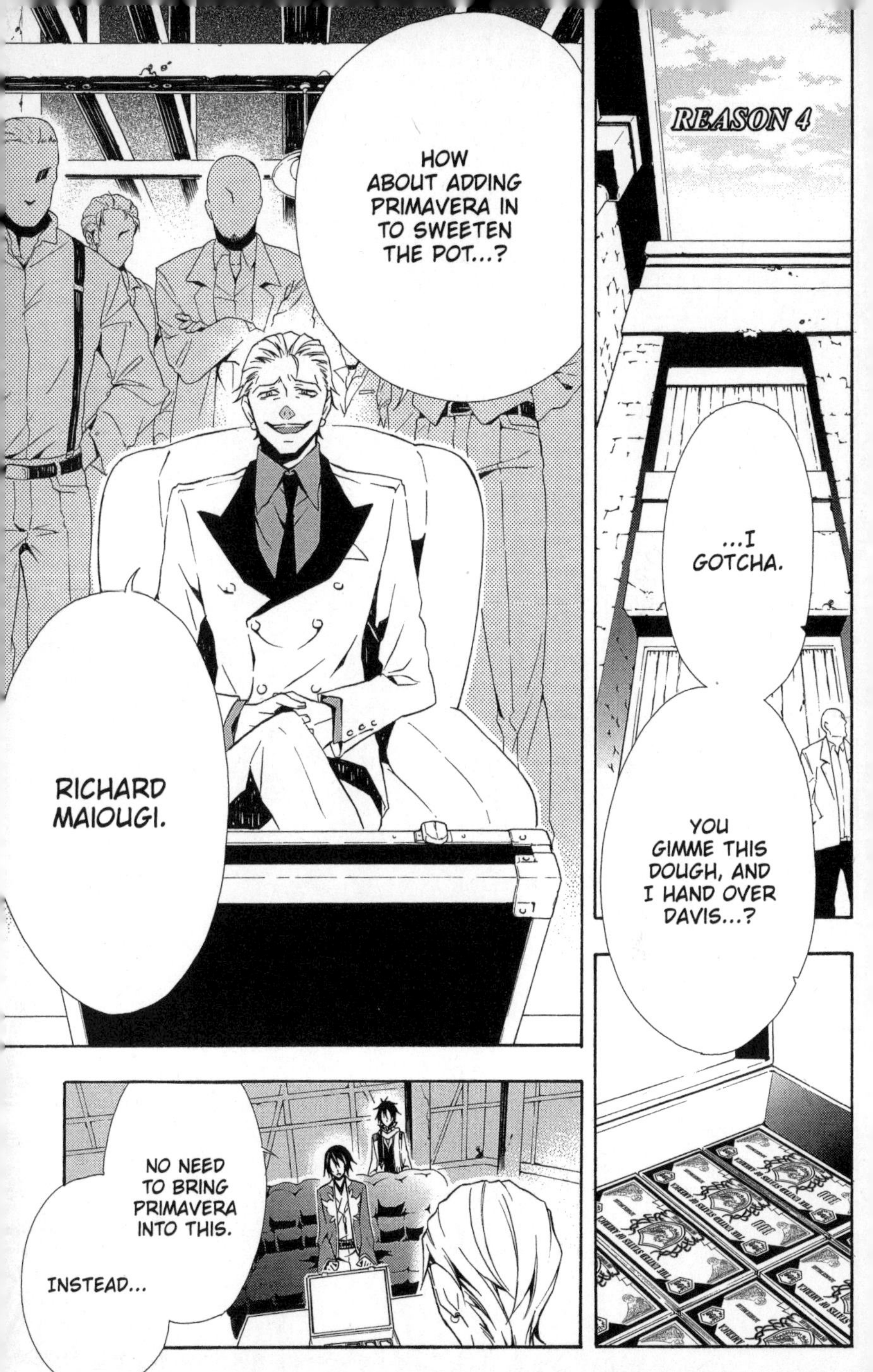
REASON 4
...I GOTCHA.
YOU GIMME THIS DOUGH, AND I HAND OVER DAVIS...?
HOW ABOUT ADDING PRIMAVERA IN TO SWEETEN THE POT...?
RICHARD MAIOUGI.
NO NEED TO BRING PRIMAVERA INTO THIS.
INSTEAD...

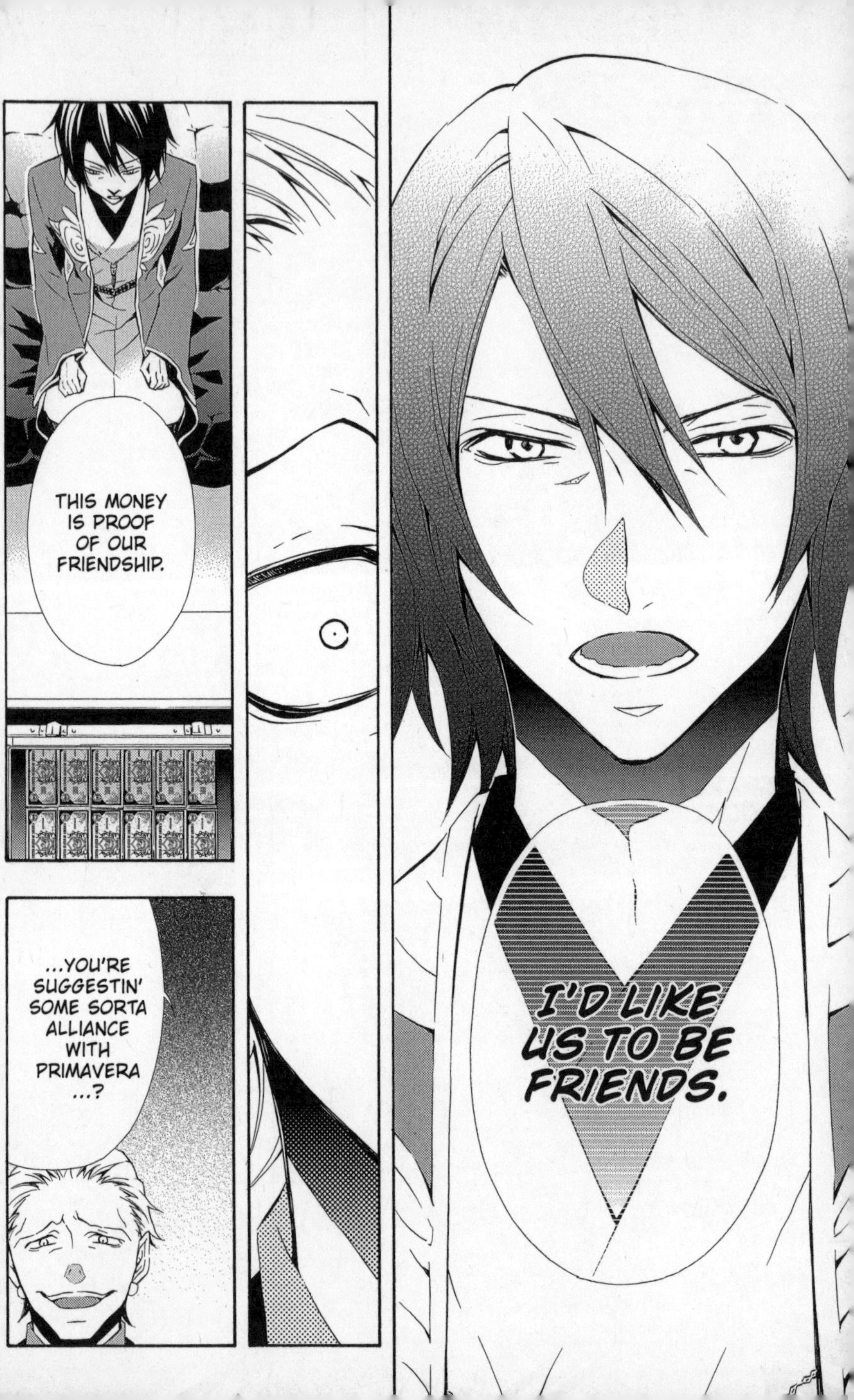
I'D LIKE US TO BE FRIENDS.
THIS MONEY IS PROOF OF OUR FRIENDSHIP.
...YOU'RE SUGGESTIN' SOME SORTA ALLIANCE WITH PRIMAVERA ...?

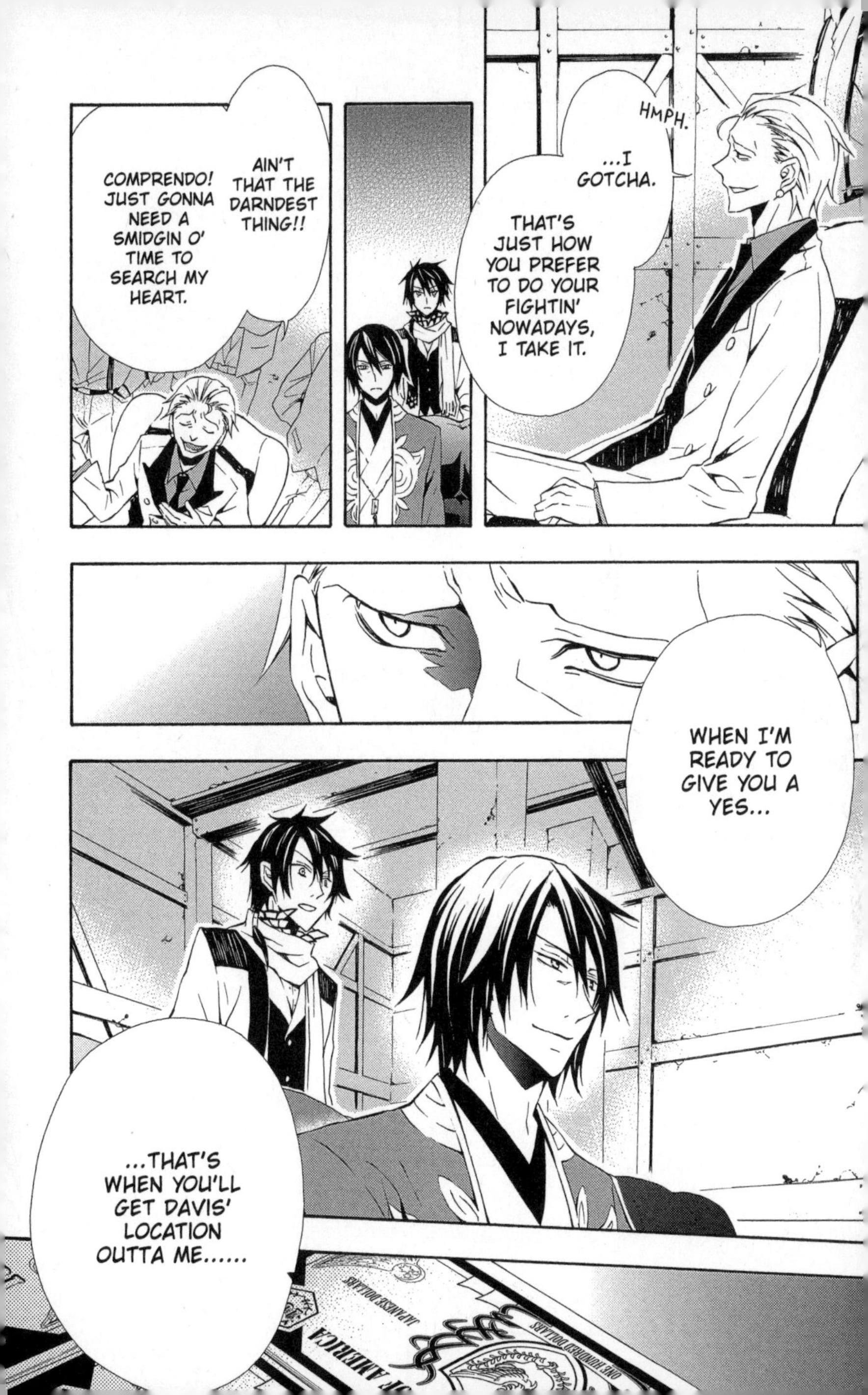
HMPH.
...I GOTCHA.
THAT'S JUST HOW YOU PREFER TO DO YOUR FIGHTIN' NOWADAYS, I TAKE IT.
AIN'T THAT THE DARNDEST THING!!
COMPRENDO! JUST GONNA NEED A SMIDGIN O' TIME TO SEARCH MY HEART.
WHEN I'M READY TO GIVE YOU A YES...
...THAT'S WHEN YOU'LL GET DAVIS' LOCATION OUTTA ME......
JAPANESE DOLLARS
ONE HUNDRED DOLLARS
OF AMERICA

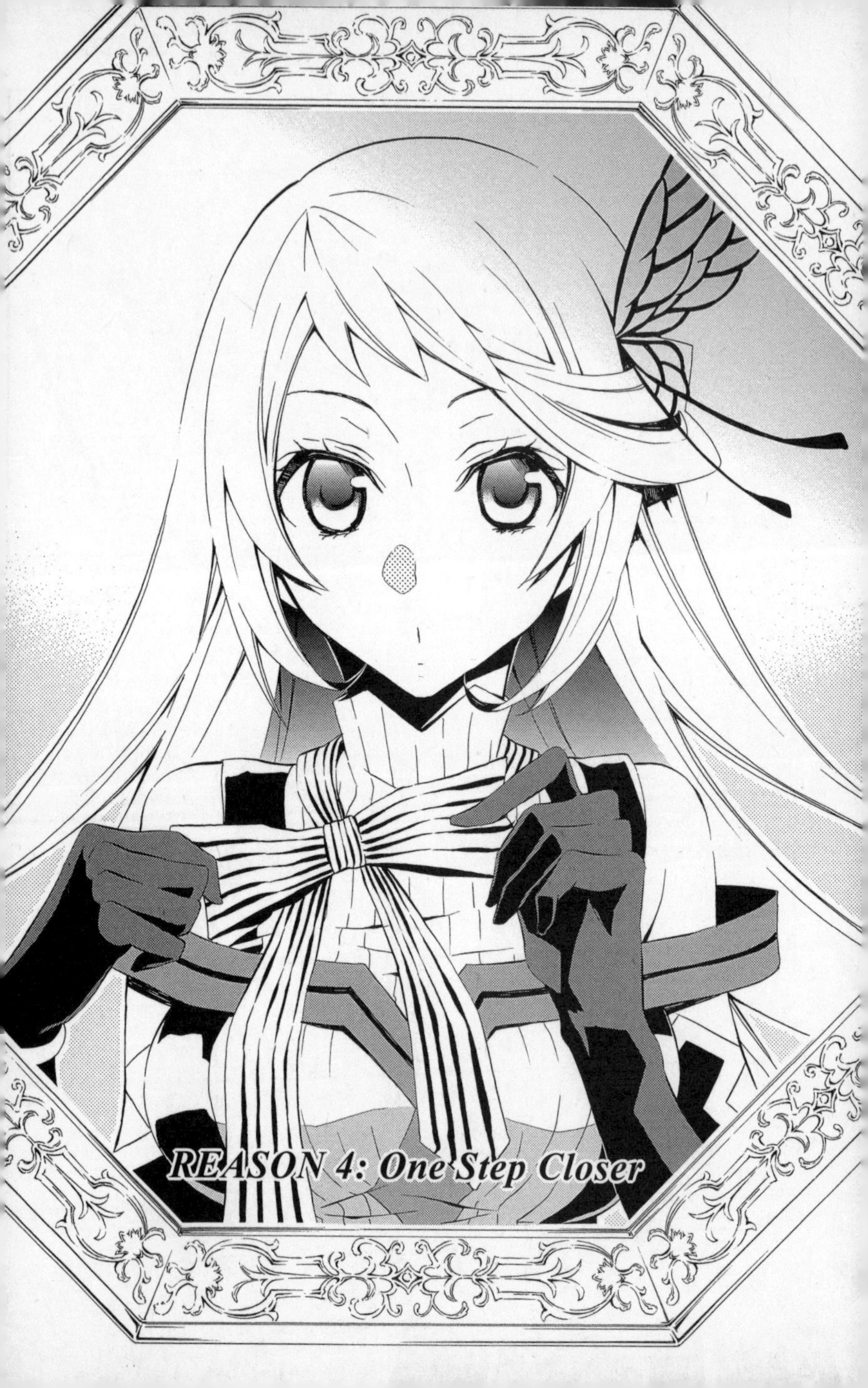
REASON 4: One Step Closer

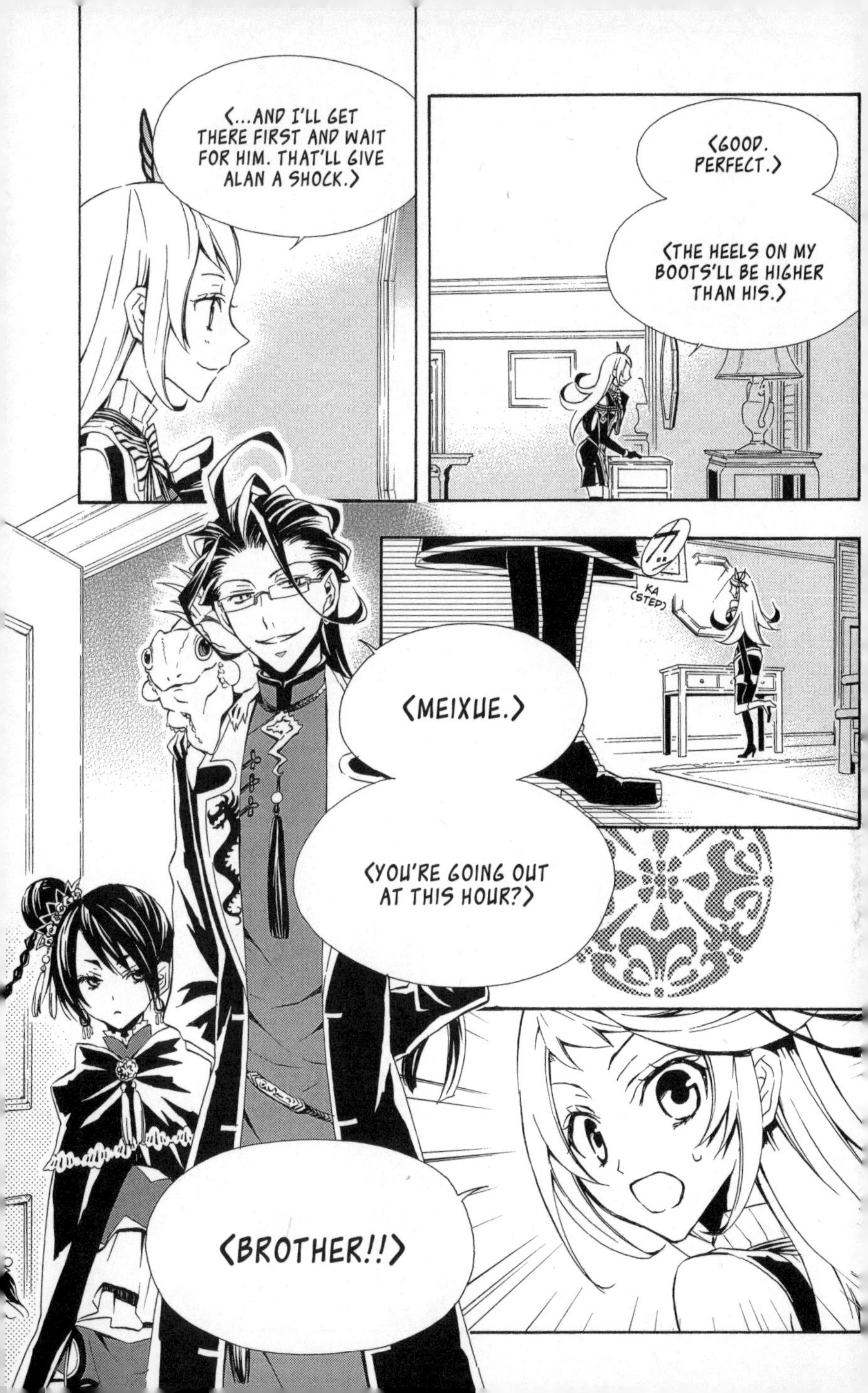
<GOOD. PERFECT.>
<THE HEELS ON MY BOOTS'LL BE HIGHER THAN HIS.>
<...AND I'LL GET THERE FIRST AND WAIT FOR HIM. THAT'LL GIVE ALAN A SHOCK.>
?!
KA (STEP)
<MEIXUE.>
<YOU'RE GOING OUT AT THIS HOUR?>
<BROTHER!!>

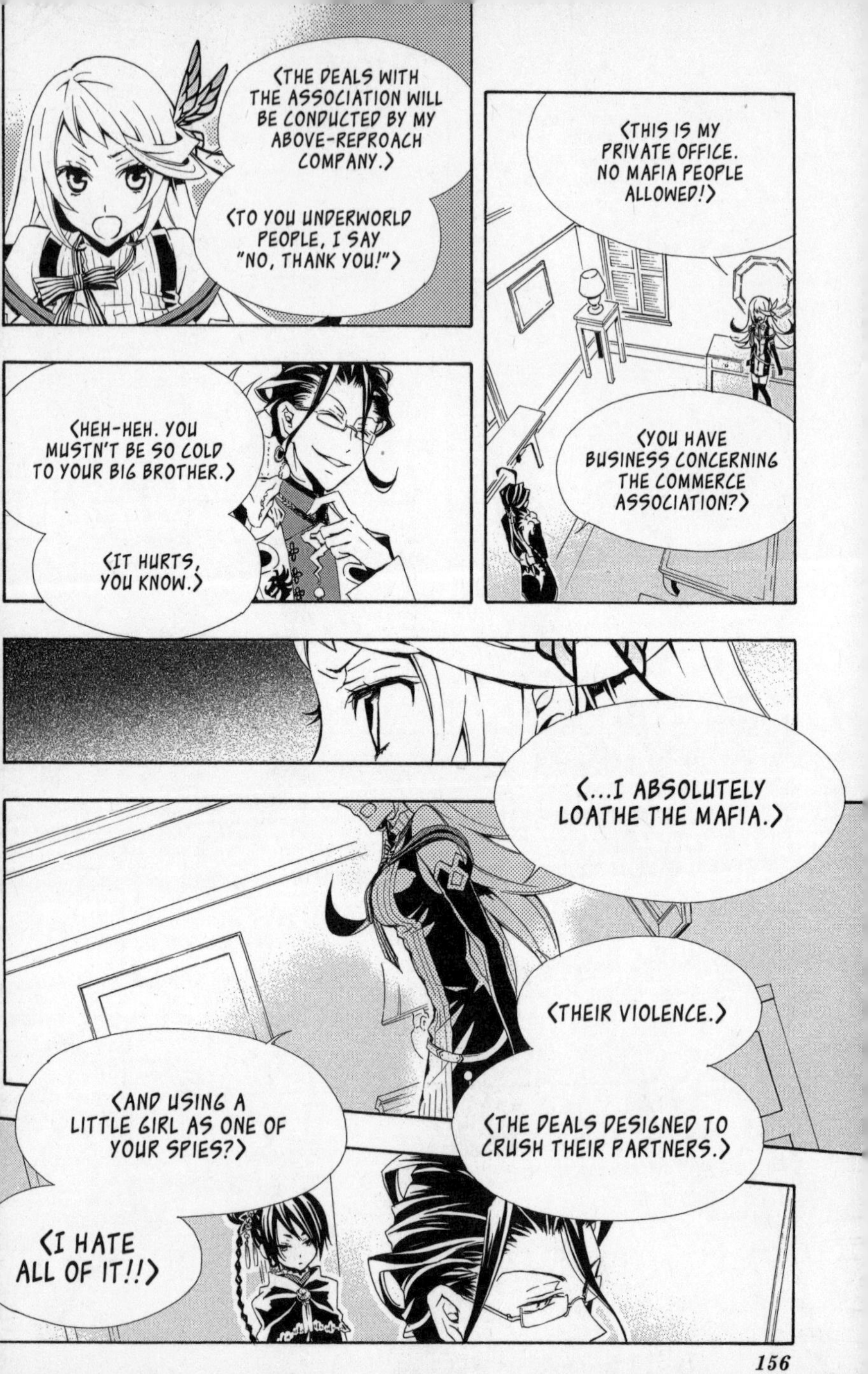
<THIS IS MY PRIVATE OFFICE. NO MAFIA PEOPLE ALLOWED!>
<YOU HAVE BUSINESS CONCERNING THE COMMERCE ASSOCIATION?>
<THE DEALS WITH THE ASSOCIATION WILL BE CONDUCTED BY MY ABOVE-REPROACH COMPANY.>
<TO YOU UNDERWORLD PEOPLE, I SAY "NO, THANK YOU!">
<HEH-HEH. YOU MUSTN'T BE SO COLD TO YOUR BIG BROTHER.>
<IT HURTS, YOU KNOW.>
<...I ABSOLUTELY LOATHE THE MAFIA.>
<THEIR VIOLENCE.>
<THE DEALS DESIGNED TO CRUSH THEIR PARTNERS.>
<AND USING A LITTLE GIRL AS ONE OF YOUR SPIES?>
<I HATE ALL OF IT!!>

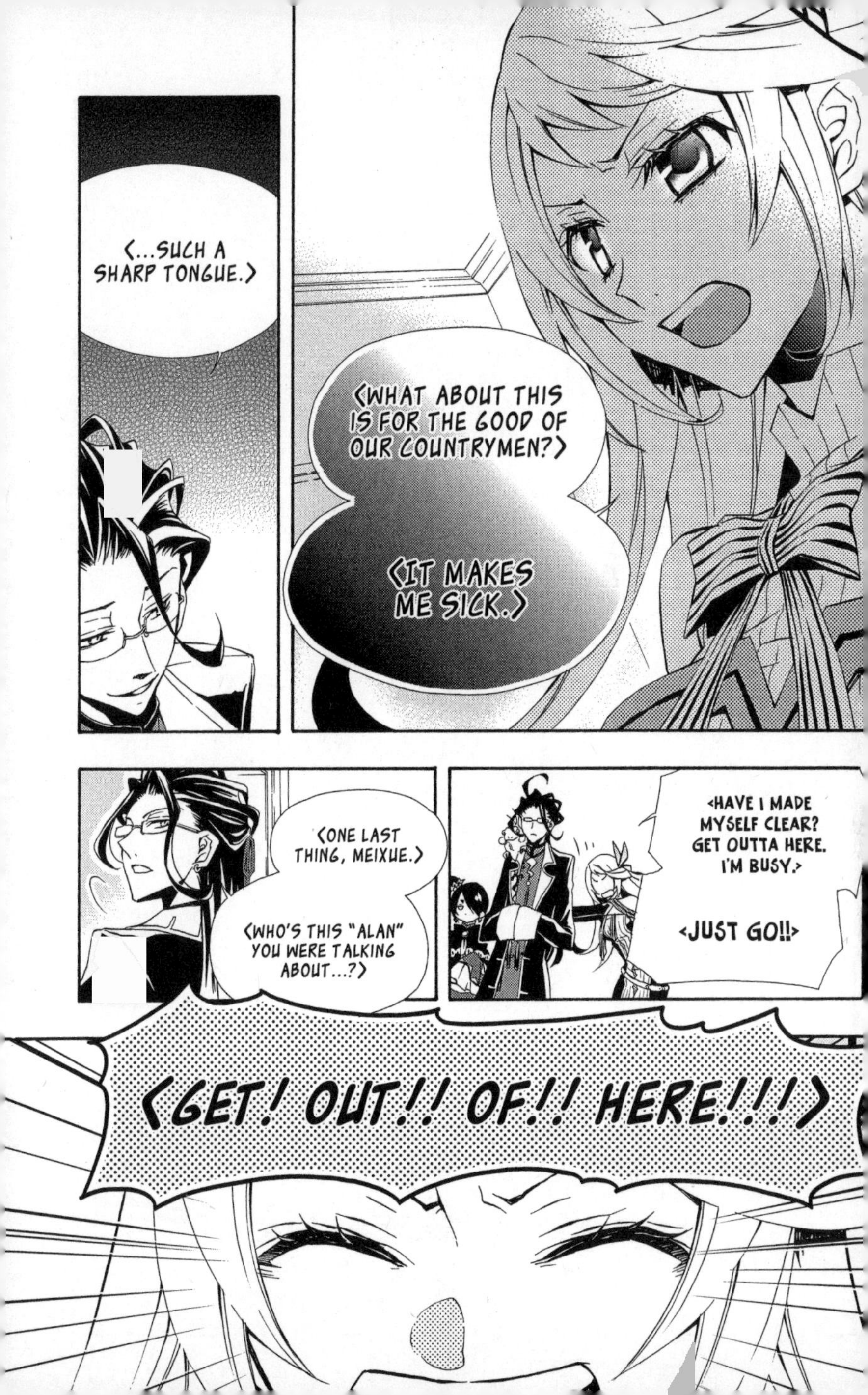
‹WHAT ABOUT THIS IS FOR THE GOOD OF OUR COUNTRYMEN?›
‹IT MAKES ME SICK.›
‹...SUCH A SHARP TONGUE.›
‹HAVE I MADE MYSELF CLEAR? GET OUTTA HERE. I'M BUSY.›
‹JUST GO!!›
‹ONE LAST THING, MEIXUE.›
‹WHO'S THIS "ALAN" YOU WERE TALKING ABOUT...?›
‹GET! OUT!! OF!! HERE!!!›

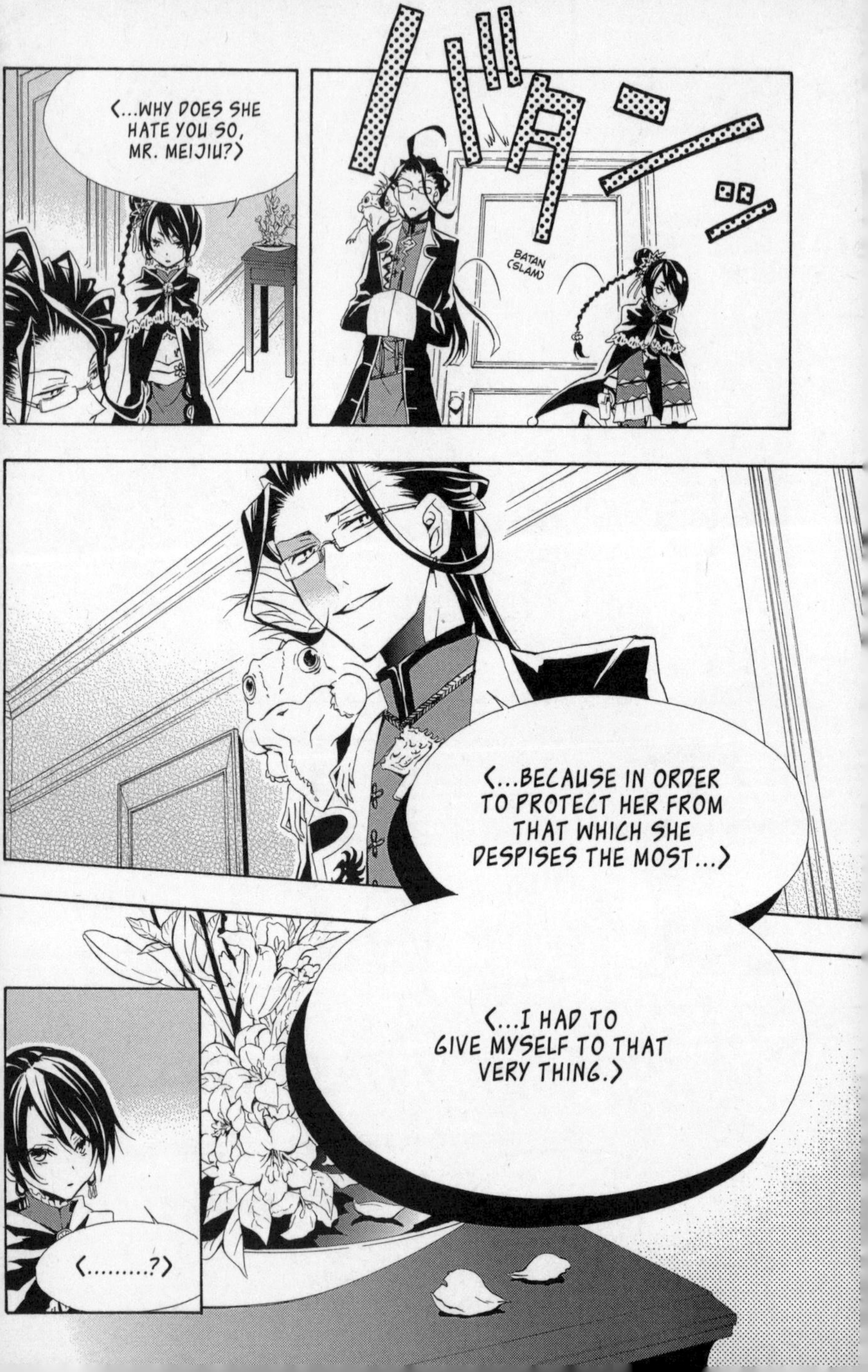

BATAN (SLAM)
〈...WHY DOES SHE HATE YOU SO, MR. MEIJIU?〉
〈...BECAUSE IN ORDER TO PROTECT HER FROM THAT WHICH SHE DESPISES THE MOST...〉
〈...I HAD TO GIVE MYSELF TO THAT VERY THING.〉
〈.........?〉

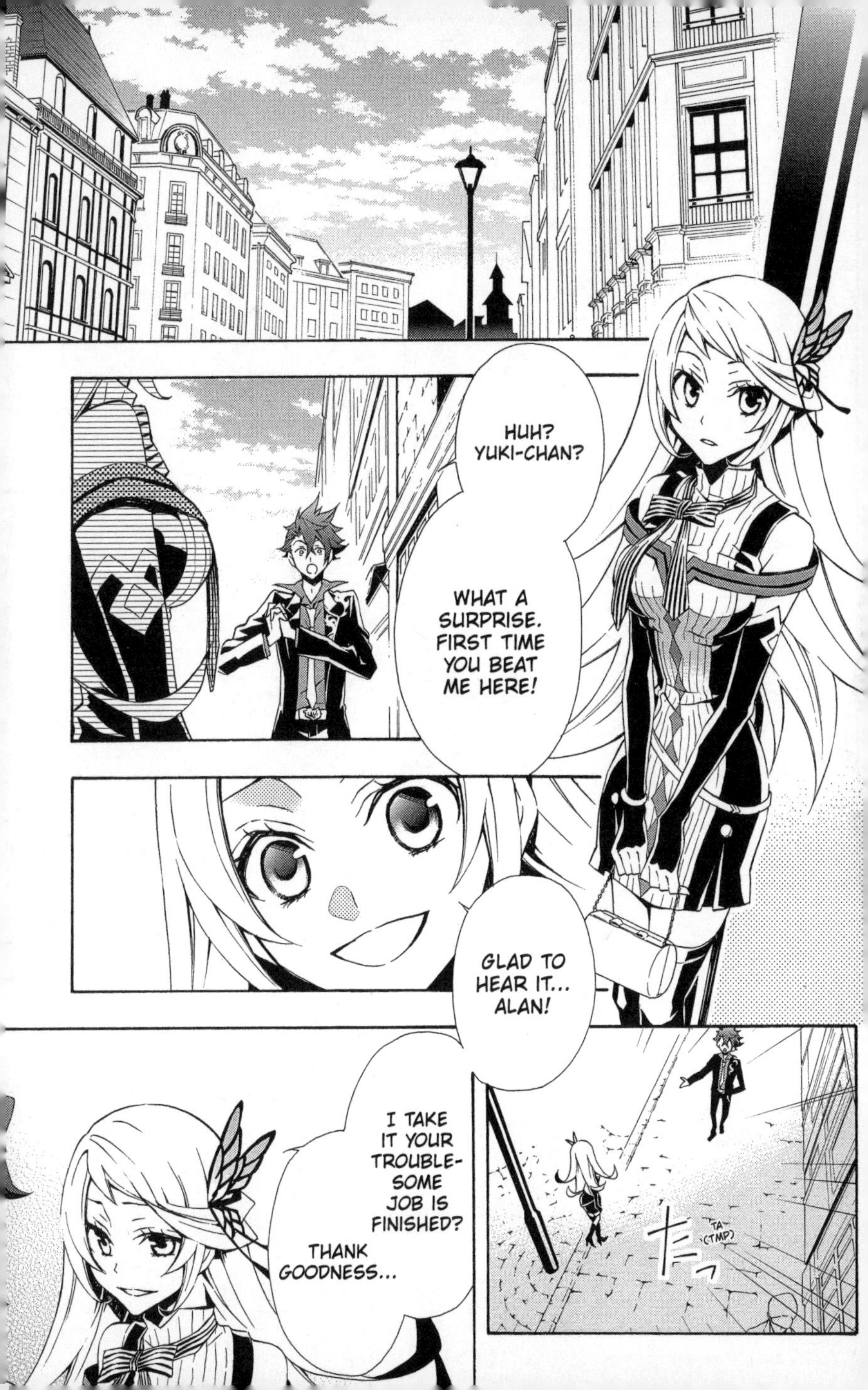
HUH? YUKI-CHAN?
WHAT A SURPRISE. FIRST TIME YOU BEAT ME HERE!
GLAD TO HEAR IT... ALAN!
TA (TMP)
I TAKE IT YOUR TROUBLE-SOME JOB IS FINISHED?
THANK GOODNESS...

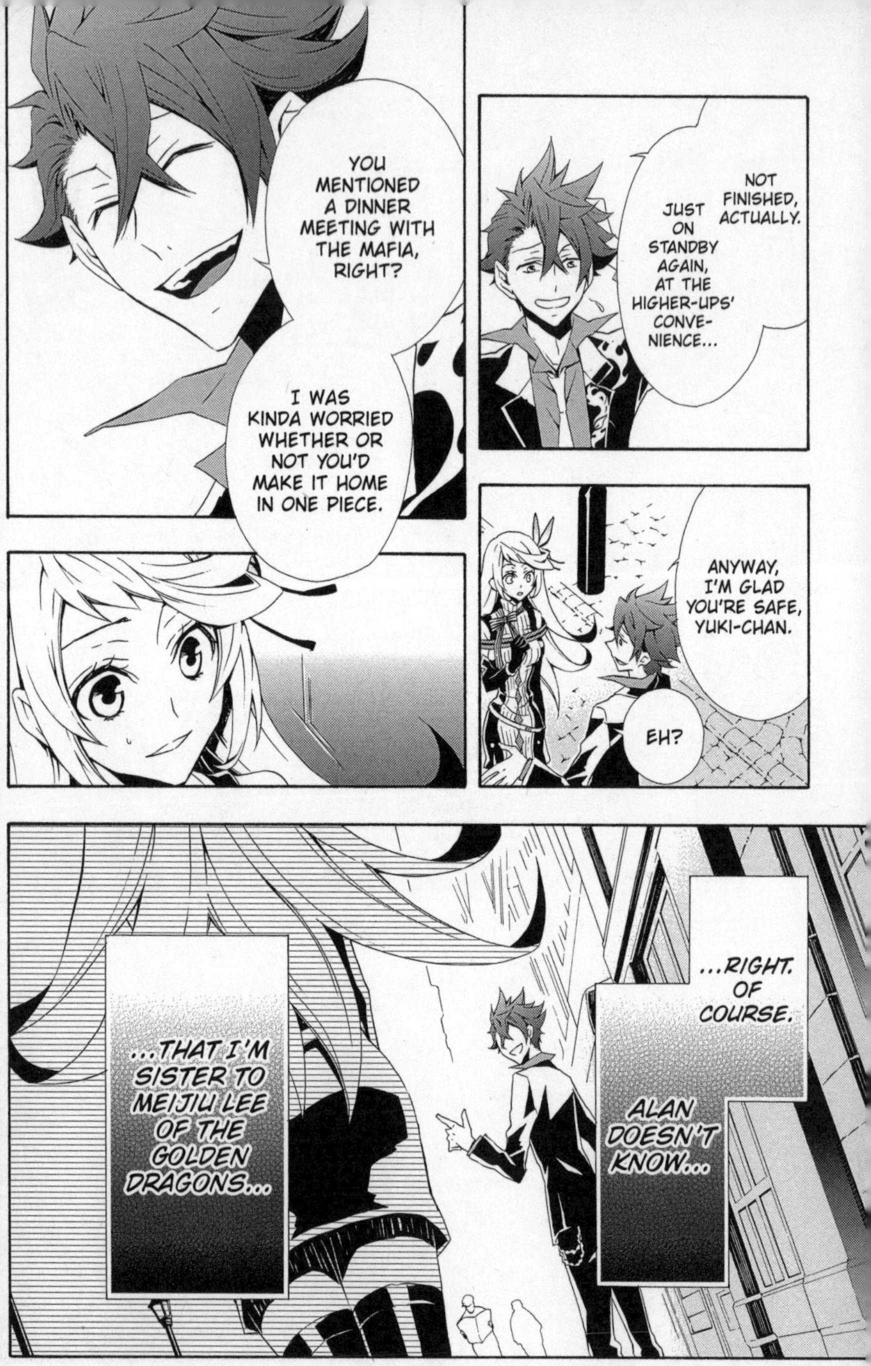
NOT FINISHED, ACTUALLY.
JUST ON STANDBY AGAIN, AT THE HIGHER-UPS' CONVE-NIENCE...
YOU MENTIONED A DINNER MEETING WITH THE MAFIA, RIGHT?
I WAS KINDA WORRIED WHETHER OR NOT YOU'D MAKE IT HOME IN ONE PIECE.
ANYWAY, I'M GLAD YOU'RE SAFE, YUKI-CHAN.
EH?
...RIGHT. OF COURSE.
ALAN DOESN'T KNOW...
...THAT I'M SISTER TO MEIJIU LEE OF THE GOLDEN DRAGONS...

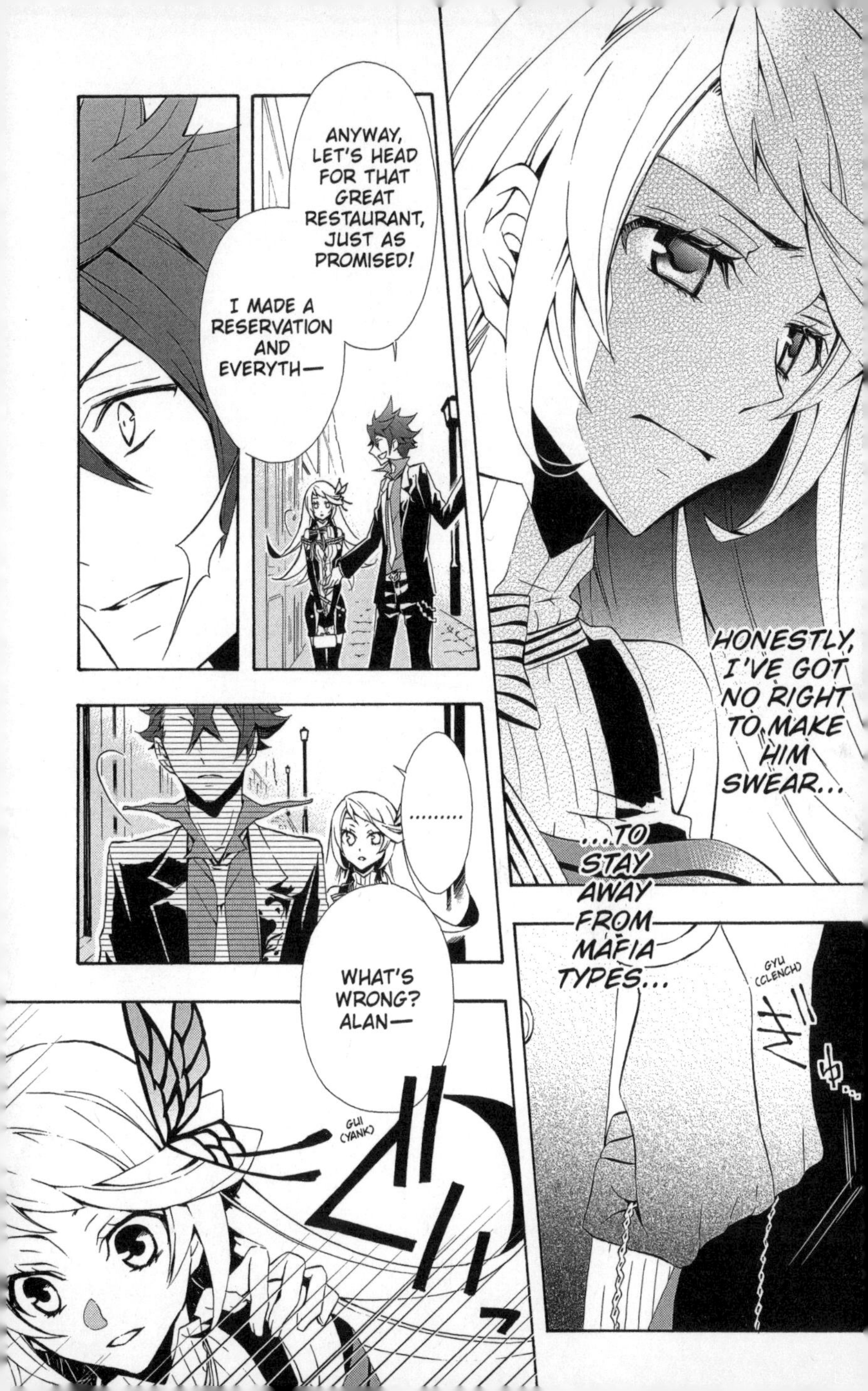
HONESTLY, I'VE GOT NO RIGHT TO MAKE HIM SWEAR...
...TO STAY AWAY FROM MAFIA TYPES...
ANYWAY, LET'S HEAD FOR THAT GREAT RESTAURANT, JUST AS PROMISED!
I MADE A RESERVATION AND EVERYTH—
....
WHAT'S WRONG? ALAN—
GYU (CLENCH)
GUI (YANK)

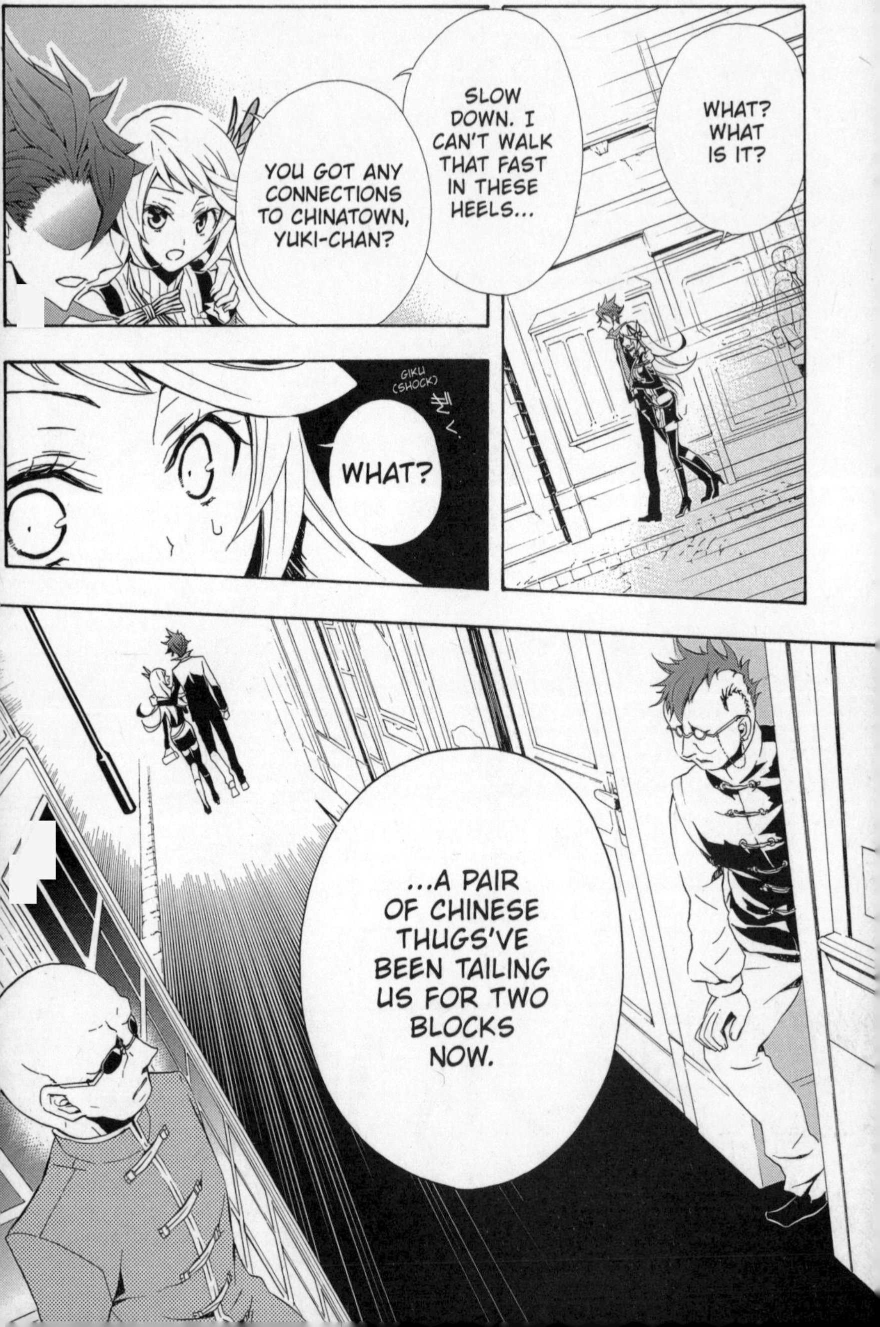
WHAT? WHAT IS IT?
SLOW DOWN. I CAN'T WALK THAT FAST IN THESE HEELS...
YOU GOT ANY CONNECTIONS TO CHINATOWN, YUKI-CHAN?
GIKU (SHOCK)
WHAT?
...A PAIR OF CHINESE THUGS'VE BEEN TAILING US FOR TWO BLOCKS NOW.

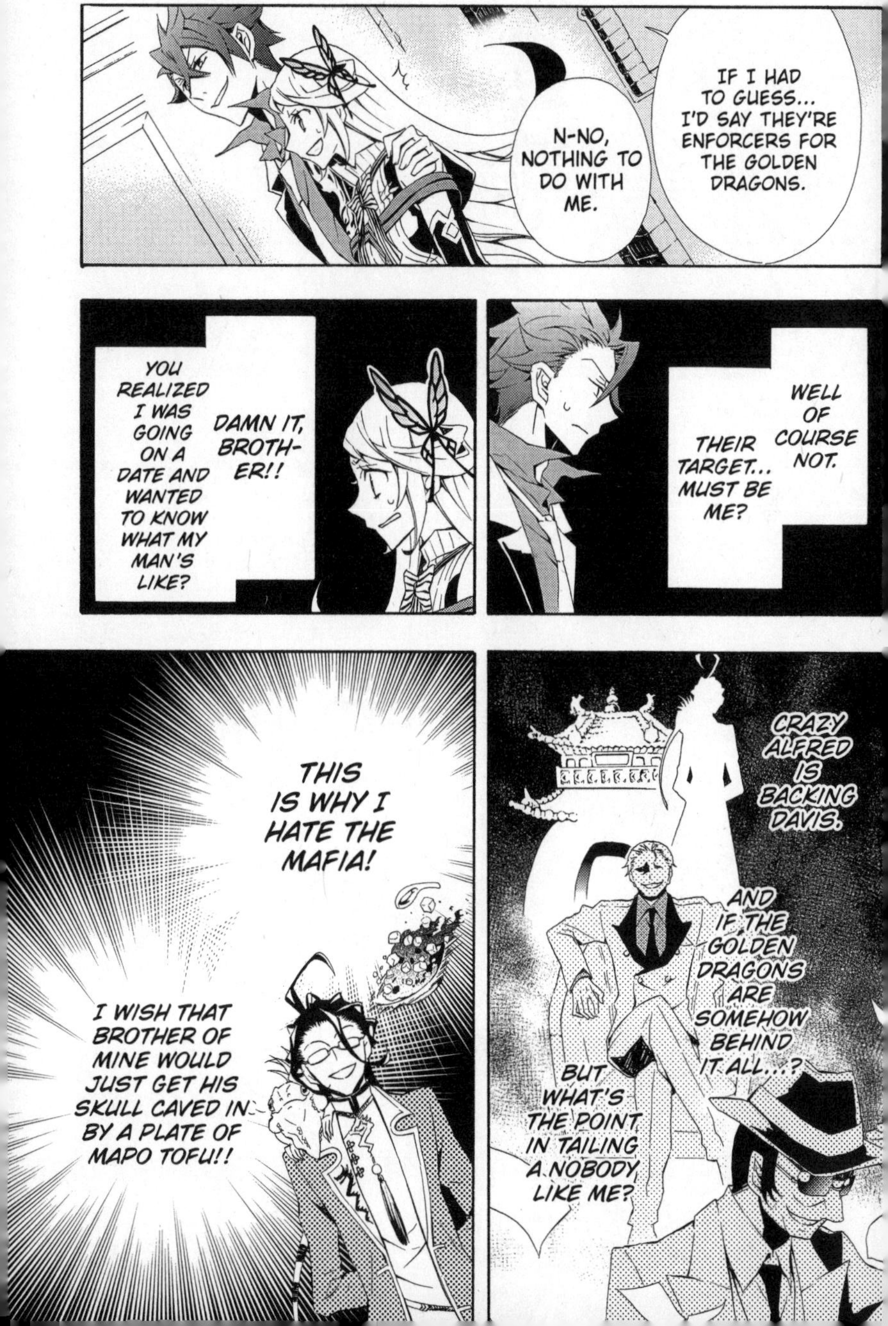
IF I HAD TO GUESS... I'D SAY THEY'RE ENFORCERS FOR THE GOLDEN DRAGONS.
N-NO, NOTHING TO DO WITH ME.
WELL OF COURSE NOT.
THEIR TARGET... MUST BE ME?
DAMN IT, BROTHER!!
YOU REALIZED I WAS GOING ON A DATE AND WANTED TO KNOW WHAT MY MAN'S LIKE?
CRAZY ALFRED IS BACKING DAVIS.
AND IF THE GOLDEN DRAGONS ARE SOMEHOW BEHIND IT ALL...?
BUT WHAT'S THE POINT IN TAILING A NOBODY LIKE ME?
THIS IS WHY I HATE THE MAFIA!
I WISH THAT BROTHER OF MINE WOULD JUST GET HIS SKULL CAVED IN BY A PLATE OF MAPO TOFU!!

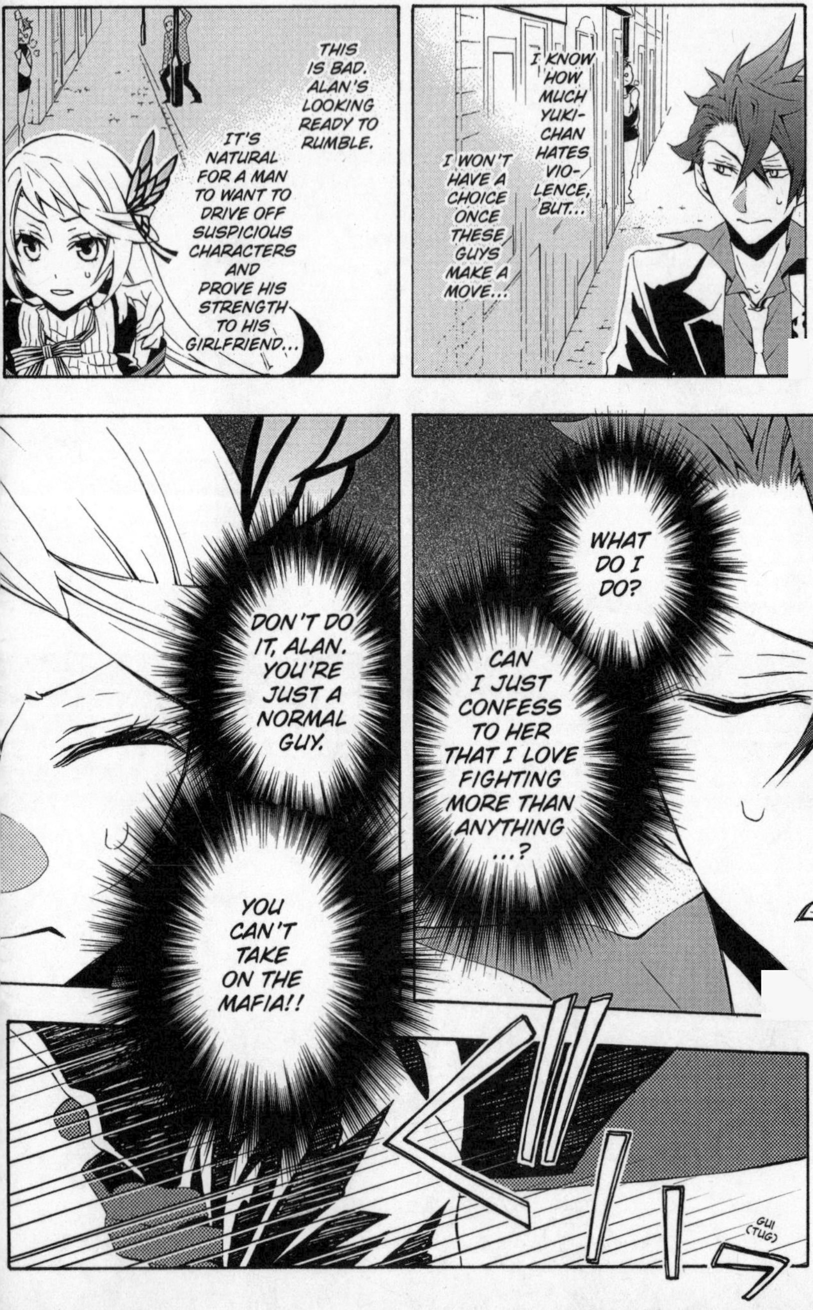
I KNOW HOW MUCH YUKI-CHAN HATES VIO-LENCE, BUT...
I WON'T HAVE A CHOICE ONCE THESE GUYS MAKE A MOVE...
THIS IS BAD. ALAN'S LOOKING READY TO RUMBLE.
IT'S NATURAL FOR A MAN TO WANT TO DRIVE OFF SUSPICIOUS CHARACTERS AND PROVE HIS STRENGTH TO HIS GIRLFRIEND...
WHAT DO I DO?
CAN I JUST CONFESS TO HER THAT I LOVE FIGHTING MORE THAN ANYTHING ...?
DON'T DO IT, ALAN. YOU'RE JUST A NORMAL GUY.
YOU CAN'T TAKE ON THE MAFIA!!
GUI (TUG)

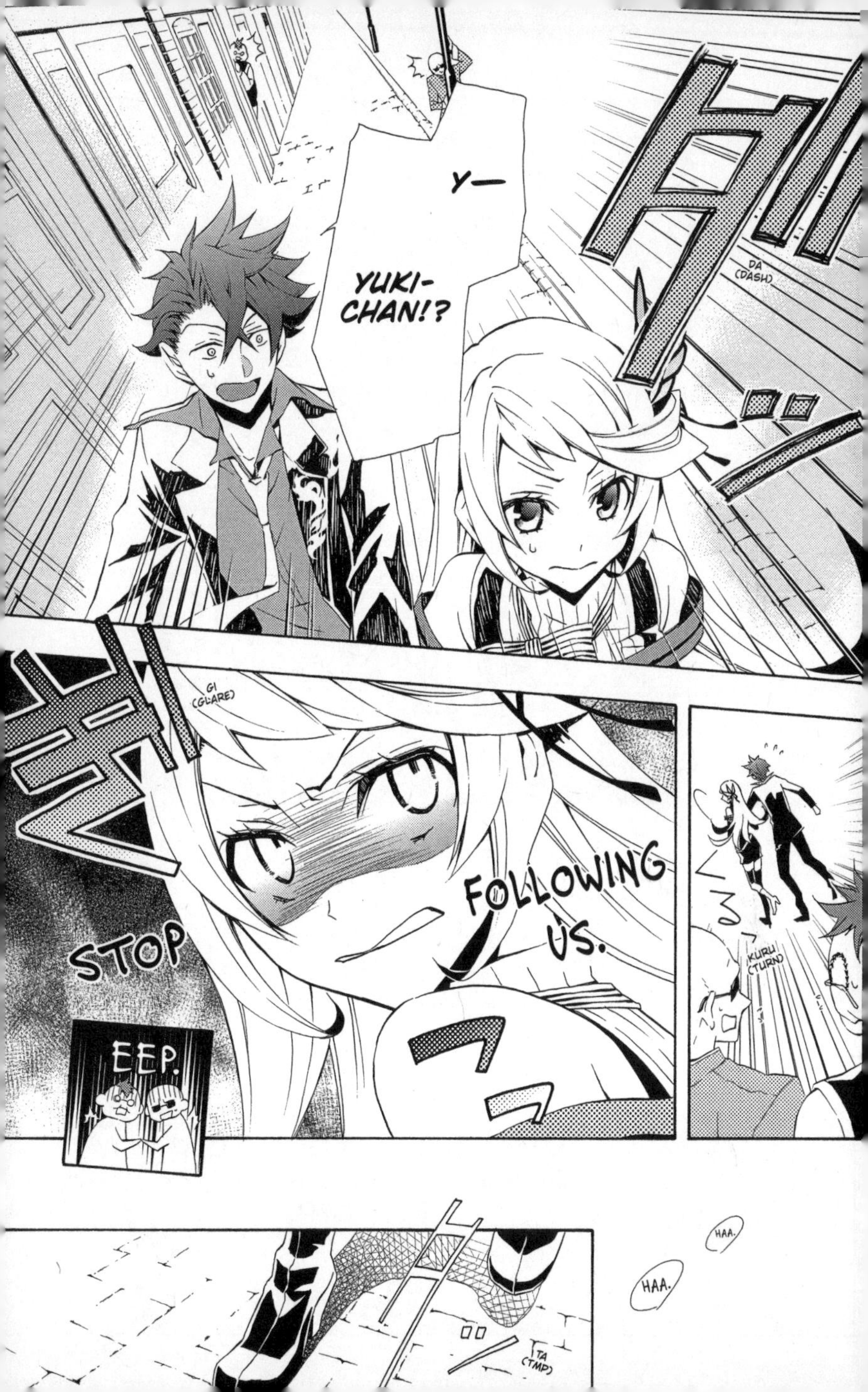
Y—
YUKI-CHAN!?
DA (DASH)
KURU (TURN)
FOLLOWING US.
GI (GLARE)
STOP
EEP.
HAA.
HAA.
TA (TMP)

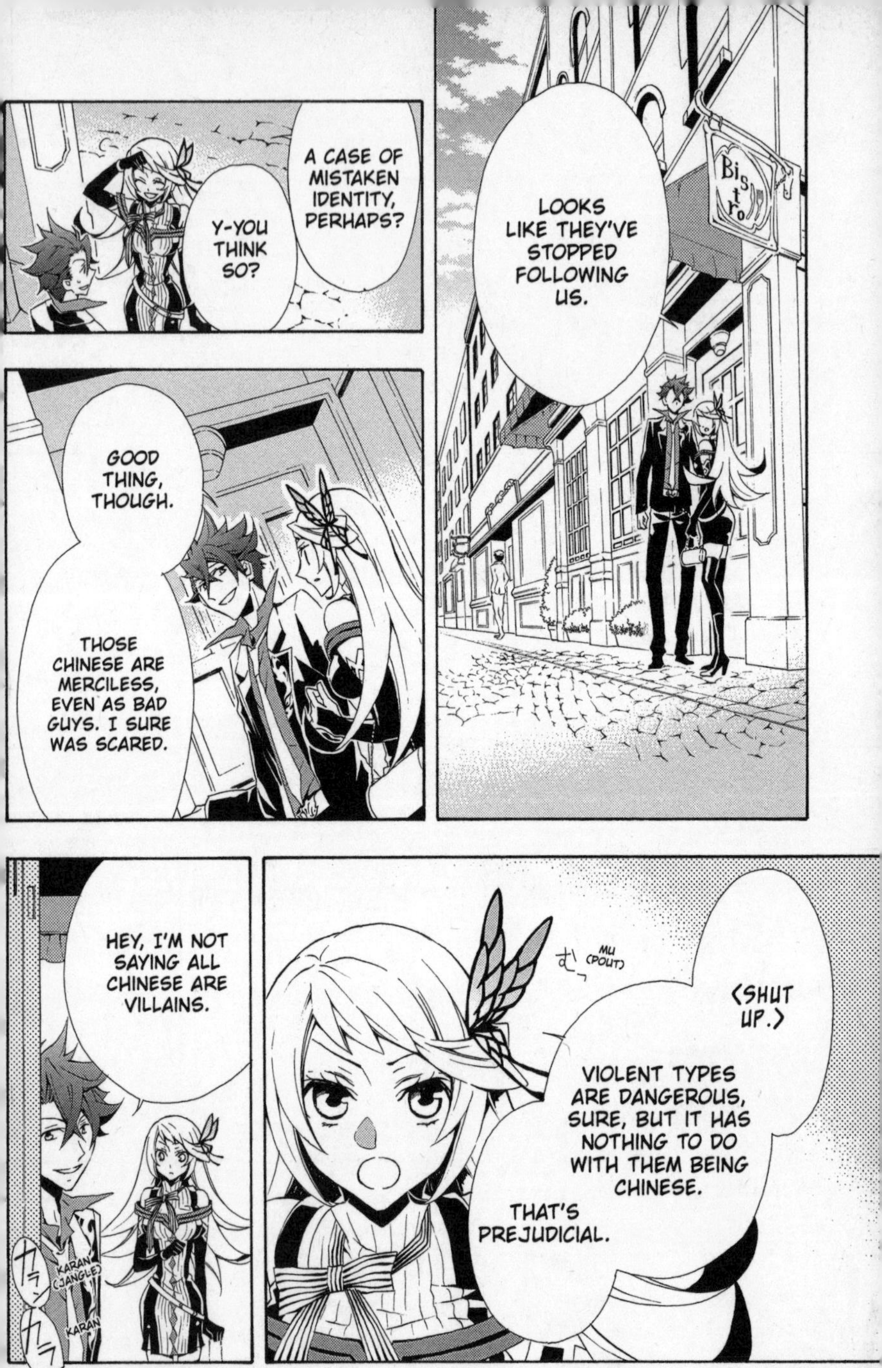
Bistro
LOOKS LIKE THEY'VE STOPPED FOLLOWING US.
A CASE OF MISTAKEN IDENTITY, PERHAPS?
Y-YOU THINK SO?
GOOD THING, THOUGH.
THOSE CHINESE ARE MERCILESS, EVEN AS BAD GUYS. I SURE WAS SCARED.
むっ
MU (POUT)
<SHUT UP.>
VIOLENT TYPES ARE DANGEROUS, SURE, BUT IT HAS NOTHING TO DO WITH THEM BEING CHINESE.
THAT'S PREJUDICIAL.
HEY, I'M NOT SAYING ALL CHINESE ARE VILLAINS.
カラン
KARAN (JANGLE)
カラン
KARAN

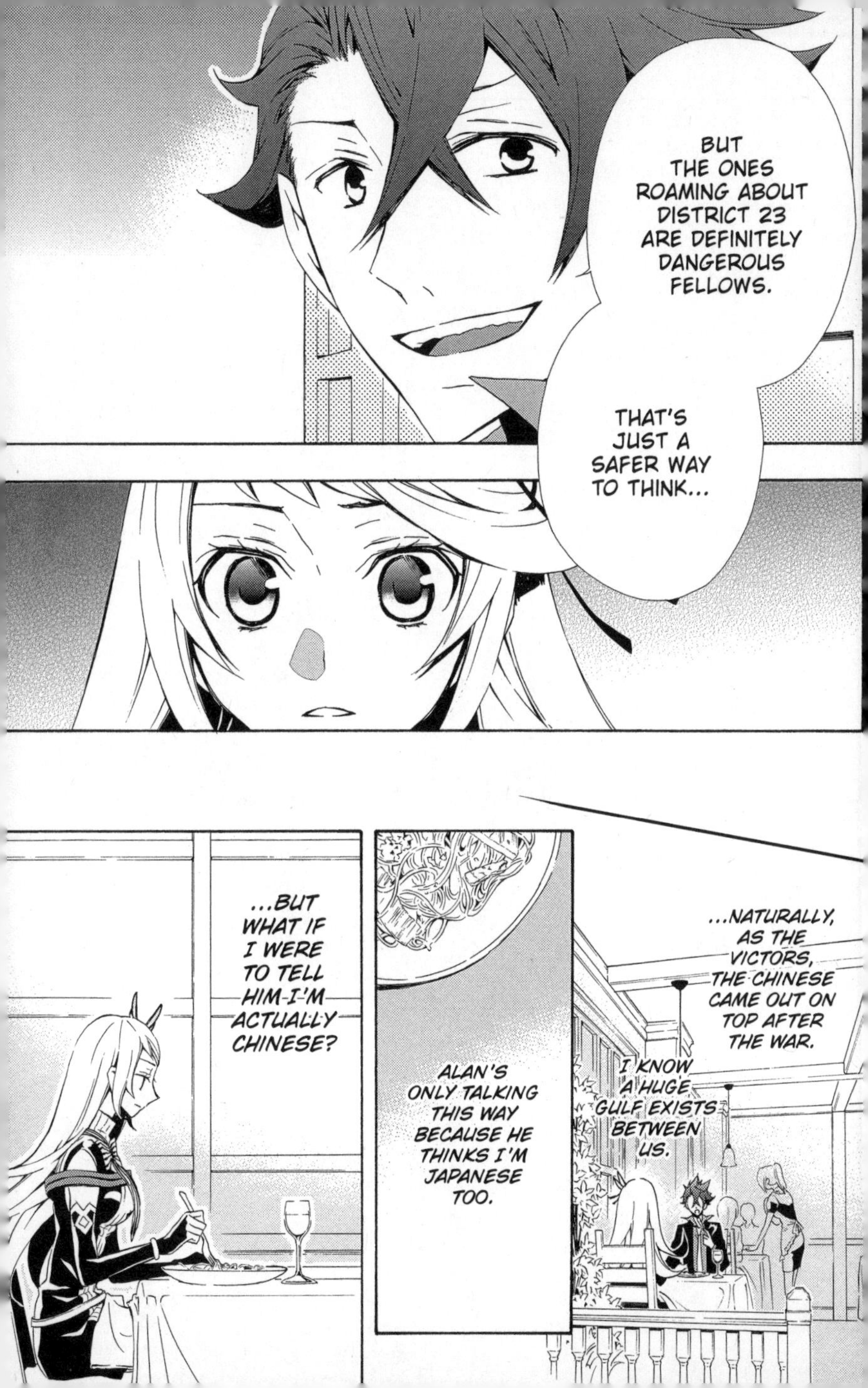
BUT THE ONES ROAMING ABOUT DISTRICT 23 ARE DEFINITELY DANGEROUS FELLOWS.
THAT'S JUST A SAFER WAY TO THINK...
...NATURALLY, AS THE VICTORS, THE CHINESE CAME OUT ON TOP AFTER THE WAR.
I KNOW A HUGE GULF EXISTS BETWEEN US.
ALAN'S ONLY TALKING THIS WAY BECAUSE HE THINKS I'M JAPANESE TOO.
...BUT WHAT IF I WERE TO TELL HIM I'M ACTUALLY CHINESE?

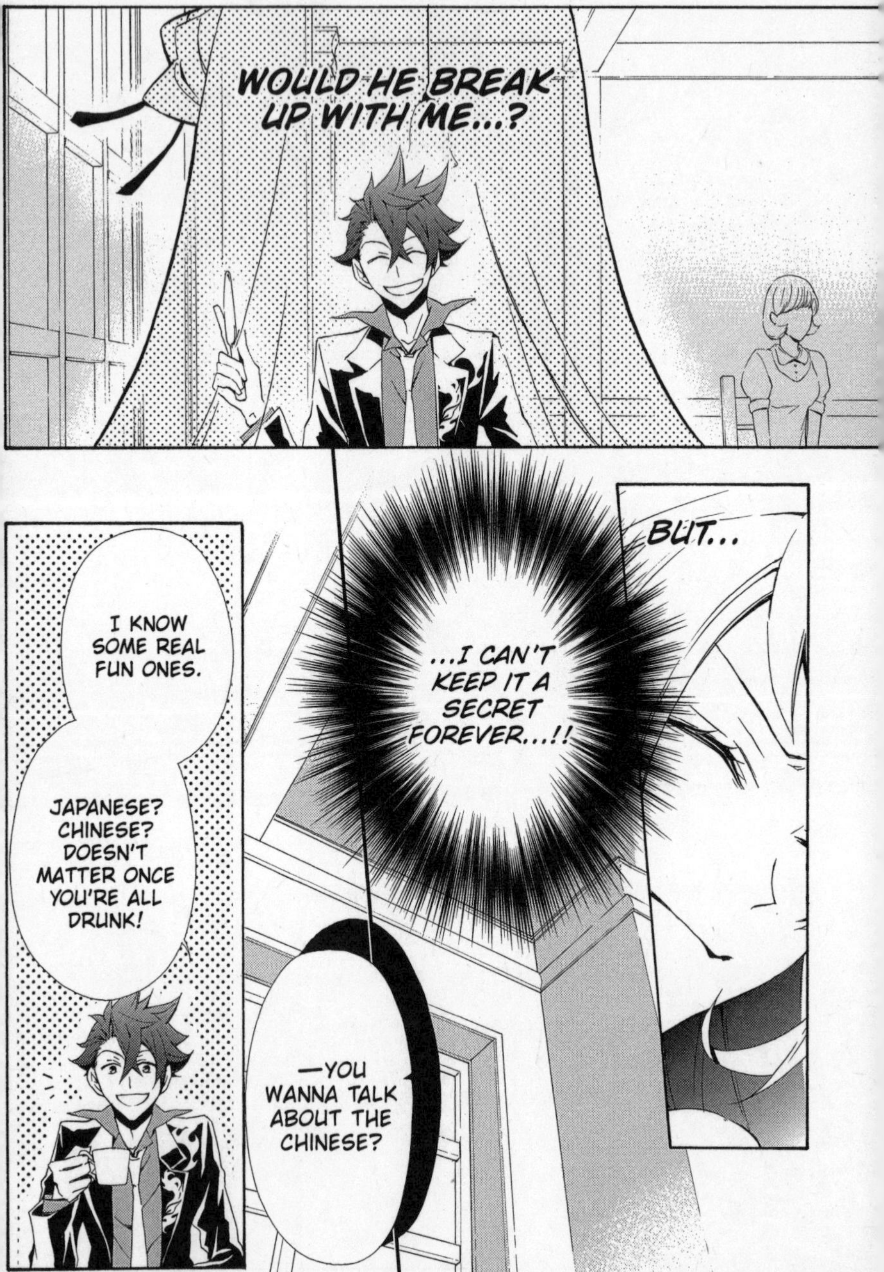
WOULD HE BREAK UP WITH ME...?
BUT...
...I CAN'T KEEP IT A SECRET FOREVER...!!
—YOU WANNA TALK ABOUT THE CHINESE?
I KNOW SOME REAL FUN ONES.
JAPANESE? CHINESE? DOESN'T MATTER ONCE YOU'RE ALL DRUNK!

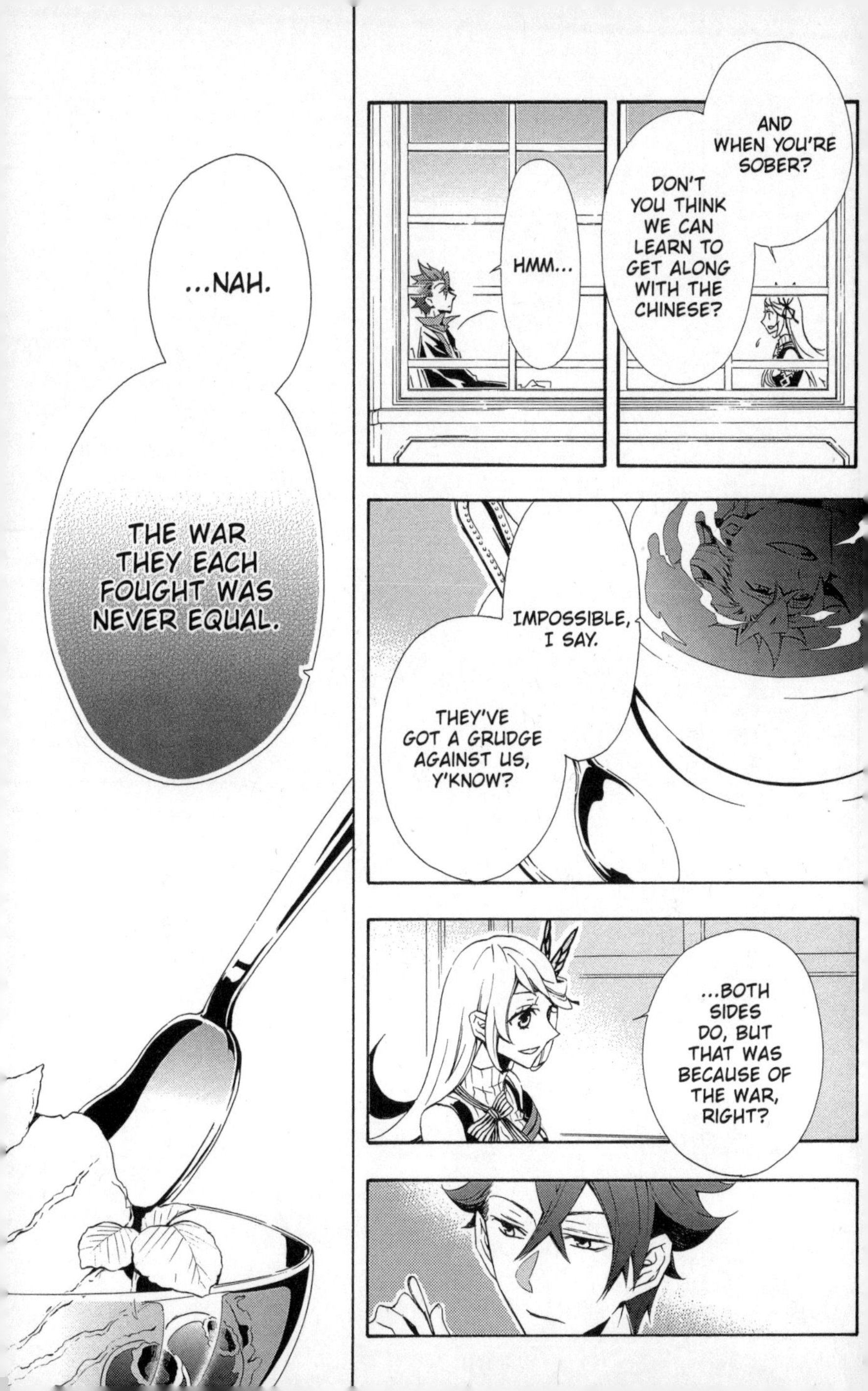
AND WHEN YOU'RE SOBER?
DON'T YOU THINK WE CAN LEARN TO GET ALONG WITH THE CHINESE?
HMM...
IMPOSSIBLE, I SAY.
THEY'VE GOT A GRUDGE AGAINST US, Y'KNOW?
...BOTH SIDES DO, BUT THAT WAS BECAUSE OF THE WAR, RIGHT?
...NAH.
THE WAR THEY EACH FOUGHT WAS NEVER EQUAL.

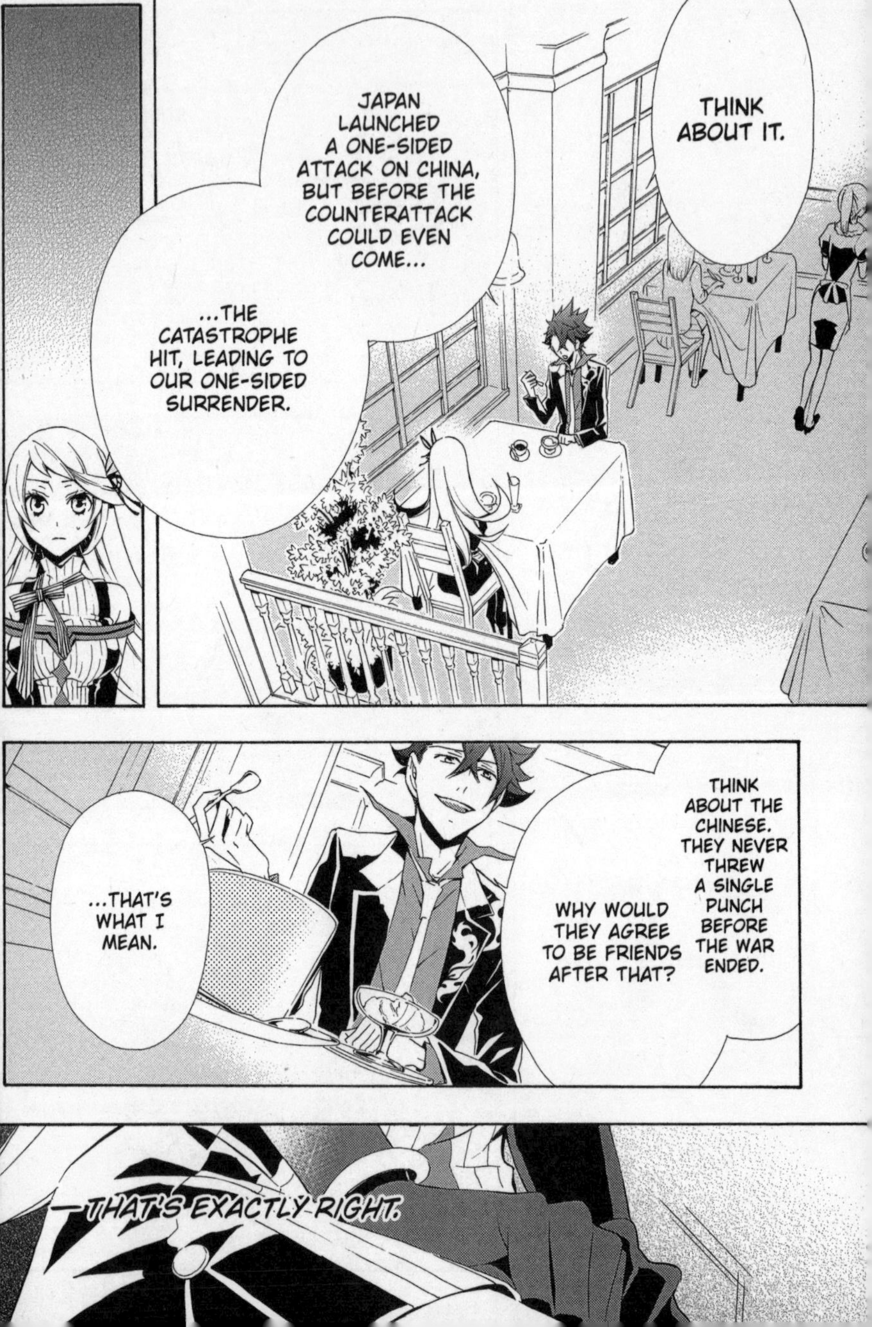
THINK ABOUT IT.
JAPAN LAUNCHED A ONE-SIDED ATTACK ON CHINA, BUT BEFORE THE COUNTERATTACK COULD EVEN COME...
...THE CATASTROPHE HIT, LEADING TO OUR ONE-SIDED SURRENDER.
THINK ABOUT THE CHINESE. THEY NEVER THREW A SINGLE PUNCH BEFORE THE WAR ENDED.
WHY WOULD THEY AGREE TO BE FRIENDS AFTER THAT?
...THAT'S WHAT I MEAN.
—THAT'S EXACTLY RIGHT.

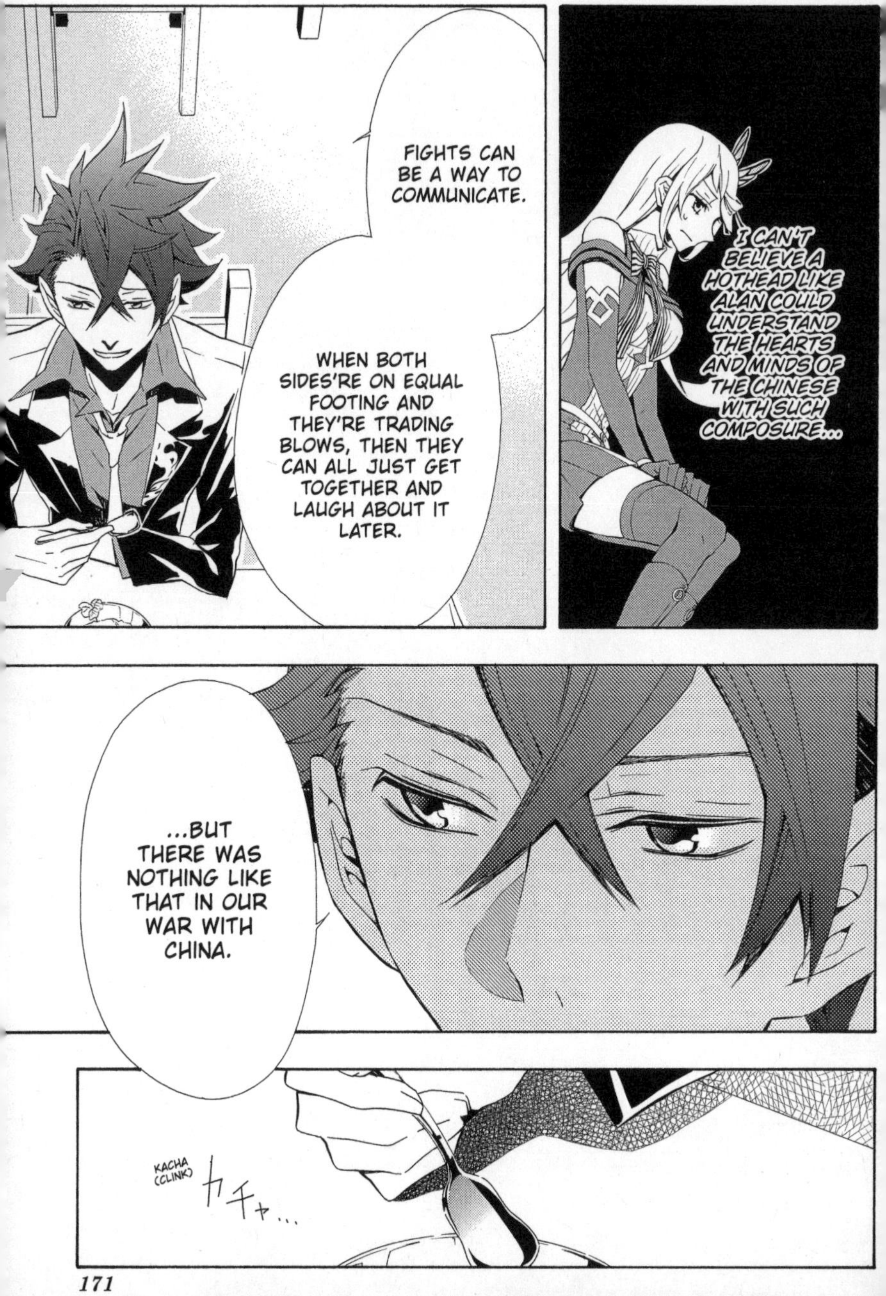
I CAN'T BELIEVE A HOTHEAD LIKE ALAN COULD UNDERSTAND THE HEARTS AND MINDS OF THE CHINESE WITH SUCH COMPOSURE...
FIGHTS CAN BE A WAY TO COMMUNICATE.
WHEN BOTH SIDES'RE ON EQUAL FOOTING AND THEY'RE TRADING BLOWS, THEN THEY CAN ALL JUST GET TOGETHER AND LAUGH ABOUT IT LATER.
...BUT THERE WAS NOTHING LIKE THAT IN OUR WAR WITH CHINA.
KACHA (CLINK)
カチャ...

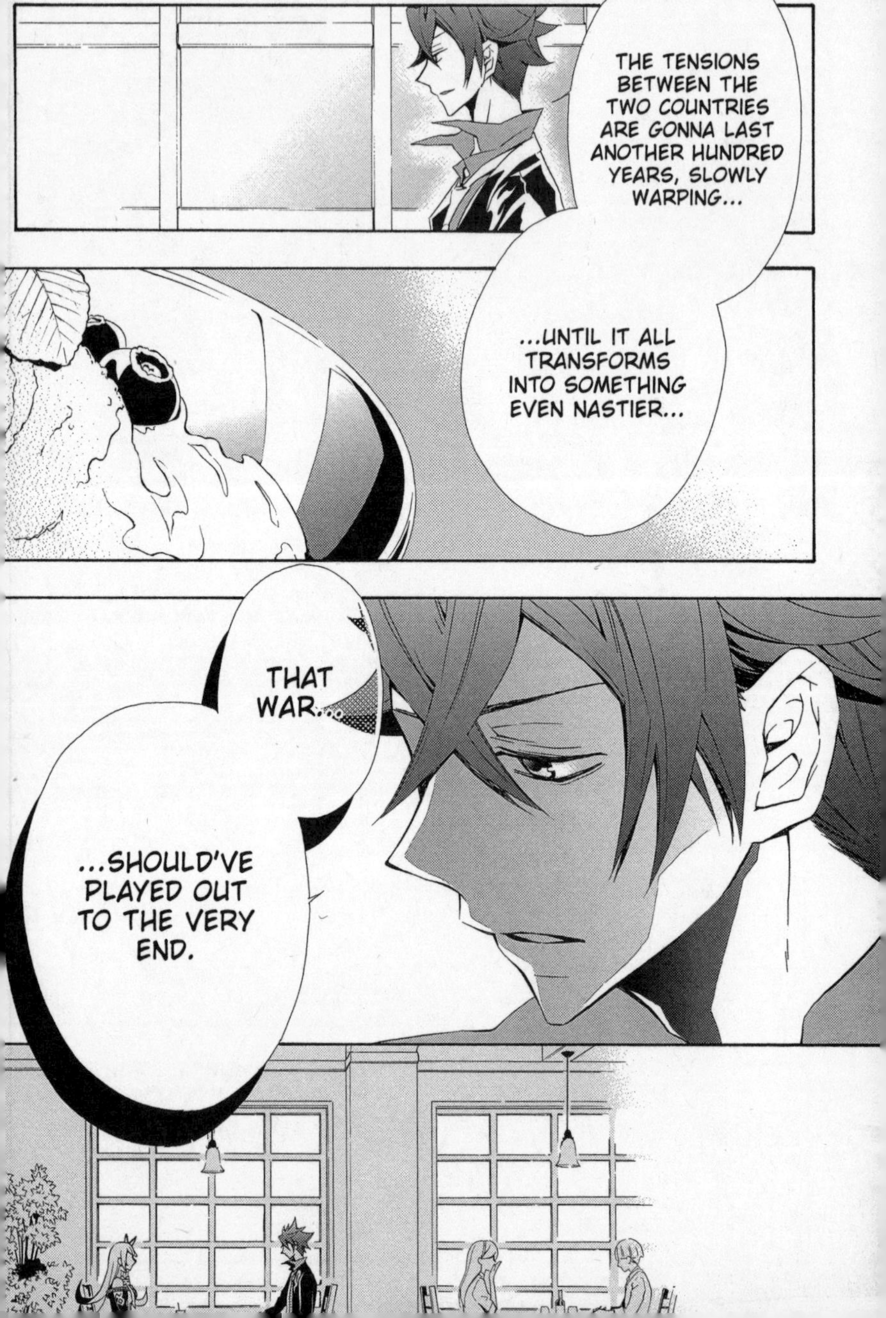
THE TENSIONS BETWEEN THE TWO COUNTRIES ARE GONNA LAST ANOTHER HUNDRED YEARS, SLOWLY WARPING...
...UNTIL IT ALL TRANSFORMS INTO SOMETHING EVEN NASTIER...
THAT WAR...
...SHOULD'VE PLAYED OUT TO THE VERY END.

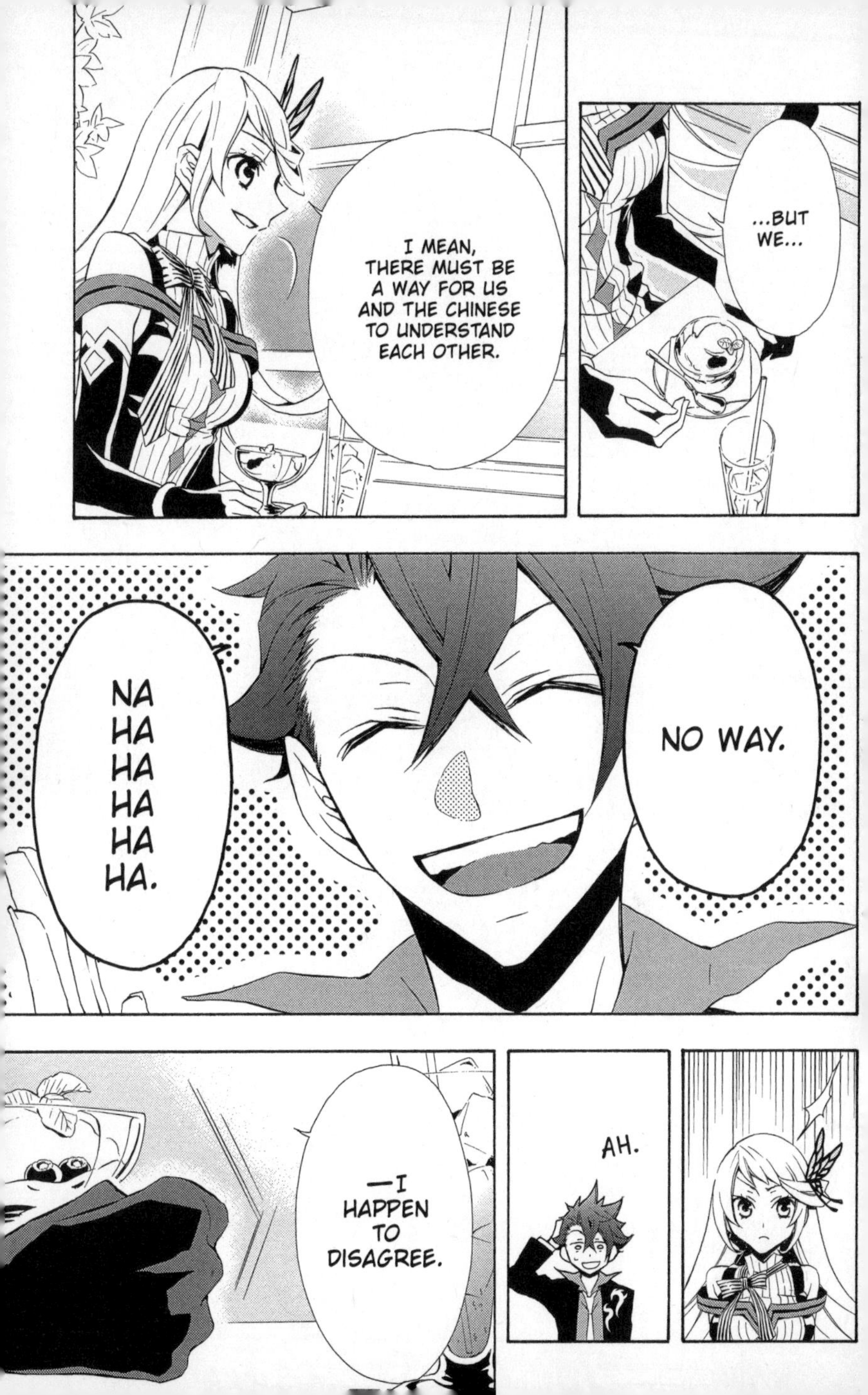
...BUT WE...
I MEAN, THERE MUST BE A WAY FOR US AND THE CHINESE TO UNDERSTAND EACH OTHER.
NO WAY.
NA HA HA HA HA HA.
AH.
—I HAPPEN TO DISAGREE.

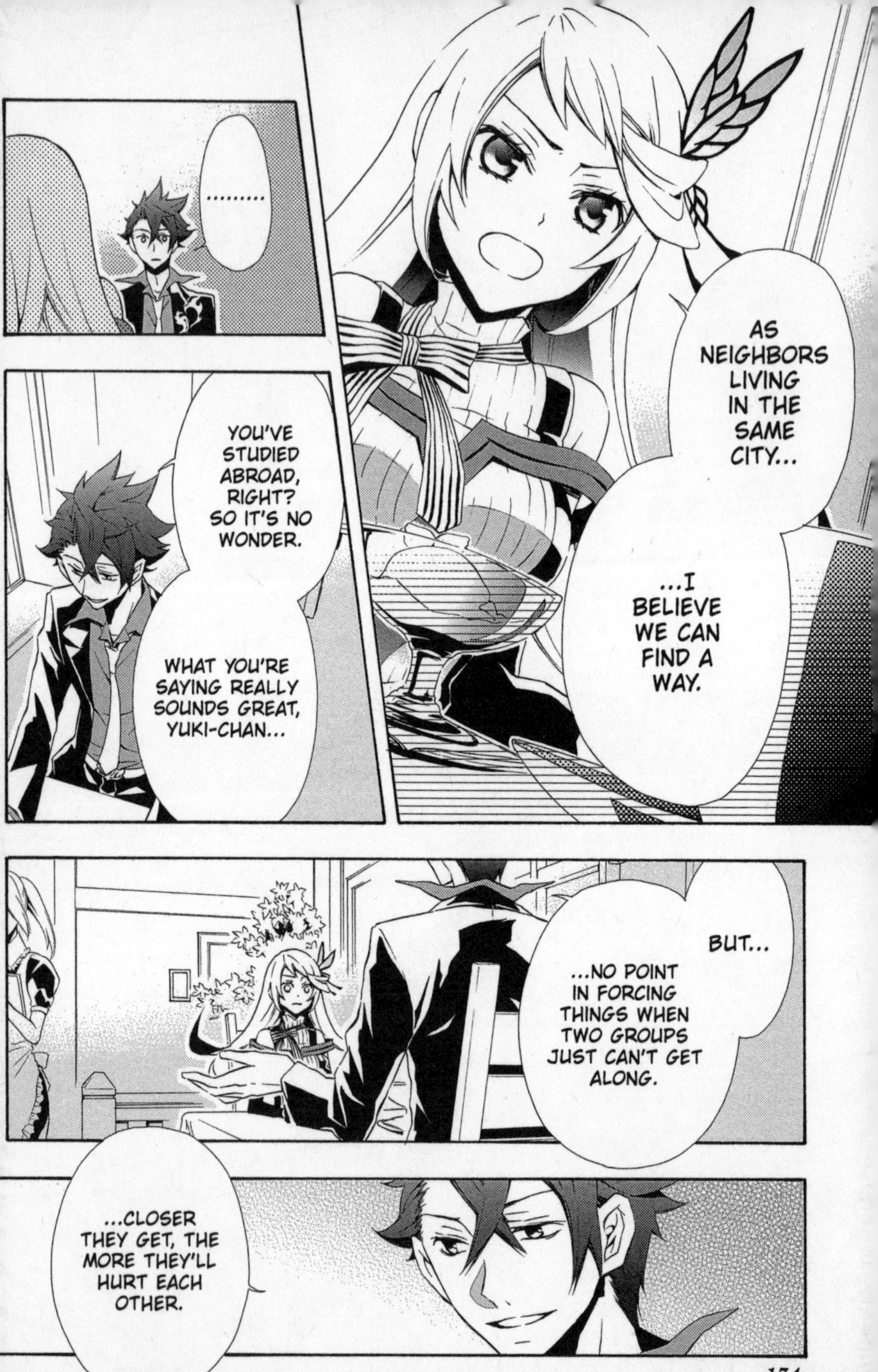
AS NEIGHBORS LIVING IN THE SAME CITY...
...I BELIEVE WE CAN FIND A WAY.
....
YOU'VE STUDIED ABROAD, RIGHT? SO IT'S NO WONDER.
WHAT YOU'RE SAYING REALLY SOUNDS GREAT, YUKI-CHAN...
BUT...
...NO POINT IN FORCING THINGS WHEN TWO GROUPS JUST CAN'T GET ALONG.
...CLOSER THEY GET, THE MORE THEY'LL HURT EACH OTHER.

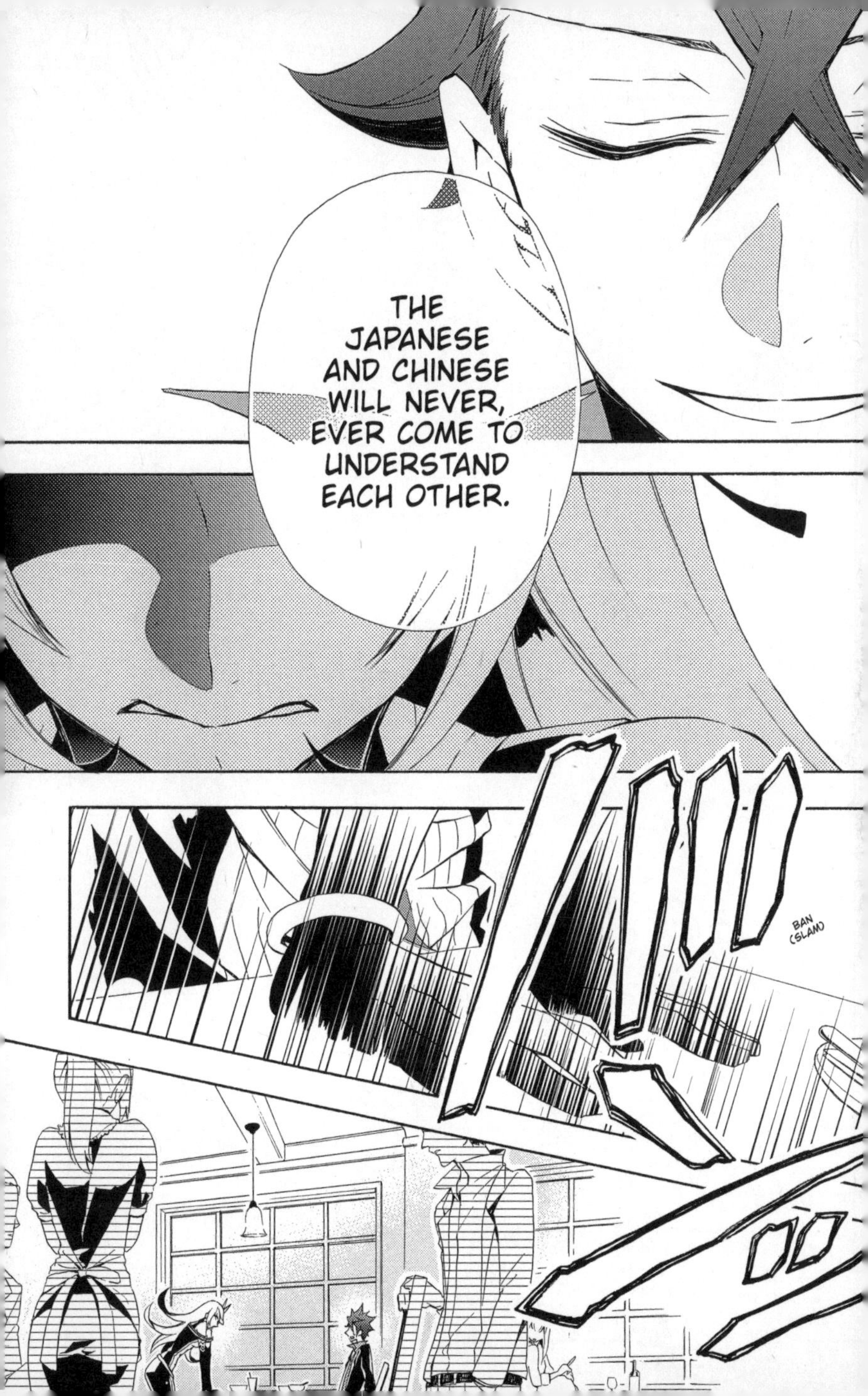
THE JAPANESE AND CHINESE WILL NEVER, EVER COME TO UNDERSTAND EACH OTHER.
BAN (SLAM)

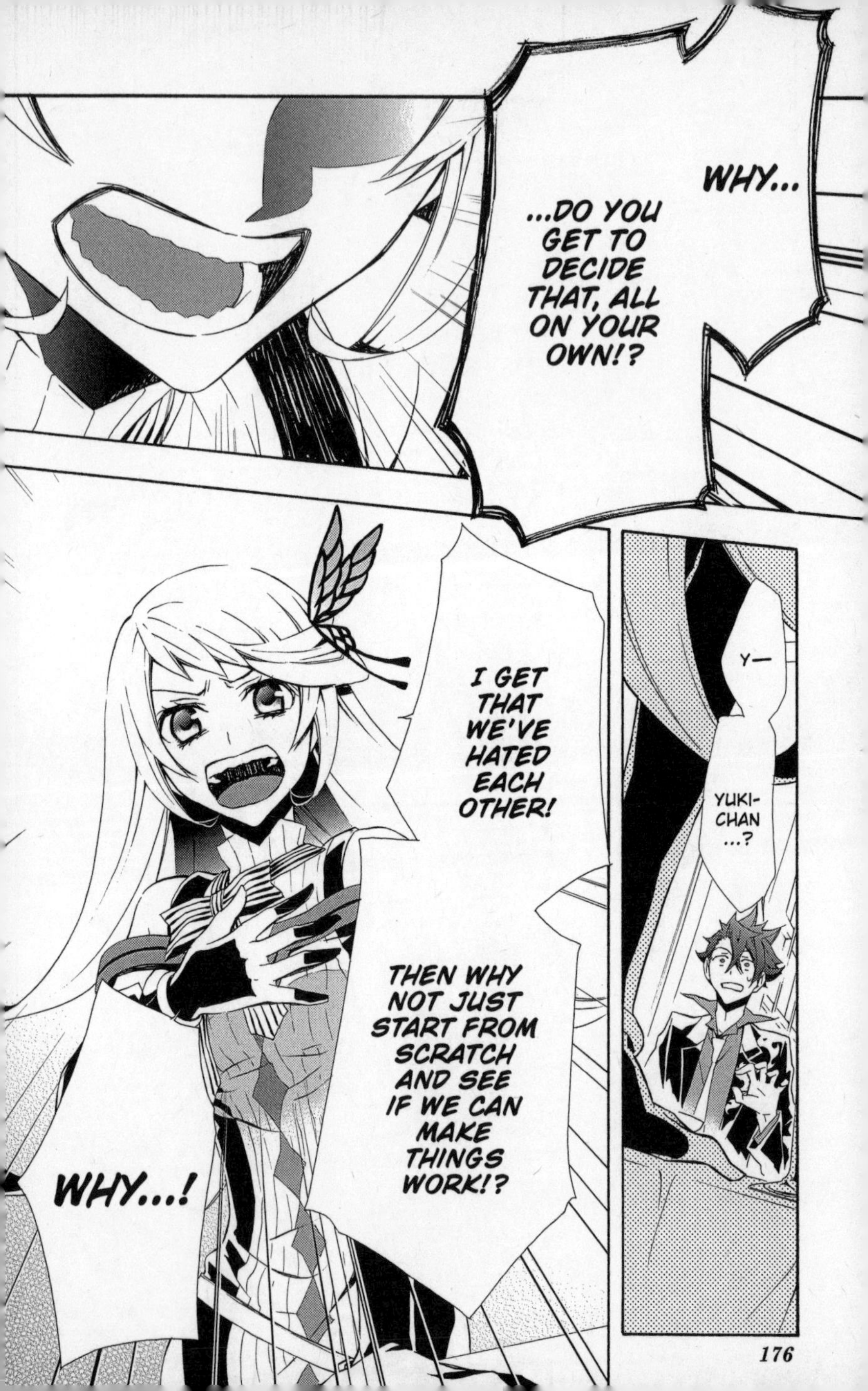
WHY...
...DO YOU GET TO DECIDE THAT, ALL ON YOUR OWN!?
Y—
YUKI-CHAN ...?
I GET THAT WE'VE HATED EACH OTHER!
THEN WHY NOT JUST START FROM SCRATCH AND SEE IF WE CAN MAKE THINGS WORK!?
WHY...!

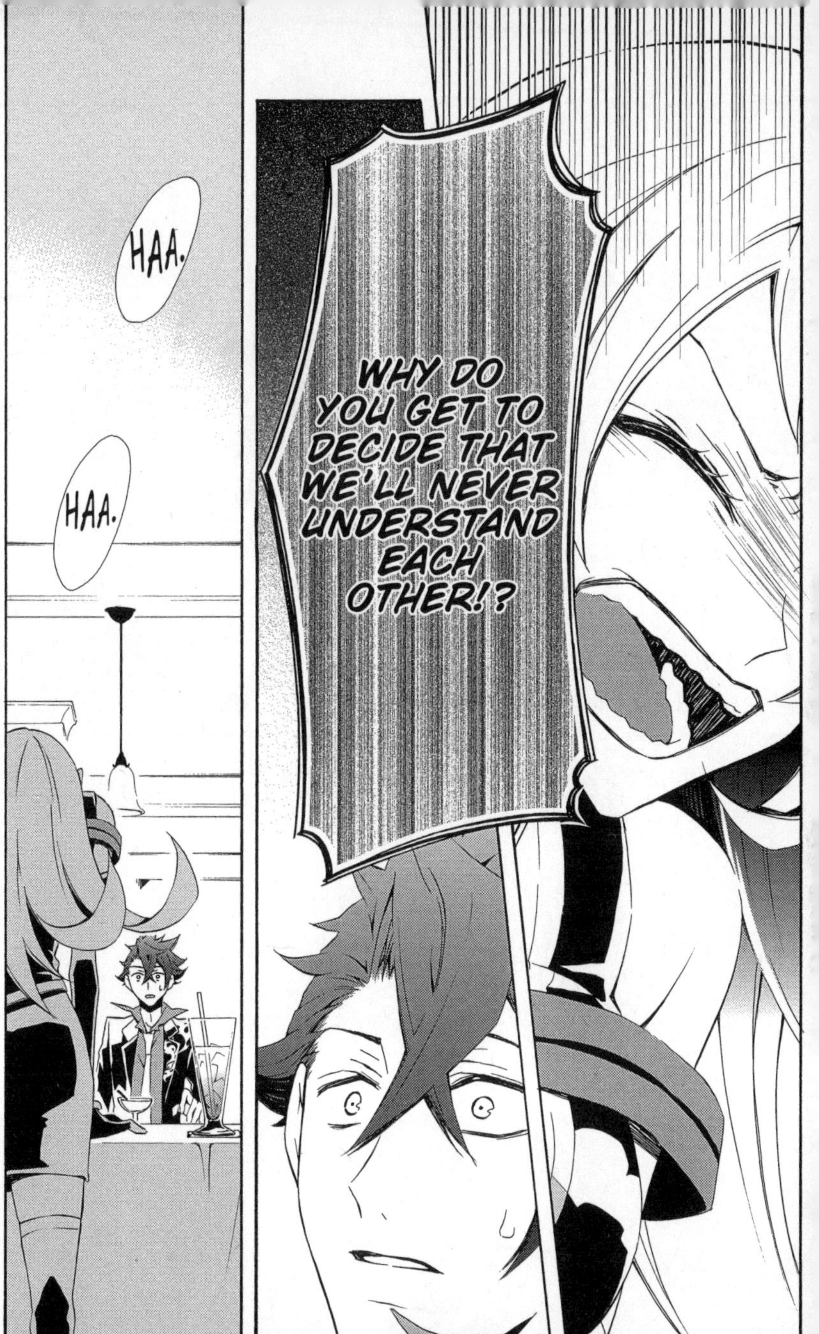
WHY DO YOU GET TO DECIDE THAT WE'LL NEVER UNDERSTAND EACH OTHER!?
HAA.
HAA.

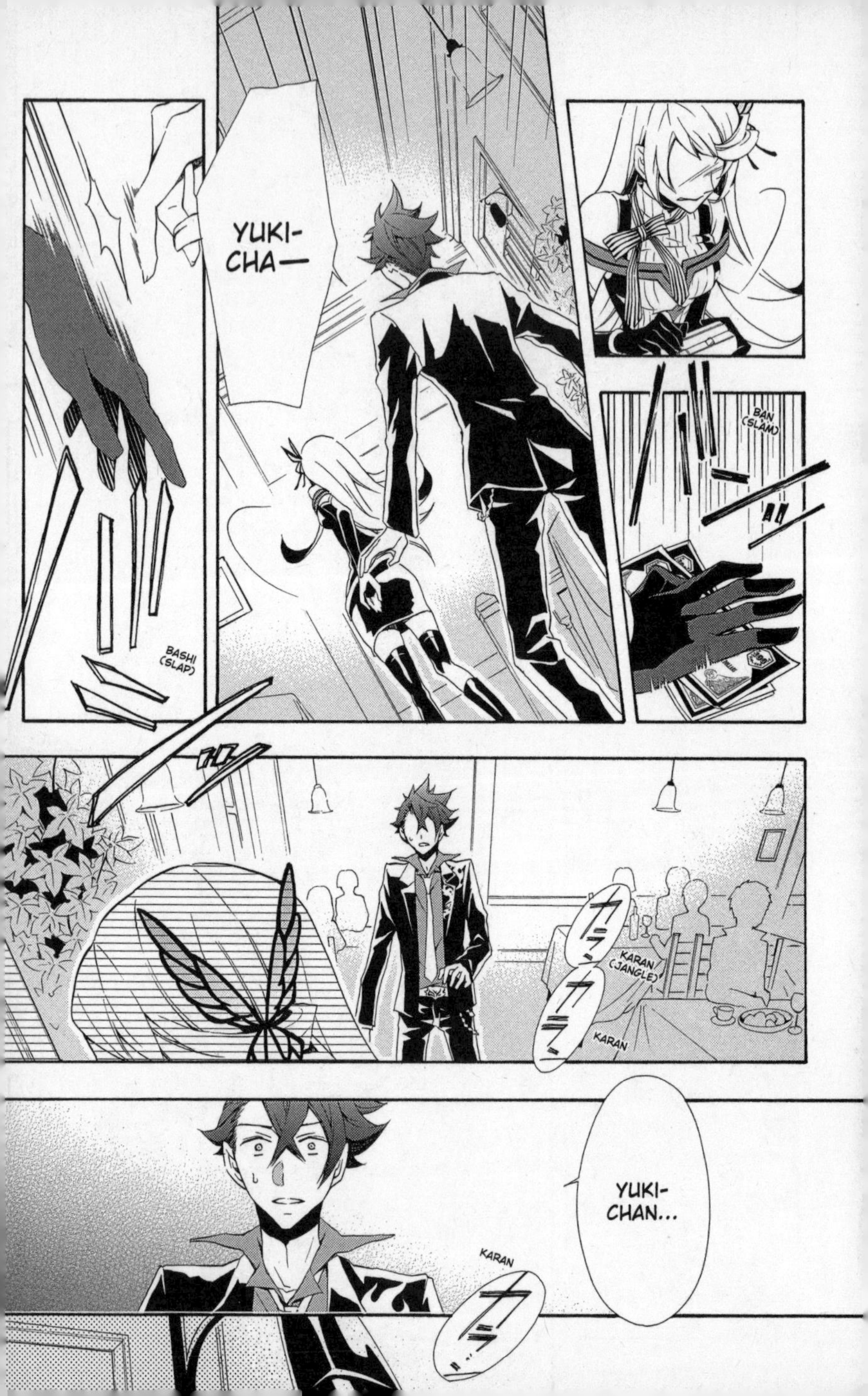
BAN (SLAM)
YUKI-CHA—
BASHI (SLAP)
KARAN (JANGLE)
KARAN
YUKI-CHAN...
KARAN

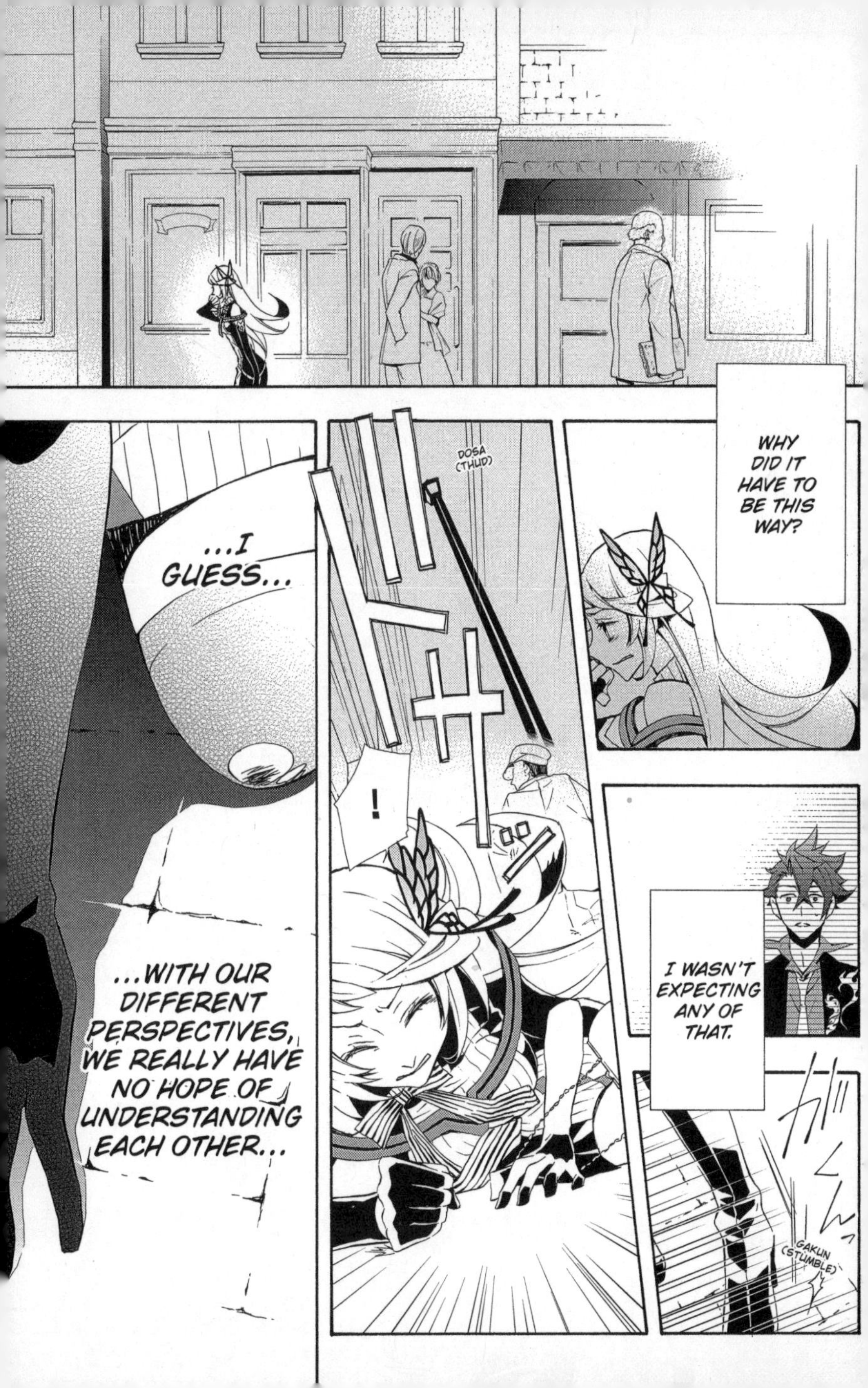
WHY DID IT HAVE TO BE THIS WAY?
I WASN'T EXPECTING ANY OF THAT.
GAKUN (STUMBLE)
DOSA (THUD)
!
...I GUESS...
...WITH OUR DIFFERENT PERSPECTIVES, WE REALLY HAVE NO HOPE OF UNDERSTANDING EACH OTHER...

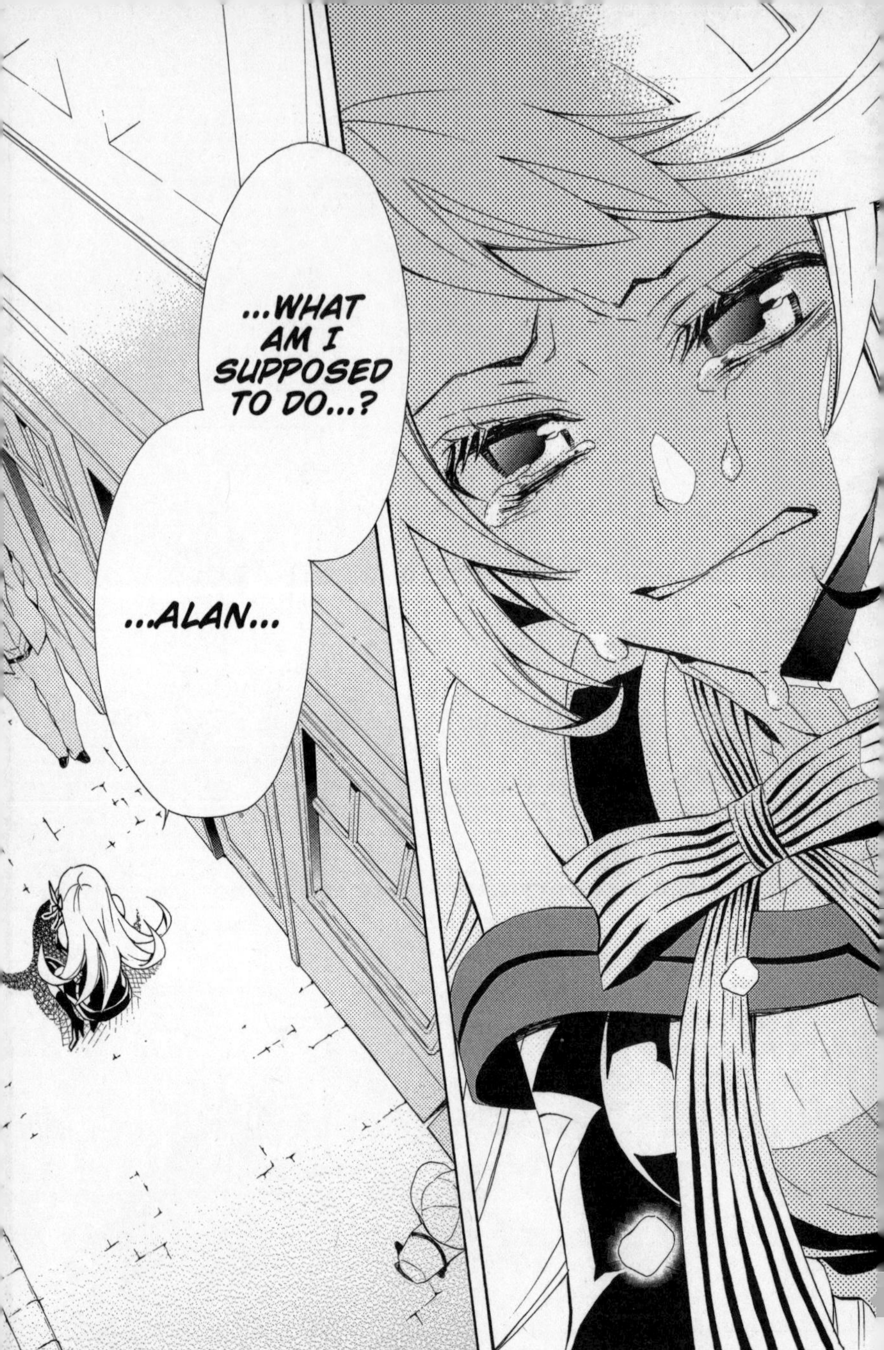
...WHAT AM I SUPPOSED TO DO...?
...ALAN...

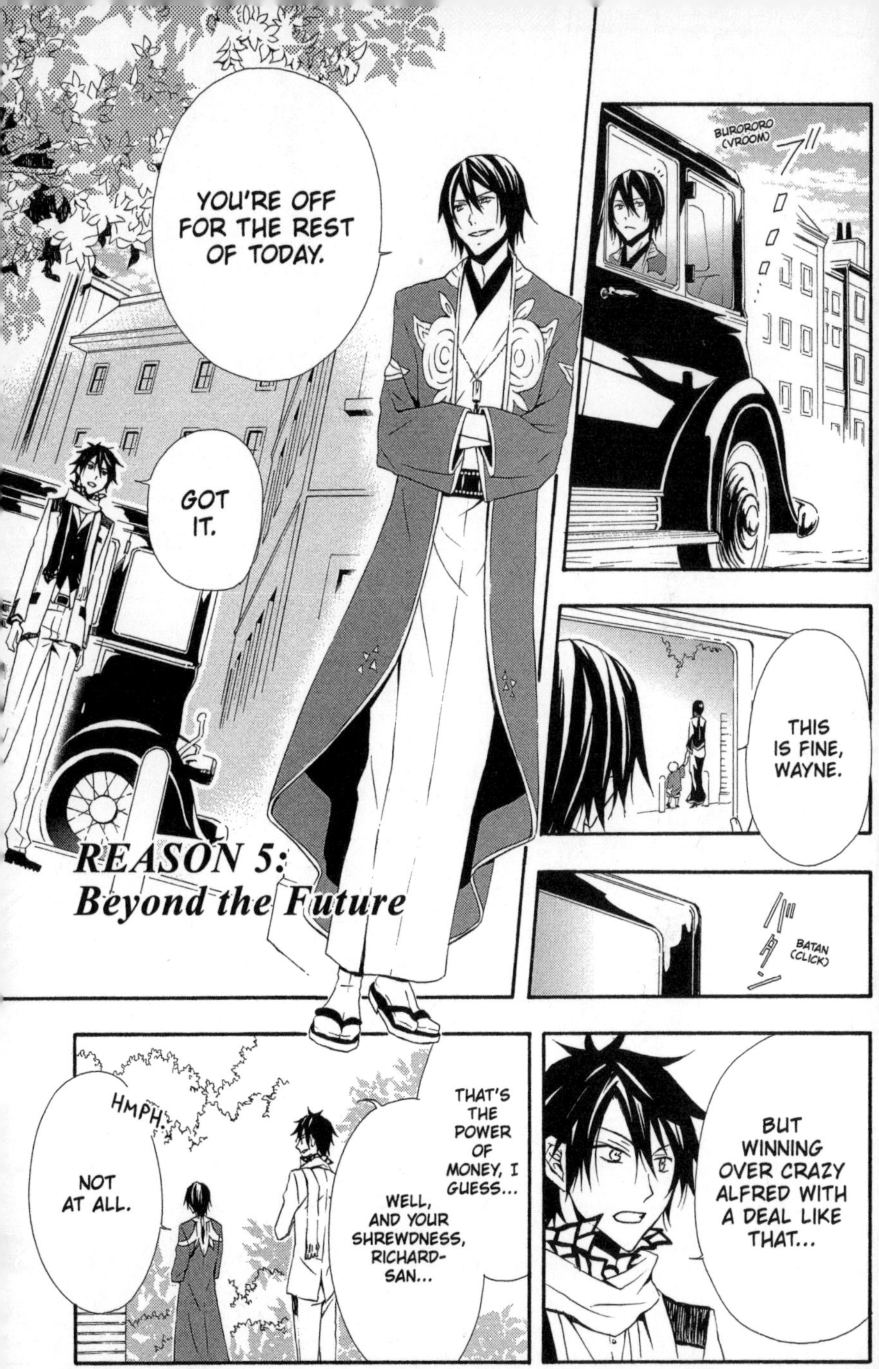
BURORORO (VROOM)
THIS IS FINE, WAYNE.
BATAN (CLICK)
YOU'RE OFF FOR THE REST OF TODAY.
GOT IT.
REASON 5: Beyond the Future
BUT WINNING OVER CRAZY ALFRED WITH A DEAL LIKE THAT...
THAT'S THE POWER OF MONEY, I GUESS...
WELL, AND YOUR SHREWDNESS, RICHARD-SAN...
HMPH.
NOT AT ALL.

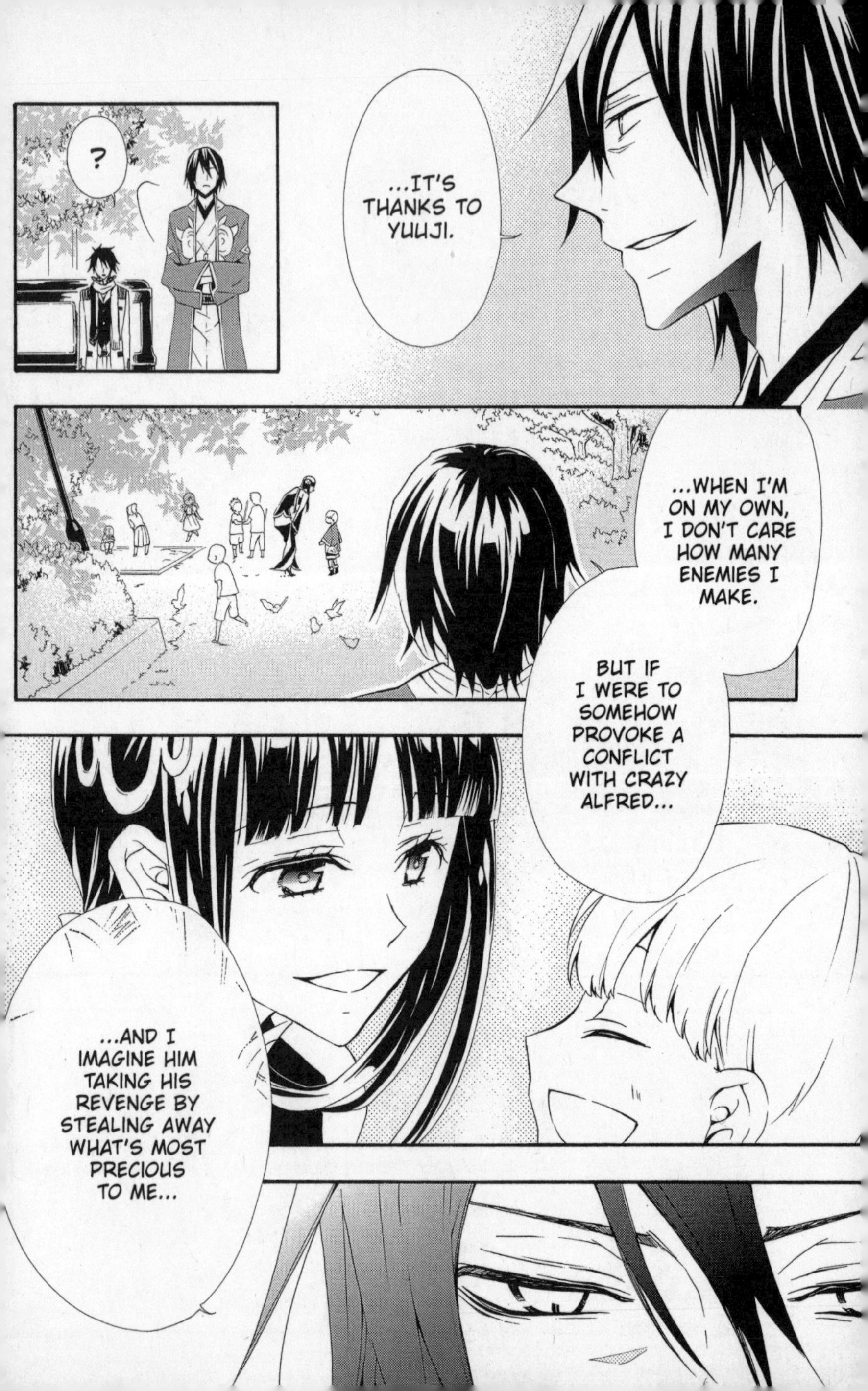
...IT'S THANKS TO YUUJI.
?
...WHEN I'M ON MY OWN, I DON'T CARE HOW MANY ENEMIES I MAKE.
BUT IF I WERE TO SOMEHOW PROVOKE A CONFLICT WITH CRAZY ALFRED...
...AND I IMAGINE HIM TAKING HIS REVENGE BY STEALING AWAY WHAT'S MOST PRECIOUS TO ME...

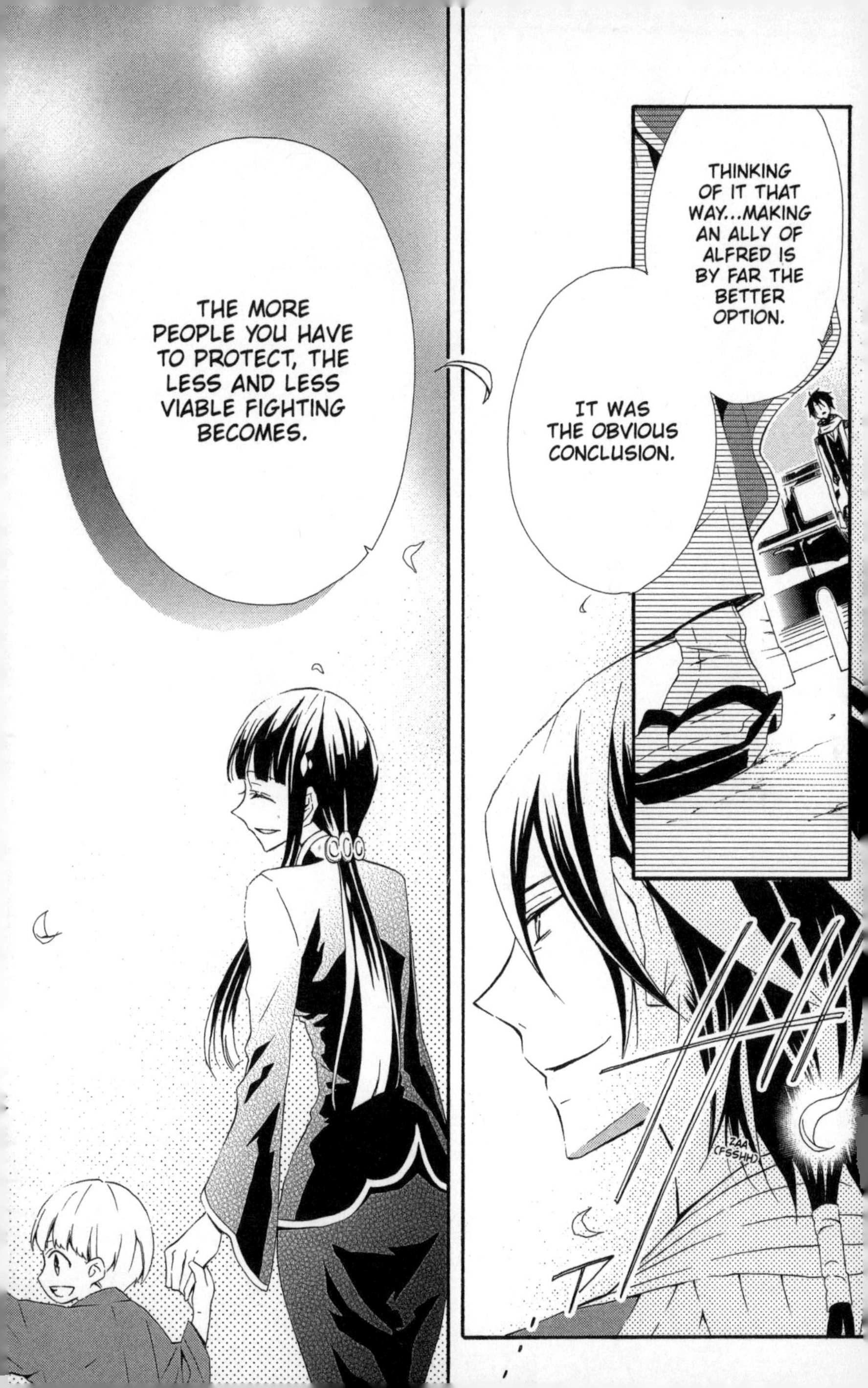
THINKING OF IT THAT WAY...MAKING AN ALLY OF ALFRED IS BY FAR THE BETTER OPTION.
IT WAS THE OBVIOUS CONCLUSION.
ZAA (FSSHH)
THE MORE PEOPLE YOU HAVE TO PROTECT, THE LESS AND LESS VIABLE FIGHTING BECOMES.

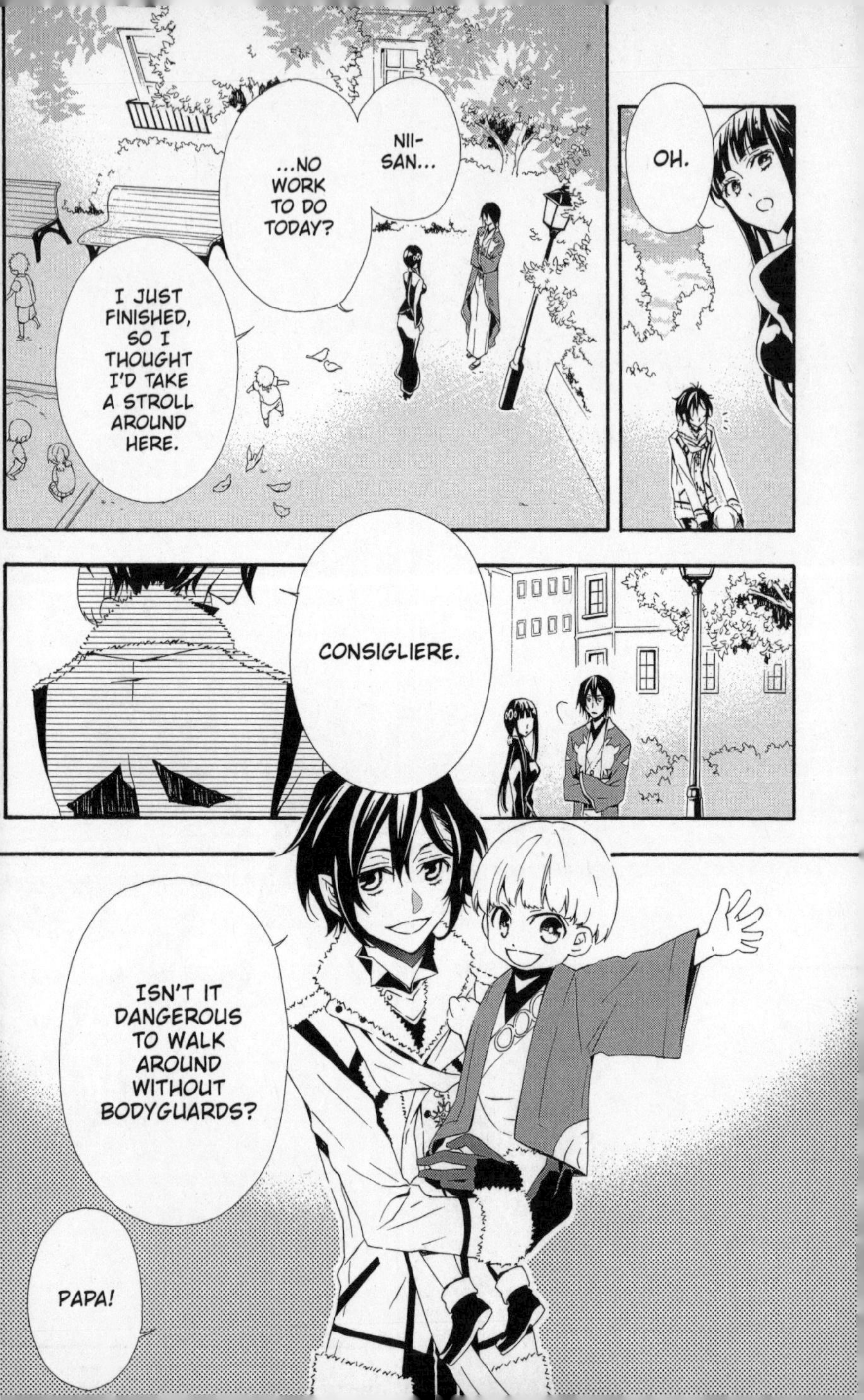

OH.
NII-SAN...
...NO WORK TO DO TODAY?
I JUST FINISHED, SO I THOUGHT I'D TAKE A STROLL AROUND HERE.
CONSIGLIERE.
ISN'T IT DANGEROUS TO WALK AROUND WITHOUT BODYGUARDS?
PAPA!

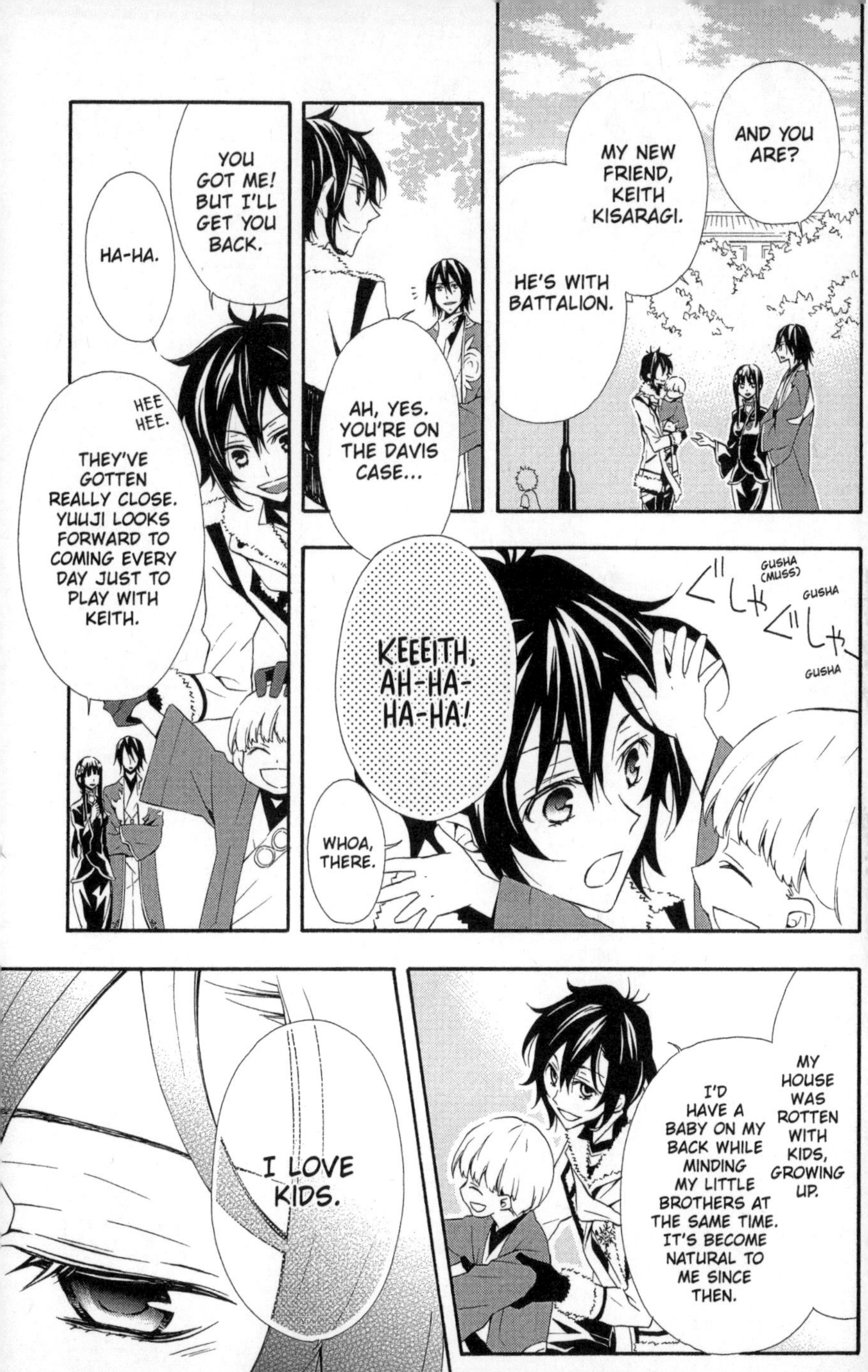
AND YOU ARE?
MY NEW FRIEND, KEITH KISARAGI.
HE'S WITH BATTALION.
AH, YES. YOU'RE ON THE DAVIS CASE...
ぐしゃ GUSHA (MUSS)
ぐしゃ GUSHA
GUSHA
KEEEITH, AH-HA-HA-HA!
WHOA, THERE.
YOU GOT ME! BUT I'LL GET YOU BACK.
HA-HA.
HEE HEE.
THEY'VE GOTTEN REALLY CLOSE. YUUJI LOOKS FORWARD TO COMING EVERY DAY JUST TO PLAY WITH KEITH.
MY HOUSE WAS ROTTEN WITH KIDS, GROWING UP.
I'D HAVE A BABY ON MY BACK WHILE MINDING MY LITTLE BROTHERS AT THE SAME TIME. IT'S BECOME NATURAL TO ME SINCE THEN.
I LOVE KIDS.

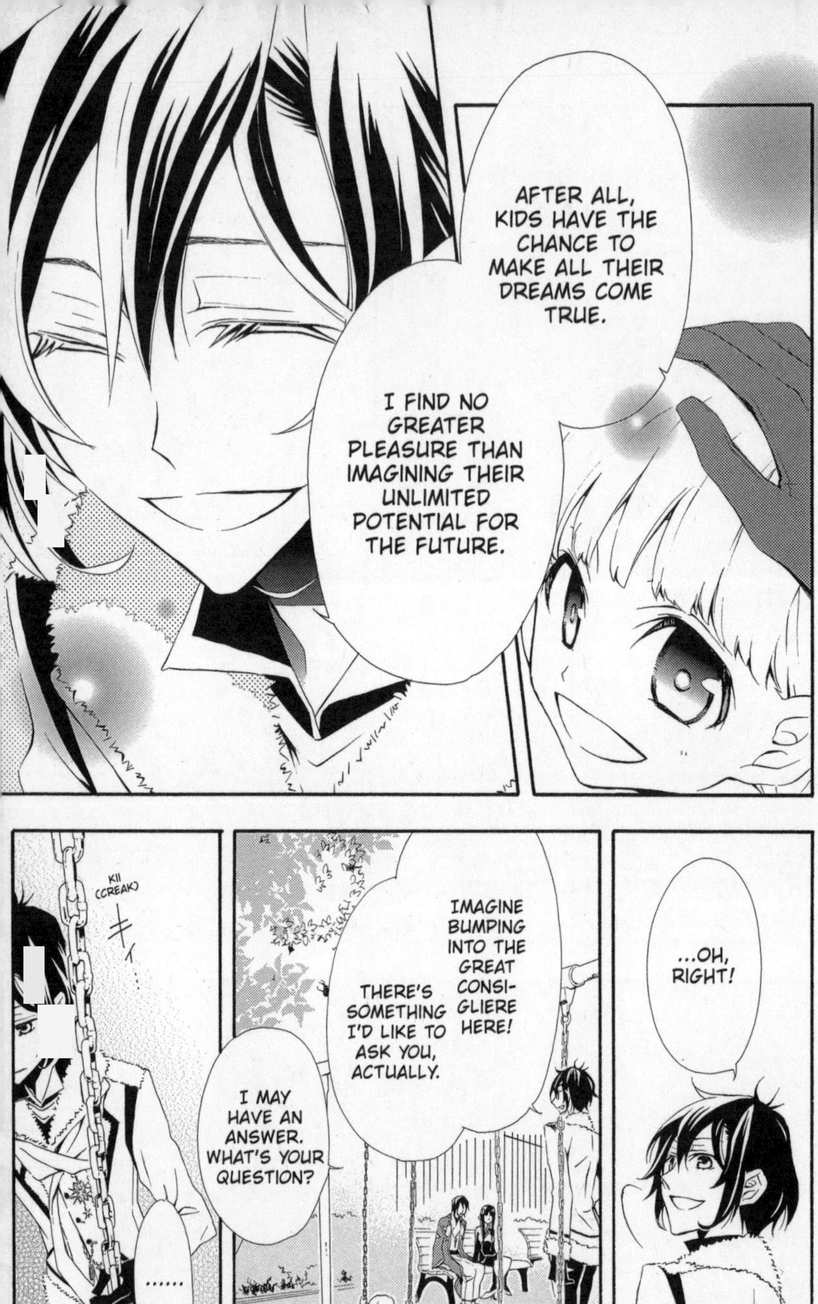
AFTER ALL, KIDS HAVE THE CHANCE TO MAKE ALL THEIR DREAMS COME TRUE.
I FIND NO GREATER PLEASURE THAN IMAGINING THEIR UNLIMITED POTENTIAL FOR THE FUTURE.
...OH, RIGHT!
IMAGINE BUMPING INTO THE GREAT CONSI-GLIERE HERE!
THERE'S SOMETHING I'D LIKE TO ASK YOU, ACTUALLY.
I MAY HAVE AN ANSWER. WHAT'S YOUR QUESTION?
KII (CREAK)
......

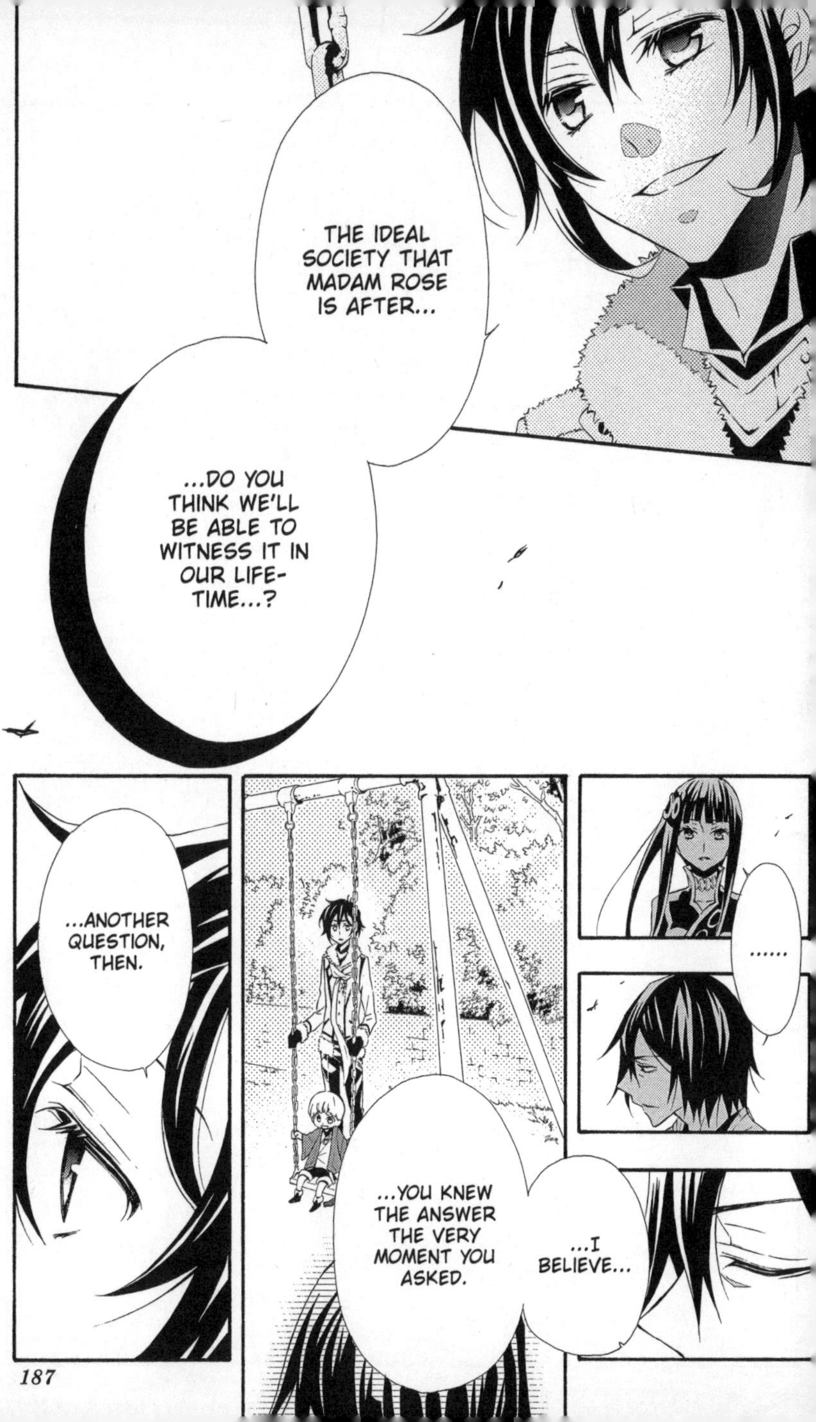
THE IDEAL SOCIETY THAT MADAM ROSE IS AFTER...
...DO YOU THINK WE'LL BE ABLE TO WITNESS IT IN OUR LIFE-TIME...?
......
...I BELIEVE...
...YOU KNEW THE ANSWER THE VERY MOMENT YOU ASKED.
...ANOTHER QUESTION, THEN.

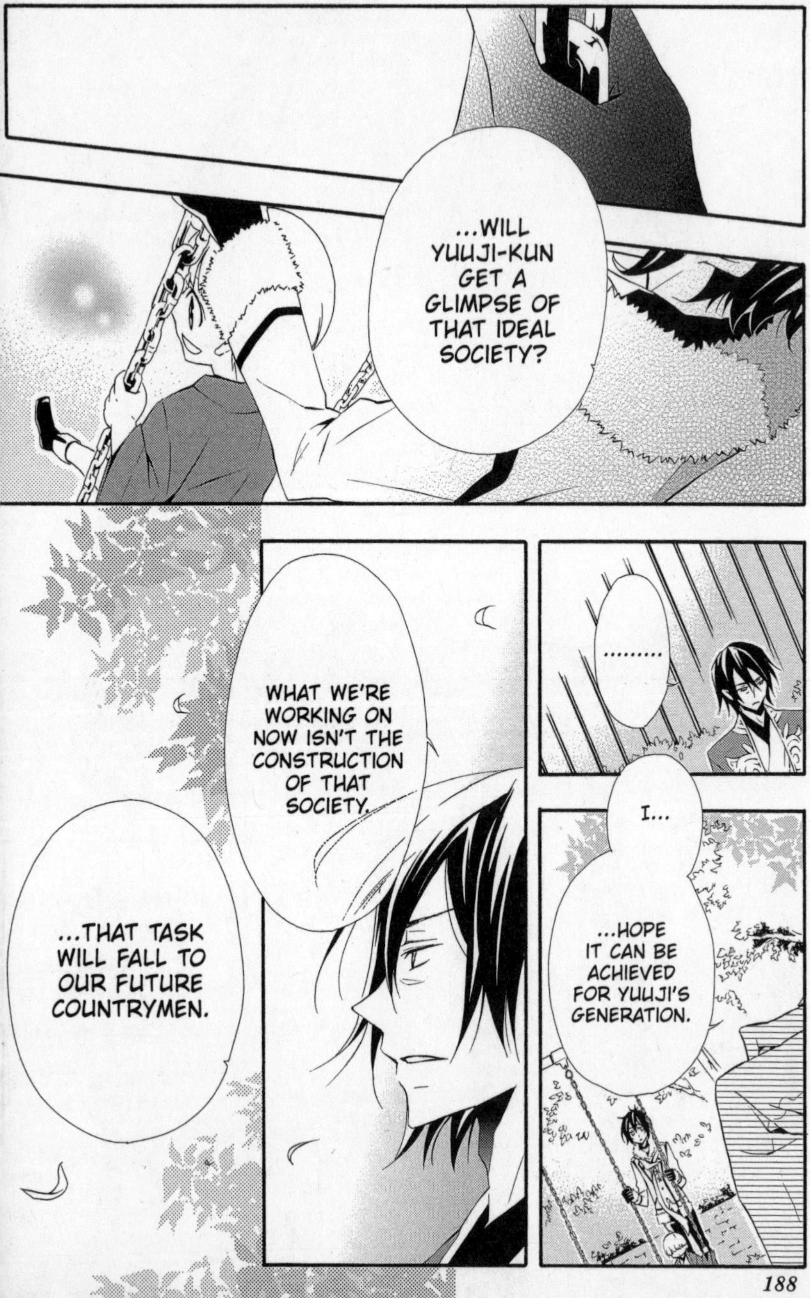
...WILL YUUJI-KUN GET A GLIMPSE OF THAT IDEAL SOCIETY?
....
I...
...HOPE IT CAN BE ACHIEVED FOR YUUJI'S GENERATION.
WHAT WE'RE WORKING ON NOW ISN'T THE CONSTRUCTION OF THAT SOCIETY.
...THAT TASK WILL FALL TO OUR FUTURE COUNTRYMEN.

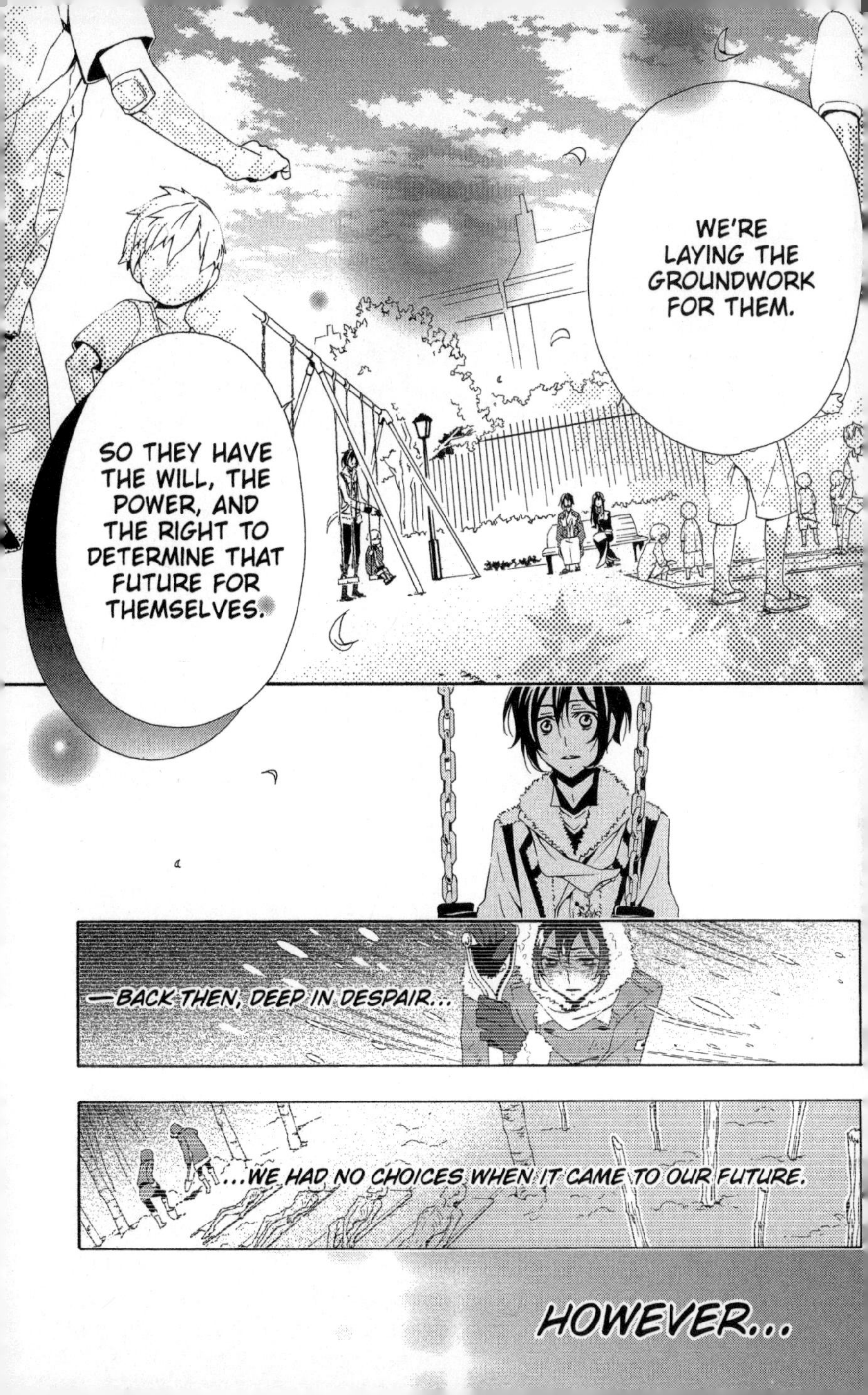
WE'RE LAYING THE GROUNDWORK FOR THEM.
SO THEY HAVE THE WILL, THE POWER, AND THE RIGHT TO DETERMINE THAT FUTURE FOR THEMSELVES.
—BACK THEN, DEEP IN DESPAIR...
...WE HAD NO CHOICES WHEN IT CAME TO OUR FUTURE.
HOWEVER...

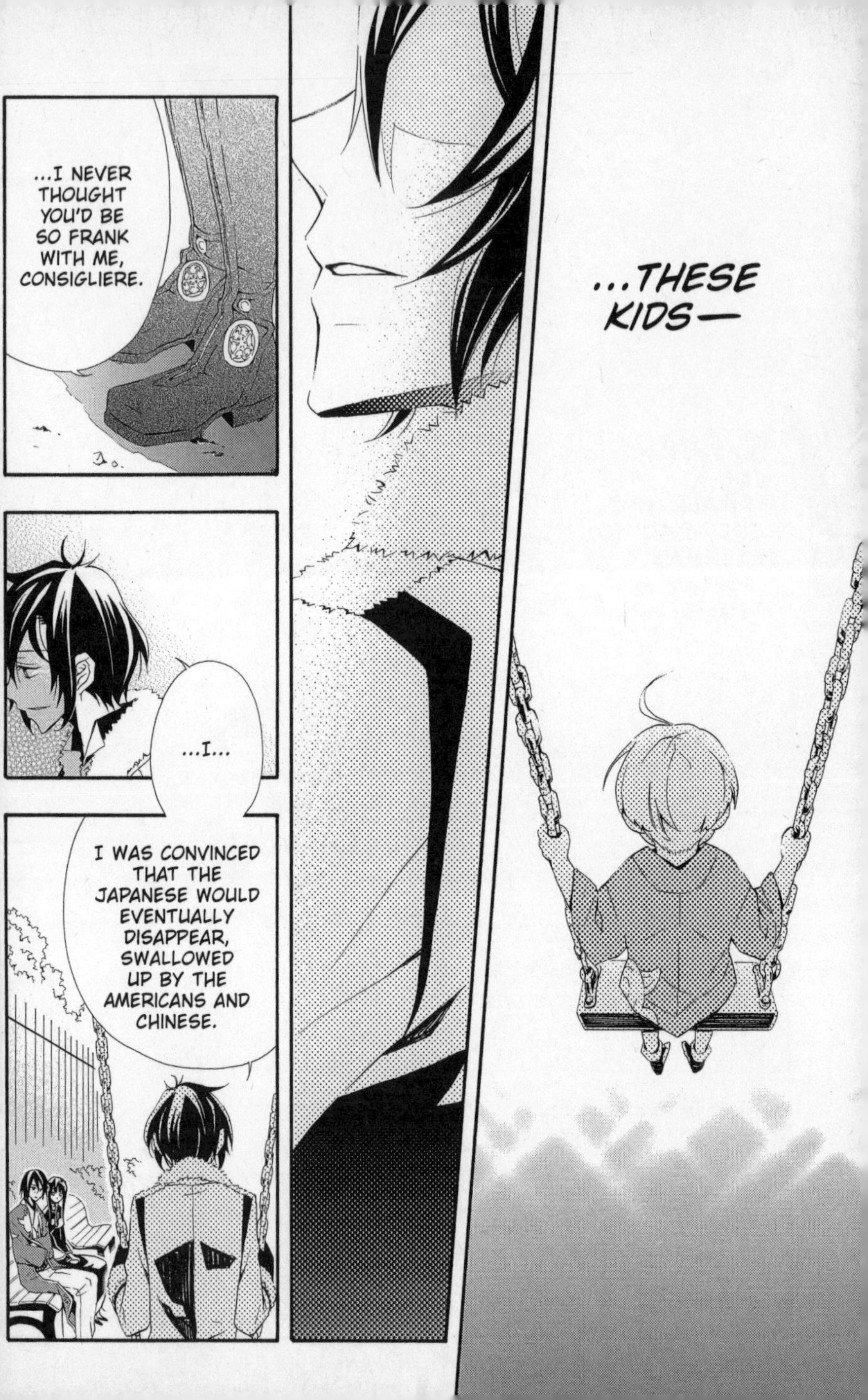
...THESE KIDS—
...I NEVER THOUGHT YOU'D BE SO FRANK WITH ME, CONSIGLIERE.
...I...
I WAS CONVINCED THAT THE JAPANESE WOULD EVENTUALLY DISAPPEAR, SWALLOWED UP BY THE AMERICANS AND CHINESE.

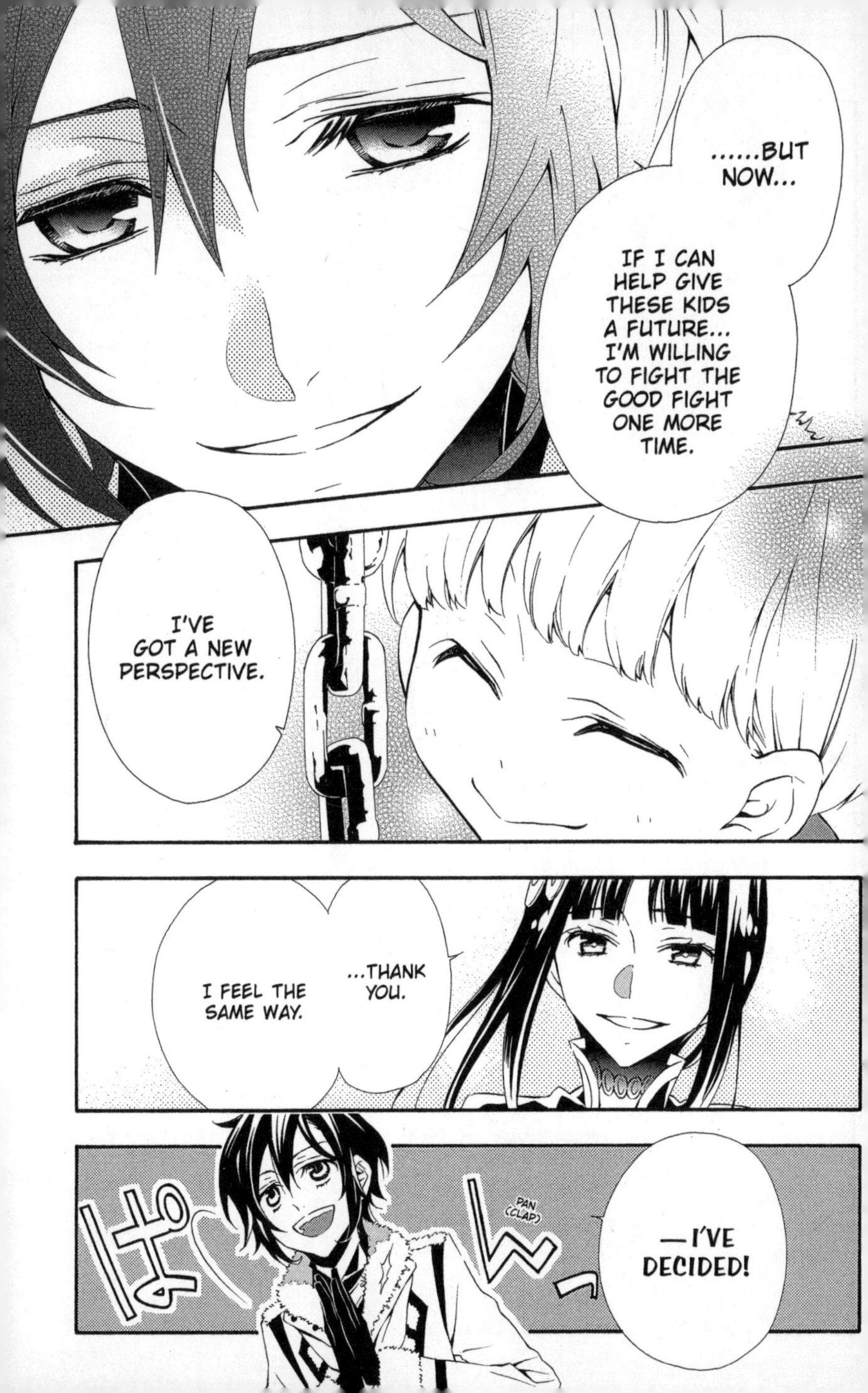
......BUT NOW...
IF I CAN HELP GIVE THESE KIDS A FUTURE... I'M WILLING TO FIGHT THE GOOD FIGHT ONE MORE TIME.
I'VE GOT A NEW PERSPECTIVE.
...THANK YOU.
I FEEL THE SAME WAY.
—I'VE DECIDED!
PAN (CLAP)
ぱん

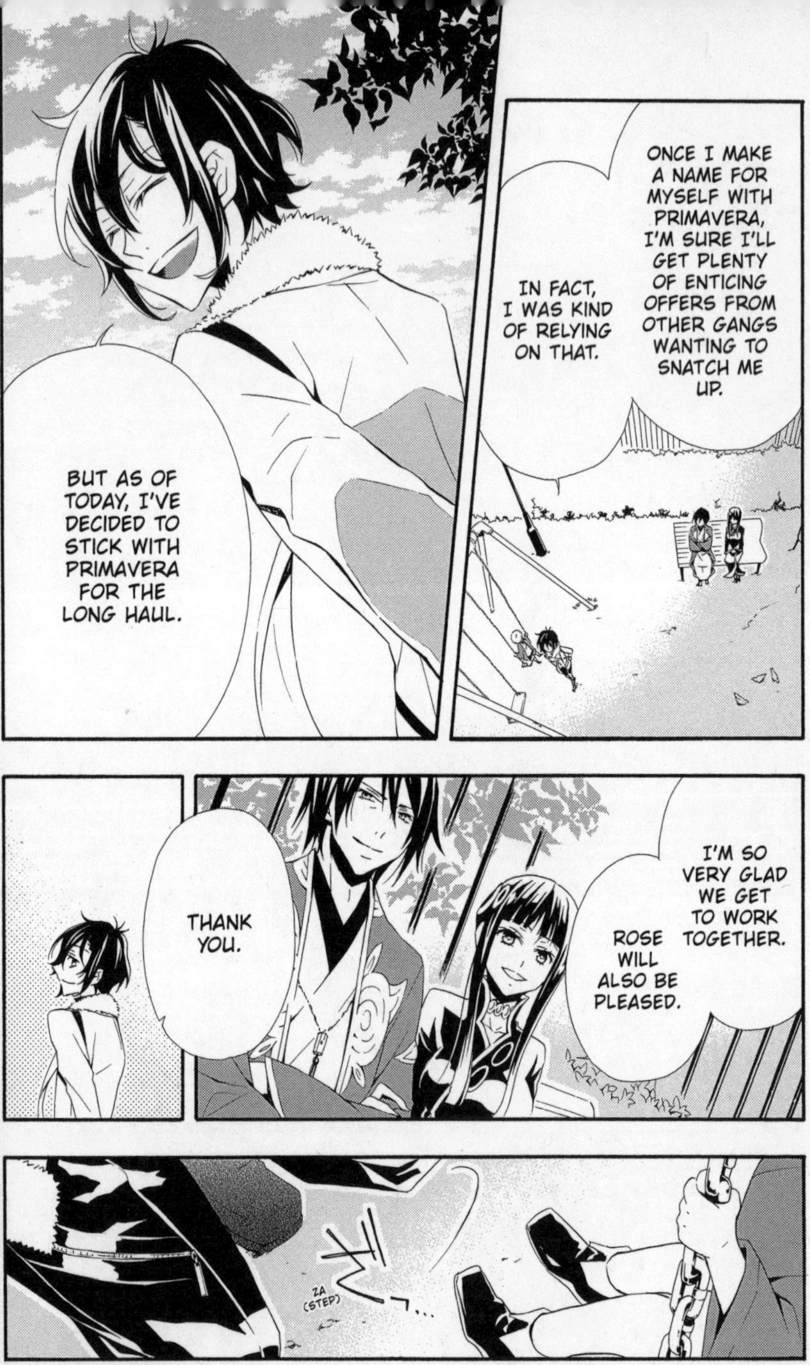
ONCE I MAKE A NAME FOR MYSELF WITH PRIMAVERA, I'M SURE I'LL GET PLENTY OF ENTICING OFFERS FROM OTHER GANGS WANTING TO SNATCH ME UP.
IN FACT, I WAS KIND OF RELYING ON THAT.
BUT AS OF TODAY, I'VE DECIDED TO STICK WITH PRIMAVERA FOR THE LONG HAUL.
I'M SO VERY GLAD WE GET TO WORK TOGETHER.
ROSE WILL ALSO BE PLEASED.
THANK YOU.
ZA (STEP)

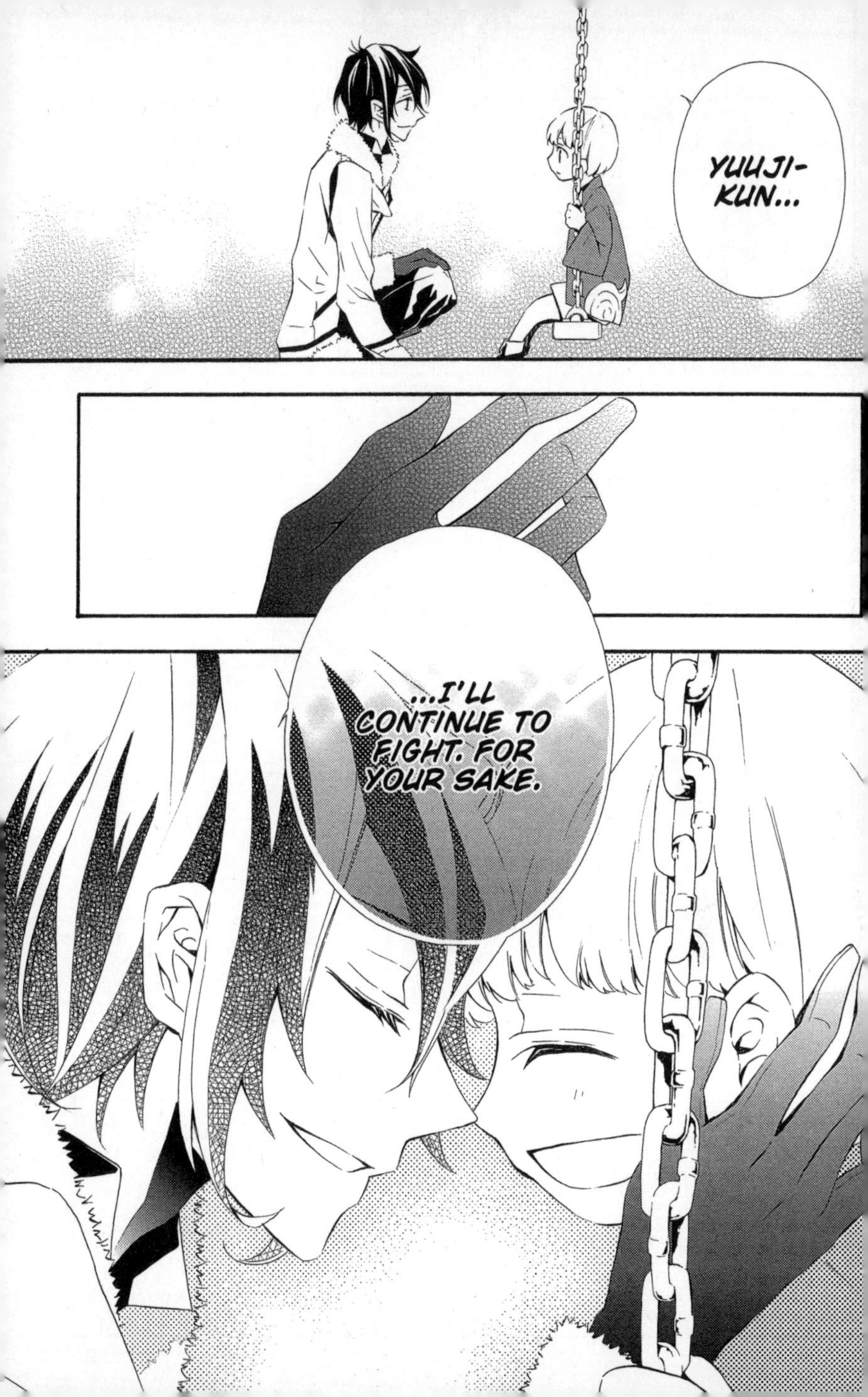
YUUJI-KUN...
...I'LL CONTINUE TO FIGHT. FOR YOUR SAKE.

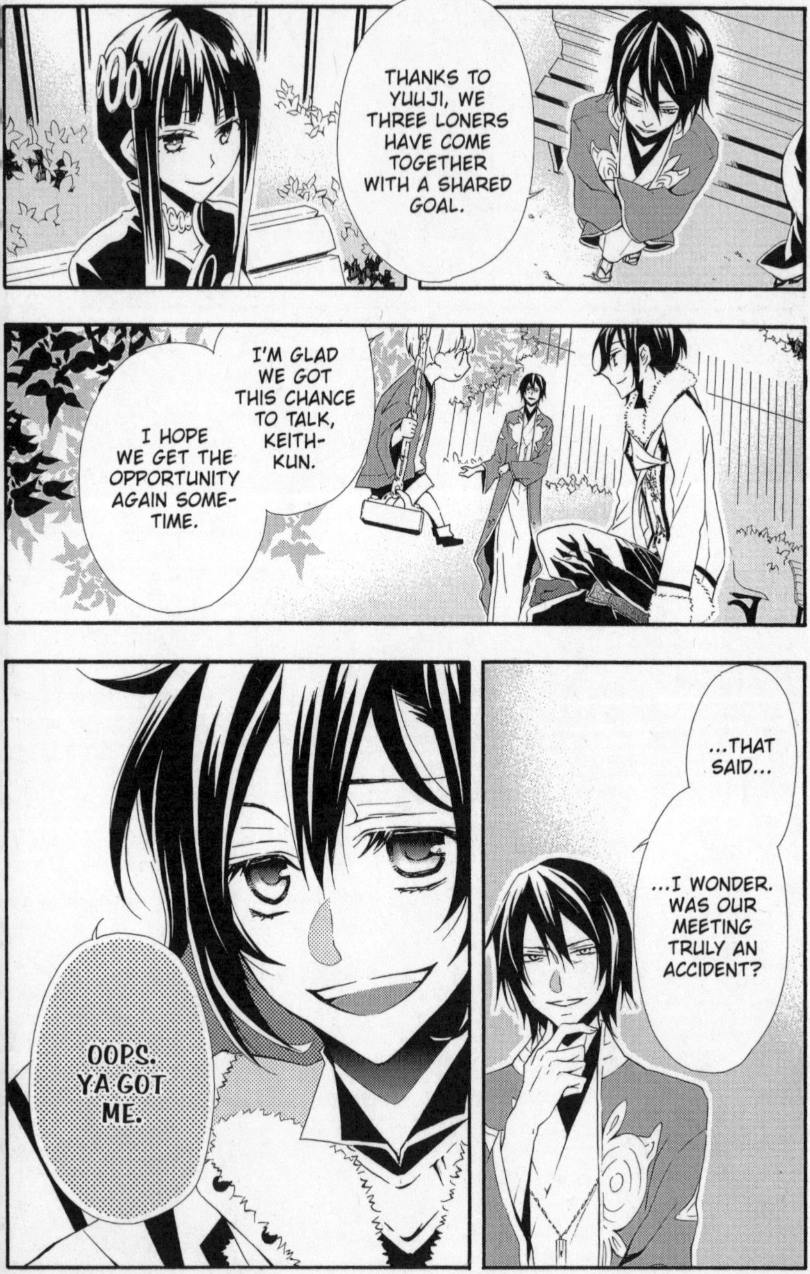
THANKS TO YUUJI, WE THREE LONERS HAVE COME TOGETHER WITH A SHARED GOAL.
I'M GLAD WE GOT THIS CHANCE TO TALK, KEITH-KUN.
I HOPE WE GET THE OPPORTUNITY AGAIN SOME-TIME.
...THAT SAID...
...I WONDER. WAS OUR MEETING TRULY AN ACCIDENT?
OOPS. YA GOT ME.

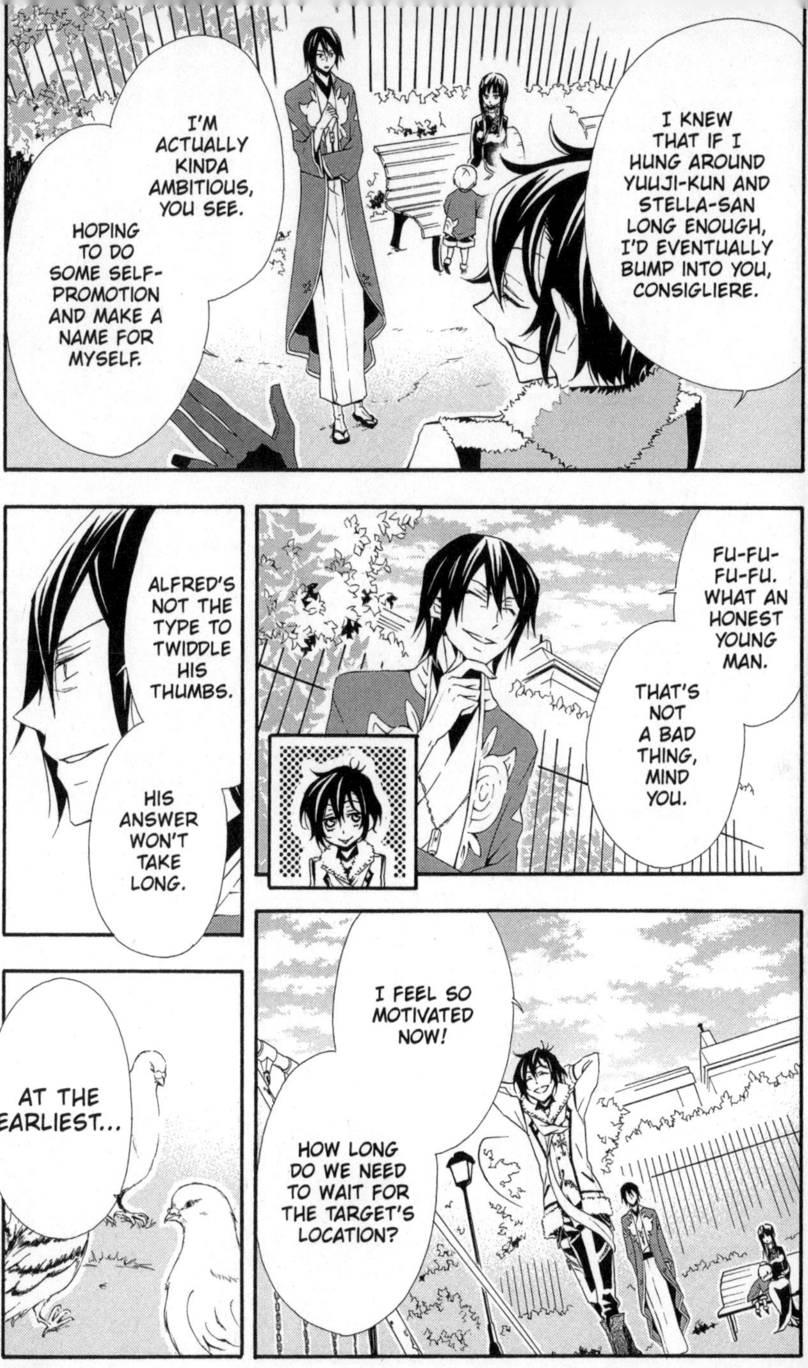
I KNEW THAT IF I HUNG AROUND YUUJI-KUN AND STELLA-SAN LONG ENOUGH, I'D EVENTUALLY BUMP INTO YOU, CONSIGLIERE.
I'M ACTUALLY KINDA AMBITIOUS, YOU SEE.
HOPING TO DO SOME SELF-PROMOTION AND MAKE A NAME FOR MYSELF.
FU-FU-FU-FU. WHAT AN HONEST YOUNG MAN.
THAT'S NOT A BAD THING, MIND YOU.
ALFRED'S NOT THE TYPE TO TWIDDLE HIS THUMBS.
HIS ANSWER WON'T TAKE LONG.
I FEEL SO MOTIVATED NOW!
HOW LONG DO WE NEED TO WAIT FOR THE TARGET'S LOCATION?
AT THE EARLIEST...

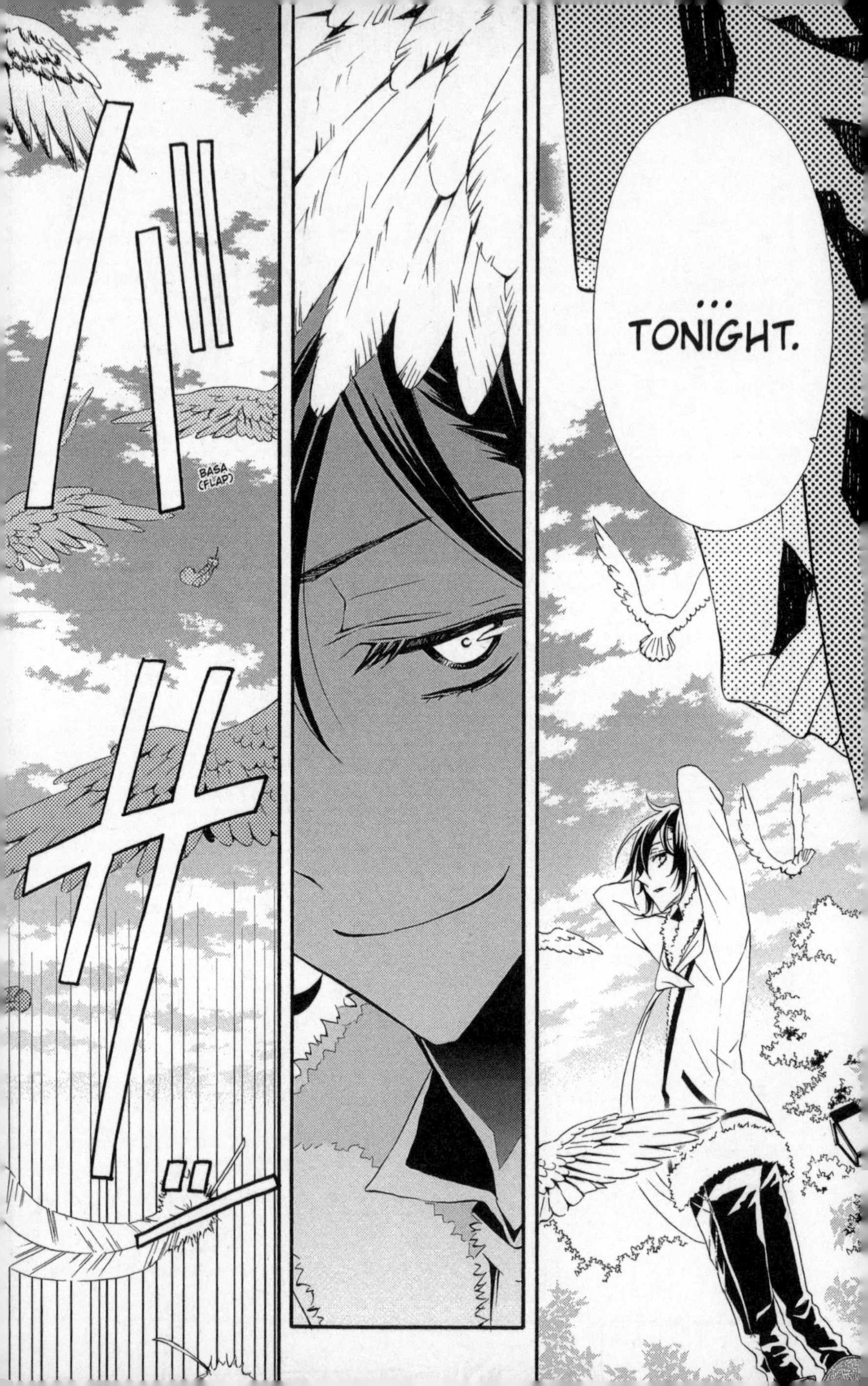
...TONIGHT.
BASA
(FLAP)

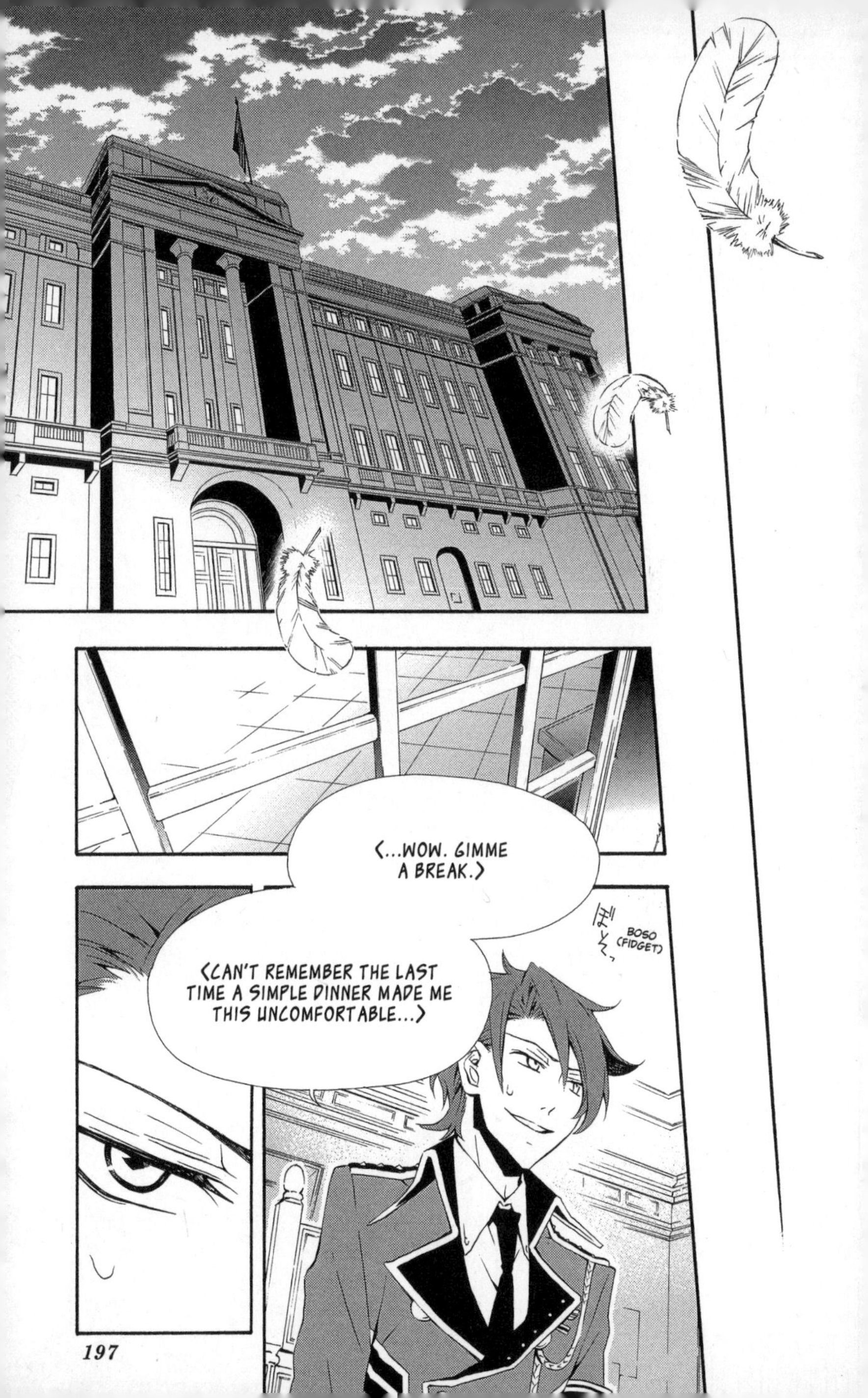
〈...WOW. GIMME A BREAK.〉
BOSO (FIDGET)
〈CAN'T REMEMBER THE LAST TIME A SIMPLE DINNER MADE ME THIS UNCOMFORTABLE...〉

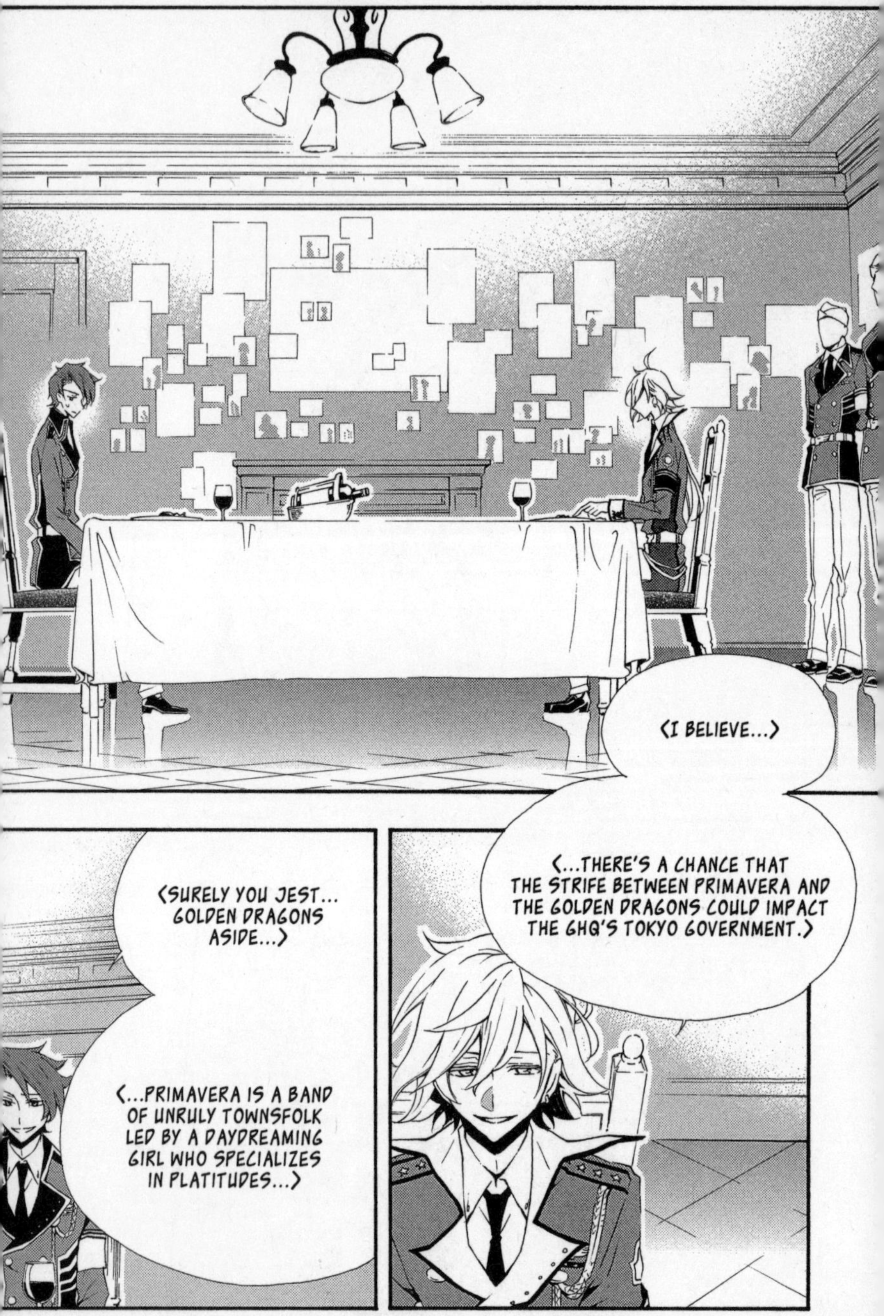

<I BELIEVE...>
<...THERE'S A CHANCE THAT THE STRIFE BETWEEN PRIMAVERA AND THE GOLDEN DRAGONS COULD IMPACT THE GHQ'S TOKYO GOVERNMENT.>
<SURELY YOU JEST... GOLDEN DRAGONS ASIDE...>
<...PRIMAVERA IS A BAND OF UNRULY TOWNSFOLK LED BY A DAYDREAMING GIRL WHO SPECIALIZES IN PLATITUDES...>

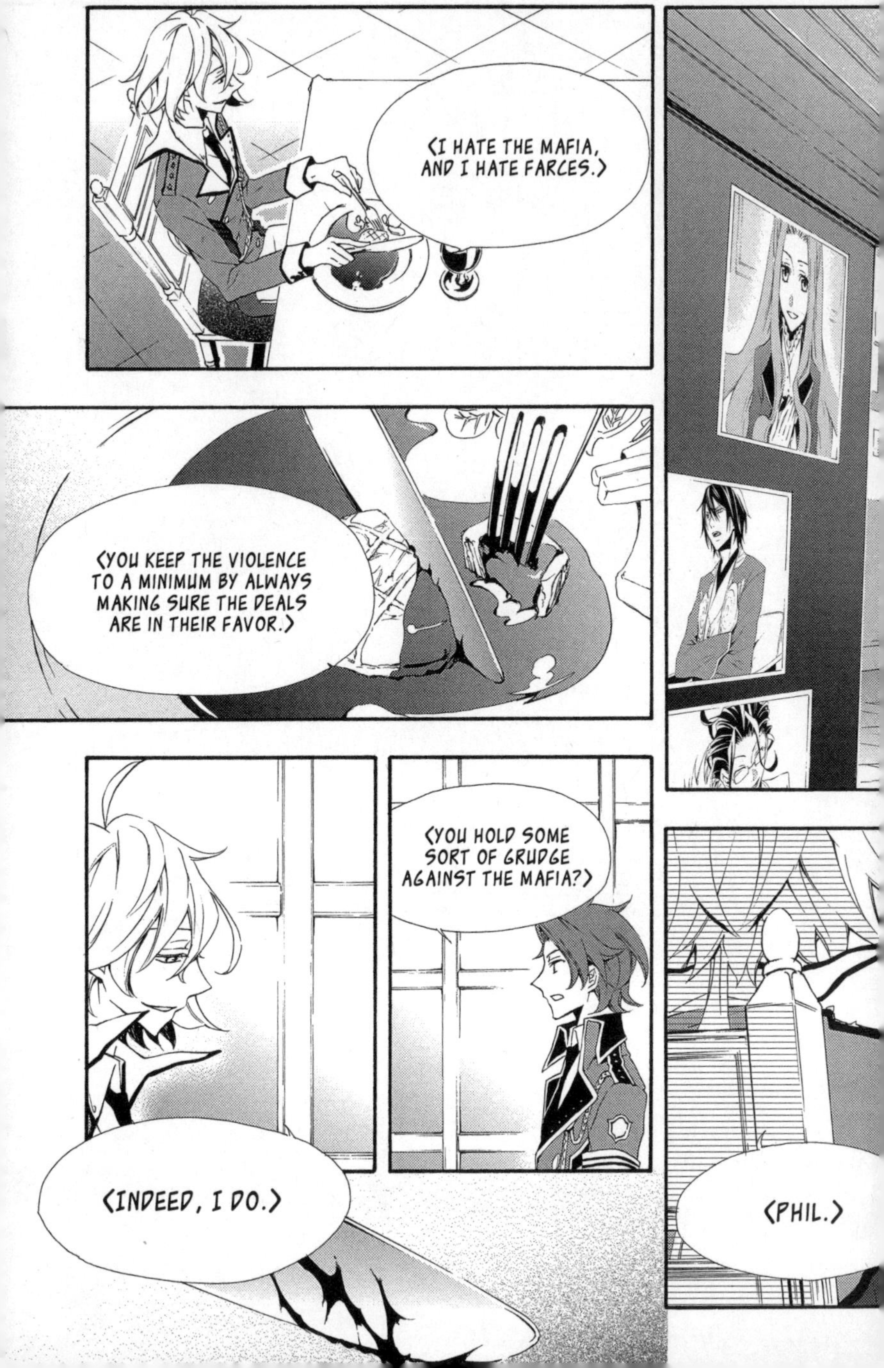
〈I HATE THE MAFIA, AND I HATE FARCES.〉
〈YOU KEEP THE VIOLENCE TO A MINIMUM BY ALWAYS MAKING SURE THE DEALS ARE IN THEIR FAVOR.〉
〈PHIL.〉
〈YOU HOLD SOME SORT OF GRUDGE AGAINST THE MAFIA?〉
〈INDEED, I DO.〉

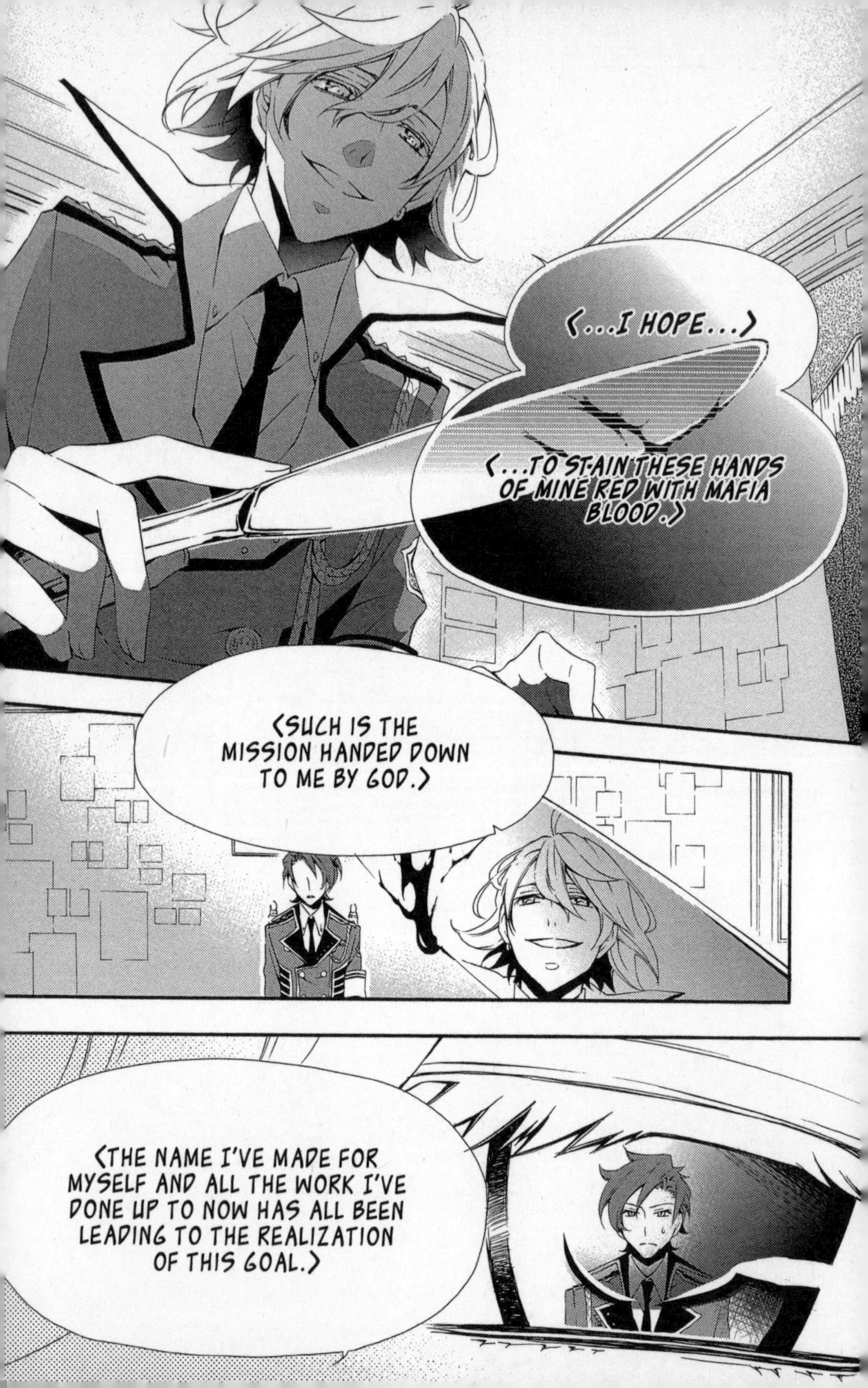
<...I HOPE...>
<...TO STAIN THESE HANDS OF MINE RED WITH MAFIA BLOOD.>
<SUCH IS THE MISSION HANDED DOWN TO ME BY GOD.>
<THE NAME I'VE MADE FOR MYSELF AND ALL THE WORK I'VE DONE UP TO NOW HAS ALL BEEN LEADING TO THE REALIZATION OF THIS GOAL.>

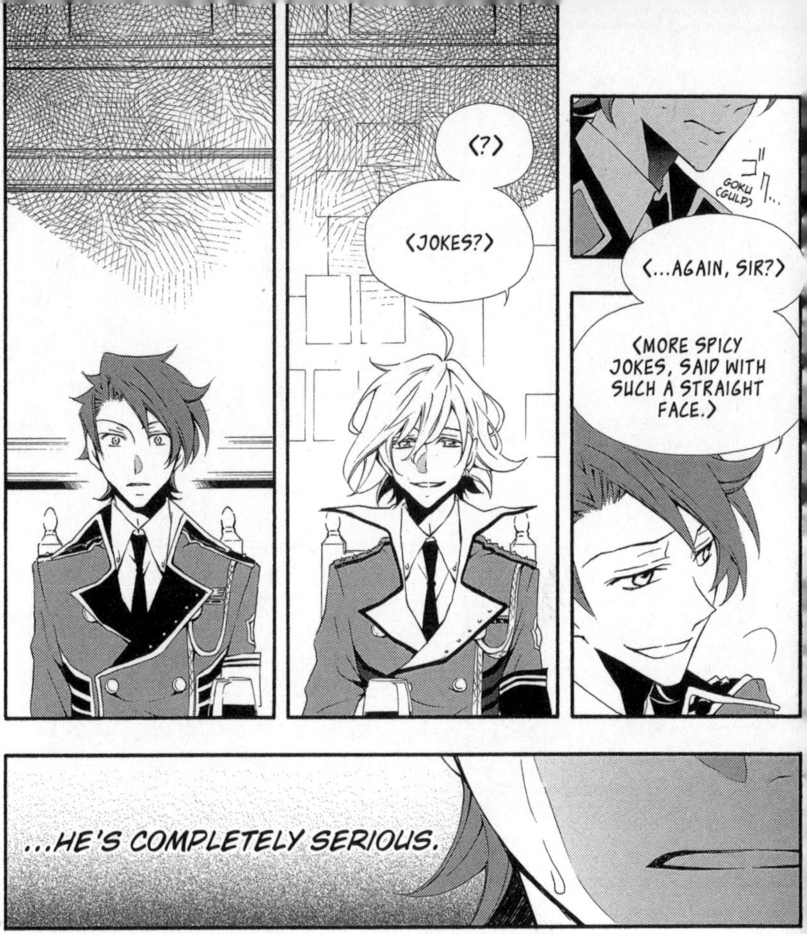
ゴク…
GOKU (GULP)
〈...AGAIN, SIR?〉
〈MORE SPICY JOKES, SAID WITH SUCH A STRAIGHT FACE.〉
〈?〉
〈JOKES?〉
...HE'S COMPLETELY SERIOUS.

—THERE'S ***NOTHING JOKING*** *ABOUT THIS MAN'S INTENTIONS.*

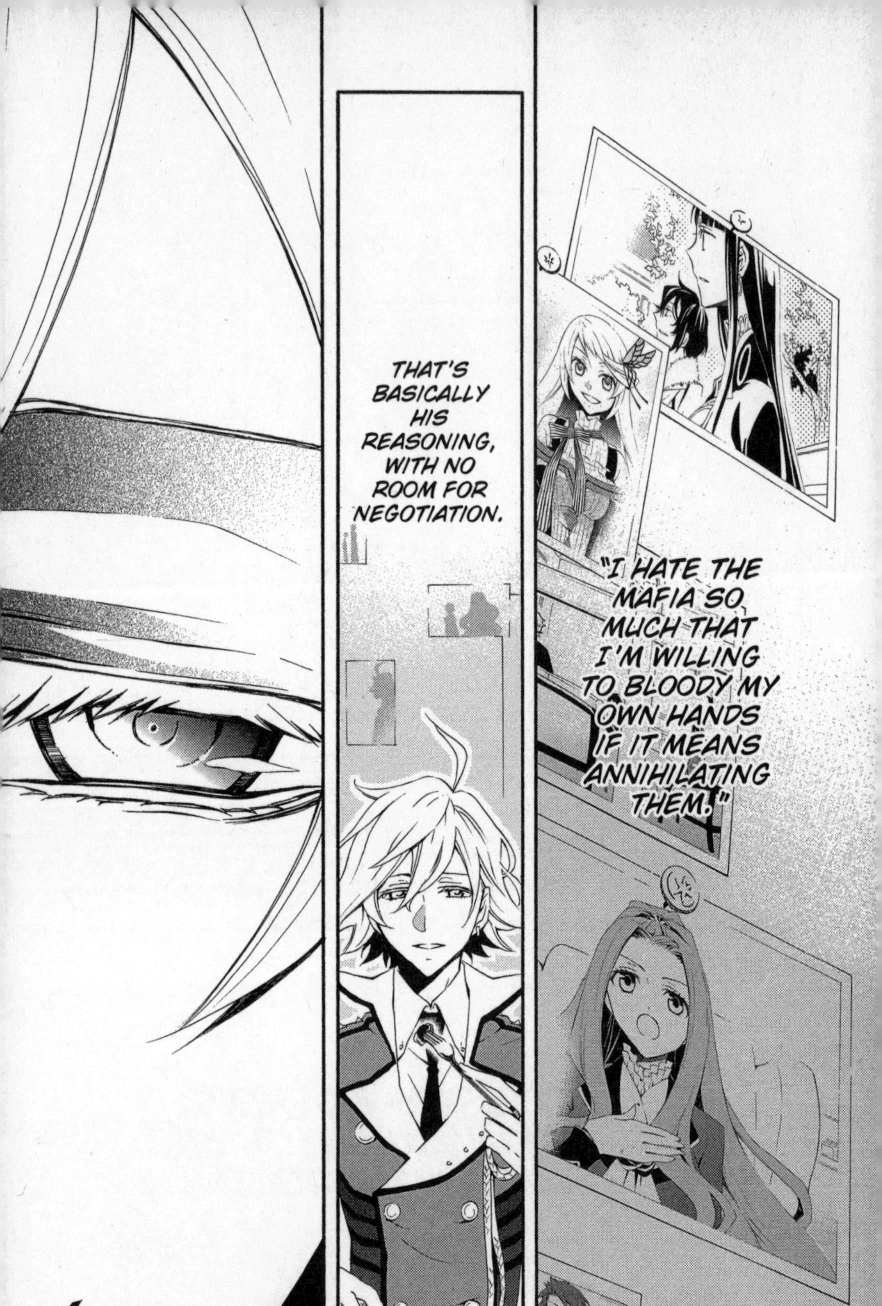
"I HATE THE MAFIA SO MUCH THAT I'M WILLING TO BLOODY MY OWN HANDS IF IT MEANS ANNIHILATING THEM."
THAT'S BASICALLY HIS REASONING, WITH NO ROOM FOR NEGOTIATION.

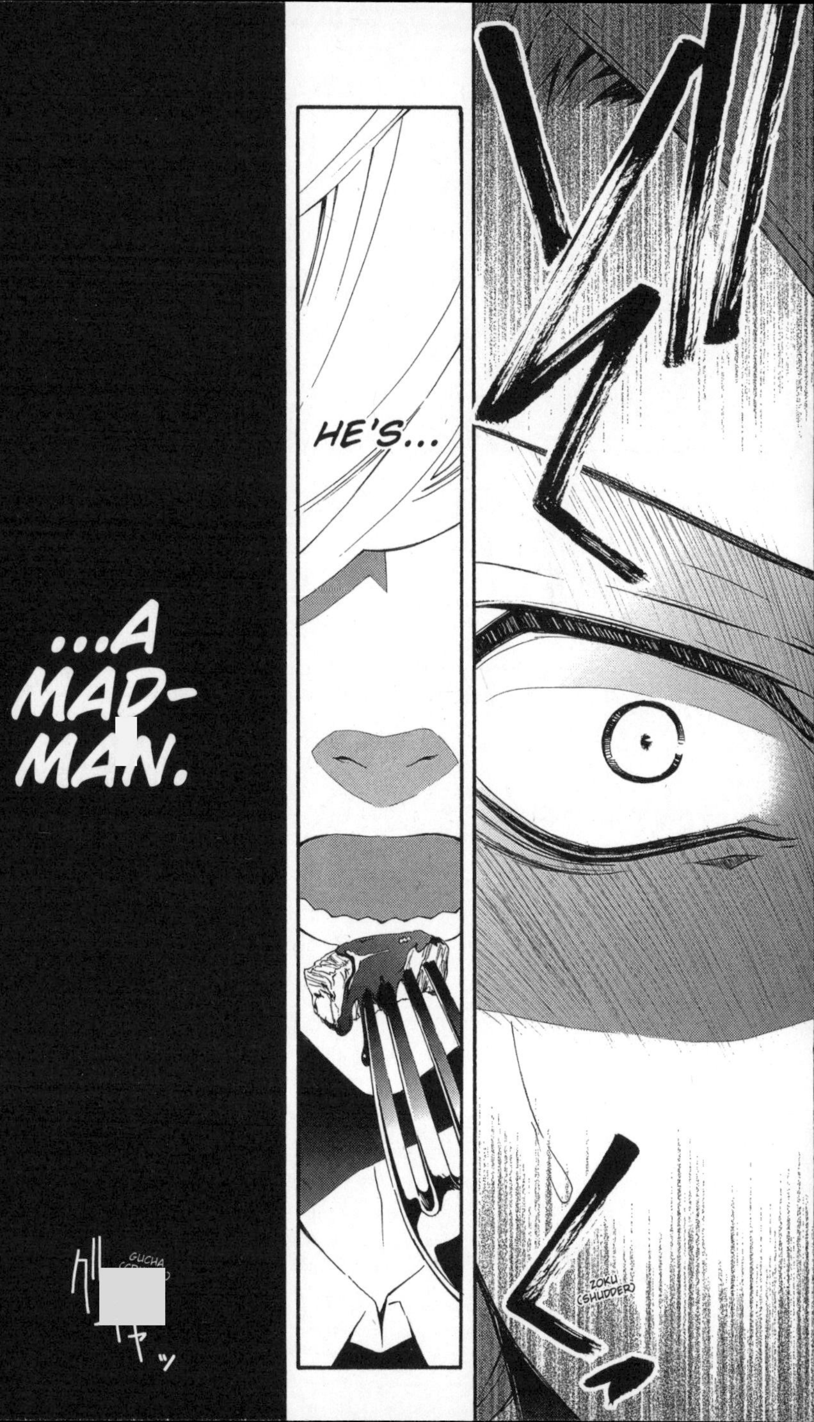
ZOKU (SHUDDER)
HE'S...
...A MAD-MAN.
GUCHA

⟨...TO THAT END...⟩

⟨...YOU WILL BE MY INSTRUMENT, PHIL.⟩

⟨......HUH.⟩

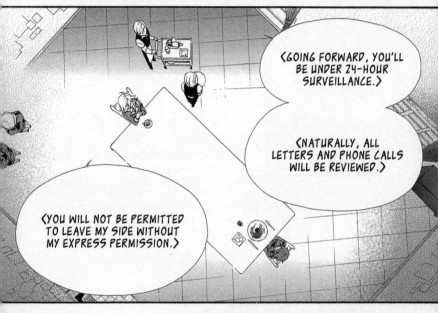

⟨GOING FORWARD, YOU'LL BE UNDER 24-HOUR SURVEILLANCE.⟩

⟨NATURALLY, ALL LETTERS AND PHONE CALLS WILL BE REVIEWED.⟩

⟨YOU WILL NOT BE PERMITTED TO LEAVE MY SIDE WITHOUT MY EXPRESS PERMISSION.⟩

⟨I WOULD LIKE TO KEEP YOU FROM EATING AND SLEEPING WITHOUT MY PERMISSION TOO...BUT I'M NOT QUITE SUCH AN OGRE.⟩

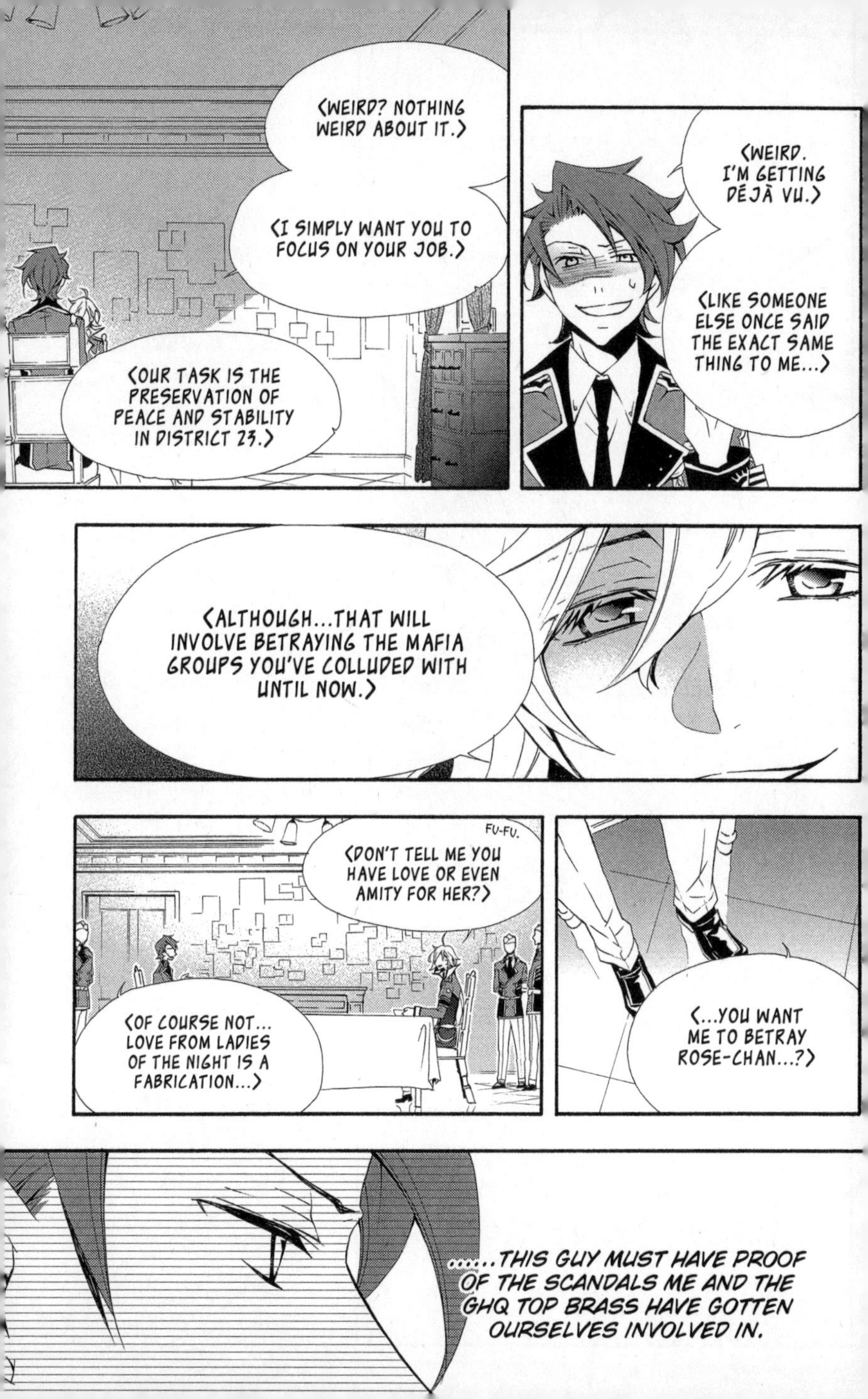

〈WEIRD. I'M GETTING DÉJÀ VU.〉
〈LIKE SOMEONE ELSE ONCE SAID THE EXACT SAME THING TO ME...〉
〈WEIRD? NOTHING WEIRD ABOUT IT.〉
〈I SIMPLY WANT YOU TO FOCUS ON YOUR JOB.〉
〈OUR TASK IS THE PRESERVATION OF PEACE AND STABILITY IN DISTRICT 23.〉
〈ALTHOUGH...THAT WILL INVOLVE BETRAYING THE MAFIA GROUPS YOU'VE COLLUDED WITH UNTIL NOW.〉
〈...YOU WANT ME TO BETRAY ROSE-CHAN...?〉
FU-FU.
〈DON'T TELL ME YOU HAVE LOVE OR EVEN AMITY FOR HER?〉
〈OF COURSE NOT... LOVE FROM LADIES OF THE NIGHT IS A FABRICATION...〉
......THIS GUY MUST HAVE PROOF OF THE SCANDALS ME AND THE GHQ TOP BRASS HAVE GOTTEN OURSELVES INVOLVED IN.

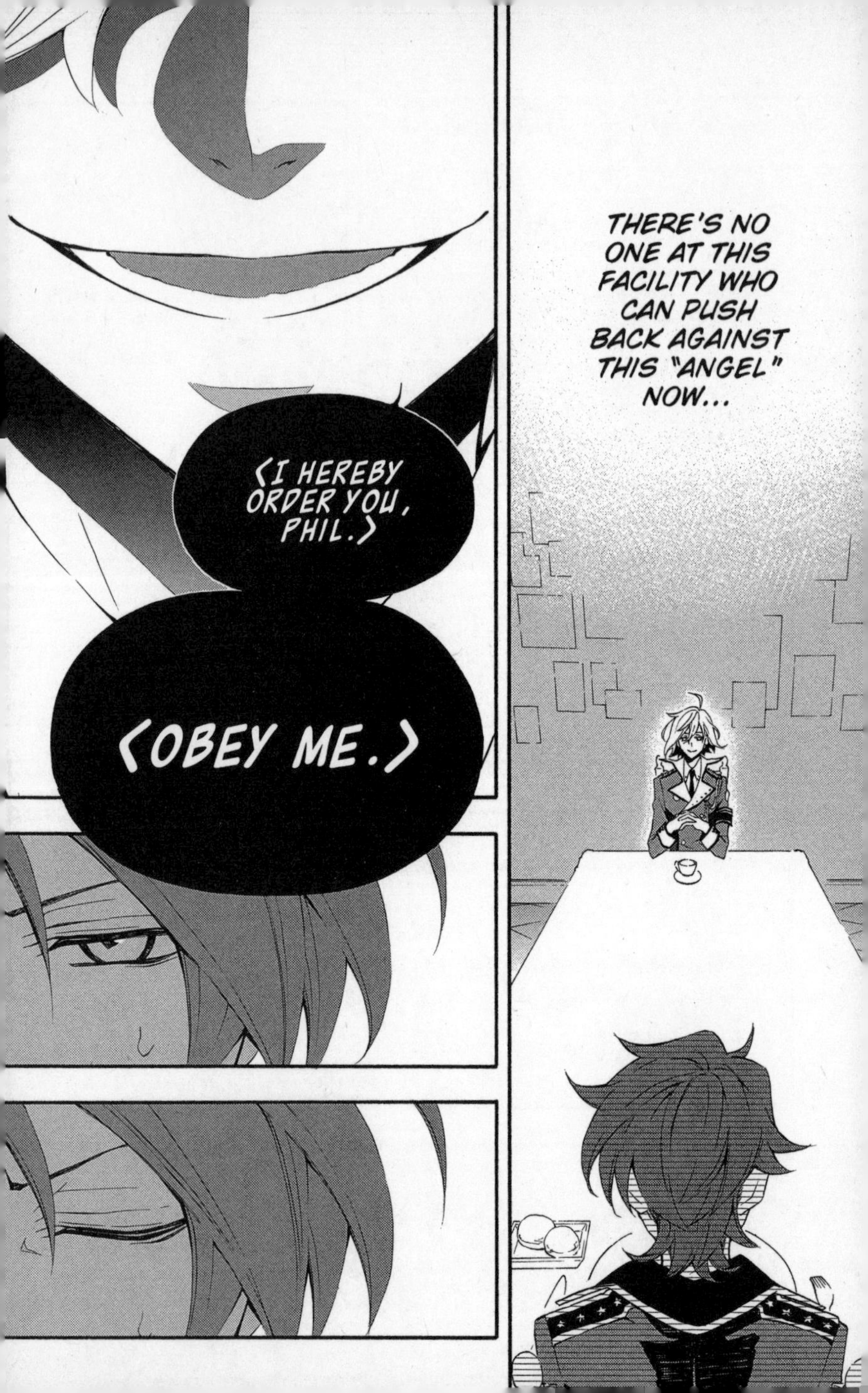
THERE'S NO ONE AT THIS FACILITY WHO CAN PUSH BACK AGAINST THIS "ANGEL" NOW...
<I HEREBY ORDER YOU, PHIL.>
<OBEY ME.>

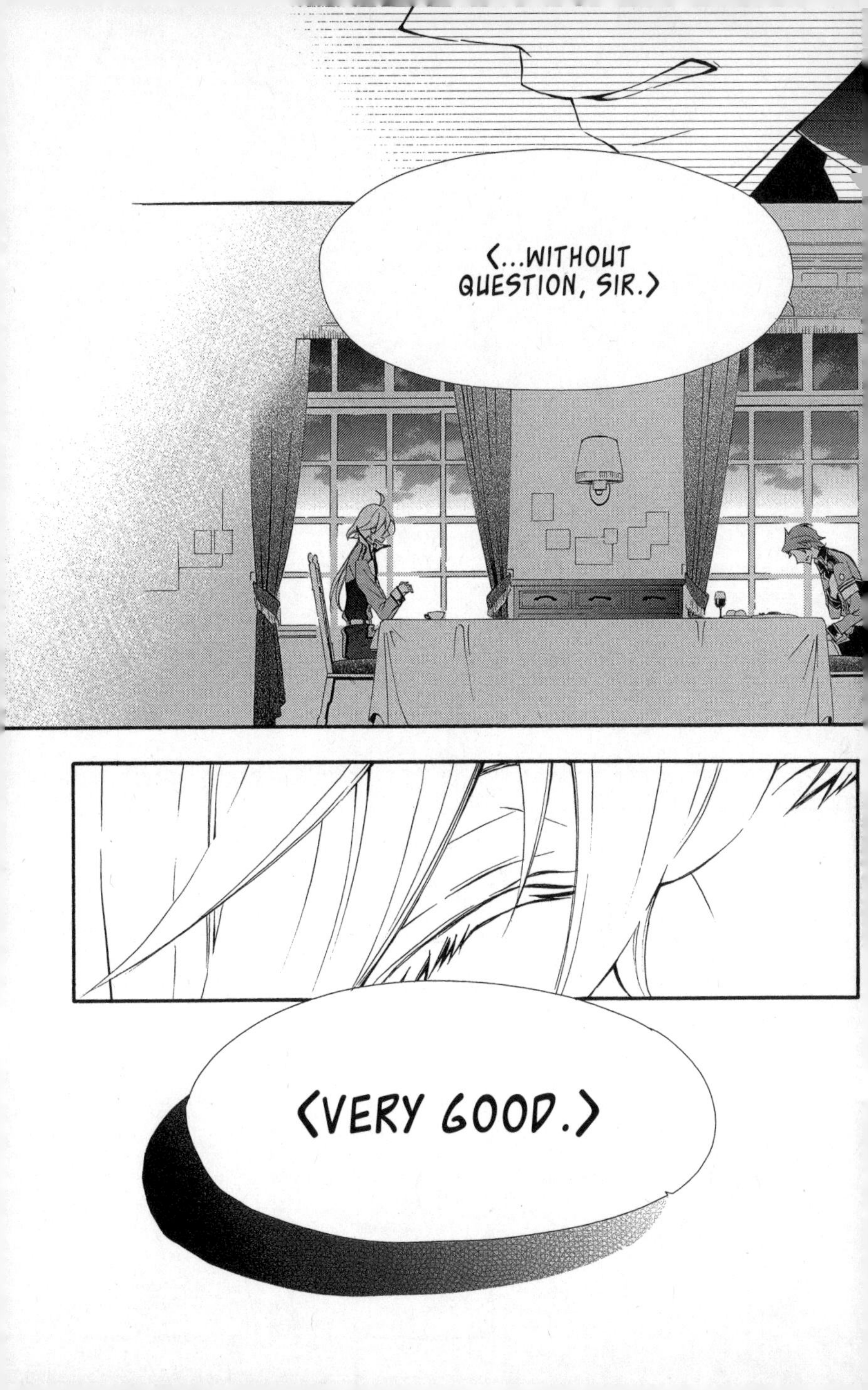
<...WITHOUT QUESTION, SIR.>
<VERY GOOD.>

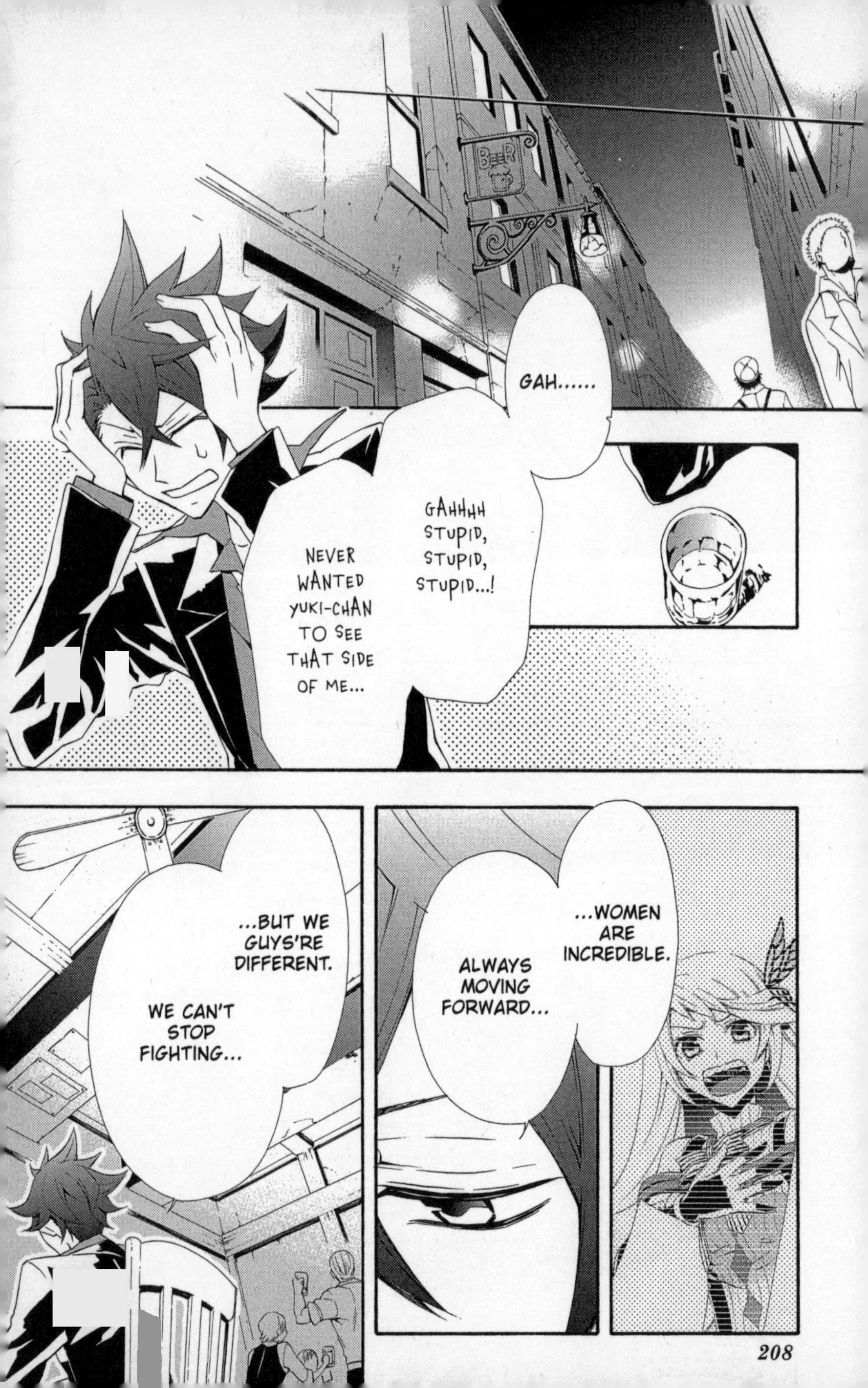
GAH......
GAHHHH STUPID, STUPID, STUPID...!
NEVER WANTED YUKI-CHAN TO SEE THAT SIDE OF ME...
...WOMEN ARE INCREDIBLE.
ALWAYS MOVING FORWARD...
...BUT WE GUYS'RE DIFFERENT.
WE CAN'T STOP FIGHTING...

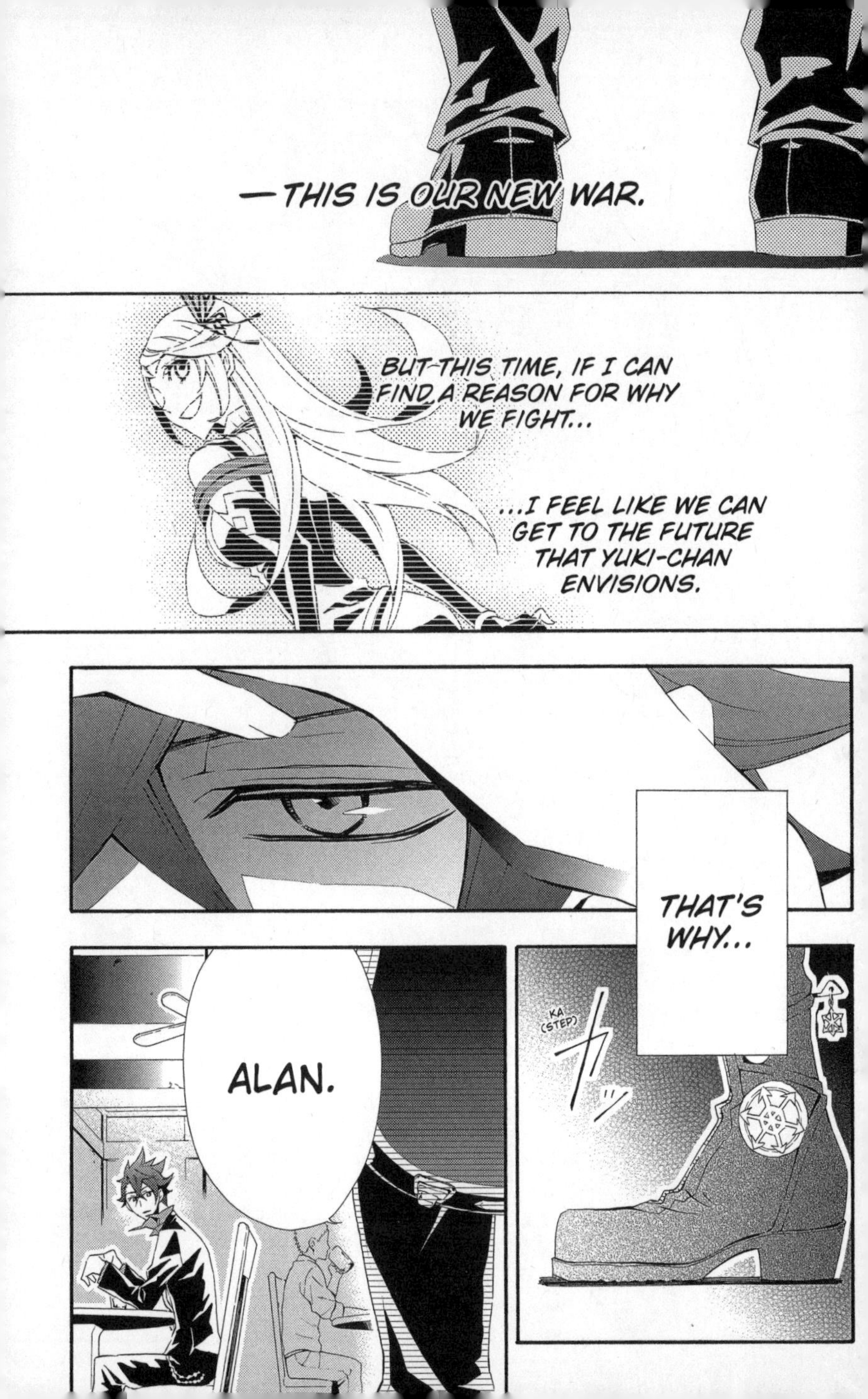
—THIS IS OUR NEW WAR.
BUT THIS TIME, IF I CAN FIND A REASON FOR WHY WE FIGHT...
...I FEEL LIKE WE CAN GET TO THE FUTURE THAT YUKI-CHAN ENVISIONS.
THAT'S WHY...
KA (STEP)
ALAN.

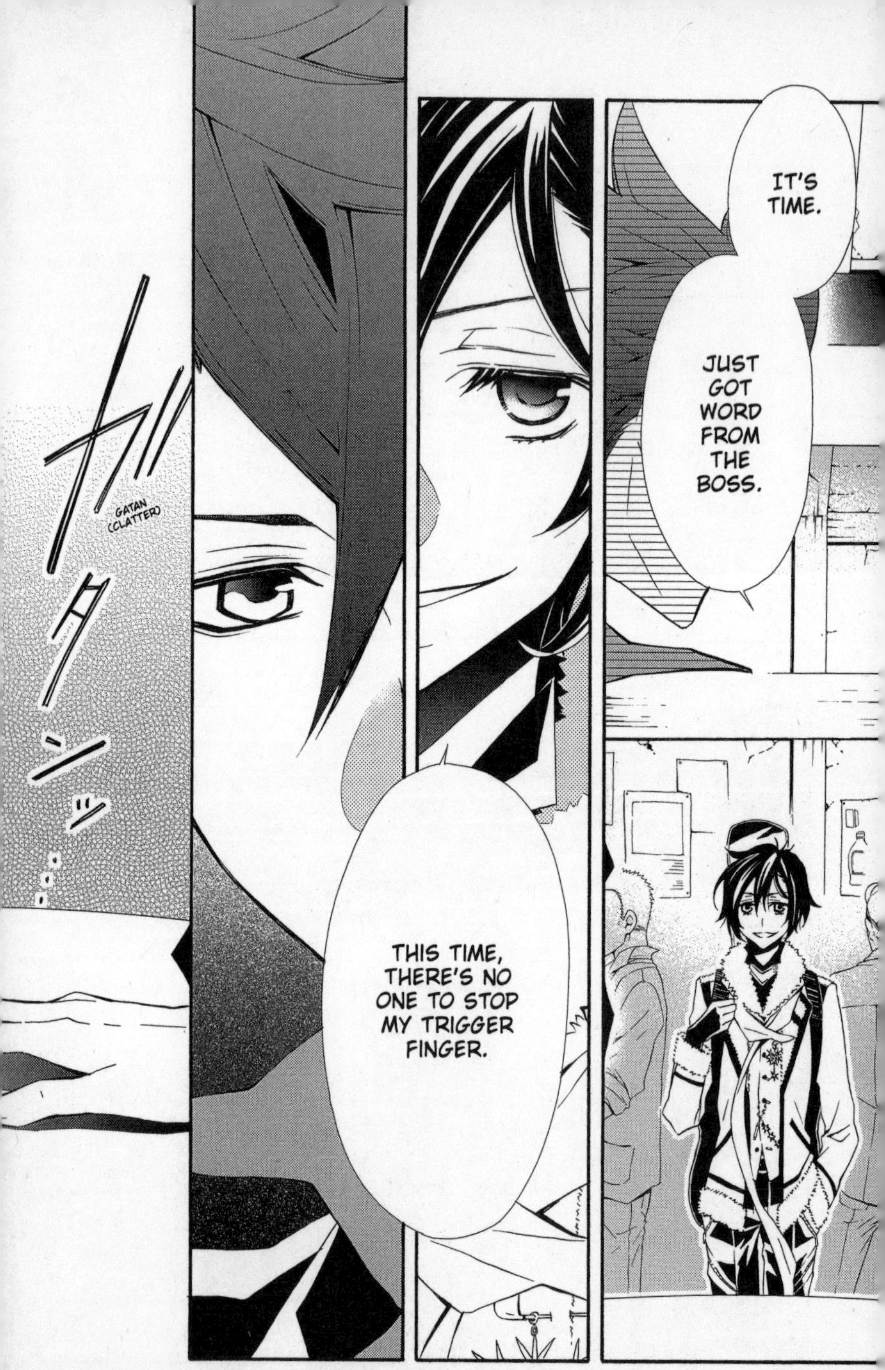
IT'S TIME.
JUST GOT WORD FROM THE BOSS.
THIS TIME, THERE'S NO ONE TO STOP MY TRIGGER FINGER.
GATAN (CLATTER)

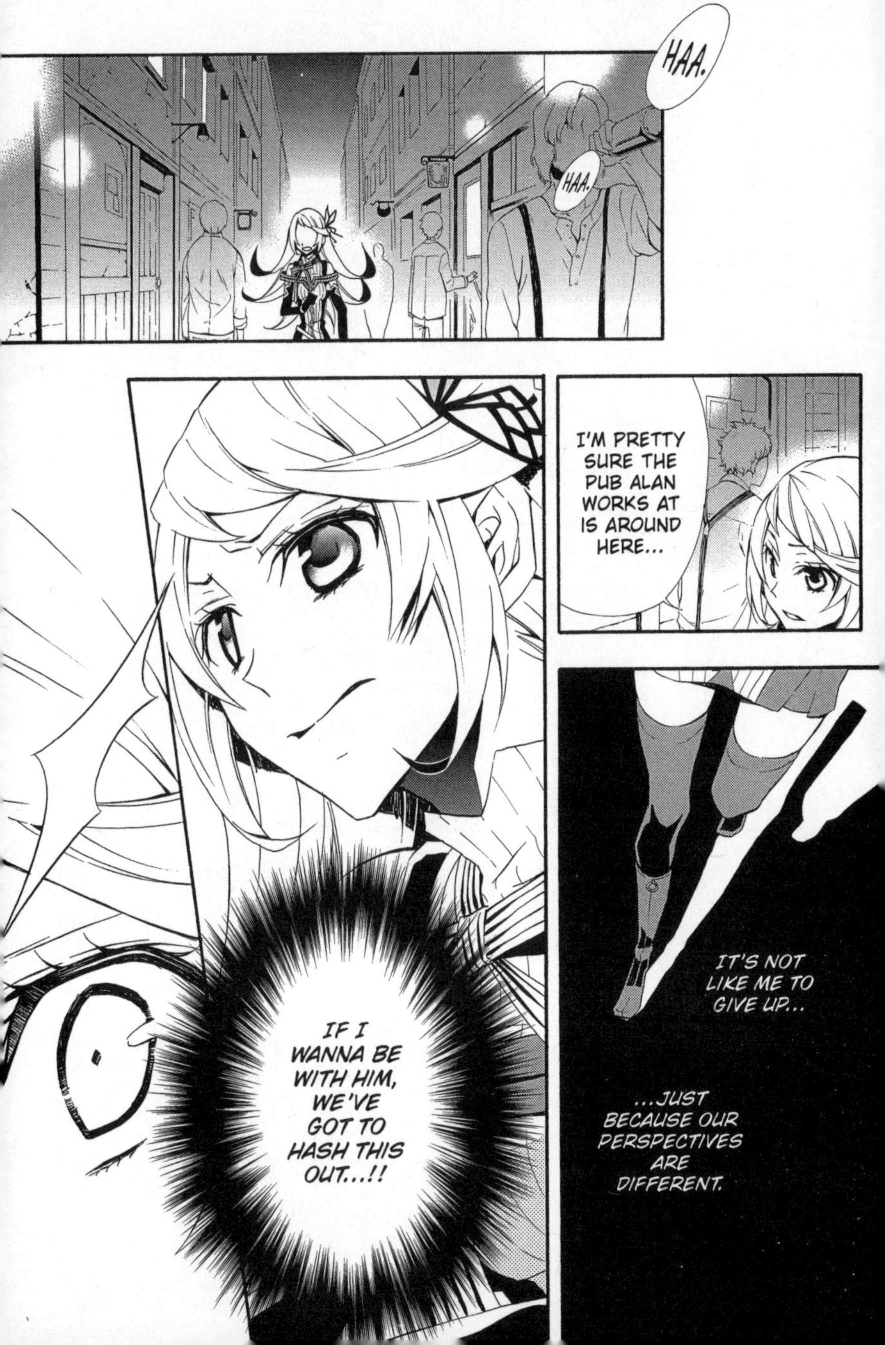
HAA.
HAA.
I'M PRETTY SURE THE PUB ALAN WORKS AT IS AROUND HERE...
IT'S NOT LIKE ME TO GIVE UP...
...JUST BECAUSE OUR PERSPECTIVES ARE DIFFERENT.
IF I WANNA BE WITH HIM, WE'VE GOT TO HASH THIS OUT...!!

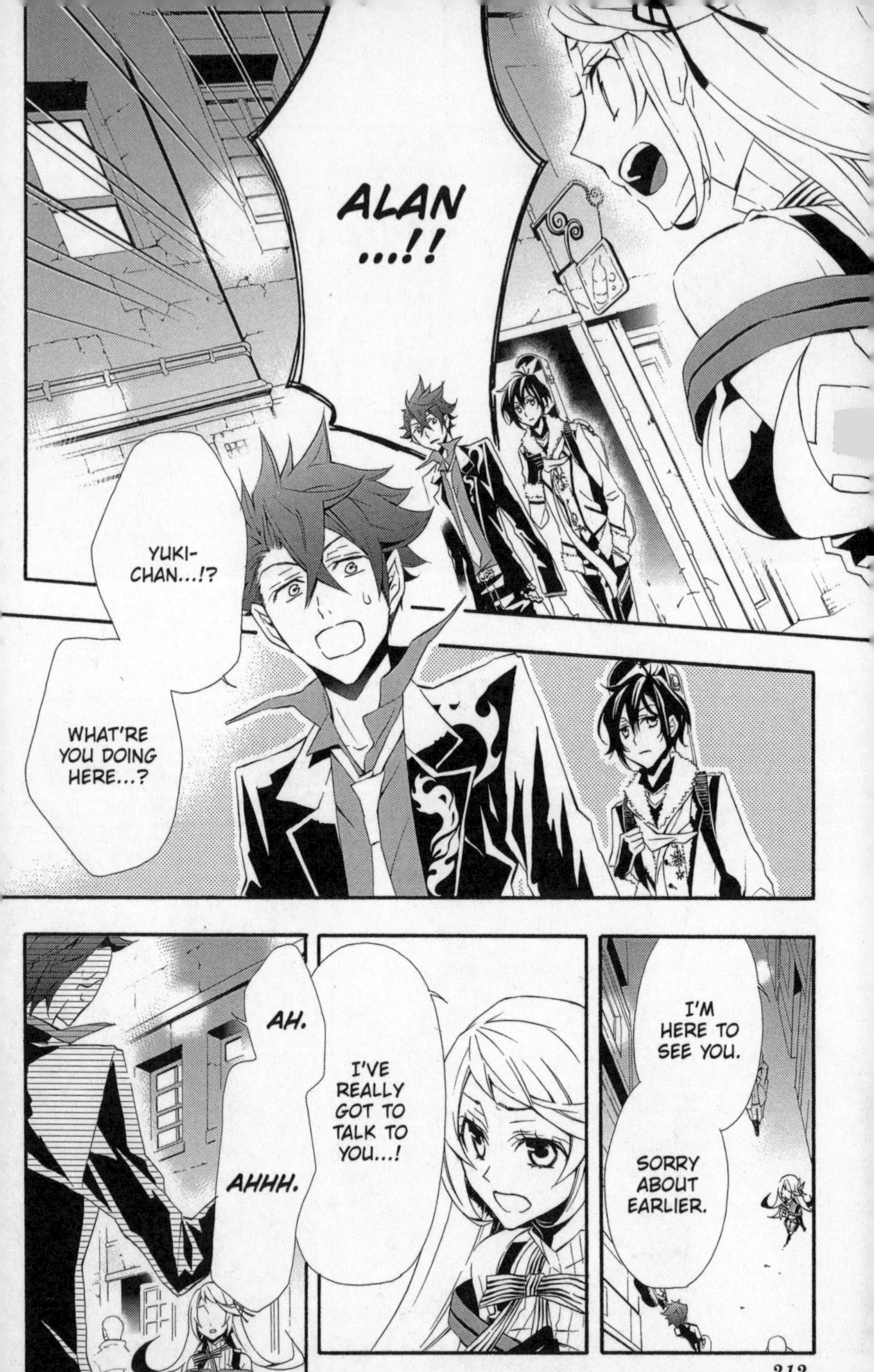
ALAN ...!!
YUKI-CHAN...!?
WHAT'RE YOU DOING HERE...?
I'M HERE TO SEE YOU.
SORRY ABOUT EARLIER.
I'VE REALLY GOT TO TALK TO YOU...!
AH.
AHHH.

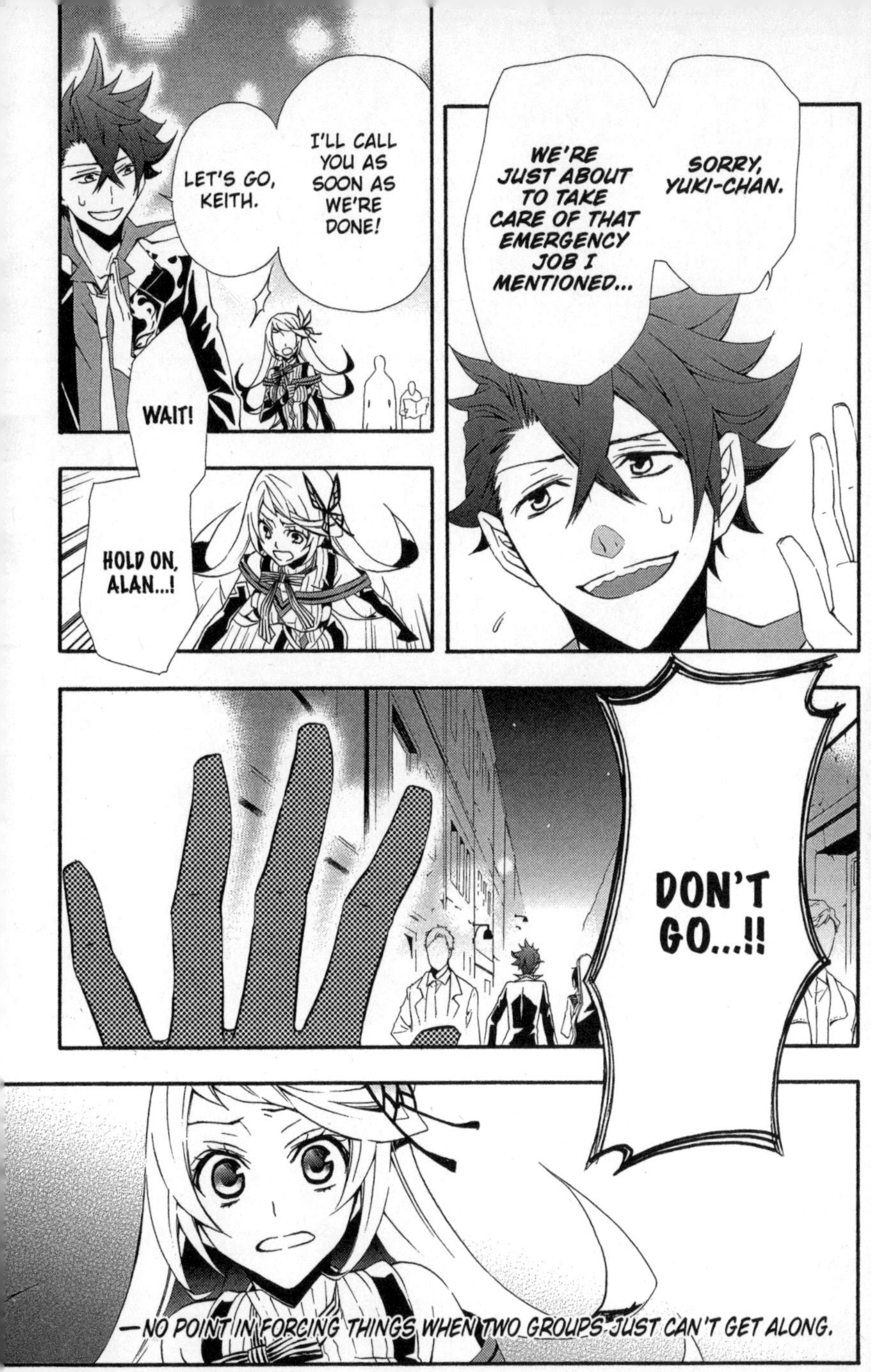
SORRY, YUKI-CHAN.
WE'RE JUST ABOUT TO TAKE CARE OF THAT EMERGENCY JOB I MENTIONED...
I'LL CALL YOU AS SOON AS WE'RE DONE!
LET'S GO, KEITH.
WAIT!
HOLD ON, ALAN...!
DON'T GO...!!
—NO POINT IN FORCING THINGS WHEN TWO GROUPS JUST CAN'T GET ALONG.

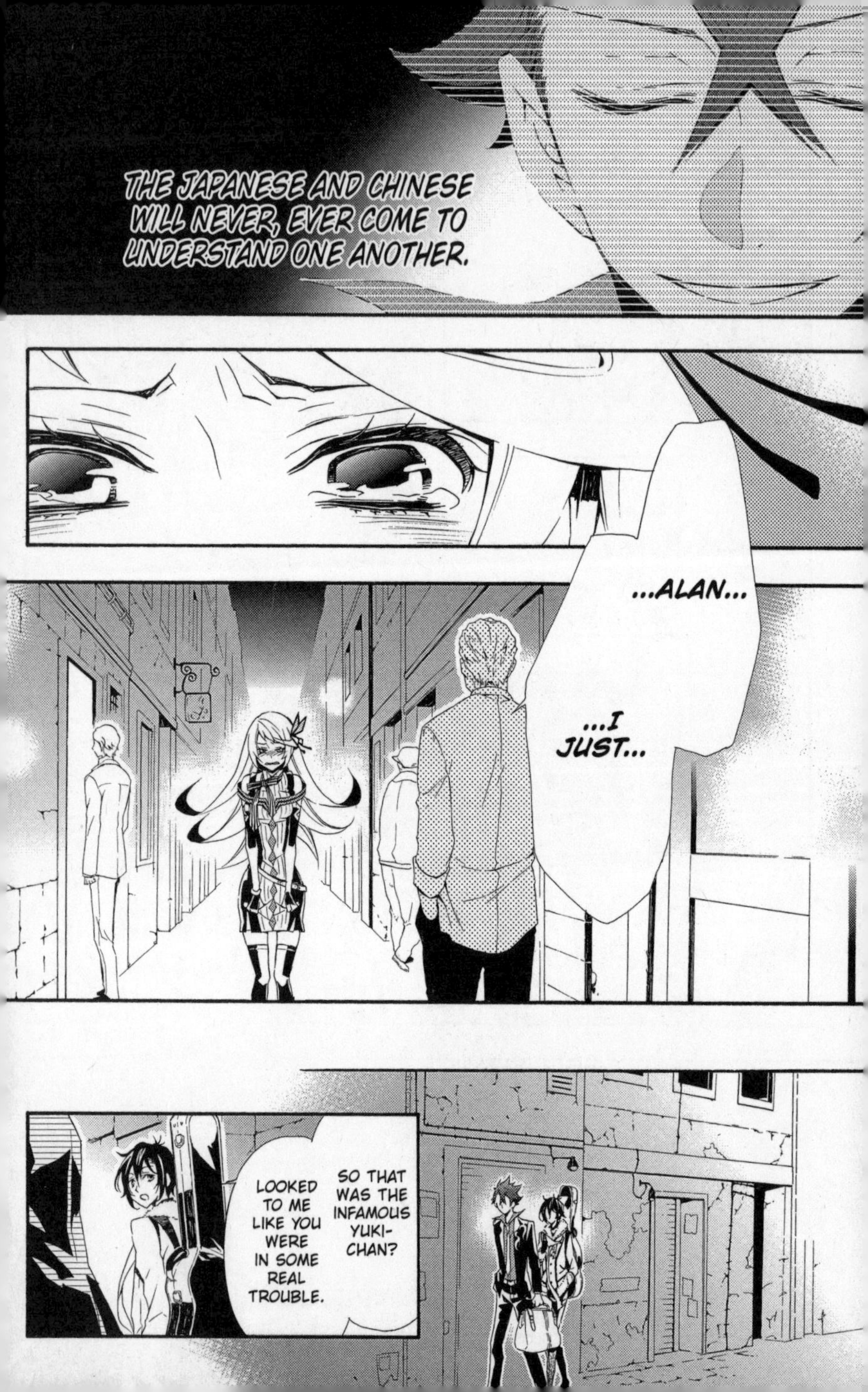
THE JAPANESE AND CHINESE WILL NEVER, EVER COME TO UNDERSTAND ONE ANOTHER.
...ALAN...
...I JUST...
SO THAT WAS THE INFAMOUS YUKI-CHAN?
LOOKED TO ME LIKE YOU WERE IN SOME REAL TROUBLE.

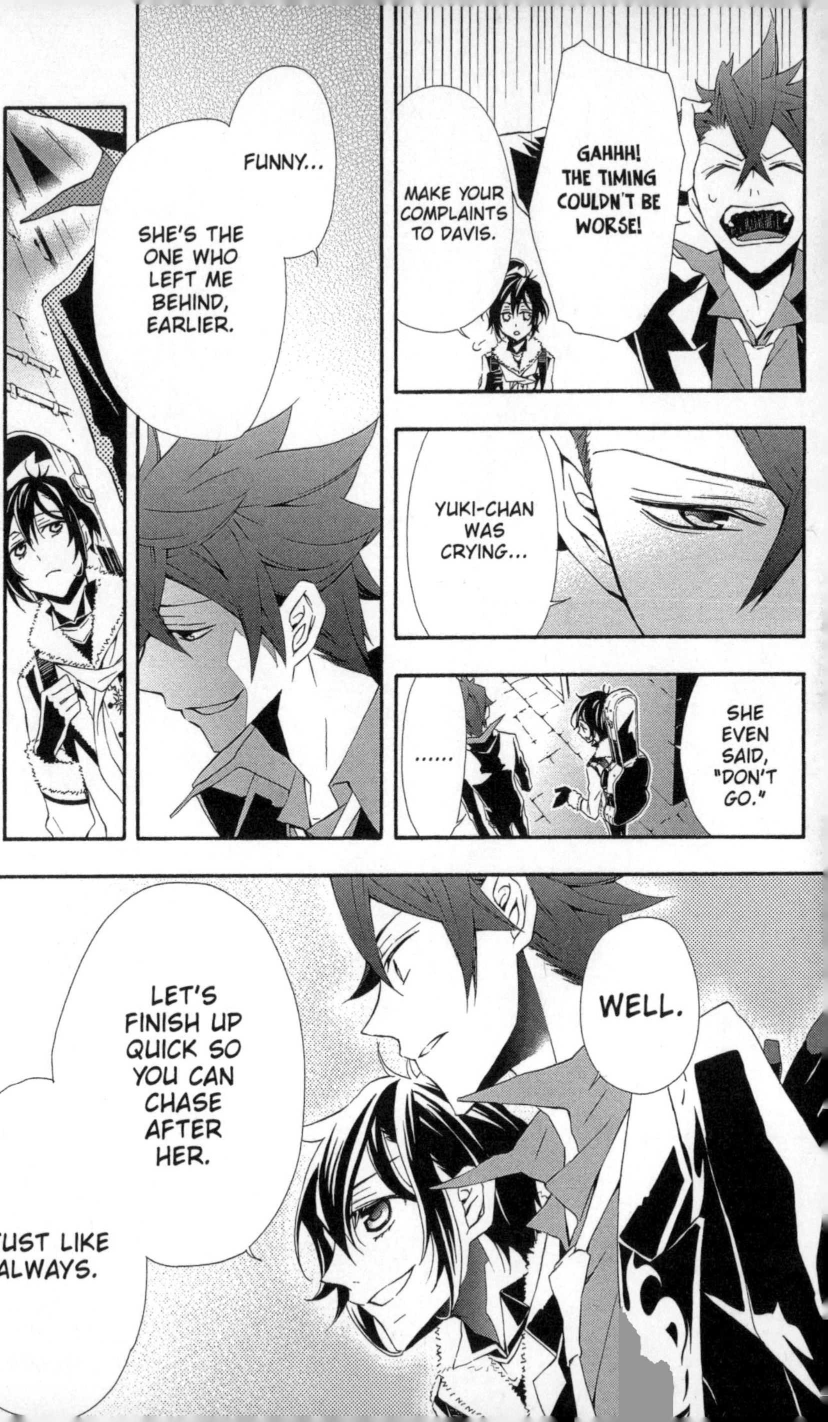
GAHHH! THE TIMING COULDN'T BE WORSE!
MAKE YOUR COMPLAINTS TO DAVIS.
YUKI-CHAN WAS CRYING...
SHE EVEN SAID, "DON'T GO."
......
FUNNY...
SHE'S THE ONE WHO LEFT ME BEHIND, EARLIER.
WELL.
LET'S FINISH UP QUICK SO YOU CAN CHASE AFTER HER.
JUST LIKE ALWAYS.

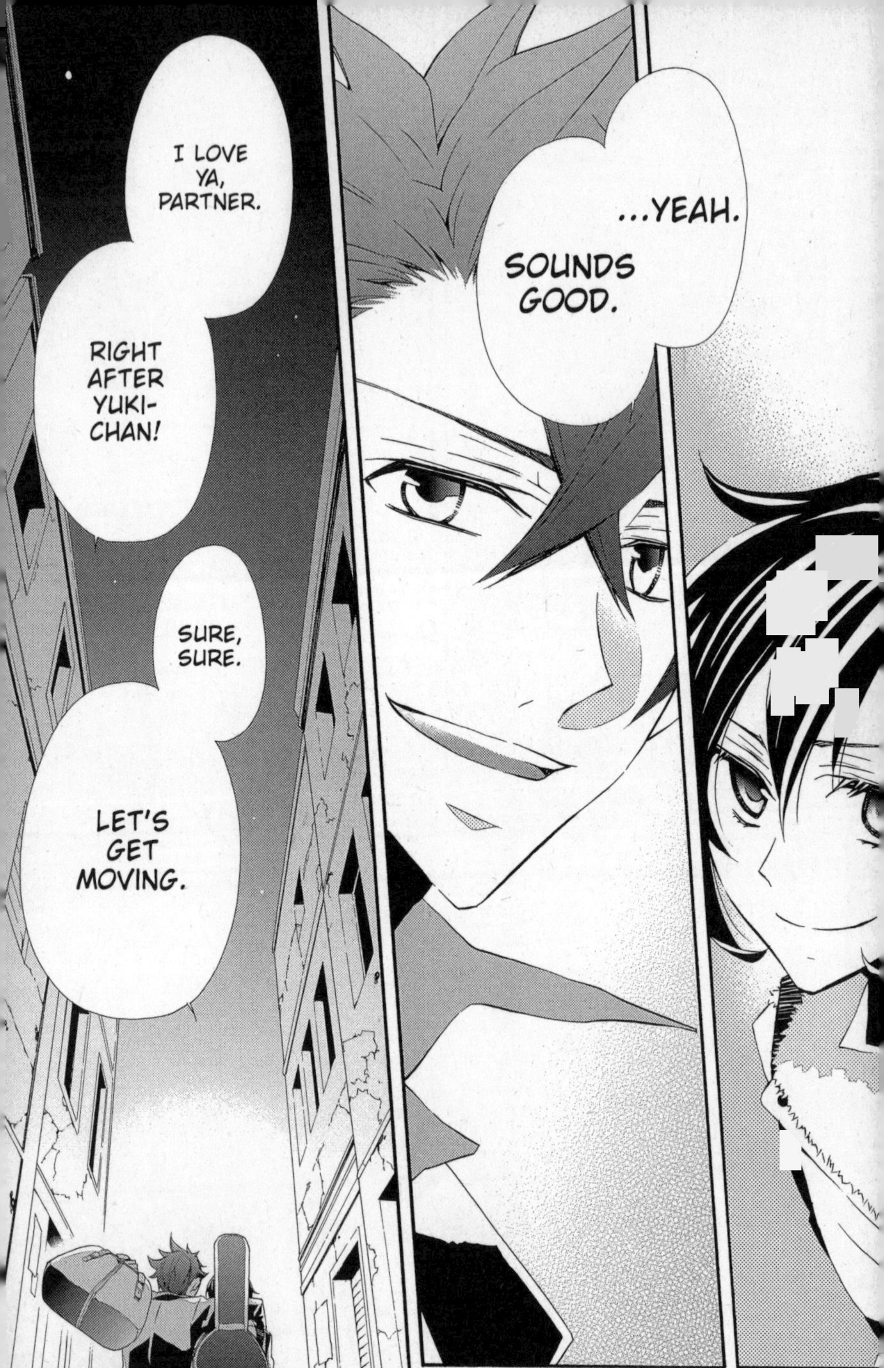
...YEAH.
SOUNDS GOOD.
I LOVE YA, PARTNER.
RIGHT AFTER YUKI-CHAN!
SURE, SURE.
LET'S GET MOVING.

ROSE GUNS DAYS Season 3 1 END

ROSE GUNS DAYS

Season 3

From the original writer and supervisor, Ryukishi07

Hi there. Ryukishi07 here.

Our heroes Alan and Keith hit the streets running in Season 3, and once again, this season features developments unlike any other. Both protagonists are charming, reliable guys, and I had a lot of fun writing them. Fresh and exciting characters like these are just the way to make the story pop!

The attention paid to Alan and Keith throughout Season 3 is most of what makes it so fun. Make sure you don't miss how the impending tragedies give them trials to overcome and tie the story together.

In this manga version, Alan and Keith are about 200% more charming, even! Omura-sensei has taken these characters—whose appeal originally had to come across via nothing but dialogue— and, through the fabulous art, has allowed even me, the author, to re-discover how charming they can be! I hope you'll keep tuning in to read what happens next during the adventures of these two inseparable friends!

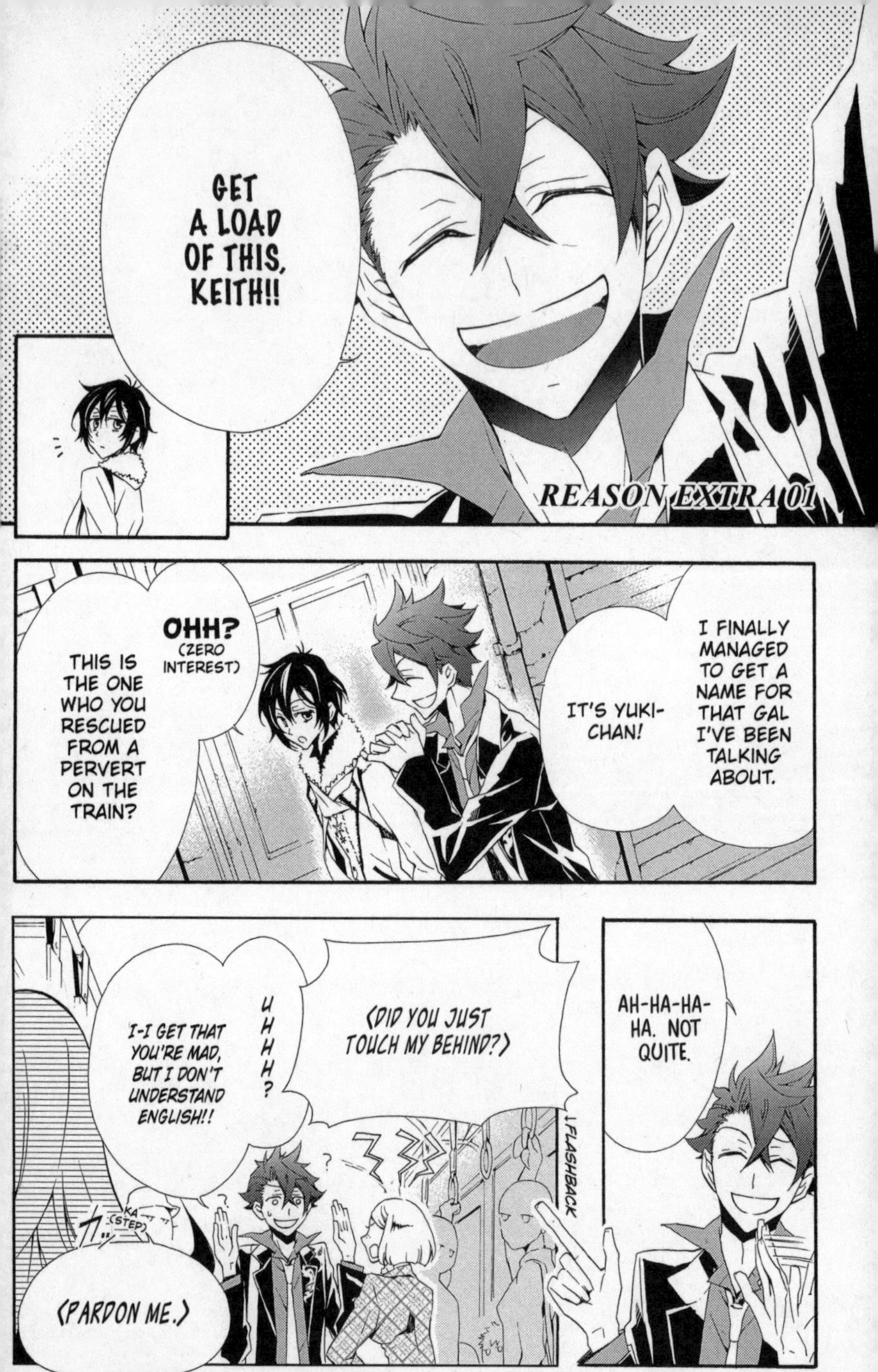
GET A LOAD OF THIS, KEITH!!
REASON EXTRA 01
I FINALLY MANAGED TO GET A NAME FOR THAT GAL I'VE BEEN TALKING ABOUT.
IT'S YUKI-CHAN!
OHH?
(ZERO INTEREST)
THIS IS THE ONE WHO YOU RESCUED FROM A PERVERT ON THE TRAIN?
AH-HA-HA-HA. NOT QUITE.
FLASHBACK
〈DID YOU JUST TOUCH MY BEHIND?〉
UHHH?
I-I GET THAT YOU'RE MAD, BUT I DON'T UNDERSTAND ENGLISH!!
KA
(STEP)
〈PARDON ME.〉

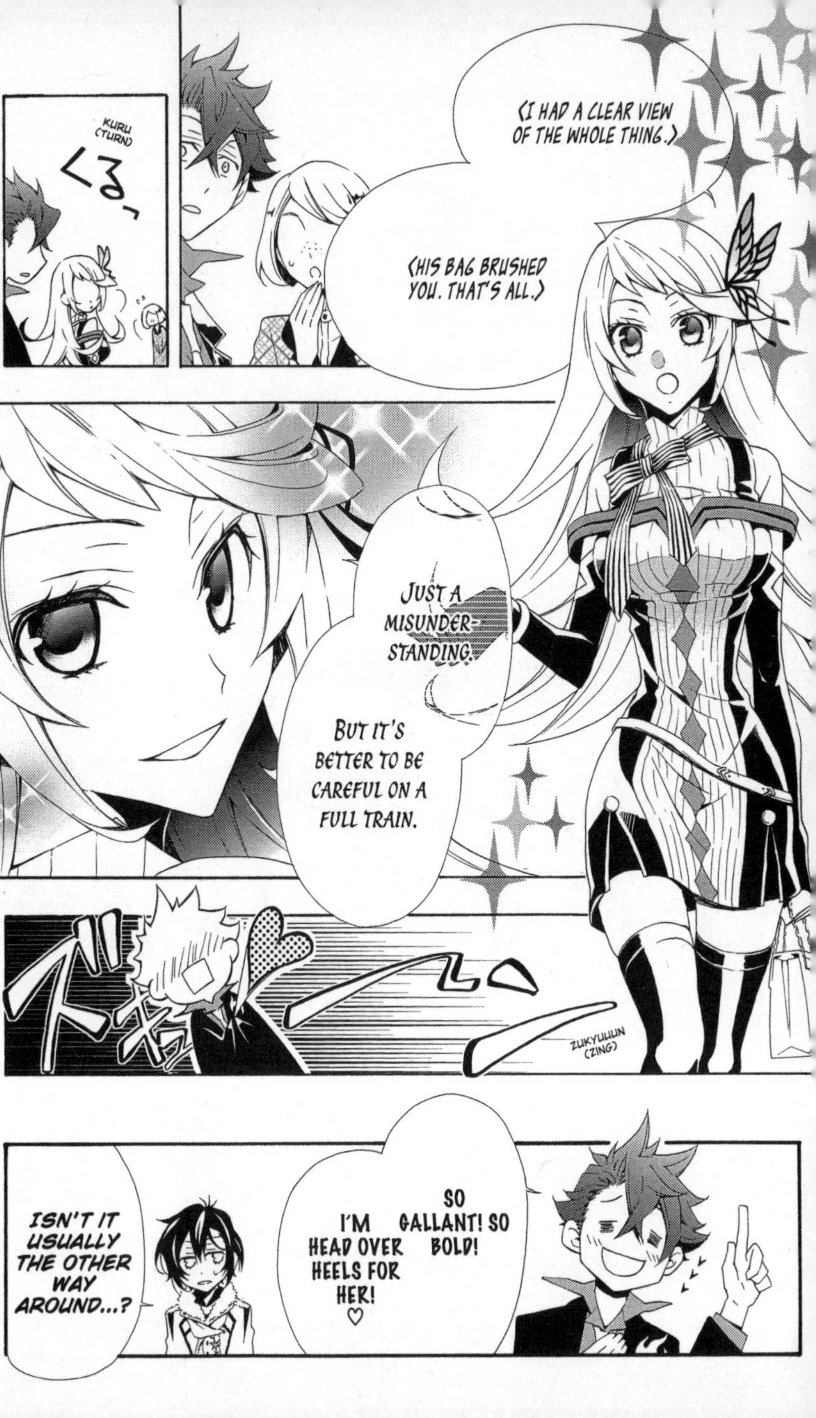
<I HAD A CLEAR VIEW OF THE WHOLE THING.>
<HIS BAG BRUSHED YOU. THAT'S ALL.>
KURU (TURN)
くる
JUST A MISUNDERSTANDING.
BUT IT'S BETTER TO BE CAREFUL ON A FULL TRAIN.
ZUKYUUUN (ZING)
SO GALLANT! SO BOLD! I'M HEAD OVER HEELS FOR HER! ♡
ISN'T IT USUALLY THE OTHER WAY AROUND...?

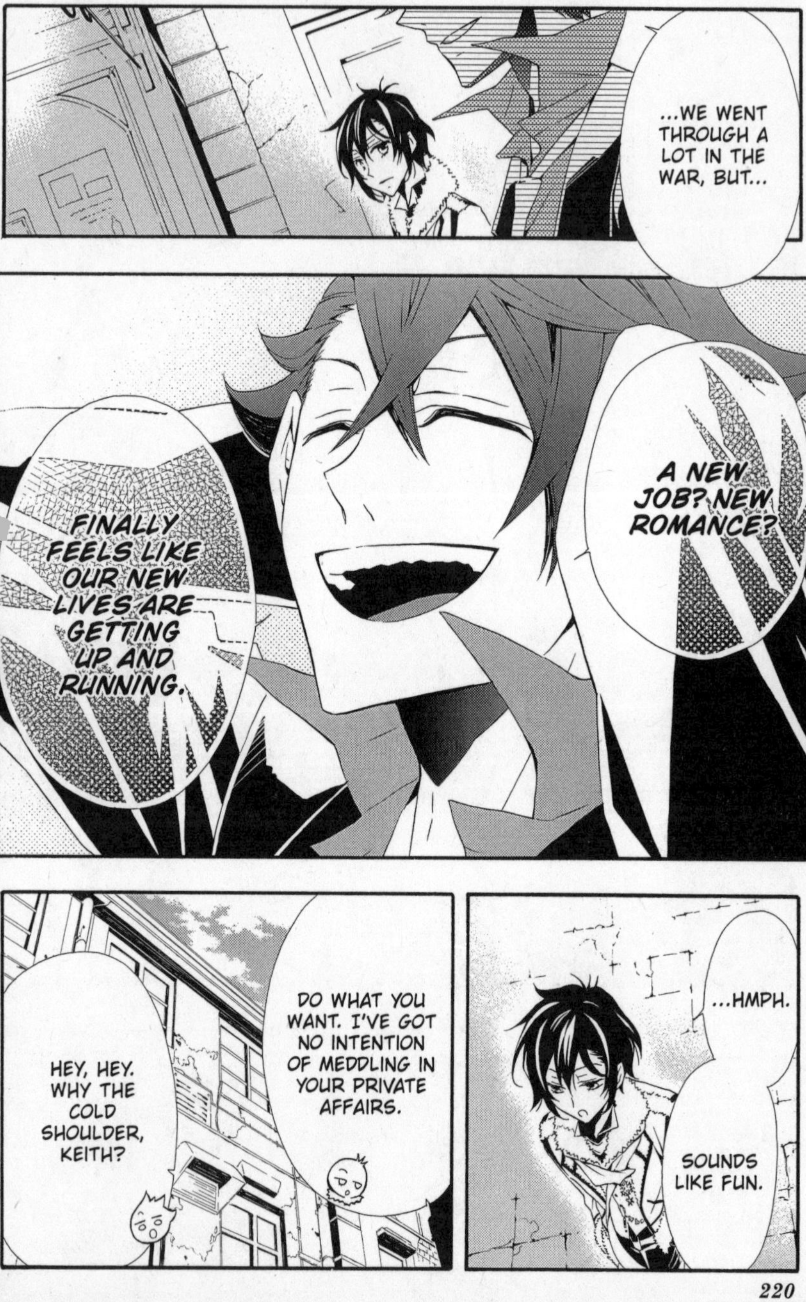

...WE WENT THROUGH A LOT IN THE WAR, BUT...
A NEW JOB? NEW ROMANCE?
FINALLY FEELS LIKE OUR NEW LIVES ARE GETTING UP AND RUNNING.
...HMPH.
SOUNDS LIKE FUN.
DO WHAT YOU WANT. I'VE GOT NO INTENTION OF MEDDLING IN YOUR PRIVATE AFFAIRS.
HEY, HEY. WHY THE COLD SHOULDER, KEITH?

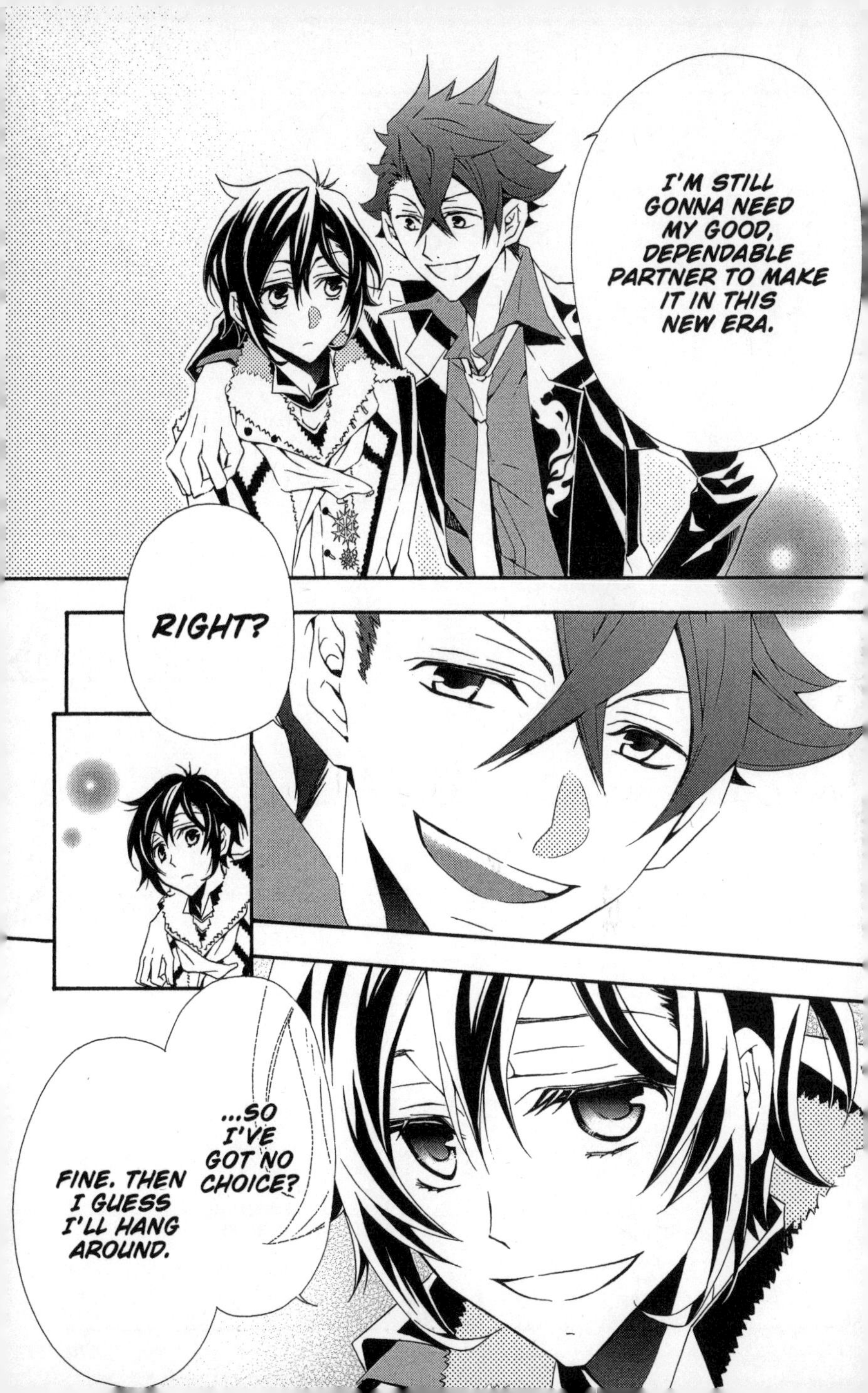
I'M STILL GONNA NEED MY GOOD, DEPENDABLE PARTNER TO MAKE IT IN THIS NEW ERA.
RIGHT?
...SO I'VE GOT NO CHOICE?
FINE. THEN I GUESS I'LL HANG AROUND.

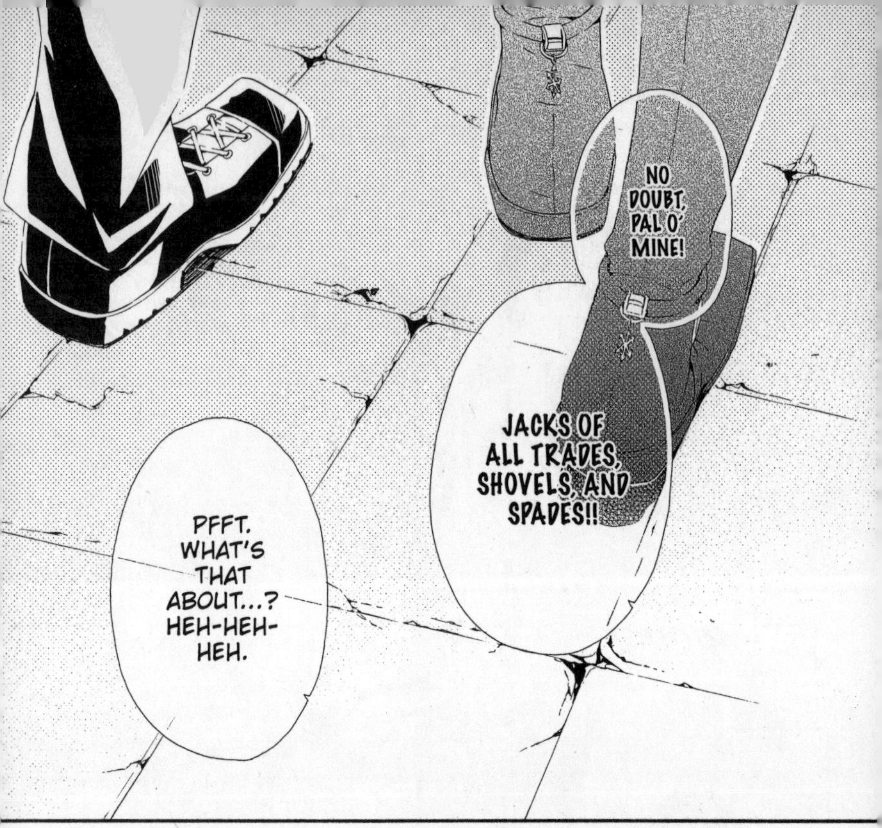
NO DOUBT, PAL O' MINE!
JACKS OF ALL TRADES, SHOVELS, AND SPADES!!
PFFT. WHAT'S THAT ABOUT...? HEH-HEH-HEH.

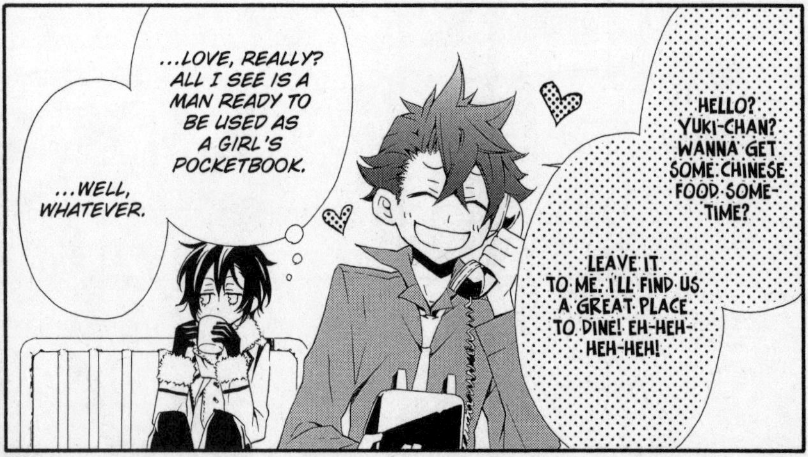
HELLO? YUKI-CHAN? WANNA GET SOME CHINESE FOOD SOME-TIME?
LEAVE IT TO ME. I'LL FIND US A GREAT PLACE TO DINE! EH-HEH-HEH-HEH!
...LOVE, REALLY? ALL I SEE IS A MAN READY TO BE USED AS A GIRL'S POCKETBOOK.
...WELL, WHATEVER.

END

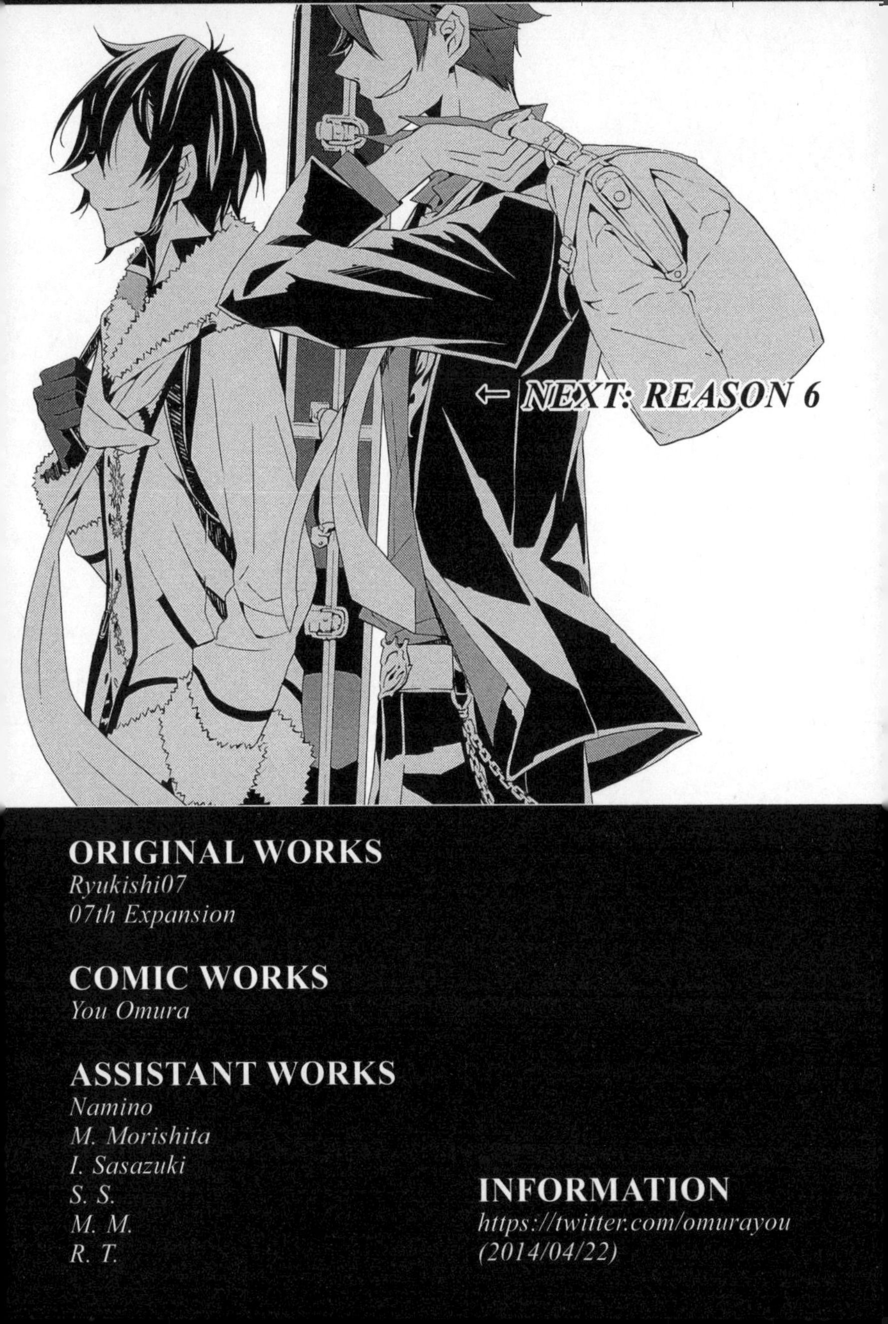
← NEXT: REASON 6

ORIGINAL WORKS
Ryukishi07
07th Expansion

COMIC WORKS
You Omura

ASSISTANT WORKS
Namino
M. Morishita
I. Sasazuki
S. S.
M. M.
R. T.

INFORMATION
https://twitter.com/omurayou
(2014/04/22)

TRANSLATION NOTES

COMMON HONORIFICS

no honorific: Indicates familiarity or closeness; if used without permission or reason, addressing someone in this manner would constitute an insult.

-san: The Japanese equivalent of Mr./Mrs./Miss. If a situation calls for politeness, this is the fail-safe honorific.

-sama: Conveys great respect; may also indicate that the social status of the speaker is lower than that of the addressee.

-kun: Used most often when referring to boys, this indicates affection or familiarity. Occasionally used by older men among their peers, but it may also be used by anyone referring to a person of lower standing.

-chan: An affectionate honorific indicating familiarity used mostly in reference to girls; also used in reference to cute persons or animals of either gender.

-senpai: A suffix used to address upperclassmen or more experienced coworkers.

PAGE 23

Soumen (thin white noodles) and **chashu-men** (ramen with roasted pork) don't mean anything special here. It's all just one of Alan's nonsense rhymes.

PAGE 102

The second kanji of **Meixue's name** is the character for "snow," which is read as *yuki* in Japanese. Hence her alias.

ROSE GUNS DAYS

Season 3

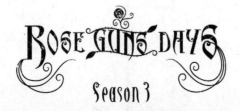

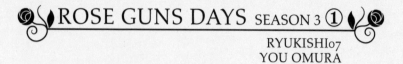

ROSE GUNS DAYS SEASON 3 ①

RYUKISHI07
YOU OMURA

Translation: Caleb D. Cook • Lettering: Katie Blakeslee and Lys Blakeslee

ROSE GUNS DAYS Season 3 vol. 1
© RYUKISHI07 / 07th Expansion
© 2014 You Omura / SQUARE ENIX CO., LTD.
First published in Japan in 2014 by SQUARE ENIX CO., LTD.
English translation rights arranged with SQUARE ENIX CO., LTD.
and Yen Press, LLC through Tuttle-Mori Agency, Inc.

English translation © 2017 by SQUARE ENIX CO., LTD.

Yen Press
1290 Avenue of the Americas
New York, NY 10104

Visit us at yenpress.com
facebook.com/yenpress
twitter.com/yenpress
yenpress.tumblr.com
instagram.com/yenpress

First Yen Press Edition: September 2017

Yen Press is an imprint of Yen Press, LLC.
The Yen Press name and logo are trademarks of Yen Press, LLC.

The publisher is not responsible for websites (or their content) that are not owned by the publisher.

Library of Congress Control Number: 2017939212

ISBNs:
978-0-316-44103-2 (paperback)
978-0-316-52003-4 (ebook)

10 9 8 7 6 5 4 3 2 1

BVG

Printed in the United States of America